KU-778-353

CONSTITUTIONAL LAW OF IRELAND

The Law of the
Executive Legislature and Judicature

DAVID GWYNN MORGAN

LL.M. (Lond.), of the Middle Temple, Barrister-at-Law,
Statutory Lecturer in Law, University College, Cork

THE ROUND HALL PRESS

The typesetting of this book was produced by
Keystrokes Limited, 38 Merrion Square, Dublin 2
for The Round Hall Press Limited,
Kill Lane, Blackrock, County Dublin, Ireland.

© David Gwynn Morgan 1990

ISBN 0-947686-57-6
ISBN 0-947686-58-4

ACKNOWLEDGMENT
The publishers acknowledge the permission of the Controller, Stationery Office
to reprint in this book pages 35 and 36 of *Revised Estimates for Public Services
for the year ending 31 December 1983* (Pl. 1407).

First edition 1985
Second edition 1990

BRITISH LIBRARY CATALOGUING IN PUBLICATION DATA

Morgan, David Gwynn
    Constitutional law of Ireland.—2nd ed.
    1. Ireland (Republic). Constitution, history
    I. Title
    344.1702

Printed in Great Britain by BPCC Wheatons Ltd, Exeter

TO MY PARENTS

Contents

Preface

It is curious that, although at least four accounts of the Irish Free State Constitution* and the organs of government which it created, were published, by contrast no comprehensive work has yet appeared dealing exclusively with the institutions of government established by *Bunreacht na hÉireann,* the Constitution of Ireland, 1937. Possibly the reason for this is that the authors who might otherwise have undertaken the task have concentrated their attention on the far-reaching developments in the other portion of constitutional law, namely, the judicial review of legislation against the standards laid down in the 1937 Constitution. In any case, the fact is that there is no full-length treatment of the law constituting the framework of our system of government, that is, the law of the executive, legislature and judicature. It is this gap which the present work attempts to fill.

The book is very much a work of description and analysis with suggestions for improvement being kept to a minimum: the first step in any reform is after all to understand the *status quo*. If there is any ideology underlying this work, it is that a fair, open and predictable system of government does lead to better-quality government decisions and more decent government practice. Such a view may appear a shattering glimpse of the obvious but after the events of 1982, *annus horribilis* in the history of Irish constitutional government, it is no harm to re-state it.

Because of the exigencies of publishing economics in a small jurisdiction, the book attempts to meet the needs of several types of reader, namely, students of law, public administration or civics, lawyers, public servants and members of the Oireachtas as well as that rare bird, the intelligent layperson. Different readers will require varying levels of detail to try to accommodate their varying tastes. I have adopted the compromise — ungainly, as is often the way with compromises — of telescoping a certain amount of qualification, explanation, and even speculation into the endnotes, which also contain fairly full references. In addition, topics adequately covered elsewhere have been omitted or summarised and lengthy quotations from Bunreacht na hÉireann kept to a minimum, on the assumption that the reader has a copy. Again in the interests of brevity, Chapters 7-11, on the legislature, focus chiefly on the Dáil, and

---

*Darrell Figgis, *The Irish Constitution* (Dublin 1922); J. Swift McNeill, *Studies in the Constitution of the Irish Free State* (Dublin 1925); Barra Ó Briain, *The Irish Constitution* (Dublin 1929); Leo Kohn, *The Constitution of the Irish Free State* (London 1932).

where the position in the Senate differs this has been mentioned only briefly. (In these Chapters, the abbreviations DSO and SSO have been employed to refer to the Dáil and Senate Standing Orders.)

I have endeavoured to state the law in the light of the materials available in June 1984, though in the isle of unreported judgments I may not always have succeeded. I should be grateful to anyone who points out any omissions or errors.

Necessarily, a book concerned as much with lore as with law required the help of experienced practitioners in the field. The bulk of this help was given, without stint, by civil servants of the State in the Oireachtas and civil servants of the Governments in the relevant departments. Where serving civil servants are involved, it is better to acknowledge gratefully without identifying precisely. I can, however, record that Senators Jim Dooge, Sean O'Leary and Brendan Ryan; Deputies Bertie Ahern and Seamus Brennan; Lord Elystan Morgan; Professor John A. Murphy (UCC History Department); and Messrs Brian Farrell (UCD Department of Ethics and Politics), Michael Kilroy (retired civil servant) and Dick Walsh (*The Irish Times*) assisted me with various queries, whilst Mr John Dunne (Institute of Public Administration), Professor Bryan Murphy (UCC Law Department) and Dr Michael Adams (Irish Academic Press) offered useful suggestions and, at different stages, shared some of the task of proof-reading with me. Dr Adams also bore the burden of preparing the index and tables. Miss Valerie O'Connell and Miss Marcella Doyle, the UCC Law Department secretaries, uncomplainingly typed and re-typed a manuscript which was, at its best, crabbed. For all this assistance, I am profoundly grateful. I should also like to thank my wife, Deirdre, for her encouragement and good company and for relieving me of so many parental and domestic duties.

1

Introduction

R.T.C. LIBRARY, LETTERKENNY

1.1 CONSTITUTIONAL LAW

The scope of the subject — and of the book Constitutional law comprises three parts. The central element consists of the rules dealing with the structure, composition, functions and inter-relationships of the principal organs of state, *viz.* the Government, the Oireachtas (Parliament) and the Courts. In the Irish context, this segment of constitutional law — and incidentally the subject-matter of this book — may be summarised as follows. The head of state is the President who also has other functions as 'Guardian of the Constitution.' (Chapter 3) The executive power of the State is exercised by or on the authority of the Government which consists of the Taoiseach and fourteen other members. The detailed administration of the executive function is carried out by the departments of state each of which consists of a number of civil servants headed by a minister (Chapter 4). There is a multitude of other agencies — State-sponsored bodies, local authorities, Gardaí — which discharge specialised executive functions and which fall outside the scope of the present work. The Government is responsible to, and may be removed by, the Dáil (Chapter 5) which is the lower House of the Oireachtas but is not responsible to the Senate or upper House (Chapter 6). While bills almost all emanate from departments, acts of the Oireachtas must be 'made' by way of a complicated procedure in the two Houses, followed by the assent of the President (Chapter 7). Considerable modifications apply to this procedure in the case of financial legislation (Chapter 8). As in other parliaments, each House follows a detailed procedure (Chapter 9), intended to ensure fair and thorough debate of public affairs, and is protected by privileges (Chapter 10) designed to ensure that debate is free. Each House is elected albeit in very different ways (Chapter 11). Finally, the least dangerous arm of government — the judicial branch — is housed in a system of four principal courts (Chapter 12).

Secondly, it is customary to treat as part of constitutional law the basic rights of the individual. Where, as in Arts. 40-44 of the Irish Constitution, there is a fairly comprehensive statement of fundamental rights in the written constitution, then the case for inclusion of these rights becomes conclusive, although this can lead to overlap (e.g. in regard to the right of association, between constitutional law and labour law). A further reason for treating fundamental rights as part of constitutional law is that while these rights may be invoked against a private individual, in fact it usually happens that they are opposed to some state organ (the legislature or the executive) and thus, viewed from one perspective, they may be regarded as a limitation on the powers of state organs. The fundamental rights are not covered in detail in this book, but a summary of the case law on a specimen right is provided in Section 2 of this Chapter.

Thirdly — and this is less important than the other two parts — a written constitution frequently states national beliefs, ideals or aspirations. In Bunreacht na hÉireann, examples are to be found in the Preamble, Arts. 2 and 3 ('The national territory consists of the whole island of Ireland') and 45 ('Directive Principles of Social Policy'). In this context, it may be noted, too, that a written constitution can also constitute a symbol of the State and a focus of the citizens' loyalty, in the same way as the national flag or national anthem.

Sources   Like most States (though not the United Kingdom), Ireland has a written constitution, i.e. a single document embodying the most important constitutional laws. It is difficult to amend[1] and, consonant with this, ordinary law which conflicts with the Constitution is invalid.[2] Very frequently, the reason for a written constitution is the need to establish the foundations of the machinery of government in a newly-independent State and this was true of the Irish Free State Constitution in 1922. The inspiration behind the establishment of Bunreacht na hÉireann in 1937 was the desire to have a constitution which was completely free of all marks (however symbolic or trivial) of subservience to the former colonial power. In a sense, therefore, the 1937 Constitution consisted of the completion of unfinished business left over from 1922. Accordingly, as might have been expected, there was much more continuity than change in 1937. The institutions were barely altered and the language by which they were described in the later Constitution is often taken *verbatim* from the 1922 Constitution. In these circumstances, it has seemed only realistic, in the present work, to treat the Irish State, from 1922 to the present, as a continuous system. It is also important, from a comparative perspective, that, at Independence, the Irish institutions were closely modelled on their British counterparts. This is true both of formal governmental structures and administrative processes and of the informal institutions of party politics. As has been observed by Mr Brian Farrell, 'Irish political culture developed into an established and sturdy parliamentary mould prior to political indpendence.'[3] This carries obvious advantages in that the British constitutional scene affords a convenient reservoir of models and precedents. However, the similarities can also act as a trap in that the differences are subtle and, thus, liable to be overlooked (see, for example, parliamentary privilege: Chapter 10.1).

Johnston J observed in *The State (Burke) v. Lennon*:[4] 'that a further Constitution — an unwritten one — was [not] intended by the People of Éire to exist side by side with this written Constitution . . .'. However this stark statement must be read in the light of the context in which it was made (the issue of whether Art. 34.4.3° authorised an appeal against a grant of habeas

12

corpus) and subject to the considerable *caveat* that it only applies where the subject area concerned is comprehensively covered in Bunreacht na hÉireann. For, in fact, the Búnreacht is only one of the sources (albeit the most important source) of constitutional law and thus the word 'Constitution' is ambiguous in that it can be used, narrowly, to refer exclusively to the Bunreacht or, more widely, to comprise all the sources of constitutional law. As with other areas of law, some parts of constitutional law result from acts of the Oireachtas and some from judicial decisions. At the risk of some inaccuracy, it may be said that legislation is a more important source of law in regard to the organs of the State (legislature, executive and judicature), for example, the Ministers and Secretaries Act, 1924[5] — whereas case law has come into its own in controlling the State-individual relationship, by way of the creative interpretation of the fundamental rights established by the Constitution.

Conventions In Britain, a most important source of constitutional rules is the 'conventions of the constitution'.[6] These are unwritten constitutional rules which are enforced, not by a court, but by the influence of educated public opinion and, more concretely, by the fear that the Government may lose votes at the next election if it breaks a convention. Ultimately, this sanction is as strong or as weak as informed opinion and a sense of constitutional morality in the community. These conventions are a natural product of the evolutionary history and moderate character of the British constitution. The spirit underlying them was explained by Lord Radcliffe in a Privy Council case:

. . . the practical application of these principles to a given situation if it arose in the United Kingdom, would depend less upon any simple statement of principle than upon the actual facts of that situation and the good sense and political sensitivity of the main actors called upon to take part.[7]

In Britain, the following requirements are conventional rules: the Monarch must assent to bills duly passed; ministers must be members of either the Commons or the Lords; money bills must be introduced in the House of Commons. In Ireland, by contrast, such central rules as these are regulated either in the Bunreacht or, if not, in some other law; and, in consequence, there is less need for conventions. Nevertheless it is possible at least to suggest (for, of their nature, it is impossible to be dogmatic about conventions) that some conventions may have crystallised, in Ireland. For instance, there may be a convention that the chairman of the Dáil Public Accounts Committee — and half of its membership — must be members of Opposition parties. Another possibility, as a convention, is the practice by which the draft bill drawing up constituency boundaries is devised on the recommendation of an independent Dáil Éireann Constituency Commission.[8] The background to this practice is that up to and including the Electoral (Amendment) Act, 1974, successive Governments had used their majority in the Oireachtas to design constituency boundaries which gave their own party an advantage.

13

The adverse reaction (admittedly, some of it politically motivated) which arose in 1976 when the Minister for Defence publicly insulted the President, who thereupon resigned,[9] at least suggests that there is a convention that the President should not be publicly criticised by the Government. Again, it seems to be accepted that there is a conventional doctrine of individual ministerial responsibility,[10] though it is a rule which has been honoured more in the breach than in the observance. Whilst Taoisigh sometimes appoint senators who are not supporters of the Government party(ies), there is certainly no equivalent of the British practice of allowing the Leader of the Opposition to nominate a certain number of life peers. However, the first incumbent of the office of Ombudsman was nominated following consultation with the Leader of the Opposition. There is no rule controlling the appointment of judges or members of State-sponsored bodies or An Bord Pleanála; Governments usually appoint their own supporters to these posts (without, in any way, undermining the independence of the judiciary).[11] However, there was substantial public reaction against appointments to such posts being made by a Government after it had been defeated at a general election (in 1977, and in December 1982). Formerly there was said to be a convention that at least one Protestant judge should be nominated to the High or Supreme Court. However, as the need to reassure members of the minority religion has diminished, so, correspondingly, has the need for such a convention.

The usefulness of conventions was illustrated by the difficulties created by their absence or, at any rate, the absence of any generally agreed rules, in 1989, when the 26th Dáil failed, at first, to nominate a Taoiseach. Some of the substantive questions, raised by this situation, are discussed in the Supplement to Chapter 5, *infra*. For present purposes, however, the significant issue is the method by which satisfactory rules might best be developed. One solution is a court action. However, there are manifest disadvantages in drawing a court into such a peculiarly political area. Not that conventions offer an easy answer either: they lack an impartial arbiter to determine content; they are slow to crystalize; and the sanction for a breach is at best flimsy.

However, it is possible to suggest that one convention emerged from the 1989 episode. Following the Dáil's failure to re-nominate Mr Haughey as Taoiseach at the first time of asking, it was generally agreed that the Constitution required his resignation, as substantive Taoiseach. The point of disagreement, however, was whether he must resign forthwith or whether, as Mr Haughey claimed, he was allowed a few days' grace. Nonetheless, following concerted opposition protest and the threat of a motion of no confidence, within a few hours Mr Haughey did indeed resign. This incident will probably be regarded as a precedent for holding that a Taoiseach in this situation is obliged to resign forthwith.

Arts. 40-44 of the Constitution consist of short, positive statements of the minimum rights essential for an acceptable life as an individual in a constitutional polity, e.g. free speech, freedom of assembly, freedom to practise religion. All laws which conflict with the fundamental rights are invalid.[13] This primacy belongs not only to the fundamental rights but also to the other articles of the Constitution, but there have been, and probably will continue to be, far more cases involving the fundamental rights than the other articles.

This is not a book about fundamental rights. However, because of the impact which the fundamental rights have made upon the wider questions of government, it is necessary to examine the subject briefly and best to do so by reference to one specimen right. The unspecified personal rights (conjured from Art. 40.3.1°) have been selected not only because of the wealth of the case law which they have attracted but also because they present so many characteristic features and problems.

Ryan v. A.G.[14]   By Art. 40.3 of the Constitution:

1° The State guarantees in its laws to respect, and, as far as possible, by its laws to defend and vindicate the personal rights of the citizen.

2° The State shall, in particular, by its laws protect as best it may from unjust attack and, in the case of injustice done, vindicate the life, person, good name and property rights of the citizen.

The seminal judgment on this area is that of Kenny J in the High Court in *Ryan*. Before *Ryan*, save for a few judicial straws in the wind,[15] it was generally assumed that the phrase 'personal rights' in Art. 40.3.1° simply provided a head-line to herald the slightly more specific formulation ('life, person, good name and property rights . . .') in the following subsection, and in the other sections of the Article. Kenny J's principal reason for rejecting this conventional wisdom was that the Constitution sets up a 'Christian and democratic state' from which it follows that the citizens of that State should enjoy all the personal rights which are appropriate in such a State. To the extent that these are not mentioned in the Constitution, then Art. 40.3.1° may be regarded as a reservoir of unspecified rights to make up this deficiency, for example the right to bodily integrity, right to free movement (the right to a passport) and the right to marry.

The immediate question in *Ryan* was the constitutionality of the Health (Fluoridation of Water Supplies) Act, 1960 under which fluoride was put in the public water-supply consumed by, among others, the plaintiff. The plaintiff alleged that fluoride was damaging to health. After the hearing of sixty-five days' evidence, this contention was rejected. However, in spite of this, Kenny J went on to examine the legal position, on the basis that the plaintiff's contention had succeeded, and held that, on this assumption, the compulsory

15

fluoridation would have violated the plaintiff's right to bodily integrity, which was one of his unspecified personal rights. A question which went unexplored in *Ryan* was whether the right to bodily integrity was not already embraced within the citizen's specified right (in Art. 40.2.2°) to have his 'person' protected. If this suggestion were correct, the facts alleged in *Ryan* would not have called for any discussion of unspecified rights.

In American jurisprudence,[16] what is known in Ireland as the right to bodily integrity has been invoked in cases involving searches of the rectal cavity; compulsory blood testing or vaccination; and artificial preservation of a human body so that the organs might be used for spare-part surgery (the so-called 'right to die').

It is now proposed to move on from the right to bodily integrity to outline some of the other major latent personal rights which have been divined by the courts.

(i) Privacy No case has yet arisen on privacy *simpliciter*, i.e. the right not to be spied upon, but the specialised right to marital privacy was successfully invoked in *McGee v. A.G.*[17] Marital privacy means, according to U.S. law, 'the right of the individual to make for himself — except where a good reason exists for placing the decision in the Government's hands — the fundamental decisions that shape family life, whom to marry, whether and when to have children.[18] The question at stake in *McGee* was the constitutionality of section 17 of the Criminal Law Amendment Act, 1935 which made it a crime to sell, or import, any contraceptive. The effect of section 17, according to three members of the Supreme Court,[19] would be to violate Mrs McGee's right to marital privacy, and the section was therefore unconstitutional. It seems clear that this decision would apply even to healthy married ladies and was not conditional on the fact that an additional pregnancy would have endangered Mrs McGee's health.

In *Norris v. A.G.*[20] the plaintiff argued that the laws making homosexual activity a crime were unconstitutional. His strongest argument was an extended definition of the right to privacy as a ban on state interference with private, personal conduct where no compelling state interest was involved. While apparently accepting the definition, the Supreme Court majority (of 3:2) found, as a matter of fact, that private homosexual acts lead to increased depression and venereal disease; promote marital breakdown; and undermine the Christian moral order. And thus intervention by the law was justifiable.

(ii) Right of the unmarried mother and child It has been held that Arts. 41 and 42 which establish certain rights in the field of the family and education are confined to the married family and the legitimate child.[21] Into the resulting breach in regard to the illegitimate child and its mother stepped Art. 40.3.1°. According to O'Higgins CJ in *G. v. An Bord Uchtála*:

As a mother [the plaintiff] has the right to protect and care for and to have the custody

16

of her infant child . . . . The right is clearly based on the natural relationship which exists between a mother and child. It arises in my view from the mother's natural determination to protect and sustain her child . . . . The child also has natural rights . . . . Having been born the child has the right to be fed and to live, to be reared and educated.[22]

The specific point at issue in G. arose from the Adoption Act, 1974, by which, in certain circumstances, the consent of the natural mother to adoption could be waived by the High Court by reference to the criterion of 'the best interests of the child to do so.' The Supreme Court held that, read, or rather glossed, in the light of the natural mother's constitutional right to custody, the statutory test should be taken to mean that the High Court could only waive the mother's consent where this was being capriciously withheld.

(iii) Right to litigate   This is the right to have recourse to the courts to assert a legal cause of action. The right was first enunciated by Kenny J in *Macauley v. Min. for Posts*[23] in which the plaintiff sought a declaration that the Minister was obliged to provide a proper telephone service. He was barred, at a preliminary stage, by the refusal of the Attorney General to grant his *fiat* (permission) which was required, under the Ministers and Secretaries Act, 1924,[24] before any action could be taken against a minister. The right to litigate was deduced from Art. 34.1.1° which grants the High Court 'full original jusrisdiction in and powers to determine all matters and questions . . . civil or criminal.' As a result, the requirement of a *fiat* was held unconstitutional. The other context in which the right has been invoked is to hold that certain of the statutory periods of limitation (which provide that action to enforce a legal right must be brought within a specified period) are unreasonably short and, hence, unconstitutional.[25]

Although the right to litigate has only been applied, so far, in two areas, it may have a considerable potential as a vehicle by which the judiciary could re-shape any procedural or evidential law which could be characterised as plainly unreasonable.

(iv) Right not to be unreasonably interfered with in earning an adequate living   It must be emphasised that this is not a positive right to employment but a negative right, which protects the individual against unreasonable interference. In *Murtagh v. Cleary*[26] the right was successfully invoked to prevent the defendant trade union from picketing a hotel because the trade union objected to the employment of female bar staff. It has also been suggested that the closed shop — an agreement between an employer and a trade union by which only members of that trade union will be employed by the employer — is unconstitutional.[27]

The Incorporated Law Society's limitation on the numbers entering the solicitor's profession raises a similar question. Since the right to earn a living is not an unqualified right, a court's approach, if it were confronted with this

17

issue, would be to weigh up the interests of the various people affected by the limitation — would-be solicitors; existing solicitors and members of the public — in order to decide whether the limitation were justifiable.

As with the other fundamental rights, it will be necessary more often to assert the right to work against the State than against a private body or individual. This is what happened in the unlikely case of *Landers v. A.G.*[28] in which the father of a singing prodigy aged eight was convicted for allowing the child to sing in public contrary to the Prevention of Cruelty to Children Act 1904. His argument that the Act was unconstitutional was rejected. The judge stressed that the restriction only applied to persons below the age of eleven, appearing after 9 p.m. and that Master Landers was perfectly free to undergo training for his chosen career. Thus, though the right was restricted to an extent, the restriction was justifiable.

(v) Free legal and medical assistance   *The State (Healy) v. O'Donoghue*[29] arose out of a court case in which the accused had been convicted of crimes of dishonesty and sent to prison. The key points were that the accused was poor, uneducated and not represented by a lawyer. In quashing his conviction, the Chief Justice held that where an uneducated accused faces a serious criminal charge and requires the assistance of a lawyer, which the accused is unable to afford, then there is a constitutional right to be provided with a lawyer at state expense. (This right is usually met by the operation of the Criminal Justice (Legal Aid) Act, 1962, though this was not the case in *Healy*.) This finding was alternatively based on Art. 38.5 and Art. 40.3.1° and 2° (constitutional justice). In *State (C) v. Frawley*[30] it was assumed that Art. 40.3.1° created a duty to provide medical treatment for prisoners provided that the cost was not prohibitive. Taking *Frawley* and *Healy* together, it is possible to suggest that the High Court might be prepared to impose a duty on the State to provide free medical treatment to a certain standard for indigent people. If this right were to come into existence, it might have significant implications for a Government seeking to cut back on free medical services.

Comment   As already mentioned, the unspecified personal rights were chosen as specimen fundamental rights because they illustrate so many of these rights' characteristic features and problems.

1. Because of the brevity with which the fundamental rights are formulated (nowhere more so than in the case of the *unspecified* personal rights) the wording of the Constitution offers only a little help in determining the scope of the rights. Consider the following judicial explanation (given by Henchy J in *McGee*[31] of how the personal rights are to be identified:

. . . it must be . . . a right that inheres in the citizen in question by virtue of his human personality. The lack of precision in this test is reduced when[Art. 40.3.1°] is read (as it must be) in the light of the Constitution as a whole and, in particular, in the

R.T.C. LIBRARY, LETTERKENNY

light of what the Constitution expressly or by necessary implication, deems to be fundamental to the personal standing of the individual in question in the context of the social order envisaged by the Constitution.

But '. . . the social order envisaged by the Constitution' (even if updated to meet the needs of contemporary society) is a rather vague standard. It is submitted that the reality of the matter was captured in the observation, made by Miss Justice Carroll in *Morgan v. Park Development*,[32] that '. . . no law which can be described as 'harsh and absurd' or which the courts could say was unreasonable and unjustifiable in principle . . . could also be constitutional.'

2. Decisions in the field of government are the product of a complex balance between a number of competing interests and values. The result is that all of the fundamental rights are qualified. When Art 40.3 was quoted, the alert reader will have noticed the cautious phrases, 'as far as practicable' and 'as best it may.' The other fundamental rights, too, are qualified by similar, if differently formulated exemptions. Many of the cases rehearsed above resulted in a law being upheld because, although it violated the right, it was within the exception authorised by the Constitution. It follows that, in most cases, in this area, the judge's task is to balance up the individual right and the exception, as it is defined in the Constitution, and then to scrutinise the law under review to see if it accords approximately with this balance.

3. The first basis for criticism of the new judicial activism in striking down unconstitutional law is that of democracy itself: judges are appointed and not elected; thus, it is urged, it is not for them to make, or unmake, laws passed by the elected Oireachtas. This line of attack is at its strongest where one is dealing not with fairly small-scale decisions (such as periods of limitation or the right to be provided with a passport) but with decisions which have a wider effect, sending ripples throughout society. Examples, *par excellence*, of cases in this second category are cases about fundamental moral questions, like *McGee* or *Norris*, or cases involving large sums of public money, for example *The State (Healy)* or the land-mark decision in *Murphy v. A.G.*[33] in which the spirit underlying Art. 41 ('The Family') was invoked to strike down the tax law by which a married couple were given only the same allowances, tax bands etc. as a single person. In cases involving large sums of money, the fixing of the balance between governmental income and expenditure and the choice among different types of expenditure are surely such far-reaching decisions as to be better left to the Oireachtas and the Government, save in extreme cases.

4. There is also the practical difficulty that courts of law are not well-adapted to decide the sort of governmental decisions which arise in certain fundamental rights cases. A court lacks the specialist advice in fields like economics, sociology etc. which is available to a minister. (In the *Norris* case, evidence from theologians, psychiatrists etc. was called by the plaintiff, but ignored

19

40025561

by the majority of the Supreme Court.) Even where specialist evidence is heard and heeded, a court, with its adversarial procedure and evidential rules, is not well-designed as a place in which to carry out the sort of comprehensive survey which the unmaking of important law should entail. Moreover, a court has to decide the validity of a law in the context of a single case presenting only one instance, among many, of the law's operation. And — in the old legal adage — hard cases make bad law.

5. The courts have shown themselves aware of these types of argument. One line of defence has been to observe a self-denying ordinance, 'the presumption of constitutionality.' This was explained by Kenny J in *Ryan*, as follows:[34]

the Oireachtas has to reconcile the exercise of personal rights with the claims of the common good and its decision on the reconciliation should prevail unless it was oppressive to all or some of the citizens or unless there is no reasonable proportion between the benefit which the legislation will confer on the citizens or a substantial body of them and the interference with the personal rights of the citizen.

The result of this approach is that the legislature is allowed some tolerance and a law will only be struck down if it is clearly unconstitutional. The doctrine has sometimes been justified in the language of the 'separation of powers', by reference to 'that respect which one great organ of the State owes to another.'[35]

6. The best justification on offer for judicial activism in the constitutional field may be, simply, that it is done *faute de mieux*, because of the inertia of the legislature. The changes brought about, for instance in *McGee* and *Murphy v. A.G.* (the married women's tax case) and, almost, in *Norris* were all changes made, in Britain, through Parliament. The need for a judicial mission to bring the laws into line with the needs and values of contemporary society stems from the conservative nature of Irish politics. And this, in turn, derives from such factors as the influence of the Church in social and sexual matters; and the fact that, as a result of the Civil War, the two major political parties are divided on a pro- and anti-Treaty basis rather than a progressive/conservative line of cleavage so that a clear majority for, or against, change fails to emerge in the Oireachtas. In the context of politicians as reformers, it is notable that, following the *McGee* case, no fewer than four unsuccessful legislative attempts were made to reform the law on family planning before the Health (Family Planning) Act, 1979 was finally passed. Again, during 1966-67, a Committee of Oireachtas members sat to review the Constitution.[36] (This was the first, and, so far, only, fruit, of Mr Sean Lemass' idea that the Constitution ought to be reviewed every twenty-five years.) The principal recommendations on which they were able to agree were: the removal of the claim of the Six Counties, the ban on divorce and the special position of the Church.[37] All but the last of these were deemed too controversial to be taken any further.

Within the United Kingdom context, the general election of 1918 is significant as a landmark on the long march to universal adult suffrage. It was the first time that all men over the age of twenty-one, and women over the the the age of thirty, had the right to vote; in Ireland, the electorate rose from seven hundred thousand in 1910 to almost two million in 1918. This sea-change was one reason why, at the election, seventy-three seats out of a total of one hundred and five Irish seats were won by members of Sinn Féin, who had been elected on a pledge to withdraw from Westminster and to establish a constituent assembly within Ireland as 'the supreme national authority.' This promise was honoured by the convening of the Assembly of Ireland or *Dáil Éireann* as it was known from the first. It is from the first meeting of the First Dáil at the Mansion House, on 21 January 1919 that Irish constitutional theory dates the establishment of the new State.[39] Only twenty-seven members were present at this meeting since a number of Sinn Féin members were in prison and the members of the other parties refused to attend. Nevertheless the following documents were approved: Declaration of Independence; Message to the Free Nations of the Free World; and Democratic Programme. In addition, a short provisional constitution was adopted which established an executive government (the 'Government of Dáil Éireann') consisting of a prime minister and four other ministers. The First Dáil also established a system of courts, 'the Dáil Courts', partly in order to bolster its claim to be internationally recognised as the Government of the State and partly for the practical purpose of administering justice in the parts of the country where the ordinary courts were prevented from operating. The Dáil Courts functioned regularly in the south and west of the country.[40]

In 1920, the Westminster Parliament enacted the Government of Ireland Act which provided for two separate political units, 'Southern Ireland' and 'Northern Ireland' (each with legislature, executive and judicature) between which the only connection would have been an all-Ireland Court of Appeal and a Council of Ireland. The Council never came into being and the Court only existed during the period 1921-22. In Belfast, the forms of government established by the 1920 Act lasted until 1972, when Stormont was abolished.[41] But, in Dublin, the 1920 Act was entirely rejected as offering an inadequate measure of devolution and it was formally repealed, so far as the southern part of Ireland was concerned, at the time of the constitutional settlement in 1922.[42] However, the Act had been invoked in 1921 when, pursuant to it, the U.K. Government called elections to 'the Parliament of Southern Ireland.' The First Dáil, while declaring the 1920 Acts to be 'illegal,' resolved that these elections be regarded as elections to Dáil Éireann and that the First Dáil dissolve upon the new body being summoned by the President. And this was how the Second Dáil was constituted.

There was another consequence of the 1920 Act. The Act provided that if less than half the members of the Parliament took their seats, then the

Parliament would be dissolved and Southern Ireland governed as a crown colony. Such a change would have shifted the War of Independence, which had commenced in 1920, to an even more serious plane. This increased the pressure on both sides for a settlement and led to a truce which, after one false dawn, resulted in the negotiations in Downing Street which produced the final constitutional settlement, the Anglo-Irish Treaty, in late 1921.[43]

Under Art. 18, the Treaty had to be submitted for approval to both the U.K. Parliament and the Second Dáil. In January 1922, the Dáil[44] accepted the Treaty, by sixty-four votes to fifty-seven votes.[45] The minority left the Dáil immediately, and from some of its members sprung, in 1926, the modern Fianna Fáil Party. The remaining members elected the Provisional Government which was to organise the transfer of power. In June 1922, an election was held for the Third Dáil and, in spite of the confusion created by the Collins-de Valera election pact,[46] the election is generally regarded as having been won by the pro-Treaty members, who in the spring of 1923 formed the Cumann na nGael Party (which, in 1933, became the modern Fine Gael Party). Immediately after the election, the split between the pro- and anti-Treaty groups, which had existed since the Treaty was signed, finally turned into a civil war, which sputtered to an end in 1923. Art. 17 of the Treaty provided that the provisional institutions were only to remain in force for a limited period. Consequently the first elections under the Irish Free State Constitution were held in August 1923.[47]

It is appropriate to consider the making of the Irish Free State Constitution in a little more detail. First, a Constitution Committee was set up consisting of the head of the Provisional Government and nine other members. Following a study of eighteen foreign constitutions,[48] they produced three schemes in a single month's deliberation. On the basis of these schemes, another draft was prepared by the Provisional Government but was found unacceptable by the British Government. A further draft was produced, agreed with the British and introduced into the Third Dáil sitting as a constituent assembly.

Professor Kohn has summarised the contents of the Irish Free State Constitution thus:

The arrangement . . . follows the established order of Continental models. It opens with a chapter of fundamental declarations, which is followed by the traditional sections on the composition, and the functions of the Legislature, the Executive and the Judiciary. A concluding chapter of transitory provisions regulates the legal, administrative, judicial and fiscal succession of the new regime, the composition of the first Parliament and the mode of promulgation.[49]

In the Constituent Assembly, the clauses implementing the Treaty or safeguarding minorities (proportional representation; fundamental rights) were treated as if they were part of a Government measure; free votes were allowed in regard to the other clauses. As a result, the bill was considerably amended, in particular in regard to the representation of the universities in the Dáil (which was transferred to the Senate); the method of constitutional amendment;

and the original, radical proposals for a-political extern ministers.[50]

The Constitution and Treaty were incorporated as the first and second schedules, respectively, to the Constitution of the Irish Free State (Saorstát Éireann) Act.[51] In the event of any conflict between the Treaty and the Constitution, the Treaty was to prevail. A number of the controversial, international features of the settlement were included in the Treaty. For instance, it was Arts. 1 and 2 of the Treaty which provided that Ireland was to have the same constitutional status in the 'Community of Nations known as the British Empire' as the other dominions and that the same law and usage were to govern Ireland's relations with the Imperial Parliament and Government as applied in the case of Canada.

Not surprisingly, in view of both its troubled birth and the fact that it could be amended by simple act of parliament, no fewer than twenty-seven amendments were made to the 1922 Constitution during its fifteen-year existence. As Professor Chubb has written, 'until 1932, most of the changes were concerned with the reform of the Senate or the removal of those devices which had been grafted on to the cabinet system (initiative, referendum, extern ministers) and had not "taken."'[52] In 1932, Fianna Fáil came to power and, apart from the abolition of the Senate in 1936,[53] most of the twelve amendments made after this date were designed to remove from the Constitution the symbols and procedures of British Commonwealth and the relics of the British connection which had been imposed at the time of the Treaty. Thus, in 1933, the Constitution was amended: to terminate the right of appeal from the Irish courts to the Judicial Committee of the Privy Council;[54] to remove the Governor General's power to reserve bills;[55] and to excise the oath which had to be taken by all members of the Oireachtas, a requirement which had caused so much acrimony.[56]

Until 1936, the King — operating through his representative, the Governor General — occupied a lofty, though symbolic, position as head of state in the Irish Constitution: executive authority in the State was vested in him and his consent was necessary to the making of acts of the Oireachtas.[57] By the last amendment to the 1922 Constitution, which was made on 11 December 1936, the day after the abdication of King Edward VIII, all but one trace of the King was removed from the Constitution.[58] His place in the polity was largely taken by the office of President, which was established by Bunreacht na hÉireann (about the establishment of which more will be said in the next Section). However, both the 1922 Constitution (as amended in 1936) and the 1937 Constitution accommodated the possibility that the King might be used as the symbol of the State for 'the exercise of any executive functions of the State in or in connection with its external relations.'[59] This possibility was realised by the Executive Authority (External Relations) Act, 1936.[60] This last tenuous link with the Crown, coupled with the absence of the pregnant word 'republic' from the 1937 Constitutional was designed, said Mr de Valera, to provide 'a bridge over which the Northern Unionists might one day walk.'[61] The final stage of development came with The Republic of Ireland

Act, 1948 which explicitly declared Ireland a republic, repealed the 1936 Act and provided that 'the executive powers . . . in or in connection with [the State's] external relations' [may be exercised by] the President, acting on the advice of the Government. In fact, most of such functions (e.g. the signing of treaties) are discharged directly by the Government as permitted by Art. 29.4.°, whilst the President only accredits Irish diplomats.

In spite of all these developments, including the 1937 Constitution, the United Kingdom did not protest that there had been any breach of the Treaty and continued to regard Ireland as a member of the Commonwealth until 1949, when The Republic of Ireland Act came into effect. The Irish view was that Ireland had left the Commonwealth in 1937 and for the next twelve years was only externally associated with it, for the limited purposes contemplated by the Executive Authority (External Relations) Act, 1936.[62]

Apart from the relics of the British connection already mentioned, the 1922 constitutional settlement had given rise to dissatisfaction on two principal scores. The first of these was that, under Arts. 6 and 7 of the Treaty, the Irish Free State was to afford certain facilities to the British armed forces (including the bases at Cobh, Berehaven and Lough Swilly). She had also, in effect, forfeited her right to undertake her own coastal defence. By the Anglo-Irish Agreement of 1938 these articles were deleted. This change was necessary (as it transpired) to make Irish neutrality in the forthcoming Second World War feasible.

The second difficulty was the boundary and status of the six northern counties. Under Arts.11 and 12 of the Treaty, the Irish Free State's jurisdiction was not be to exercisable over Northern Ireland for one month (commencing 6 December 1922) and during the so-called 'Ulster month,' both Houses of the Northern Ireland Parliament (constituted under the Government of Ireland Act 1920) took advantage of their right to present a petition to the King asking to be excluded from the Irish Free State and instead to be governed under the 1920 Act. In addition, Art. 12 provided for the setting up of a boundary commission to 'determine in accordance with the wishes of the inhabitants, so far as may be compatible with economic and geographic conditions, the boundaries between Northern Ireland and the rest of Ireland.' Such a commission was set up in 1924, but its report seemed likely to be unfavourable to the Irish Free State. Accordingly, the Free State member of the commission (Eoin MacNeill) resigned and the report was not published until 1969.[63] Instead, in 1925, it was agreed by the representatives of the Free State, Northern Ireland and the United Kingdom, that the *status quo* should prevail, which decision was implemented in domestic law by the Treaty (Confirmation of Amending Agreement) Act, 1925.[64] The 1937 Constitution, however, states that the Republic's Government and Parliament have the right to exercise jurisdiction over the entire national territory and that this consists of the whole island. However, descending to practicalities, the Constitution also states that 'pending the re-integration of the national territory . . . the laws enacted by [the Oireachtas]' are to have effect only over the twenty-six counties.[65]

24

The Irish Free State Constitution　A question which arises in connection with any State is: whence does its basic law derive its authority? To elaborate: it is clear that a statutory instrument is law because it is made (usually) by a minister under authority granted by an act of the Oireachtas and the act is law because it is enacted by the Oireachtas. And the reason why the Oireachtas — unlike any other group of persons — has the capacity to pass acts is that it was given this capacity by the Bunreacht in Art. 15.2.1°. But this only leads us back to the fundamental question which underlies all other questions of law and government in the State: on what authority does the Bunreacht rest. In regard to this field of legal-political inquiry, the British early twentieth-century writer, Bryce remarked:

The question who is legal sovereign stands quite apart from the question why is he sovereign? And who made him sovereign? The historical facts which have vested power in any given sovereign as well as the moral grounds on which he is entitled to obedience lie outside the questions with which law is concerned; and belong to history or to political philosophy; or to ethics; and nothing but confusion is caused by intruding them into the purely legal questions of the determination of the sovereign and the definition of his powers.'

This positivist attitude is both convenient and characteristically British. Unfortunately it will not do in Ireland, for, as will appear, these fundamental questions had a peculiarly practical importance in relation to the 1937 Constitution. To understand why this should be, it is necessary to go back to the 1922 Constitution. Broadly speaking, there are two alternative types of answer to the question of sovereignty and each of them was offered, in different courts, during the life of the Irish Free State. The first answer is possible if (as was the case with Ireland) the State was originally part of another legal system and then split off to form its own separate legal system. In this case, it may be possible to argue that the State's authority rests ultimately on some authorisation by the parent legal system, specifically, in the case of the Irish Free State, upon the Irish Free State Act 1922 passed by the Westminister Parliament. This is the approach which was adopted by the (British) Judicial Committee of the Privy Council in *Moore v. Att. Gen. for the Irish Free State*.[66] Art. 50 was the amending article of the Constitution and the net question for decision in this case was the validity of the Constitution (Removal of Oath) Act, 1933, which purported to alter Art. 50 so that the Oireachtas' power of amendment was no longer confined to amendments which were 'within the terms of the Scheduled Treaty.' Thus the essence of the matter was whether the Oireachtas was empowered to remove what appeared to be a fetter upon its own power of amendment.

The Privy Council held that the Oireachtas did possess this power. The premise of the Privy Council decision was that the basis of the Irish legal system was a British act, the Irish Free State Constitution Act 1922. This act has been passed by the Westminster Parliament, a few months after the Third Dáil had enacted the Constitution of the Irish Free State (Saorstát Éireann) Act to which the Constitution was a schedule. The entire body of the Irish act together with its schedules were, in turn, incorporated as a schedule to the British act. Thus, said the Privy Council:

> ... the Constituent Act and ... the Constitution of the Irish Free State derived [their] validity from the Act of the [Westminster] Parliament, the Irish Free State Constitution Act, 1922. This Act established that the Constitution ... should be the Constitution of the Irish Free State ... The action of the [Third Dáil] was thereby ratified; *apart from such ratification that body had no authority to make a Constitution ...*[67] (my italics).

Granted this premise, the Privy Council's conclusion followed uncontroversially: for if the Constitution derived its validity from the Westminster Parliament then the same Parliament must also have the authority to remove any fetters from the Constitution. What happened was that, in 1931, the Westminster Parliament passed the Statute of Westminster by which the Oireachtas was given the power to pass an act repugnant to any British act. Given the assumption that the Constituent Act was to be regarded as a British act, it followed that the Oireachtas was granted, by the Statute of Westminster, the authority to amend the Constituent Act, even to remove the requirement that any constitutional amendment could not conflict with the Treaty.

Whilst the result of *Moore's* case was welcome to most Irish people, the reasoning was not. Its implication was obvious: the independence which Westminster had given, Westminster could take away, a view which was actually stated by the Privy Council in relation to the Dominion of Canada.[68] Such a view may be expected from British judges who are under a mandate to accept and enforce whatever law emanates from the British legislature. Nevertheless, such a view flies in the face of reality, specifically the ultimate historical fact of Irish (or Canadian) independence. Moreover, Irish judges in Irish courts are under a similar mandate to enforce the acts of their own law-making body. In *The State (Ryan) v. Lennon*[69] the Supreme Court members differed on the effect of an amendment to the 1922 Constitution, extending the time during which amendments could be made by way of ordinary legislation.[70] But all three judges agreed[71] that the validity of the 1922 Constitution was based on an Irish statute, the Constitution of the Irish Free State (Saorstát Éireann) Act, 1922 (to which the Constitution was scheduled) and that this Act owed its authority to the fact — which was proclaimed in its Preamble — that it had been 'decree[d] and enact[ed by] . . . Dáil Éireann sitting as a Constituent Assembly in the Provisional Parliament.' (As Kennedy CJ pointed out in *The State (Ryan)*, the 1922 Act was not an act of the Oireachtas, the Oireachtas not yet having come into existence). The consequences of this view for the paramount authority of the

Treaty were spelt out by Kingsmill Moore J in the following passage from his judgment in *In re Employers Mutual Insurance*:

The Articles of Agreement for a Treaty are to control the interpretation and operation of the Constitution and the restriction remains so long as s.2 of the Constituent Act [*sc.* Constitution of the Irish Free State (Saorstát Éireann) Act 1922] is in force. But in 1933 an attempt was made to repeal this section by s.2 of the Constitution (Removal of Oath) Act, 1933 (No. 6 of 1933). Was such purported repeal effective? If I apprehend correctly the judgments in *The State (Ryan and Others) v. Lennon and Others* the Constituent Act and the Constituent Act alone gave validity to the Constitution and the Oireachtas is merely a creation of the Constitution and so of the Constituent Act. I am unable to see how the creature can repeal or destroy the creator.'[72]

On this view, the British Statute of Westminster 1931 and the new source of power it granted the Oireachtas was irrelevant because the 'one and all sufficient root of title',[73] was an Irish, not a British, act. Thus the 1922 Constitution remained bound by the Treaty.

Búnreacht na hÉireann   The premise of *Moore's* case and the consequence of *Ryan's* case were each anathema to many Irish people. For this reason, Mr de Valera decided that the 1937 Constitution should not be cast as an amendment of the 1922 Constitution, but rather should involve a complete break with it.[74] Thus the process for the enactment of the new Constitution was carefully designed to avoid contamination by the 1922 Constitution or its creation, the Dáil. The first step was that the Dáil sat as a constituent assembly (the Senate, having been extinguished) to examine the draft Constitution in detail. But while, for convenience, the same procedure as for a bill (the different stages etc.) was followed, the motion put to the House at the final stage was: 'That the Draft Constitution, 1937 be and is hereby *approved* by Dáil Éireann.' By the Plebiscite (Draft Constitution) Act, 1937, the draft Constitution was submitted to a plebiscite of the people held in July 1937 (as it happened, on the same day as the general election).[75] The theoretical danger that anyone might argue before a court that the entire process and the Constitution which resulted from it were invalid in the sight of the 1922 Constitution was also countered: Art. 58 of the new Constitution provided that the judges in office, at the time when the Constitution came into force, 29 December 1937, could remain in office only if they took an oath to uphold the Constitution, and the same oath was required (by Art. 34.5) in the case of new judicial appointments.

Sovereignty of the People   To anticipate: the 1937 Constitution is authoritative because it was made by the People and the People are the sovereign authority in the State. The fundamental proposition that the People are sovereign was established by the Supreme Court in *Byrne v. Ireland*[76] by deduction from the Constitution. The Court relied on: the fact of the plebiscite by which the Constitution was created; the Preamble to the Constitution ('We,

27

the people of Éire . . . do hereby, adopt, enact and give to ourselves this Constitution'); Art. 1 by which 'The Irish nation affirms its . . . sovereign right to choose its own form of Government;' Art. 6 which states that 'All powers of government . . . derive, under God, from the people, whose right it is to designate the rulers of the State and, in final appeal, to decide all questions of national policy . . .;' and the involvement of the people in the amending procedure, under Arts. 46 and 47. In sum:

. . . the State is the creation of the People and is to be governed in acordance with the provisions of the Constitution which was enacted by the People and which can be amended by the People only, and . . . the sovereign authority is the People.[77]

The State (or Ireland) is thus the result of the will-act of the People but it is both subordinate to and separate from, the People. It is worth noticing this since, until *Byrne*, an alternative analysis was possible. That alternative is to regard the State as the body which represents and incorporates the People, in other words, the People in their political manifestation. This alternative view seems to have been accepted by Kingsmill Moore J in *Comyn v. A.G.*[78] However, relying on the wording of the Constitution, this view was implicitly rejected in *Byrne*. In parenthesis, it may be observed that this was another instance of a tendency, not uncommon in the judiciary, to impose a precise, legal meaning on words of the Constitution which common sense would indicate were used in a political, exhortatory sense.[79] In any case, it is suggested that since both the State and the People are artificial entities, with no clear demarcation of purpose between them, it was merely complicating the issue, to no advantage, to analyse them as legally distinct bodies.[80]

The implications of this duality have yet to be worked out, though it was relied upon in *Byrne*[81] to support the deduction that whatever types of powers, functions and prerogatives are caught by Art. 49, they are vested not in the State, but in the People. This conclusion raises, but does not answer, the question of how the People (as distinct from the State or its organs) can actually exercise these powers.

A more straightforward application of the principle of popular sovereignty formed one of the bases of the Supreme Court's recent decision in *In re Art. 26 of the Constitution and the Electoral (Amendment) Bill, 1983.*[82] The Bill would have given to British citizens, the right to vote in Dáil and Presidential elections and in referenda. At first sight, the issue might appear to be settled in favour of the bill's constitutionality, by a simple logical argument, *viz.* the Constitution enunciates a positive proposition (that is, 'every citizen . . . [has] the right to vote . . .')[83] and there is no reason in logic to deduce, from the proposition, its converse (i.e. nobody but citizens may vote). Nor is there any policy reason for such a deduction since the constitutional provision makes perfectly good sense, without any glosses, if it be read as attempting to ward off the possibility that (say) some religious minority would be denied the vote.

However, the Supreme Court turned the flank of this argument by referring to the doctrine of popular sovereignty established by the Constitution. The Chief Justice relied, in particular, on Art. 6 (quoted earlier). He said:

There can be little doubt that 'the people' referred to [. . . *sc.* in Art. 6] are the people of Ireland by and for whom the Constitution was enacted. In short, this Article proclaims that it is the Irish people who are the rulers of Ireland and that from them, under God, all powers of government derive and by them the rulers designated and national policy decided. It is not possible to regard this Article as contemplating the sharing of such powers with persons who do not come within the constitutional concept of the Irish people in Article 6.'[84]

Political-moral foundations The influence of the sovereignty of the People showed itself in the 1922 Constitution in such anti-parliamentary features as the referendum and initiative,[85] which made little impact in practice. In the 1937 Constitution, there remains only the participation of the People in the creation and amending of the Constitution and, thus, the recent pro-life amendment may be regarded as a rare example of popular sovereignty in action. (Even if the franchise for the Dáil is extended to foreigners resident in Ireland, it will remain the case that only citizens may vote to amend the Constitution.) The idea of popular sovereignty has always been a strand in the Republican tradition. This reverence for the People arises, in part, as Dr Kohn wrote, from:

the association, deeply ingrained in Irish mentality, from time immemorial, of the conception of government with the notion of external domination. In the consciousness of the people, the anti-democratic has ever been identical with the anti-national . . . . Anything that might tend to detract from the powers of the Executive or to demonstrate its constitutional subjection to the will of the people would, therefore, appear as an additional expression and safeguard of the new liberty.[86]

We have said that the Bunreacht identifies the People as its creator and as the sovereign authority. But that amounts to a *circulus inextricabilis*: the Constitution is authoritative because it was made by the People; the People are sovereign because the Constitution says so. To break this cycle, to understand, finally, why the Bunreacht is legitimate or worthy of respect, we have, as Bryce advised in the passage quoted at the start of this Section, to look beyond the constitutional and legal system. We have to pay regard to the history leading up to the creation of the Constitution and to focus not on the people as an abstraction but rather on the needs and moral values of the actual people (with a small 'p') whom the Constitution is designed to serve, the Irish citizens. First, notwithstanding the wording of the Preamble ('. . . We, the people of Eire . . .'), at the plebiscite in 1937, only 38.6% of the electorate voted in favour of the Constitution with 29.6% voting against and 31.8% either abstaining or spoiling their vote. Whilst the fact of majority support at a plebiscite must carry considerable weight with anyone who subscribes to democracy as the basic political value, these figures cannot be regarded as conclusive in view of the number of Irish citizens who either abstained or voted against the Constitution. The second type of argument on which a constitution can call for support is Locke's idea of the social contract by which a government can claim that it is entitled to such power over its citizens, and only such power, as is necessary, for the well-being of the community (including the maintenance of law and order). In other words, a constitution underpins the entire legal system. It thus deserves the same respect, writ large, as ordinary law commands in the community and warrants the allegiance of all those who reject a state of anarchy. But the social contract theory grants this claim subject to a condition and this condition is that the power entrusted to the Government should be used in the interests of the community and that the Government should respect the position of any minority group and the fundamental rights of the citizen.[87] To judge by the Preamble and, more briefly, Art. 6.1, the Bunreacht seems to accept this political theory and to rest its claim to legitimate authority on the achievement of the sort of standards mentioned in the last sentence. For the Preamble states that the Constitution was enacted in order:

to promote the common good, with due observance of Prudence, Justice and Charity, so that the dignity and freedom of the individual may be assured, true social order attained, the unity of our country restored, and concord established with other nations.

Earlier, the Preamble reinforced this claim in a slightly different way. It invokes the Almighty and implies the natural law idea that the only laws and governmental actions authorised by the Constitution are those which accord with His standards. The Preamble commences with these words: 'In the name of the Most Holy Trinity, from Whom is all authority and to Whom, as our final end, all action both of men and States must be referred, . . .'In short, the Constitution's principal claim to legitimacy is that its content conforms to a certain moral standard.

1.5 AMENDMENT[88]

As a convenient shorthand, constitutions are sometimes ranged on a 'flexible-rigid' spectrum, according to the ease with which they can be amended. On this criterion, the 1922 and 1937 Constitutions are at opposite ends of the scale. It was provided, by Art. 50 of the 1922 Constitution, that amendment would require a referendum of all the voters. However, Art. 50 also stated that, for the first eight years of its existence, the Constitution could be amended by legislation passed by the Oireachtas in the ordinary way, and it was held[89] that such legislation did not even have to be explicitly labelled as a constitutional amendment. During this initial period, the amending article was itself amended by extending the period of eight years to sixteen years[90] and this change was upheld, by a majority, in the Supreme Court in *The State (Ryan) v. Lennon*.[91] By contrast, the 1937 Constitution is, both in form and

R.T.C. LIBRARY, LETTERKENNY

in fact, a rigid constitution. It lays down a two-stage amending process: first, every proposal must be passed in the form of a bill, expressed to be 'An Act to amend the Constitution,' which shall not contain any other proposal and which must be initiated in the Dáil. Secondly, true to the idea of 'Sovereignty of the People' the proposal for an amendment must be approved by a majority at a referendum at which every citizen who has the right to vote at a general election may vote. The bill is then signed by the President and promulgated as a law.[92] The Report of the Committee on the Constitution in 1967[93] drew attention to the fact that there is no provision requiring that those who vote in favour of the proposal, at the referendum, should amount to any particular percentage of the electorate (as would have been the case with the 1922 Constitution,[94] after the sixteen-year initial period had elapsed). The Report concluded, however, that there was no danger in this since it was anticipated that a proposal to amend the Constitution would always generate sufficient interest to attract a substantial vote.

However, Art. 51, which was one of the Transitory Provisions of the Constitution, allowed for the amendment of the Constitution merely by ordinary act of the Oireachtas, subject to two provisos: first the amendment had to be made within three years of the date when the first President took office; secondly, in the opinion of the President, the proposal had to be *not* 'of such a character and importance that the will of the people ought to be ascertained by Referendum.' Two amendments were made under this dispensation.[95] The First Amendment of the Constitution Act 1939 was passed at the outbreak of World War II ('The Emergency') and its effect was to widen the scope of Art. 28.3.3 (the subsection which shelters emergency law from challenge for unconstitutionality) to encompass situations in which Ireland is not a belligerent. The Second Amendment of the Constitution, 1941 was introduced, following a stock-taking in regard to the Constitution by each of the departments of state. It made changes in sixteen articles, including a further widening of Art. 28.3.3.

Apart from these two 'teething' amendments, there were no changes until 1972, since three bills which had been passed by the Oireachtas (all proposing changes in the electoral system) were rejected by the People in 1959 and 1968. Three proposals were approved at referenda in 1972: entry into EEC; votes at 18; and termination of the special position of the Catholic Church. Two further proposals were accepted in 1979: the first was a by-product of the long-running saga of the reform of higher education and allowed for the re-distribution of the university seats in the Senate; the second rendered adoption orders made by the Adoption Board immune from the requirement that justice must be administered by a court[96] and thus excluded the possibility that adoption orders might be characterised as an 'administration of justice' and struck down for unconstitutionality. In 1983, the pro-life amendment was added to the Constitution. And, in 1984, the Constitution was amended so as to empower the Oireachtas to extend the franchise in Dáil elections to non-citizens.[97]

31

Three observations may be made on these amendments: first, whilst the pro-life amendment, the termination of the Catholic Church's special position and, possibly, the introduction of votes at eighteen may be regarded as the outcome of a specific desire to develop the Constitution, the other four amendments were either the result of a more general decision which incidentally impacted on the Constitution (entry into EEC, reform of higher education) or were designed to neutralise a consequence which was probably not foreseen in 1937 (adoption orders' and foreign electors' amendments). Secondly, as has already been noted, constitutions generally contain rules of two types. First, there are those which regulate the composition and functions of the major organs of government. All the amendments, so far, have been of this type, apart from the pro-life amendment and the termination of the special position of the Church. Secondly, a constitutional provision may set down an aspiration, policy or value which is so significant as to warrant a statement in the fundamental law. It appears likely that any major amendments which might be proposed in the foreseeable future would be of this type and would deal with such matters as the ban on divorce or the constitutional right to property. As a final observation, it may be mentioned that, apart from the pro-life amendment, the other amendments enjoyed the support of a consensus among the two major parties and other significant institutions and were passed by overwhelming majorities.

In any case, the conclusion must be that, chiefly because of the difficulty of the amending process, there have been few formal amendments and that these have been fairly insignificant. In view of this, it is necessary to notice that there are other ways, apart from formal amendment, by which changes of a constitutional nature may be brought about. The most obvious of these is by way of an act of the Oireachtas. However, as noted in Section 2, the Oireachtas has been very reticent in the field of social, family or religious reforms which is the field in which change is likely to be demanded in the short- or medium-term future. Undoubtedly, in Ireland, as in the U.S.A., the greatest contribution to constitutional development in the field of individual rights has come not from the legislature but by way of judicial interpretation of the Constitution, in particular, the fundamental rights. The final, indirect, source of reform of the law and Constitution is the European Convention on Human Rights, which is administered by the European Commission of Human Rights and, ultimately, by the European Court of Human Rights. A decision of the Court has already led to the introduction of a civil legal aid scheme and to the vesting in the Circuit Court of jurisdiction to grant divorce *a mensa et thoro*.[98] Pending before the Commission, or soon to be brought before it, are cases in which it will be submitted that the constitutional ban on divorce and the criminalisation of homosexual activity between consenting adults are in conflict with the Convention.

2

Separation of Powers and Rule of Law

At the root of the separation of powers is Acton's dictum that 'Power tends to corrupt and absolute power corrupts absolutely.'[2] It follows from this dictum that one way of encouraging limited government is to divide governmental authority among more than one body, with each body having some degree of independence so as to be able to act as a counter-balance against the others. There are, of course, many ways in which governmental power may be divided. One example, not adopted in Ireland, is federalism, in which the power is divided among different, territorial organs of government. Again, in bygone centuries, in Britain, the three estates in Parliament (Lords, Commons and Clergy) were seen as checking and balancing each other. However, one particular arrangement for the division of power has attracted most attention from the writers who have concerned themselves with the matter (including Plato, Locke and Montesquieu). It is this model which has secured for itself the title of the 'separation of powers' and which, in its purest model, has been outlined, by Professor de Smith in the following passage:

1. There are three main classes of governmental functions: the legislative, the executive and the judicial.
2. There are (or should be) three main organs of government in a State: the Legislature, the Executive and the Judiciary.
3. To concentrate more than one *class* of function in any one person or organ of government is a threat to individual liberty. For example, the Executive should not be allowed to make laws or adjudicate on alleged breaches of the law; it should be confined to the executive functions of making and applying policy and general administration.

It is an easy, though not very useful, exercise to demonstrate that, apart from the three exceptional provisions to be noted below, in most of its features the Irish Constitution does not conform to the strict model of the separation of powers outlined in the passage quoted. For instance, the major element in the Constitution is the fused legislative-executive; formally the legislature is supposed to control the executive; the reality is usually the other way round; either way, the separation of powers is not followed. There is also a significant overlap of personnel, with all ministers being members of one or other House of the legislature. Again, even where the most independent organ, the judicature, is concerned, the judges (although they are ineligible to sit in either House) are appointed by the President, on the advice of the Government, and may be removed only by the legislative Houses. In addition, there are some instances of the judicial and (on one interpretation of the word) 'legislative' functions being vested in the executive, a point to which we shall return later. Thus, as regards the precise match of a particular govermental function with one specialised organ, the Irish Constitution does not follow the strict model of the separation of powers outlined in the quotation. However, the modern view is that this is not an important aspect of the doctrine. For it is surely more dangerous to liberty to concentrate a large quantum of power derived from the same govermental function in one organ than it is to combine in the same organ, analytically distinct, but less important, functions. As has been suggested already, the quintessence of the separation of powers is the existence of branches of government which are sufficiently independent of each other (total independence may be undesirable for other reasons) to act as counterweights controlling each other. Comparing the Irish Constitution with this standard, the independence of the judiciary can be seen as a vital element of the separation of powers. As regards the executive-legislature relationship, it may be suggested that the Irish polity would be improved if the legislature enjoyed sufficient independence of the executive to enable it to exercise at least the power of criticism.

It is a defect in the pure model of the separation of powers, that there is a lack of communication between the distinct branches of government which it envisages. There is thus no direct way for one branch to control another which is exercising its power improperly. A related idea which modifies the separation of powers, in an attempt to meet this criticism, is the notion of 'checks and balances,' by which each organ of government is equipped to exercise some control over the other organs in that it plays a part in the exercise of their functions and may thus be able to restrain an abuse of power. This idea has been adopted, at some points, in the Irish Constitution. Thus, as has been noted in the previous paragraph, formally the Government is responsible to, and may be removed by, the Dáil. Again, the Oireachtas may impeach the President or remove the judges, though it does not, as the U.S. Senate does, enjoy a power of veto over the appointment of ambassadors or Supreme Court justices.

It will be useful here to give a general account of the three, classic functions into which all governmental activity has been analysed. The *legislative* function refers to the making of a law, i.e. a generalised norm which applies not to a single group or situation but rather to a potentially unlimited group of persons or situations falling within a common category. To apply a law in a concrete case, two further processes (which constitute the *judicial* function) are required. First the facts of the matter may be in dispute between interested parties, and therefore the rival accounts must be investigated, weighed against each other and authoritatively resolved. The need for the second process arises from the fact that no law — unless it be unbearably long — can anticipate and cater

34

precisely for all possible contingencies. Thus, in order to bridge the gap between the pre-existing law and the precise decision which is necessary to settle the dispute before the court, an act of interpretation or adjustment may be required. Whether this action requires a sufficient degree of creativity to be regarded as, strictly speaking, an act of law-making is perhaps unimportant; for practical purposes, it is a task which has always been left to the judiciary simply because it is they who decide concrete cases.

Whereas the legislative and judicial functions involve (at least at the centre) fairly solid concepts, the peculiar characteristics of the *executive* function are more elusive and at some points difficult to demarcate from the judicial function. One British authority has offered the following description:

The executive or administrative function is the general and detailed carrying on of government according to law, including the framing of policy and the choice of the manner in which the law may be made to render that policy possible. In recent times, especially since the industrialisation of most civilised countries, the scope of this function has become extremely wide. It now involves the provision and administration or regulation of a vast system of social services — public health, housing, assistance for the sick and unemployed, welfare of industrial workers, education, transport and so on — as well as the supervision of defence, order and justice, and the finance required therefor, which were the original tasks of organised government.[4]

We have already described the chief purpose of the separation of powers, namely the idea of dividing power among more than one organ and, thus, reducing the danger to freedom which is inherent in all government. There is also a subsidiary purpose which is significant in the Irish Constitution. It arises from the fact that each of the three functions (just explained) requires a different procedure and process and thus, it is assumed, a different organ, To take, first, the case of the judicial function it can be seen that it is appropriate for it to be exercised through a system which is characterised by openness and by conspicuous uniformity and fairness, both as regards substance and procedure. It is thus desirable for the entire judicial function to be located in its own distinct arm of government. What, for example, is the point of creating a fine, independent judiciary if all the important judicial decisions could be located elsewhere, even in some cats-paw of the executive?

Similar considerations apply in regard to the question of why the function of legislating is exclusively vested in a specialised legislature. The idea of appropriate procedure means that in a constitutional democracy it is of the essence that the process of law-making should be preceded by an examination of the draft law and the possible alternatives to it, and that this scrutiny should be conduced in public and reported in the news media. This notion of appropriate process is the only possible reply to the question: given that the executive controls a reliable majority in the legislature, what is the need for an elaborate law-making ceremony which has little effect on the content of the law?

Finally, as regards the executive function, it can be said that, of its nature, this function needs to be discharged privately, quickly, flexibly and (often) by way of a multiplicity of routine administrative actions. These characteristics explain the need for an organ to house the executive which is distinct from the other two organs.

2.2 SEPARATION OF POWERS IN THE IRISH CONSTITUTION

In Ireland, the practical significance of the classic functions of government stems from the three deep marks which the separation of powers has left on the Constitution.

Art. 34.1   First, subject to two exceptions to which we shall return, Art. 34.1 provides that justice must be administered in the courts of law and only in the courts.[5] This principle has two consequences of which the first is that the other organs of government[6] (legislature and executive) may not trespass upon the judicial process, as for example by way of an act of the Oireachtas which specifically settles the results of a pending court case.[7] A less spectacular example occurred in *Maher v. A.G.*[8] in which the Supreme Court considered a section which provided that a certificate, stating that a specimen of a person's blood contained a specific concentration of alcohol, was to be taken as '*conclusive* evidence' of that fact (my italics): the section was held unconstitutional because the Constitution reserves to the courts, 'the determination of all the essential ingredients of any offence charged against an accused person.'[9] Again, 'the selection of punishment is an integral part of the administration of justice'; thus it was held in *Deaton v. A.G.*[10] that a provision was unconstitutional because it provided that the punishment for a revenue offence was 'either treble the value of the goods . . . or one hundred pounds *at the election of the* [*Revenue Commissioners*]' (my italics). Nor can it be left to the Minister for Justice to decide whether a prisoner should undergo hard labour or not.[11]

The principle under discussion has also been applied to the rule that the executive — the Government or a department of state — could not be compelled to produce documents or give oral evidence in any court case where such disclosure was against the public interest. It was formerly the case that the certificate of a minister or secretary of a department that disclosure would violate the public interest was unreviewable by a court. Whilst accepting that there may be a public interest in confidentiality, the courts have recently held that there is also a public interest in the disclosure of all the evidence in a court case and — this is the most important point — that if a conflict arises between these two aspects of the public interest, in the context of a court case, then it is for the court, not a minister, to balance the two aspects. For: 'Power to compel the attendance of witnesses and the production of evidence is an inherent part of the judicial power of government of the State and is the ultimate safeguard of justice in the State.'[12]

Art 34.1 means, secondly, that save for the exceptions to be mentioned later justice cannot be administered anywhere other than a court. A straightforward example is *Cowan v. A.G.*[13] in which a statute was held unconstitutional because it vested all the powers and duties formerly possessed by the High Court sitting as an 'election court,' in a tribunal made up merely of a practising barrister of at least seven years' standing. Again, in the multi-faceted case of *In re Haughey,*[14] the Supreme Court held that it would be unconstitutional to vest, in a committee of the Oireachtas, the function of certifying the facts on which the criminal offence of failing to answer the committee's questions were based.

One disadvantage of this rule is that it prevents the vesting of a judicial function even in an independent tribunal, although this may be desirable in certain specialised subject areas. An especially grave instance was the danger that the adoption orders — on which the legal relationship between twenty five thousand adopted children and adoptive parents rested — would be held unconstitutional and invalid[15] because the adoption orders were made not by a court but by An Bord Uchtála (The Adoption Board). This particular danger was met by a constitutional amendment which made it clear that adoption orders were outside the sweep of Art. 34.1[16]

'Limited functions . . . of a judicial nature' The other and more general exception to Art 34.1 is Art 37. The immediate reason for the creation of Art. 37 was the suggestion that Art. 64 of the 1922 Constitution (the equivalent of Art 34.1) might render the Irish Land Commission unconstitutional, in particular as regards its power of considering objections to the compulsory acquisition of land. Whilst this submission was rejected, after extensive consideration, by the Supreme Court in *Lynham v. Butler (No. 2),*[17] the very suggestion caused a shock to the Irish body politic. The response was the inclusion in the 1937 Constitution of Art. 37 which was designed to protect, among other things, the Land Commission. Art 37.1 read as follows:

Nothing in this Constitution shall operate to invalidate the exercise of limited functions and powers of a judicial nature, in matters other than criminal matters, by any person or body of persons duly authorised by law to exercise such functions and powers, notwithstanding that such person or such body of persons is not a judge or a court appointed or established as such under this Constitution.

Many cases[18] have been decided on the basis of Art. 37, the use of which means that there is no need for a court to wrestle with the difficult question of what constitutes an 'administration of justice.' The most significant case on Art. 37 is *In re Solicitors Act, 1954*[19] in which it was held that the powers to strike off an erring solicitor, which had been vested in a tribunal (the Disciplinary Committee of the Incorporated Law Society) amounted to an administration of justice. The issue, which divided the Supreme Court from the High Court, was the interpretation of Art. 37. According to the High Court, the Disciplinary Committee's jurisdiction was limited in two ways: first because there was an appeal to the Chief Justice against an order striking off a solicitor. Disagreeing on this point, the Supreme Court said that, even if there had been an untrammelled right of re-hearing (which was not the case), 'the existence of an appeal to the Court's cannot restore constitutionality to a tribunal whose decisions, if unappealed, amounted to an administration of justice.'[20] Nevertheless, on this important practical point, there remains some authority in favour of the opposite view.[21] On the other, central point, the High Court held that the power given to the Disciplinary Committee was limited in the sense that it was exercised only over a limited group of persons. This approach was rejected by the Supreme Court, in a passage which has often been followed by later courts:

It is the 'powers and functions' which must be 'limited', not the ambit of their exercise. Nor is the test of limitation to be sought in the number of powers and functions which are exercised. The Constitution does not say 'powers and functions limited in number.' ... Again it must be emphasised that it is the powers and functions which are in their own nature to be limited. A tribunal having a few powers and functions but those of far-reaching effect and importance could not properly be regarded as exercising 'limited' powers and functions. The judicial power of the State is by Article 34 of the Constitution lodged in the Courts, and the provisions of Article 37 do not admit of that power being trenched upon, or of its being withdrawn piecemeal from the Courts. The test as to whether a power is or is not 'limited' in the opinions of the Court, lies in the effect of the assigned power when exercised. *If the exercise of the assigned powers and functions is calculated ordinarily to affect in the most profound and far-reaching way the lives, liberties, fortunes or reputations of those against whom they are exercised they cannot properly be described as 'limited.*[22] (my italics).

The Court concluded that since a solicitor's livelihood was involved the situation fell outside Art. 37.

In a rather different context, in *Central Dublin v. A.G.*[23] (which was decided before the loss of most of the Minister for the Environment's adjudicatory powers in the planning field to *An Bord Pleanála*) it was held that the Minister's decision as to what constitutes exempted development was a 'limited function . . .' in that the Minister's decision does not finally settle whether the development can be carried out or not, but only whether permission is required.

Administration of Justice Great uncertainty exists regarding the meaning of the other phrase which delineates Art. 34.1's sphere of operation — the 'administration of justice.' The same type of difficulty has arisen in the context of other constitutions and Geoffrey Marshall has said that it entails asking:

Over what range of activities is it an essential protection of liberty to have liabilities finally determined by the traditional methods of common law courts acting judicially? That, of course, is a policy question wrapped in a very large preliminary question of definition.[24]

Because of the variety of different powers with which the legislature may equip a tribunal in considering whether a tribunal is administering justice it is necessary first to scrutinise the tribunal to see whether it possesses some at least of the characteristics of the judicial organ.[25] This raises the fundamental question of what these characteristics are. One attempt at a definition is that of Davitt P in *The State (Shanahan) v. A.G.*:

. . . there can be gleaned from the authorities certain essential elements of that power. It would appear that they include, 1, the right to decide as between parties disputed issues of law or fact, either of a civil or criminal nature or both; 2, the right by such decision to determine what are the legal rights of the parties as to the matters in dispute; 3, the right, by calling in aid the executive power of the State, to compel the attendance of the necessary parties and witnesses; 4, the right to give effect to and enforce such decision, again by calling in aid the executive power of the State. Any tribunal which has and exercises such rights and powers seems to me to be exercising the judicial power of the State.[26]

This definition is especially worthy of attention since it coincides (approximately) with the list of characteristics offered by Kenny J in *McDonald v. Bord na gCon*;[27] we shall use it as a framework for the following discussion. One of the ideas behind the first element in the passage quoted is that the judicial function applies a pre-existing rule to present or past facts; by contrast, where the decision is reached by drawing upon the decision-maker's view of the public interest, then the judicial function is not involved.[28] This distinction has been important in a number of cases. In *Central Dublin v. A.G.*[29] it was held that the Minister's decision as to what constitutes 'exempted development' was an 'administration of justice' (albeit a limited function) because it involved the application of settled legal standards. By contrast, the Minister's decision in regard to planning applications appeals was determined by reference to his idea of 'proper planning . . .' and this was a policy question rather than an 'administration of justice.' A second example of this distinction is afforded by the Report of the Kenny Committee on the Price of Building Land.[30] This Report proposed a system for the compulsory acquisition of land in which the criteria for the acquisition should be whether the land's market value had been inceased by public works and whether the land would be likely to be used for house-building. The Committee regarded these as sufficiently clear-cut criteria to make the decision on acquisition an 'administration of justice' which would, therefore, have to be vested in a court.

The second of the 'essential elements' in Davitt P's catalogue is that the decision should be conclusive: a body which merely makes a recommendation is not exercising the judicial power, for it makes no determination affecting rights at all. There is no case law on this criterion,[31] but it would obviously serve to exclude inquiries in which a court-style procedure was being followed by a body which is only empowered to make recommendations — for example, an inquiry, held under the Housing Act, 1966, Third Schedule, to advise the Minister for the Environment whether to confirm a local authority compulsory purchase order.

The third on the list of characteristics of the judicial function is the power to sub-poena witnesses, and this was relied upon in *In re Solicitors Act, 1954.* Dealing with the question of whether the disciplinary system for solicitors constituted an administration of justice, Kingsmill Moore J regarded it as relevant that the 1954 Act vested in the Disciplinary Committee:

> . . . *the powers, rights and privileges vested in the High Court or a judge thereof on the occasion of an action* in respect of the enforcement of the attendance of witnesses and their examination on oath or otherwise and in respect of the compelling of the production of documents[32] (italics in original).

Finally, the criterion of whether the tribunal in question enjoys the rights to call in aid the executive power of the State to enforce its decision was supplemented by the High Court, in *McDonald v. Bord na gCon,*[33] by the requirement that the order made by the Tribunal should be one which 'as a matter of history is an order characteristic of Courts in this country.' *McDonald* involved a disciplinary tribunal, Bord na gCon, which had made an exclusion order prohibiting the person named from being on a greyhound track. According to Kenny J in the High Court,

> . . . a body or tribunal which may lawfully execute its orders by physical force or authorise others to do so does not differ from a Court in this respect. The effect of an exclusion order is that the licensee of any greyhound race track or those authorised by him may remove by force any person against whom the order is made from the track and may thereby override his contractual rights. Lastly, an exclusion order seems to me to be similar in form and in effect to an injunction against trespass and such an injunction is an order characteristic of Courts in this country.[34]

However, whilst the Supreme Court provisionally accepted the 'characteristic' features of the 'administration of justice' as enunciated in the High Court, it reversed the actual decision. The point of difference lay in the fact that the Supreme Court emphasised that it was the licensee of the greyhound track himself, rather than Bord na gCon, who could use reasonable force to remove the person to whom the order applied or could seek a court injunction to exclude him. Since this remedy was not exercisable directly by the Bord itself, the Supreme Court held that the Bord was not administering justice.[35]

Art 15.2 The second manifestation of the separation of powers in the Constitution lies in the plain rule that only the Oireachtas has power to make laws for the State (Art. 15.2). The difficulty which this provision entails is the need to reconcile it with the existence of several annual volumes of statutory instruments, regulations, rules and orders. The courts' approach to this problem was stated as follows by the Supreme Court in *Cityview v. An Comhairle Oiliúna*[36]:

> The giving of powers to a designated Minister or subordinate body to make regulations or orders under a particular statute has been a feature of legislation for many years . . . Sometimes, as in this instance, the Legislature, conscious of the danger of giving too much power in the regulation or order-making process, provides that any regulation or order made should be subject to annulment by either House of Parliament. This retains a measure of control, if not in Parliament as such, at least in the two Houses. Therefore, it is a safeguard. Nevertheless, the ultimate responsibility rests with the courts to ensure that constitutional safeguards remain, . . . In discharging that responsibility, the Courts will have regard to where and by what authority the law in question purports to have been made. In the view of this Court, the test is whether that which is challenged as an unauthorised delegation of parliamentary power is more than a mere giving effect to principles and policies which are contained in the statute itself. If it be, then it is not authorised, for such would constitute a purported exercise of legislative power by an authority which is not permitted to do so under the Constitution. On the other hand, if it be within the permitted limits — if the law is laid down in the statute and details only filled in or completed by the designated Minister or subordinate body — there is not unauthorised delegation of legislative power.

The point of issue in *Cityview* involved the Industrial Training Act, 1967, s.21 which authorises the defendant (AnCO) to 'make an Order . . . imposing a levy on the employers' in a particular industry to be used for the training of recruits to that industry. The Court held the levy order to be constitutional: the Act, it was said, contained (in the long title) a clear declaration of policies and aims and, thus, the actual determination, in the levy order, of the amounts of the levy was characterised as being merely a 'final detail' (notwithstanding that the statute contained no precise guidelines, by which to calculate the amount of the levy — for example, turnover or number of employees).

Recently, in *Cooke v. Walsh*,[37] the Supreme Court has drawn on Art. 15.12 to strike down a regulation. The parent section provided, widely, that: 'Regulations under this section may provide for any service under this Act [the Health Act, 1970] being made available only to a particular class of the persons who have eligibility for that service.' The regulation in question, which purported to be made under this section, excluded from full eligibility for free medical services, victims of road accidents, who receive compensation in respect of their injuries. The Court held that the regulation varied the principle stated in the 1970 Act in that it created a category of persons who could not enjoy full benefits under the Act. It thus made 'law' in the sense explained in the passage from *Cityview* quoted. Read at its full width, the parent section would probably have authorised the making of the regulation and would thus itself have been unconstitutional. However, the Court read the parent section in the light of the presumption of constitutionality. This had the effect of narrowing its scope and thus of: (i) making it constitutional; but (ii) rendering the regulation in question *ultra vires* and invalid.[38] (As regards the question of what utility this surgery left to the parent section, the Chief Justice suggested tentatively that it might enable a particular health board or boards to be exempted from the duty to provide particular services.)

Art. 28.2   The last of the marks which the separation of powers has left on the Irish Constitution is the requirement that 'The executive power of the State . . . [must] be exercised by or on the authority of the Government' (Art. 28.2; *cf.* Art. 29.4.1°). This provision has not yet been fully explored. It has, however, been emphasised by Walsh J in two authorities — *The State (C) v. Minister for Justice*[39] and *Murphy v. Dublin No. 1*[40] — that the fact that a statutory function is vested in a minister or other agent of the executive does not, *ipso facto*, mean that the function is an executive function (a proposition which would seem to be indisputable). Thus, for instance, in *Murphy*, the learned judge characterised the function of the Minister for Local Government, in adjudicating on a dispute between a local authority and a landowner whose land is being compulsorily acquired, as judicial or quasi-judicial, rather than executive. On a different aspect, it seems clear that an 'executive power of the State' may constitutionally be vested in a single minister (as indeed commonly occurs) without violating Art. 28.2 by which such powers must be exercised 'by or *on the authority* of the Government.' The reason is that it is always open to the Government to direct a minister as to how a decision should be taken, although that decision has been vested in a single minister.[41]

2.3   RULE OF LAW[42]

Like the separation of powers, the rule of law is an idea, or sometimes an ideal, about the nature of government. However, while the separation of powers offers a means by which the rule of law may be achieved, the rule of law is closer to being an end.

As a preliminary, one should note that the 'Rule of Law' is often written with capital initials and sometimes even inverted commas, in order to indicate that this important expression does not refer to any specific, concrete legal rule; rather it describes a standard to which some systems of government aspire and which few achieve completely. At the heart of the rule of law are three inter-related notions:

1. Everyone, even the Government and its servants, is subject to the law.
2. The law must be public and precise.
3. It must be enforced by some independent body, principally the court system.

Government subject to law   The idea of 'a government of laws and not of men' goes back to Aristotle. It is the antithesis of the capricious, unlimited ruler portrayed in the novel, *Nineteen Eighty Four*. It is a significant theme in British constitutional history. It surfaced, for example, in the remark of the thirteenth-century writer, Bracton, which Coke, Chief Justice of the

Common Pleas, took pleasure in retailing to James I in 1607: *quod Rex non debet esse sub homine sed sub Deo et lege quia lex facet regem* (= the King ought not be under man but under God and the law, for it is the law which makes him King). More recently, the principle received graphic affirmation in the impeachment proceedings against President Nixon which were initiated in 1974, by the House Judiciary Committee and which forced the President to resign.[43] On a much less spectacular level, in Ireland the excision in *Macauley v. Minister for Posts and Telegraphs*,[44] of the pre-condition that the Attorney General's fiat (permission) was a necessary pre-condition to an action against a minister of the Government could be regarded as a triumph for the rule of law. (It should be noted, though, that the fiat had only been refused in a couple of cases in the history of the State.)[45]

The greatest difficulty with the rule of law arises from the need to re-state the principle in order to accommodate the modern *dirigiste* State with its manifold interference with the rights of the individual. Since the mid-nineteenth century, the comprehensive functions which the State has undertaken have necessitated sweeping compulsory powers of, for example, taxation, regulation, inspection, registration and land acquisition. Whilst the legal principles applicable to official and to private, acts have elements in common, — for example the law of contract or tort — the developments which have just been mentioned mean that it is no longer possible (if it ever was) to say that public officials are subject to the same law as the individual. (Moreover, even where the law is the same, the huge differences in scale between the activities of the State and an individual in regard to say placing orders for goods gives the State bargaining power which is tantamount to a statutory power.)[46]

The result of these developments is that over large areas of government activity, the rule of law is represented by 'the principle of legality,' which has been defined as follows:

Every act of governmental power, *i.e.* every act which affects the legal rights, duties or liberties of any person, must be shown to have a strictly legal pedigree. The affected person may always resort to the courts of law, and if the legal pedigree is not found to be perfectly in order the court will invalidate the act, which cannot then affect him.[47]

Examples of this principle in operation will be given in Chapter 12.5.

It must be emphasised that the rule of law requires everyone and not merely the Government (in its various forms) to obey the law. Breach of the law by individuals or groups (pickets; employers withholding their employees' income tax; punters placing illegal bets; or householders refusing to pay ground-rent or water-rates etc.) is dangerous to the rule of law both for itself and because it weakens the principle of respect for the law throughout the community. The reasons why most of the discussion in this area — including the present short account — has focussed on the Government is simply the enormous powers over the individual which the Government genuinely needs and the unique potential for abuse which this creates.

Law: public and precise The object of this element of the rule of law is that the law should be ascertainable and its operation predictable. Thus the power which the law assigns to the Government and the freedom which it leaves to the individual are known and fixed. An individual can arrange his behaviour to conform to the law; he can be secure in the knowledge that, for example, only a predictable amount of his money can be taken in the form of tax. In the criminal law and procedure, the rule of law is especially important: it means that the citizen can only be detained or arrested on specified grounds and that he can only be punished if he commits specific acts. This is the reason why criminal law is, or ought to be, precisely defined and why the Nazi law of 1935, which made a crime of any act 'which is deserving of penalty according to the fundamental conceptions of a penal law and sound popular feeling' is anathema. This is the reason, too, why criminal law which operates retrospectively — that is, applies to acts which occurred before the law was passed — is banned by the Constitution.[48] Where non-criminal law is concerned there is a well-established rule of statutory interpretation requiring a judge not to give a statute retrospective effect unless the wording of the statute very plainly requires it.[49]

Independent courts Thus far we have focussed on the qualities which laws must possess if they are to be regarded as conforming to the rule of law. The remaining feature bears on the system for putting laws into effect. This consists chiefly of the court system, though, in a more detailed survey, it would also be appropriate to include other institutions for the control of governmental administration and/or the enforcement of the laws, such as the Ombudsman, or tribunals like the Appeal Commissioners (who hear appeals from the Revenue Commissions) or Bord Pleanála (the Planning Board). Concentrating on the courts, we can say, first, that the judges should be impartial and free of possible pressure from the Government or any other quarter. (The independence of the judiciary is a topic to which we shall return in Chapter 12.1.) Secondly, the trials at which the law is enforced should conform to certain minimum standards of procedural justice. To state the contents of these standards would take us deeply into the law of criminal and civil procedure; in view of the exceptionally open texture of the rule of law it would also be rather subjective. However, the following matters (which are also considered important enough to be included in the Constitution) may be suggested: save in exceptional cases, trials should be heard in public;[50] the rules of constitutional justice apply to, *inter alia*, all court proceedings;[51] serious criminal trials must be heard by a jury;[52] and the accused should be provided with a lawyer, if necessary, at state expense.[53]

Caveat The widespread respect in which the rule of law is held is not always

44

accompanied by an equivalent degree of understanding, and so it is well to end on a note of qualification. In my view, unless the rule of law is to be stretched further than it ought to go to remain a serviceable concept with a definite core of meaning, it should not be regarded as an epitome of the entire range of public law. Towards such objectives of the welfare state as social justice or the need to assist the weaker and poorer members of the community, the rule of law is neutral. For it focuses on only one aspect — the negative aspect — of the conditions necessary for a decent and civilised form of government.

3

The President

The President has two functions: he is 'Guardian of the Constitution,' a role which will be dealt with below; he is also head of state — the precise wording used in the Constitution is: '[He] shall take precedence over all other persons in the State . . .'.[2] The essence of the head of state as the symbol of the nation-state was captured by the then Taoiseach, Mr de Valera, at the ceremony for the entry into office of the first President:

You are now our President, our head, freely chosen under our own laws, inheriting the authority and entitled to the respect which the Gaels ever gave to those whom they recognised to be their rightful chiefs, but which for centuries they denied to those whom a foreign law would enforce upon them. In you we greet the successor of our rightful princes and in your accession to office we hail the closing of the breach that has existed since the undoing of our nation at Kinsale.[3]

More specifically, the role of the head of state in a typical parliamentary democracy has been inimitably defined by Leo Kohn in the following passage:

The modern framework of parliamentary government requires at the apex of its pyramid a formal embodiment of executive authority, removed from the sphere of political conflict and symbolic of the continuity of the legal order of the State amidst the fluctuating changes of its political direction . . . The Head of State convokes and dissolves the legislative. He promulgates its enactments thereby converting the contentious issues of parliamentary strife into binding rules of national authority. He transmits the seals of office to the nominees of the legislature and on their recommendation appoints the judges. He interposes the permanent authority of the State in those moments of transition when the holders of executive office change their position . . .[4]

The President's functions in relation to the legislature, executive and judicature, described in this passage, will be elaborated in later chapters. In addition to these functions, the supreme command of the Defence Forces is vested in the President.[5] However, the Defence Act, 1954 provides (rather tortuously) that 'under the direction of the President [who must act on the advice of the Government] . . . the military command of and all executive and administrative powers in relation to, the defence forces, including the power to delegate command and authority, shall be exercisable by the Government . . . through and by the Minister [for Defence].'[6] The President also commissions, dismisses and receives the resignation of officers and makes appointments to the high offices, in the defence forces, specified in the 1954 Act.[7] The right of pardon and the power to commute or remit punishment imposed by any criminal court is also vested in the President and has been consistently exercised to commute the death penalty in murder cases, for the past several years.[8] In addition to these functions, conferred by the Constitution, a few other duties of an honorific, non-controversial nature have been vested in the President, for instance the *ex officio* presidency of the Irish Red Cross Society[9] and presentation of the centenarian's bounty. He is also patron of such bodies as the Civil Service Benevolent Society and the National Council for the Blind. In addition the President accredits Irish diplomatic envoys[10] and executes on behalf of the State, particularly important treaties like the Treaty of Accession to the EEC.

The most significant point is that in respect of almost all his functions, the President's role is purely formal. The Constitution states, carefully, that — save for the decisions he takes as Guardian of the Constitution — 'the powers and functions conferred on the President by this Constitution [or by law] shall be exercisable and performable by him only on the advice of the Government.'[11] Moreover, should the President fail to perform any of the powers and functions of his office as directed by the Government, then the powers and functions shall be exercised by the Presidential Commission (composed of the Chief Justice and the chairmen of each House) which is also to act in place of an absent, incapacitiated or dead President.[12]

At least one President has chafed at his largely ceremonial role and sought to capitalise on the prestige of the office to make a more positive contribution. As Professor Chubb has written,

[Erskine] Childers . . . believed that the President should openly espouse social causes that were incontrovertibly in the public interest and that he could appropriately speak on matters on which the parties and the public were virtually unanimous. He evoked a stirring of unease among politicians, particularly when he actually put a toe into dangerous Northern waters.[13]

3.2 'GUARDIAN OF THE CONSTITUTION'

This convenient if rather gradiose title, coined by Mr de Valera in the debates on the draft Constitution,[14] refers to the six[15] powers which the President exercises on his own initiative independently of the Government. Since each of these powers will be described in more detail in later chapters, they may be outlined very briefly here. The first four of the President's decisions are related to the legislative process and the first three involve situations in which the normal legislative process has been short-circuited in some way. First the President's agreement is necessary to the appointment of a Committee of Privileges, when a challenge is being mounted to the Ceannn Comhairle's certificate that a bill is a money bill.[16] Secondly, where a bill is 'urgent and immediately necessary for the preservation of the public peace and security, or by reason of the existence of a public emergency . . .', the time for its consideration in the Senate may be abridged. Whether a bill fails within this category depends in the first place, on the Government's opinion on the issue; but this opinion must be supported by both a Dáil resolution and the concurrence of the President.[17] Next, where a bill is passed (under Art. 23.1) without the consent of the Senate, then Art. 27 provides that a majority of senators plus at least one third of the members of the Dáil may petition the President, asking him not to sign the bill unless it has been approved by the people either at a referendum or at a general election. The President decides whether or not to sign according to the following criterion: whether 'the Bill contains a proposal of such national importance that the will of the people thereon ought to be ascertained.'[18] Fourthly, before signing a bill, the President may consider whether the bill ought to be referred to the Supreme Court (under Art. 26) for an examination of its constitutionality.[19] Fifthly, the President has a discretion to refuse a dissolution to a Taoiseach who does not command a majority in the Dáil.[20] Finally, he has the power to convene a meeting of either or both of the Houses of the Oireachtas.[21]

It is a tribute to successive Irish Governments that Presidents have seldom found it necessary to use these powers and have never had to do so in what might reasonably be regarded as a crisis. Indeed it is notable that only two of these discretionary functions have ever been exercised by the President. And in the case of the first of these — the summoning of a joint meeting of the Dáil and Senate (held on 2 January 1969) to commemorate the fiftieth anniversary of the first meeting of Dáil Éireann[22] — the function was not being exercised in the circumstances primarily contemplated in the Constitution. The other function to have been exercised — on seven occasions — is the power to refer bills to the Supreme Court under Art. 26.

With one exception (the decision to refuse a dissolution) the President may exercise his discretionary powers only after consultation with the Council of State. In this role,[23] the Council of State is a purely advisory body: whose term of office is the same as that of the President who appointed it; which meets only when the President summons it; and whose members have each taken an oath to 'conscientiously fulfil [their] duties' as members (a pledge which might just be important, should a conflict of interest with another office held by a member arise). The membership (which is listed in the State Directory) consists of: the existing incumbents of specified high offices of state; the past incumbents of certain of those offices provided that they are 'able and willing to act'; and finally, 'such other persons — up to a maximum of seven — as the President may appoint.'[24]

The person responsible for the President's administration and for advising the President is the secretary to the President, a civil servant of the State, who is appointed by the Government following consultation with the President. The secretary to the President is *ex-officio* secretary to the Presidential Commission and clerk to the Council of State.[25]

3.3 COMBINATION OF THE TWO ROLES

Although the President has never had to act as Guardian of the Constitution in a crisis, it is a type of role which could, some day, be crucial. Its combination in the same office as the ceremonial role of head of state invites comment (although such combination is not peculiar to Ireland[26]). The idea behind it is that the ceremonial functions will give the President the respect of the people and the aura of being 'above politics.' And this credit can be drawn upon to make it more likely that his discretionary decisions, as Guardian, will be accepted by politicians and people. This appears, to me, to be a realistic assumption, and it has led to a system which has worked satisfactorily in practice. This view needs to be stated emphatically before going on to notice a difficulty which inevitably arises from the location of these two disparate functions in the same person and which was illustrated by an episode which occurred in 1976.[27] A package of measures to control the IRA was passed following various incidents, including the murder of the British Ambassador. Among these measures was the Emergency Powers Bill 1976, which commenced with a long title connecting the Bill with the emergency resolution comtemplated by Art. 28.3.3° of the Constitution. The result, so the Government believed (wrongly as the subsequent court decision showed), would be that the Bill would be brought within the protection of Art. 28.3.3° and would be, thus, beyond challenge for unconstitutionality. Great was the surprise when the President exercised his powers under Art. 26, to refer the Bill to the Supreme Court. (This decision was probably connected with the fact that the President of the day, President Ó Dálaigh, had been Chief Justice during the Supreme Court's most creative period.) Members of the Government were disturbed by the reference which they regarded as reminiscent of Nero fiddling while Rome burned. These feelings were given public expression in a speech by the Minister for Defence in which he said that it was amazing that the President had referred the Bill to the Court and continued, according to the published version: 'in my opinion, he is a thundering disgrace. The fact is that the Army must stand behind the State.' It was accepted that the second sentence meant that the President was not loyal to the State. A few days later, moved by the Government's failure to punish the Minister, the President resigned. In a country where even ministerial resignations are rare, this unprecedented resignation made an impact.[28]

This episode illustrates the potential strain involved in giving the President the duty of belling the cat. On the one hand, high stakes may be involved in the exercise of any of the President's discretions: the fate of a Government or (as was the case with the Emergency Bill, 1976) of some badly-needed legislature measure may be involved. Even if the Government accepts the absence of political motivation on the President's part, they may still regard his decision as ill-conceived or, possibly, just inconvenient to themselves. In these circumstances, it would be quite possible that they would protest publicly, if the matter became sufficiently serious. The President might wish to reply. Yet, on the other hand, because of the President's other function as head of state, there is a need for the Government and President to present a united front, in public at least. Thus, it would have sapped the confidence of the public in their institutions of Government if in 1976, the same Government and President had continued side by side with a statement on the record, in which a minister had labelled the President as unpatriotic.

To help to maintain a common front, the Constitution gives the Government a power of veto over any message which the President, following consultation with the Council of State, may decide to communicate to the Oireachtas or nation on 'any matter of national or public importance,'[29] a description which would, presumably, cover an exercise of the President's discretionary powers.

3.4 THE PRESIDENT'S INDEPENDENCE

Certain provisions exist to emphasise and support the President's unique position. First, he is not 'answerable to any court.' This protection, however, seems only to exist so long as he is President. And it is confined to 'the exercise and performance of the powers and functions of his office or for any act done or purporting to be done by him in the exercise and performance of these powers and functions'[30] so that presumably the President is not immune in respect of his private actions. This provision was invoked in the Supreme Court in *Draper v. Ireland*[31] (the 'handicapped voters' case). It was sought to prevent the President from dissolving the Dáil on the advice of the Taoiseach in an attempt to force the Oireachtas to introduce arrangements to enable hadicapped persons to vote. O'Higgins CJ stated that the attempt to join the President as a defendant was 'in open defiance' of the constitutional provision. On the other side of the line was *The State (Walshe) v. Murphy*,[32] an action for *certiorari* against a district justice in which it was successfully claimed that the justice had not been properly appointed because he did not satisfy the statutory qualifications for appointment. The rather forlorn argument was made that, as the President had appointed the district justice, to review the validity of the warrant of appointment amounted to impugning an action of the President. This potentially far-reaching argument was rejected by the High Court because the proceedings did not directly involve the President. In addition, Finlay P suggested that the constitutional immunity does not exist in the case of judicial examination of a function which 'require[s] the President's intervention for its effectiveness in law, [but is] in fact the decision and act of the Executive.' This second point would seem to cut across the ratio in *Draper*.

The Constitution also provides that the President is not 'answerable to either House of the Oireachtas.'[33] According to the rules of parliamentary debate, the conduct of the President is not open to comment, favourable or unfavouarable, even on a debate on a motion relating to the President's emoluments.[34] As with the higher judiciary, the President's emoluments are fixed by statute; secured on the Central Fund; and may not be diminished during his term of office.[35] The President may not be a member of either House nor indeed hold 'any other office or position of emolument.'[36] But the President is not above all law. For the Constitution establishes a process by which he may be impeached for 'stated misbehaviour,' a phrase which is, to judge from U.S. practice, wider than the category of criminal offences *simpliciter*. The charge must be preferred by either House of the Oireachtas and confirmed by the other House. If the charge is made out, the President is automatically removed from office and would thus probably be amenable to proceedings before the ordinary court. The removal of the President by impeachment would be an earth-shattering and (in Ireland) unprecedented event and it is carefully designed only to be used *in extremis*. Thus a proposal to either House to prefer a charge against the President may only be even entertained if it is signed by at least thirty members of that House. It will only be adopted if a resolution is supported by two-thirds of the total membership of the House. Then the other House 'investigate[s] the charge, or causes the charge to be investigated.' The second alternative seems to contemplate that the House would convene some type of judicial inquiry, perhaps under the Tribunals of Inquiry Acts, 1921-81. In any case, the President has the right to appear and be represented at the investigation. Finally, the investigating House must pass, by at least two-thirds of its total membership, a resolution 'declaring that the charge against the President has been sustained and that the misbehaviour, the subject of the charge, was such as to render him unfit to continue in office. . .'.[37]

In addition, the Constitution provides, briefly, for the removal from office of a President whose 'permanent incapacity has been established to the satisfaction of the Supreme Court consisting of not less than five judges.'[38]

3.5 ELECTION

To mark the importance of the President he is directly elected by the same electorate as elects deputies[39] (save that in the wake of the foreign electors' constitutional amendment it seems likely that the franchise for the Dáil — but not for the Presidency — will be widened to include British citizens resident in the Republic).

The laws regulating the Presidential elections are set out in the Constitution[40] and amplified by the Pesidential Elections Act, 1937,[41] as amended by Electoral Act, 1963.[42] The qualifications for a candidate are straightforward: he or she must be an Irish citizen and aged at least thirty-five. If a member of either house of the Oireachtas be elected, then he shall be deemed to have vacated his seat. A person who holds or has held office as President is eligible for re-election once only.[43] Strangely, there seems to be no equivalent of the rules which disable certain persons — for example, those serving a prison sentence or the judges — from standing for election to the Dáil.

The rules regarding nomination seem designed to enable the larger parties to determine who may stand for the Presidency. A candidate must be nominated either by twenty members of the Oireachtas or by four county or county borough councils. However, most councillors are members of a political party and so far they have always followed the party line and left it to the members of the Oireachtas to nominate presidential candidates.[44] A former or retiring President may also nominate himself.[45] This facility, which was availed of by President O'Kelly in 1952 and President Hillery in 1983, but not by President de Valera in 1966, is presumably designed to avoid (any) embarrassment caused by a President having to solicit nominations.

As with all other central or local government elections, in Ireland, the election is held, by secret ballot, 'on the system of proportional representation, by means of the single transferable vote.'[46] However, the non-partisan nature of the job has resulted in the agreement of all political parties on a single candidate on five out of nine occasions: the election of Douglas Hyde (1938); Sean T. O'Kelly (1952); Cearbhaill Ó Dálaigh (1974); and Patrick Hillery (1976 and 1983). (The following Presidents have had to face a contest for election: Sean T. O'Kelly (1945); Eamon de Valera (1959 and 1966); Erskine Childers (1973).

If President Hillery completes a full term, there will have been no contested election between 1973 and 1990. In view of this it seems pertinent to discuss the question of whether it is necessary for the health of the body politic that there should be a contested election for the office of President rather than to devote space to an account of the rules regulating an election contest. In the first place, one should note that Ireland is unique in having a non-executive head of state, who is yet elected by universal suffrage, rather than (say) by a college composed of all members of the Parliament. In part, this anomaly is the product of the historical circumstances in which Bunreacht na hÉireann was designed. The 1930's were a period when dictators marched in many European states. In Ireland, the limited nature of the President's discretionary powers were not universally appreciated at first and one way of dispelling the inevitable suspicions was to make the Presidency an elected office.

In my view the question of whether there should be an election to the office of President turns on the correctness of the oft-repeated assertion[47] that an election is necessary because without one, the people would not regard a President as sufficiently independent of the Government to discharge his functions as Guardian of the Constitution. I respectfully disagree with this view of 'what the people think.' First, the decisions which the President has to take, as Guardian, are not 'policy' decisions but are somewhat similar to those taken by the judiciary, and there has never been any suggestion that the judiciary are less independent because they are appointed by the Government. Indeed the case is even stronger asregards the President since, where there is no election, the President, is, in effect, appointed by agreement between the parties, whereas the judges are appointed on the advice of the

52

Government on its own. Secondly, where a President is elected, this entails a divisive, nationwide battle, which carries the danger that a large number of people, including, possibly, the losing political party, may regard the President as associated with the party which supported him and, for that reason, less independent. (With the exception of Douglas Hyde, all subsequent incumbents have been former politicians from the same political party, Fianna Fáil; where there has been a contest, the runner-up has always been a member of Fine Gael.)

4

Government, Taoiseach, Ministers and Departments

The Constitution says only that the Government shall have seven to fifteen members (in practice, there always are fifteen members) with the Taoiseach at its head.[1] Professor Chubb writes, more informatively, that

The Government (sometimes called the Cabinet) consists, then, of those parliamentary leaders of the party or combination of parties, that has won a majority in the Dáil. These leaders meet as a committee to decide the major issues of public policy and the measures they intend to present to the Oireachtas for approval, to coordinate the work of the departments they control, and generally to manage the affairs of the State.[2]

In examining the Government from a legal perspective, we shall deal, in this Chapter, first with the Taoiseach and his Department and his special position *vis-à-vis* other members of the Government; and, secondly, with the appointments, removal and status of other members and junior ministers. The same person is almost always both a member of the Government and a minister of the Government,[3] and we shall conclude the Chapter with a sketch of the minister as corporation sole and of his relations with his department.

We ought to refer briefly to the Attorney General, who is associated with the Government as its chief legal adviser.[4] In constituting this office, the Constitution provides that the Attorney General is not a member of the Government but also states that the holder of the office is to be appointed by the President on the nomination of the Taoiseach and must retire with the Taoiseach (although he is to carry on his duties until a successor to the Taoiseach has been appointed).[5]

4.1 THE TAOISEACH AND HIS DEPARTMENT

Department of the Taoiseach[6]   Since the Taoiseach is the head of the Government, it is natural that his Department should act as the Government Secretariat. From a legal point of view this allocation can be justified by reference to the Ministers and Secretaries Act, 1924 (described later) which gives the Department of the Taoiseach responsibility for all the public services which are not allocated to any other department. Formerly, the Secretary and Assistant Secretary of the Department were always the Secretary and Assistant Secretary to the Government. In 1980, this practice was broken by the appointment of separate incumbents to each post. Nevertheless, the Secretariat remains within the Department and is financed by the same Vote as the rest of the Department. The Secretariat prepares the agenda of items to be discussed at Government meetings. It also services any Government committee[7] which may be set up. To assist in the effective presentation and consideration of items, there exists a thirty-page confidential code of (non-legal) rules variously known as the *Procedure in Government* or the *Cabinet Procedure*. This covers such questions as: how Government business must be framed; what information must be circulated beforehand; and the procedure which must be followed to attempt to resolve inter-departmental disputes before, as a final resort, appeal is made to the Government. It also regulates the course of consultation to be followed in regard to Government legislation.[8] The Government Secretary takes the minutes of Government meetings,[9] and is responsible, afterwards, for conveying the decisions taken to the minister(s) affected and monitoring their implementation. Until recently, a distinction used to be made, in the agenda for a Government meeting, between Government items, which are the matters vested in the Government by the Constitution or other law (for example, advising the President to appoint a judge), and, on the other hand, Cabinet items which encompass all other matters (for example, considering legislation). To the bafflement of future researchers, this division was reflected in the existence of separate Government and Cabinet Minutes.

Secondly, the Department is involved in overseeing the policy and performance of the other departments. This function equips the Taoiseach to exercise better-informed powers of surveillance over his Government's activity. It represents a radical break with the past, as can be seen from the increase in the number of higher civil servants in the Taoiseach's Department. For instance, according to the Directory of State Services, the authorised numbers of principals in 1979 and 1983 were three and ten, respectively. (In 1983, five of the principals were working in the Economic and Social Policy Division, headed by an Assistant Secretary, which had effectively originated in 1980, on the demise of the Department of Economic Planning and Development.) This expansion can be attributed to such factors as: the economic crisis; the personalities of the incumbents of the office since 1979 (Mr Haughey and Dr Fitzgerald); and the need for the Taoiseach to be fully briefed on the entire range of Government activities for meetings of EEC Heads of Government. Consonant with this change, the ministers of state to the Department increased from one to three, in late 1982. Traditionally, the minister of state in the Department is the Government Chief Whip who deals with the management of Government business and party discipline, in the Dáil. In late 1982, two other ministers of state, dealing with Women's Affairs and Arts and Culture, respectively, were assigned to the Department.

In a media-conscious age, it is also significant that the Department includes the Government Information Service which was first set up in 1934 (as the Government Information Bureau) to supply information on the work of the Government to the print and broadcasting media. The head of the Service

55

is often a temporary civil servant, who leaves office at the same time as the party which appointed him.

Relations with the North loom so large in the official life of the Republic as to make the subject *sui generis*. It is dealt with chiefly by the Department of the Taoiseach. However, because of the ubiquitous nature of the subject, it is also, in part, a function of the Department of Foreign Affairs and of other departments which may have an operational connection (for example, the Department of Energy).

The remaining items in the Taoiseach's bailiwick comprise some very miscellaneous, minor functions. For instance, the Department controls the release of state papers to the State Paper Office, an ante-room of the Public Records Office. (Under the 'thirty years rule', — at the time of writing — the papers for the Administrations up to 1948-51 have been released.) In addition, the Department has varying responsibilities (including staff matters, answering Dáil questions, administering grants-in-aid) for certain non-commercial State-sponsored bodies, commissions and agencies, including the Central Statistics Office;[10] National Board for Science and Technology;[11] Arts Council (An Chomhairle Ealaoinn);[12] Attorney General's Chambers;[13] Local Appointments Commission; the National Economic and Social Council; National Planning Board (charged with the duty of drawing up and supervising a national economic plan); and Council for the Status of Women.

As can be seen, the tradition has been not to burden the Taoiseach's Department with major executive functions and this was one of the reasons why the Devlin Report, when recommending that personnel and other functions should be removed from the Minister for Finance, refrained from proposing that they should be vested in the Taoiseach.[14]

'Prime ministerial government'? The real power of the Taoiseach, in particular, his authority, *vis-à-vis* his colleagues in the Government, is a matter which is peculiarly ill-fitted to definition in a series of rules because so much depends on circumstances and personalities. The most that can be done in a book on constitutional law is to summarise the factors which determine whether — to adopt the terminology used in Britain — the Taoiseach is merely *primus inter pares* or whether we have a system of 'prime ministerial government.'[15]

The Constitution describes the Taoiseach (twice indeed[16]) as the 'head of the Government or Prime Minister.' It is he who appoints and, if necessary, dismisses members of the Government or junior ministers and who allocates portfolios.[17] The decision to dissolve the Dáil (which is formally done by the President) is vested in the Taoiseach, rather than, as is the case with most important official functions, in the Government as a whole.[18]

The Taoiseach's position at the centre of the Government is pivotal. He is the central co-ordinating figure who must take an interest in the work of all departments and the person to whom ministers naturally turn for advice when faced with large problems. His position is further strengthened by his control of the Government Secretariat and the Government Information

Service. A Taoiseach is almost always leader of his party which enables him to tap an extra source of influence. Again, the exigencies of modern public relations and the mass electorate, the majority of whom are uninterested in the details of politics, have created a pressure towards the personification of a party in its leader. In all but the most recalcitrant cases, the spotlight of publicity which thus focuses on the leader tends to increase his prestige. Both for this reason, and also because the duty of loyalty to a leader is at least as strong in Ireland as elsewhere, Churchill's observation is apt: 'The loyalties which centre on number one are enormous. If he trips, he must be sustained. If he makes mistakes, they must be covered. If he sleeps, he must not be wantonly disturbed.' The levers of power controlled by a Taoiseach or even a potential Taoiseach are considerable; and thus the difficulties confronting colleagues who might wish to remove or replace him are substantial. The amount of public upheaval that would be entailed in uprooting a Taoiseach or potential Taoiseach, who is really determined to stay, is such that sufficient deputies might shrink from the attempt (as seems to have occurred in the failure of the February 1983 party censure motion against the Leader of the Opposition, Mr Haughey).

Another factor must be considered as a determinant of the Taoiseach's authority. It is the extent to which he can command loyalty by saying: 'Do as I do or get another Taoiseach.'[19] In other words, much depends on the extent to which he is perceived as an electoral asset by his party. This point is graphically illustrated by the career of Mr Jack Lynch. After an unremarkable start (in 1966), his authority noticeably increased, because it was accepted that it was his *persona* which countered an anti-Government trend and returned Fianna Fáil to power in 1969. Then, again, at the end of his leadership, in 1979, his position (already undermined by a feeling that his resignation was imminent) was further weakened because of his party's poor showing not only in European Assembly and local authority elections but even in two Dáil by-elections (in Cork City and Cork North East, territory which was regarded as the heart-land of his support).

And yet in practice, Taoisigh have seldom used their powers to the full. Mr de Valera, for instance, always sought to achieve Government decisions which were unanimous, even if this required postponement or compromise. Again, the power of dimissal has been used only once, as late as 1970, to remove Mr Blaney and Mr Haughey at the time of the Arms Crisis.[20] Taoisigh have felt constrained by such factors as the need to respect the seniority rule or to accommodate different sections of the party. Thus, *Chairman or Chief?*, Mr Brian Farrell's survey of five Taoisigh, published in 1971, concludes that they have behaved more as chairmen than as chiefs. Since this survey was written, the only new Fianna Fáil incumbent of the office has been Mr Haughey. His periods in office are too close to the time of writing, to allow a balanced judgment. It seems reasonable to suggest, though, that his unpopularity with some sections of his own party — unprecedented, in its extent and publicity — stems from three sources: first, the methods used by his supporters in 1979 to undermine the then Taoiseach, Mr Lynch; secondly, Mr Haughey's perceived tendency to personalise the Fianna Fáil party and to develop a Presidential-style, reflected in the increased size of the Department of the Taoiseach — in all of which there was a sharp contrast with the modest, relaxed *persona* projected by Mr Lynch; thirdly, Mr Haughey's tendency, especially in his second period in office in 1982, to give office to his supporters, however ill-qualified, and to exclude critics. It seems as if Mr Haughey ignored the unspoken bargain between a Taoiseach and his party: on the one side, public loyalty and support; on the other, private consultation and restraint in the exercise of his considerable powers. The reaction to the breach tends to confirm Mr Farrell's thesis that the Taoiseach is expected to exercise a self-denying ordinance. A further factor affecting his position, which is not confined to political life, may be suggested. It is simply that times have changed and uncritical public obeisance to the leader is no longer regarded as the virtue that it once was.

Inevitably, the Taoiseach's position is weaker in a coalition government than a single party administration. In a coalition, his power has to be shared, and be seen to be shared, with the leader of the second largest party. In regard to members of the Government who belong to other parties, he lacks the real powers of appointment, dismissal,[21] replacement and allocation of portfolios, since these decisions are, in substance, taken by the leader of the party whose members are affected. Most strikingly, the Labour Party made it a condition of its participation in the Inter-Party Government of 1948-51 that the leader of Fine Gael, General Richard Mulcahy, should not be Taoiseach. However, within the Taoiseach's own party (which has always been Fine Gael) it seems that, at least since the commencement of the National Coalition of 1973-77, the Taoiseach has been able to exercise an authority similar to that of a Fianna Fáil Taoiseach. Of the most recent incumbent, it has been said: 'Dr Fitzgerald exercised [a] decisive authority in selecting his governmental team and weighting it deliberately in favour of his own supporters within the party.'[22] But it may be noted, equally, that this exercise of one of the prerogatives of his office has drawn mutterings from certain quarters in his own party. In a subdued form, this is the same feature which was noted, in the previous paragraph, in relation to Mr Haughey's period as Taoiseach.

4.2   MEMBERS OF GOVERNMENT AND MINISTERS OF STATE

Members of Government   The President appoints, as the other Government members (besides the Taoiseach), the persons who have been nominated by the Taoiseach, with the previous approval of the Dáil.[23] Each member must be either a deputy or a senator. However, befitting the seniority of the Dáil, not more than two may be senators and the Taoiseach, Tanaiste and Minister for Finance must, in any case, be deputies.[24] In fact, up to 1984, there had only ever been three ministers in the Senate.[25] Each member of the Government has the right to attend and be heard, but not vote, in the House of which he is not himself a member.[26] There is a suggestion that members of the Government are under a conventional obligation to resign from any local authority to which they may belong. Where a minister is temporarily unable to discharge the functions of his office (whether from illness, absence from Ireland or any other reason), the Government may make an order nominating another member of the Government 'to execute . . . the office of the [absentee minister]'. The replacement minister has full powers but he may if 'it appears to him to be convenient so to do' add the prefix 'acting' to his title.[27]

The President may be required, on the Taoiseach's advice, either to accept the resignation, or to terminate the appointment of any other member of the Government.[28] If the Taoiseach, himself, resigns (whether for personal reasons or in the unlikely event that he loses the support of a majority in the Dáil without the Dáil being dissolved), then the other members of the Government are deemed also to have resigned with him.[29] However, both the Taoiseach and his colleagues 'continue to carry on their duties until their successors shall have been appointed'.[30] Where there is a dissolution of the Dáil, the Constitution provides, in slightly different language, that the Taoiseach and his ministers 'shall continue to hold office until their successors shall have been appointed.'[31] In view of the fact that there is usually a hiatus of two to three weeks between a general election and the meeting of the new Dáil which is necessary to form the new Government, this is a significant provision. It probably applies, whether the party originally in Government wins or loses the election[32] and to all members, of the Government, even those who have lost their seats.[33]

The Taoiseach must select one of his colleagues as Tanaiste. If the Taoiseach is temporarily absent, the Tanaiste deputises for him. In addition, if the Taoiseach should die or become permanently incapacitated, the Tanaiste acts 'for all purposes' in his place until his successor is appointed.[34] The Tanaiste can be and always is, appointed, in addition, to be the minister of some department. As has been written by Mr Farrell: 'Despite his title, the Tanaiste has no automatic right of succession; the title is a mark of seniority rather than of favour, although it may well be that a Taoiseach is more likely to consult the Tanaiste than other ministers on politically delicate matters.'[35] In Coalition Governments, the post of Tanaiste is used as a formal acknowledgement of the leader of the second largest party forming the Government.

Ministers of state   The Ministers and Secretaries Act, 1924, provided for the appointment by the Executive Council of a maximum of seven 'parliamentary secretaries' to act as junior ministers.[36] In 1977, this provision was repealed and replaced by a measure allowing for the appointment of 'ministers of state' from among members of either House to a maximum of initially ten and, since 1980, fifteen.[37]

In spite of this change of name, the function of these junior ministers remains the same, that is, to assist the minister at the head of the department to which they are assigned by their appointment. A Government order[38] may be made on the request of a minister, delegating to his minister of state all the minister's powers and duties under a particular act or, more narrowly, any particular statutory power or duty. There are five limitations on this power of delegation. First, it may be revoked by the Government at any time, even without a request by the minister of the Government. Secondly, it automatically terminates if the identity of either the minister of the Government or minister of state changes and, for this reason, the order mentions the minister of state by his name. Thirdly, the power delegated is exercisable by the minister of state in his own name but 'subject to the general superintendence and control of the Minister.' Fourthly, the power delegated continues to be vested in the minister so that it can be exercised either by him or by the minister for state. Finally, the minister remains responsible, politically or legally, for the exercise of the power delegated.[39]

By standing orders and house practice, ministers of state are treated, for several purposes, in the same way as members of the Government, for instance in regard to presenting a bill without leave in the Dáil; or speaking in the House of which they are not members.[40]

Since the functions of a minister of state are largely the same as those formerly performed by a parliamentary secretary, the change is merely a matter of 'image', the need for which has been explained on the grounds that the title 'parliamentary secretary' gave people, both at home and internationally, the impression that a very junior minister was involved. Accordingly, the new title was decreed for the position of junior minister. Probably because of its use in Britain, the title 'minister of state' was invoked. However, the same style was already in use for 'members of the Government having charge of a Department of State,'[41] that is, Government ministers. This change therefore required a new name for Government ministers and this latter meaning is now (in respect of statutes passed after 1977), conveyed by the new title 'Minister of the Government.'[42] The increase in the number of junior ministers was explained in the Dáil on the grounds of the greater volume of government business by comparison with that in 1924. The increase also had the effect of enlarging the 'pay roll' vote.[43]

The 1977 Act states that 'the Government may, on the nomination of the Taoiseach, appoint . . . Ministers of State . . . and may at any time, on the recommendation of the Taoiseach remove a Minister of State.'[44] The wording of this provision suggests that the Government (as distinct from the Taoiseach) is allowed some discretion, in the functions of appointing or removing a minister of state.[45]

Since a parliamentary secretary was originally envisaged as having mainly parliamentary duties, he ceased to hold office on the dissolution of the House of which he was member.[46] By contrast, ministers of state are subject to broadly similar conditions to those of members of the Government in regard to leaving office. They lose office if and when they cease to be a member of

60

the Oireachtas. However, when the Dáil is dissolved, a minister of state 'continue[s] to hold office' until the successor to the Taoiseach by whom he was nominated, is appointed. If the Taoiseach resigns, the minister of state is 'to carry on his duties' until the new Taoiseach is appointed.[47]

4.3 THE LEGAL FRAMEWORK OF THE MINISTERS AND DEPARTMENTS

Apart from the Constitution, the chief source of law determining the broad framework of the executive arm of government is the Ministers and Secretaries Acts, 1924- (a code which is contemplated at Art. 28.12 of the Constitution). The code 'established . . . the several [eleven in the original 1924 Act] Departments of State . . . amongst which the administration and business of the public services in [the State] shall be distributed . . .'[48] This division is subject to the cardinal principle that 'each . . . Department . . . and the powers, duties and functions thereof shall be assigned to and administered by the Minister.' The minister is made a corporation sole,[49] that is, an artificial legal entity distinct from the holder of the office. The result of these arrangements is that the minister is not only the head of the department. In addition, as a corporation sole, the office of the minister personifies the department in law and bears responsibility for all its activities. Whenever any power (for example, the power to make regulations or to acquire land compulsorily) is vested by statute in a minister then, as one would expect, the administration entailed in the exercise of that power shall be deemed to be allocated to the department of that minister.[50] However, in recent case law, a qualification has been imposed upon this principle. It applies to a quasi-judicial function such as the confirmation of a local authority compulsory purchase order, by the Minister for the Environment, under the Housing Act, 1966, Schedule III. In that case, the function is conferred on the minister as *persona designata* and he must discharge the function personally and not through his civil servants.[51] If there is any doubt as to the minister or department in which a power is vested, the doubt is to be determined by the Taoiseach.[52]

The Ministers and Secretaries Code sets out an itemised description of the duties of each of the departments which it establishes, of which the following may be given as an example:—

(ii) The Department of Finance which shall comprise the administration and business generally of the public finance of Saorstát Éireann and all powers, duties and functions connected with the same, including in particular the collection and expenditure of the revenues of Saorstát Éireann from whatever source arising (save as may be otherwise provided by law), and the supervision and control of all purchases made for or on behalf of and all supplies of commodities and goods held by any Department of State and the disposal thereof, and also the business, powers, duties and functions of the branches and officers of the public service specified in the first part of the Schedule to this Act, [e.g. Revenue Commissioners; Paymaster General], and of which Department the head shall be, and shall be styled an t-Aire Airgid or (in English) the Minister for Finance.'[53]

A question which naturally arises is the effect of this (and parallel) statutory provisions. In the first place, it is useful, in a non-legal way, as a straightforward description of the type of work which the Department can be expected to do. This means that it could be invoked by, among others, the Comptroller and Auditor General, if he were deciding whether some item of expenditure fell outside an imprecisely-worded vote. However, the significance of the statutory description of departmental duties is limited by the fact that almost all governmental functions are created by a specific statute and such a statute would prevail against the description in the 1924 code even if it involved vesting a function in what would seem, according to the 1924 code, to be an inappropriate department, for instance if a function in the field of agriculture were vested in the Minister for Education. However, certain consequences do flow from the fact that a minister is a corporation sole: as such, for instance, a minister has the capacity to contract but to do so only for the purpose of his authorised function or purposes incidental thereto. The description in the 1924 Act would be significant in divining what these purposes were and thus in determining whether a contract were outside a minister's power to contract.

Where a new department, with its ministerial head, is established, then a statute (called a Ministers and Secretaries (Amendment) Act) is passed. A statute is necessary because the creation (or dissolution) of a corporation sole requires an act of the Oireachtas. Thus the Ministers for: Supplies,[54] Health,[55] Social Welfare,[56] the Gaeltacht,[57] Transport and Power,[58] Labour[59] the Public Service,[60] Economic Planning and Development[61] and Communications[62] were not created by the Ministers and Secretaries Act, 1924 and so each had to be created by its own amending statute. A statute also had to be passed when the office of Minister for Supplies was dissolved.[63] However, no statute was necessary when the Minister for Economic Planning was dissolved or when the Minister for Energy was constituted as a minister, distinct from the former Minister for Industry, Commerce and Energy. Each of these two changes was accomplished simultaneously, in early 1980, without the need for an act of the Oireachtas. The reason why no act was required in either case, is instructive. Under the Ministers and Secretaries (Amendment) Act, 1939, the Government has extensive powers, exercisable by order, to alter the name of any department or the title of any minister; to transfer powers between ministers and the administration of a public service between departments; to allocate to a department the administration of a public service not expressly allocated to a department; or to make rules regarding the internal organisation of a department. The Government is even empowered to make 'such adaptations of enactments as shall appear to the Government to be consequential on any thing done under [these powers].'[64] These powers were used in 1980 when an order was made transferring the functions of the Minister for Economic Planning and Development to the Minister for Finance.[65] A second order was made changing the title of the Minister for Economic Planning to the Minister for Energy and making the parallel change in the name of the Department.[66] Finally, functions relating to energy, mines, minerals and petroleum were transferred from the former Minister for Industry, Commerce and Energy to the Minister for Energy.[67] The nett result was that no ministerial corporation sole was created or dissolved and, accordingly, as mentioned already, no statute was necessary.

The 1922 Constitution allowed for a maximum of twelve ministers[68] (although in the Irish Free State only nine, ten or eleven were actually appointed) whilst the 1924 Act constituted eleven departments. By today, there are sixteen departments,[69] whilst a maximum of fifteen ministers is permitted. However, no difficulty arises from this apparent mis-match, because the Taoiseach, who determines which members of the Government are to be assigned as ministers to which department, is free to assign more than one department to the same member of the Government[70] (for example, the Departments of Health and Social Welfare are usually assigned to the same minister). The Taoiseach may also appoint a member of the Government who does not have responsibility for a department, that is a minister without portfolio.[71] Apart from this exceptional type of appointment, all members of the Government are also ministers. Members of the Government are collectively responsible to the Dáil, both for Government decisions and for the work of each other's departments.[72] For whilst it is convenient to divide up Government business, as has been described, the division is subject to the overriding constitutional provision that 'The Government . . . shall be collectively responsible for the Departments of State administered by the members of the Government.'[73] This means that it is open to the Government to direct a minister as to how a decision should be taken, although the decision has been statutorily vested in the minister. It may be added that, in fact, most functions are vested in a particular minister. It is only a few functions which because of their importance or in order to attract greater lustre, are vested, by the Constitution or some statute, in the Government.

5

Dáil, Government and Parties

The Constitution states that the Government is responsible to, and can be removed by, the Dáil. But the reality is that, in normal times, the Government controls the Dáil.[1] To understand both the origin of the formal relationship and how the reality parted from the formality, it is necessary to appreciate a modicum of British constitutional history.

5.1 THE BRITISH BACKGROUND[2]

The Great Reform Act of 1832 was the seminal constitutional event of the nineteenth century in the United Kingdom. The Act made improvements in both the franchise and the distribution of seats. And whilst the immediate result was only to increase the electorate from five to seven *per cent.* of the adult population, the Act was evidently a harbinger of things to come. The *Volksgeist* was running in favour of democracy and the reformed House of Commons was the symbol of that trend. The result was the rapid growth of the convention that the Cabinet was collectively responsible, no longer to the Monarch but, to the House of Commons. The ascendancy of the House of Commons is vividly illustrated by the following figures: out of ten changes of government during the period 1832-67, seven resulted from adverse votes in the House of Commons followed, with no intervening election, by the formation of a new Government which could command the support of a majority; only three of the Ministries continued in office from one election through to the next. Here, in this brief period of just over a third of a century — known as the 'Golden Age of Parliamentary Democracy' — is the origin of the view that the British (and, later, the Irish) executive was 'a committee of the House of Commons.' This view continued its existence long after the reality had ceased to be.[3]

A second sea-change, which unpredicted and unintended, came about in the next few years of the century. Its radical nature can be shown by the fact that, in contrast with the figures cited in the last paragraph, only one of the four changes of government between 1867 and 1885 occurred following a defeat in the House of Commons, with no intervening election. The fundamental development underlying this alteration was the new party system. Up until the Great Reform Act, parties existed as small, loosely-knit groups, mainly composed of members of parliament, peers and their family and friends. However, the Reform Act required electors to be registered before they could vote, and the need to ensure that prospective supporters were registered before polling day led to the establishment of the well-organised bands of party-workers which make up modern political parties. These parties had three features which distinguished them from their predecessors. First, they became centralised with headquarters controlling each branch and with nationally-recognised leaders. Secondly, they were based on well-defined, consistent ideologies which united the members of a party and divided them from the other parties. In each constituency, throughout the country, party supporters contributed their time to secure the return of a member who was expected to promote their interests and beliefs. Such supporters were liable to feel cheated if 'their MP' took too independent a line. Thus the third characteristic of the new type of political party, which evolved in response to the Great Reform Act and which had established itself by 1870 or so, was strict obedience to the party whip in the House of Commons. In all three of these features, the Irish Party, which originated in the 1870's, was the very model of a modern political party.[4]

The constitutional system which exists in Ireland and Britain today is essentially the same as that which originated in the last third of the nineteenth century. In each case, the consequence of the strict discipline over members of the lower House is that, once elected with a working majority, a Government can count upon being sustained in office, in good times and in bad, for the full term of the parliament, unless its leader calls an early election. This result follows from a type of code by which a party candidate attracts support not only on the basis of his personal merits but also, and more significantly, as a person who will vote consistently with his party. This duty is articulated in the form of the party pledge which each party requires its candidates to sign.[5]

The striking nature of the relationship between the executive and the legislature in Britain may be emphasised by comparing it with the position in the U.S.A. There the executive and the legislature are each elected separately, by the people, rather than being yoked together. Neither has a part in the election of the other. Thus it often happens that a Republican President must co-exist with a legislature in which the Democrats are in a majority. The saving grace of the U.S. political system is that there is no strict party discipline, as it exists in Ireland or Britain. Consequently, executive and legislature wearing different political colours can yet work together. If Irish-style party discipline were superimposed on the U.S. Constitution and if it happened that the President and the majority in the legislature were from opposing parties, the result would be paralysis.

The final feature of the relationship between the legislature and executive, as it developed in the nineteenth century and persists today, is that cabinet responsibility is collective (a feature which will be elaborated later). This means that if a Government is defeated in the House of Commons or Dáil, it must resign *en bloc* and, secondly, that, outside the Cabinet all members of the Cabinet must agree with each other.[6] Because they are relevant to the next

Section, it is convenient to make two observations about the interaction of collective responsibility and the party system. First, the outward unity of the Government, which is promoted by collective cabinet responsibility, and the unity of the Government party created by the strict party system reinforce each other.[7] A minister contemplating a public disagreement with his ministerial colleagues knows that, because of party discipline, he would be unable to win over even a fraction of the party to his side of the argument. In the opposite direction, members of the legislature who disapprove of Government policy know that if they defy the party whip and vote against the Government, they will bring the entire Government down. Secondly, the collective nature of the responsibility enormously strengthens the Government's power at the expense of the legislature. For it means that a deputy who disapproves of the action of an individual minister is not usually allowed the chance to vote to remove the minister alone. All he has is the chance to vote against, and possibly bring down, the entire Government. A supporter of the Government is likely to baulk at this, however strong his feelings about the individual minister may be. The result is that the individual ministerial responsibility doctrine is robbed of most of its effectiveness.[8]

5.2 THE IRISH FREE STATE CONSTITUTION[9]

The analysis put forward in the last paragraph was accepted by the founding fathers who designed the Irish Free State Constitution. They built in certain modifications of the Westminster model which were intended to reduce the ascendancy of the executive over the Dáil.

First, it was anticipated, in the debates on the Constitution, that the proportional representation system of election would encourage the election of Independents or members of minority parties and reduce both the strictness of the party system and the power of the executive.[10] But the reality was the Civil War of 1922-23 which split most public representatives into two camps which oppose each other regardless of issue (an arrangement which President Nyerere of Tanzania once characterised as 'football crowd politics,' when speaking generally about the multi-party system followed in the western world).

The second change attempted was to strike a balance between, on the one hand, the stability created by collective responsibility and, on the other, the greater influence left to the Dáil, which results from individual ministerial responsibility. There were to be two types of ministers. Following the traditional British system, there would be 'executive ministers', who would be members of the Executive Council which was collectively responsible to the Dáil.[11] However, the constitutional innovation was the establishment of 'extern ministers' who were not nominated by the President of the Executive Council, but, instead, were chosen by the Dáil 'so as to be impartially representative of Dáil Éireann'.[12] Each extern minister (there could be a maximum of seven in a total of twelve ministers[13]) was to be individually

66

responsible to the Dáil, for his own department only and to hold office for the full term of the Dáil, unless he was earlier removed by the Dáil.[14] It was intended that the persons selected as extern ministers, who need not be members of either House, would be experts who would pursue their own non-partisan policy, independently of the Executive Council. This assumed the existence of a department in which the policies were not controversial (for example, the Department of Agriculture with the policy of completing the buying out of the landlords) and also that parties would not oppose these policies for the sake of doing so. In the event, the Civil War and the strict party system which materialised, ensured that the conditions necessary for the real operation of the extern minister system never existed. Extern ministers were appointed, but they were approved by a Dáil vote which divided along party lines; with one exception,[15] they did accept responsibility for general government policy; and, in 1927, the Constitution was amended to enable all twelve ministers to be members of the Executive Council.[16] After that date, no extern ministers were appointed.

There were other provisions which were designed to tilt the balance of power between the legislature and the executive more in favour of the Dáil. Several of these provisions recurred in the 1937 Constitution and will be mentioned in Section 5 of this Chapter. As matters turned out, they make little practical difference because of the executive's control of the legislature by way of the majority party. One modification of the Westminster model, which was not neutralised in this way, was the rule that the Oireachtas could not be dissolved on the advice of an Executive Council which had ceased to retain the support of a majority in the Dáil.[17] But in fact this situation never arose during the 1922-37 period. By contrast, in the same circumstances, the 1937 Constitution allows the President a discretion whether to grant a dissolution.[18]

Finally, a brief mention ought to be made of the Initiative and the Referendum.[19] These were devices which were characteristic of many of the post-war constitutions and which were designed to disseminate political power, more widely, by transferring it to the ordinary voter. Whereas the Referendum was negative, the Initiative would have been a positive exercise of popular sovereignty. It is significant that the Initiative was not actually established: all that the Constitution did was to state that the Oireachtas could provide machinery for an Initiative. Certain guidelines were laid down in the Constitution: a proposal (for laws or constitutional amendments) had to be initiated by a petition signed by fifty thousand voters, the Oireachtas had then either to enact the proposal or, if it rejected the proposal, to submit it for the decision of the electorate at a referendum.

Neither device was ever fully utilised. As early as 1924, a committee of the Executive Council recommended the abolition of both Initiative and Referendum because they would enable a minority to raise fundamental issues, for debate outside Parliament, in a country riven by the aftermath of civil war. No immediate action was taken on this proposal, but in fact its execution was not long postponed. Following the assassination of Kevin O'Higgins, the

Electoral (Amendment) (No. 2) Bill, 1927 was introduced. Its objective was to terminate Fianna Fáil's abstentionist policy and it provided that every candidate for election to either House should, when nominated, swear that he would take his seat if he were elected. Because deputies who had not taken the oath were counted, Fianna Fáil were able to muster the support of two-fifths of Dáil members and thus passed the first hurdle of the referendum process. However, they failed at the second hurdle (resolution of three-fifths of the Senate or a petition signed by one twentieth of the electorate). Thus the third stage— a decision by all members of the electorate — was never reached. Consequently the measure became law and Fianna Fáil submitted to 'the empty formula' of the oath and entered the Oireachtas in 1927.

The party's other line of attack on the oath was an attempt to secure the establishment of the Initiative, with a view to using it to enact a constitutional amendment excising the oath. Following the procedure set out in the Constitution, a petition for the introduction of the Initiative, signed by ninety six thousand people, was brought before the Dáil in 1928. The Government reacted by enacting a constitutional amendment abolishing both the Referendum and the Initiative.[20]

As can be seen, none of these modifications in the Westminster system made any impact on the actual separation of the 1922 Constitution and none of them was retained in the 1937 Constitution.

5.3 COLLECTIVE RESPONSIBILITY TO THE DÁIL

At the outset, it should be stressed that the Government's responsibility is to the Dáil and not to the Senate.

The Government's responsibility embraces not only the Dáil's capacity to remove and replace a Government but also its power to appoint a Government following a general election. We shall consider these three elements separately, before going on to consider the collective nature of the Government's responsibility. Afterwards, individual ministerial responsibility is examined and the interaction of the two forms or responsbility explained.

Appointment   In theory, as has been explained, the voters elect the Dáil and the Dáil elects the Government. The Constitution reflects this theory. Art. 13.1 provides that the Dáil nominate the Taoiseach and he is appointed by the President. Then the Taoiseach nominates the other members of the Government for the approval of the Dáil and they are then appointed by the President.[20] In practice almost all deputies will be members of parties which have indicated before the election which of the two alternative Governments their candidates would support. The identity of the Government is usually clear once the constituency results are known and the Dáil is merely the device by which their vote is registered. The process has been described thus:

The new Dáil having nominated the leader of the majority of the party or group to be Taoiseach after a short and usually ritualistic debate, adjourns for a few hours while the leader calls upon the President and is formally appointed to that office. He then returns to the Dáil and puts forward the names of the members of his government. These are approved *en bloc* by the Dáil, though in the early days of the State there was some attempt to have them discussed and approved individually.[21]

It may be convenient, at this point, to address briefly the common criticism that party government is bad because it depends upon and encourages, a lack of independence among TD's. This must be accepted as being correct. But, on the other hand, party government does carry what, it is suggested, is the advantage, of enabling the voter to indicate which alternative Government he prefers; by contrast under a non-party system, he could only vote for a Dáil candidate with no certainty as to which Government his vote would favour. A similar situation to the (hypothetical) non-party system may appear to occur in Ireland when no party wins an absolute majority and the balance of power between the two biggest parties is held by smaller parties and/or Independents, who have not declared which of the two possible Governments they will support. This is essentially what happened in 1948, 1981 and 1982 (twice), and the result, in each case, was protracted post-electoral negotiation and bargaining before a Government with precarious support emerged. It is true that in these circumstances the decision as to who will form the Government can be said to be taken by deputies who are not acting on instructions from their electorate. However, there are two features which distinguish this situation from the 'Golden Age of Parliamentary Democracy.' First, it is only a few — ostensibly crucial — votes which are 'free'; the way in which most deputies vote will have been settled by the electorate. Secondly, the way in which the 'free' votes are cast depends, not on debate in the chamber or any other process related to the Dáil, but rather on the balance of party or constituency advantage. Moreover, the decision as to which way to vote will usually be taken after formal or informal consultation with the party.[22] The same considerations usually applied on the occasions (mentioned in the next Section) when a minority Government, sustained in office by minority parties or Independents, fell because of the defection of this support.[23]

Removal The Constitution states that 'The Government shall be responsible to Dáil Éireann' (Art. 28.4.1°). The teeth behind this provision are contained in another section: 'The Taoiseach shall resign from office upon his ceasing to retain the support of a majority in Dáil Éireann . . .' (Art. 28.10).

It might be expected that in a constitutional system in which the Government frequently has to rely on the votes of several different parties and of Independent deputies, the bond holding these disparate elements together would sometimes melt and the Government fall, In fact, the classic pattern — a defeat in the Dáil precipitating a general election — has only been followed on two occasions, both in 1982. In February, the inter-party coalition lost office, because one of the Independent deputies on whom it relied failed to support it. And, in November, the Fianna Fáil Government fell, after losing a vote of confidence because of the simultaneous defection of a minority party and the loss of two of its own deputies owing to death and illness. What is more significant, though, is that on several other occasions the existence of Government responsibility to the Dáil has been an influential factor in causing a Government to resign. Thus, in 1930, the Cumann na nGaedhael Government resigned when the second stage of a private member's bill on old-age pensions was carried against the opposition of the Government. The President of the Executive Council was re-elected by the Dáil without a general election.[24] And, on at least three occasions (Cumann na nGaedheal in 1927, inter-party Governments in 1951 and 1957), the Government chose to resign rather than wait for the threat of a Dáil defeat to materialise. On two occasions, in 1938 and 1940,[25] Fianna Fáil Governments welcomed the opportunity, provided by defeats on fairly minor issues, to be able to rush to the hustings and win a secure majority, whilst at the same time not appearing to be responsible for forcing an election on the country. It is clear, however, that these two elections arose from the need for a working majority in the Dáil and that this need is the consequence of the responsibility doctrine, coupled of course with the necessity to pass its legislation. Thus here, too, the responsibility rule was a factor shaping political conduct.[26]

One difficulty in this area arises in connection with the phrase 'the support of a majority in Dáil Éireann' which is used in Art. 28.10 (quoted above). How is this support or its absence to be demonstrated? Is the only acceptable evidence a vote in the Dáil? This is an issue which has caused not just controversy, but even violence, elsewhere in post-Westminster constitutions, notably in 1962 in the Western Region of Nigeria. In the crisis which had arisen there, the Governor had dismissed the premier on the basis of a letter, signed by a majority of the members of the assembly, which stated that they no longer supported the premier. In the ensuing court case[27] it was necessary to interpret a phrase similar to that used in the Irish Constitution. The Federal Supreme Court of Nigeria held that the dismissal was unconstitutional because it did not follow upon a vote in the assembly. This decision was based largely upon British practice. On appeal, the Judicial Committee of Privy Council reversed the decision, founding itself on a literal reading of the provision. Because of the possibility of this type of difficulty, the Report of the Committee of the Constitution in 1967 recommended that it should be made explicit in the Constitution that a Dáil vote is necessary to remove a Government.[28] Yet the doubt on the point, in Ireland, seems slim. In November, 1982, the Fianna Fáil Government fell (by 82-80) because one of its supporters was ill and a second had died and had not been replaced at a bye-election, to be held three weeks later, which would certainly have returned a Fianna Fáil deputy. Yet no one suggested that these circumstances would justify the Government in refusing to resign following a defeat on a vote of confidence. It seems likely that this precedent would also apply in the converse situation so that a Government would not be obliged to resign if the only evidence which showed that it had lost its majority was extra-parliamentary. In other words, the Nigerian precedent would not be followed here.

The other and more likely source of difficulty in this context is the question of what type of Dáil defeat would be necessary to show that a Government had lost the support of a majority in the Dáil. Plainly, it is not every defeat which will suffice. For instance, it is striking that in Britain, between 1905-79, the Government of the day suffered more than eighty defeats (at least fifty of them occurring after 1972). Yet Governments resigned only as a result of a Commons defeat on three occasions (twice in 1924 and in 1979).[29] Again, it was generally thought that the defeats of the Irish Government in 1930, 1938 and 1944 (mentioned above) did not require the Government to resign. Unfortunately in Ireland, as in Britain, there is no formal definition — or even usage — as to what constitutes an 'issue of confidence', that is, a matter of defeat which would require the Government to resign. Thus the following observations must be treated with caution. Certain matters are so obviously important that, if a Government is defeated on one of them, it must resign, even if they are not explicitly 'motions of confidence in the Government (or Taoiseach).' Thus it occasioned no surprise when, following a defeat on a Budget resolution in 1982, the Coalition Government resigned. Where the question is in doubt, a vote may be turned into an issue of confidence by a declaration from the Taoiseach that he so regards it. This is a device for raising the stakes, in that it increases the pressure on deputies to support the Government. Conversely in 1981, the Taoiseach carefully stated in regard to the election of the Leas Cheann Comhairle (Deputy Chairman of the Dáil) that he did not regard it as an issue of confidence[30] (though it is likely that this would not have been regarded as a matter of confidence anyway). On certain issues of intermediate importance or where the Government has been caught napping by a snap vote, it may not be under an obligation to resign immediately but rather to seek an early vote of confidence. (On most important votes, some days' notice will have been given to the Government.) An example of this sequence of events occurred in June 1982, when the Government was defeated on a private members' motion to reopen the Fieldcrest factory in Kilkenny. On the following day, a motion of confidence in the Government was debated and passed.[31]

Replacement In the nineteenth century, the House of Commons could both remove an unpopular Government and select its successor without reference to the electorate. In Ireland the Dáil's power to replace a Government which it has removed is much less than this because of Art. 28.10, by which:

The Taoiseach shall resign upon his ceasing to retain the support of a majority in Dáil Éireann unless on his advice the President dissolves Dáil Éireann and on the reassembly of Dáil Éireann after the dissolution the Taoiseach secures the support of a majority in Dáil Éireann.

This provision gives a Taoiseach, who has been defeated in the Dáil and thinks that he is unlikely to be re-appointed by that Dáil, the chance to forestall his removal by appealing, over the head of the Dáil, to the electorate. The only limitation on this is that by Art. 13.2.2°:

The President may in his absolute discretion refuse to dissolve Dáil Éireann on the advice of a Taoiseach who has ceased to retain the support of a majority in Dáil Éireann.

Such evidence as there is suggests that even in these cirumstances a President will not lightly refuse a Taoiseach's request for a dissolution. There has in fact been no refusal so far in the history of the State. Indeed, on four occasions — 1938, 1944 and 1982 (twice) — a Taoiseach, with a precarious or non-existent majority, has been defeated in the Dáil and yet been granted a dissolution by the President, within eleven, ten, eight and eight months, respectively, of the previous election. Moreover, in 1938 and 1944, it was evident that the real reason for the dissolution was not that the Government had been defeated on a major issue, but rather that it needed to improve its majority. And in November 1982, the circumstances were such — the third dissolution in eighteen months — that the President might very reasonably have exercised his discretion to refuse a dissolution.

Responsibility is collective So far we have been considering the Government's responsibility to the Dáil. The other aspect of the doctrine is that the responsibility is collective, in other words the Government stands or falls as a united entity. The doctrine was first adopted on 26 August 1922 (before the 1922 Constitution came into effect) by the Provisional Government, which decided 'that all decisions of the Cabinet should be regarded as unanimous and should be treated as strictly confidential.'[32]

The kernel of the doctrine is that if the Taoiseach resigns from office, the other members of the Government as well as the Attorney General and the ministers of state are deemed also to have resigned.[33] This rule is complemented by Art. 28.4.2° by which:

The Government shall meet and act as a collective authority, and shall be collectively responsible for the Departments of State administered by the members of the Government.[34]

One of the more unusual episodes involving this provision will be considered later in the Chapter.[35] Its more normal application is to underpin the rule that all ministers and all departments should speak with the same voice in public, in regard to the Government's policy and performance.[36]

One example of this rule's operation is to be found in an angry circular drafted but never sent by the Department of Finance in 1928. The circular complained about:

. . . a disposition . . . on the part of certain other departments to dissociate themselves from decisions of the Minister for Finance on proposals involving expenditure . . . An individual . . . affected by a proposal which the Minister finds himself unable to sanction [has frequently been] informed that the proposal had been submitted to the Minister for Finance and that the latter was responsible for its rejection . . . [The Minister's] decision must be regarded as the reflection of the financial policy of the [Government]. It therefore appears that the [Government] is collectively responsible for that decision and that it is the duty of each member of the [Government] to defend it.[37]

This duty continues to cover a person who has ceased to be a minister in respect of decisions taken in Government, save upon the issue on which he resigned.[38]

In contrast with the rule by which the Government must resign *en bloc* following a Dáil defeat, the rule requiring unanimity in public is a matter of degree, and there is no indisputable method of establishing when it has been broken, and no simple, direct sanction for its breach. In short, it is not a rule enforceable by a court but rather a convention and so subject to the frailties, already discussed,[39] to which all conventions are prey. The result is that ministers have sometimes conspicuously failed to agree, or even disagreed, with no consequential resignation. It has already been noted that the unity and strength created both by collective responsibility and by the party system tend to reinforce each other. Equally, weakness as well as strength can rub off, and so it is that when a Government is made up of a coalition of parties, collective responsibility is less consistently observed than in a Government formed from a single monolithic party.[40] But even in Fianna Fáil Governments, Taoisigh have sometimes had to describe a minister as 'speaking for himself' or 'speaking personally.' Nevertheless, the rule carries considerable weight,[41] and since Independence, twelve ministers and one parliamentary secretary[42] have resigned or been dismissed because of some form of difference between them and their colleagues. The advantages of collective responsibility are: first, that it makes it more likely that there will be a stable Government which can rely on holding office usually for a period of years. Secondly, if each member of the Government knows that he may be called to account for the irresponsibility or poor judgment of his colleagues, such behaviour is more likely to be forestalled. Finally, it assists the clear expression of decisions and allocation of responsibility.[43] But even without a collective responsibility convention, unity would usually be desirable in the Government's own interest, since a lack of public confidence is likely to be engendered if ministers are at loggerheads in public.[44]

5.4 INDIVIDUAL MINISTERIAL RESPONSIBILITY

Individual ministerial responsibility and collective responsibility There are two forms of responsibility to the Dáil: intertwined with the Government's collective responsibility is a minister's individual responsibility[45] which means that if a minister commits certain types of error, there is an obligation on him, and him alone, to resign. If the minister declines to resign of his own accord, then he must certainly do so, if a vote of no confidence in him is passed by the Dáil. The type of error which attracts this duty may be: some personal act of dishonour, indiscretion, misjudgment or incompetence (including the mismanagement of his department), possibly, a mistake made by a civil servant in his department; or the failure of some policy with which he is peculiarly associated. Whist there is no reference to individual responsibility in Bunreacht na hÉireann it has been accepted that the rule does exist here: politicians speak the language of individual responsibility[46] and the rule is probably the basis of a minister's (imperfect) obligation to answer questions in the Dáil. Nevertheless, in the whole history of the State, there has only been a single resignation which can be attributed to this strand of responsibility. This was the resignation of a parliamentary secretary in 1946 following a Tribunal of Inquiry into the affairs of a firm with which he had been involved.

Obvious difficulties arise from the fact that there is no agency (certainly not the Dáil) which can establish authoritatively that the convention of individual responsibility has been broken. Even more important (as is illustrated in the following paragraphs) the party system interferes with enforcement of the sanction for a breach. For much of the mud stirred up by a resignation, in what might well be spectacular circumstances, would be bound to rub off on the Government of which the minister were a member. To avoid this, the usual course of action is that the minister resists calls for his resignation whilst the Taoiseach declares that he regards the issue as one of confidence in the Government, thereby shifting the matter on to the plane of collective responsibility. Thus, if a motion of no confidence in the minister is debated, it will be voted down by the Government majority and the minister survives, albeit possibly with a tarnished reputation. The result is that the following comment on the British scene applies with even greater force in Ireland: a minister with a majority behind him can 'brazen out appalling indiscretions, gross errors and omissions, plans gone awry and revelations of disastrous mismanagement'.[47]

An example of the individual responsibility doctrine being swallowed by the collective responsibility rule occurred in the episode which caused the resignation of President Ó Dálaigh in 1976. The Minister for Defence made an after-lunch speech at the opening of a new army building a few days after the President had exercised his powers under Art. 26 to refer the Emergency Powers Bill, 1976 to the Supreme Court for its constitutionality to be tested. In an apparently off-the-cuff remark, the Minister attacked the President in intemperate language for making this reference.[48] One would have thought that the convivial indiscretions of a minister in an after-lunch speech were *par excellence* a matter of individual responsibility. However, the Taoiseach waved aside the Minister's offer of resignation. A few days later a Dáil motion

R.T.C. LIBRARY, LETTERKENNY

calling on the Taoiseach to request the Minister's resignation was debated and, during the course of it, the Taoiseach was specifically challenged to say the Minister's remark did not have the support of the Government. He declined to do so. This was naturally taken as an indication that the Government was putting its collective responsibility behind the Minister's comments, and the censure motion was duly voted down.

Similarly, another Taoiseach was prepared to stand over the behaviour of a minister who was alleged to have misled the Dáil during the Arms Crisis (see below) and so the Taoiseach converted what probably should have been a matter of individual responsibility into one of collective responsibility.[49]

In another constitutional dispute, the sides in the argument were reversed, with the Government arguing that the responsibility should be regarded as individual only, whilst the Opposition claimed that the Government's collective responsibility was engaged. This dispute arose out of the Arms Crisis in 1970 which gave rise to strong suspicion that two ministers — the Minister for Finance and the Minister for Agriculture and Fisheries — were implicated in a plan to use official funds for the purchase of arms and to smuggle these arms into the Republic and then on to Northern Ireland. The arms were intended to be used for the defence of the minority community in the North. The two Ministers were tried on charges of conspiring to import arms illegally (although they were later to be acquitted) and dismissed from the Government because of the suspicion which attached to them. Two other ministers and a parliamentary secretary resigned at the same time.[50] Naturally this episode led to intense discussion in the Dáil. The Government claimed that the remaining members had no previous knowledge of anything which the two dismissed Ministers may have done. The Opposition said that even if this were so the Government was collectively responsible for the actions of the two Ministers. Their argument was naturally founded upon Art. 28.4.2⁰ by which 'The Government shall meet and act as a collective authority, and shall be collectively responsible for the Departments of State administered by the members of the Government.' Deputy Corish said:

'The Taoiseach alleged . . . that the two Ministers had acted without Government approval or knowledge. In such circumstances should not the Taoiseach have resigned and asked the people to decide on the issues . . . . I believe the collective responsibility principle to be a guarantee against the adventurism of individual ministers . . .'.[51]

'If Deputy Blaney or Haughey is guilty so also is Deputy Lynch and every single remaining Minister in the cabinet.'[52]

Art. 28.4.2⁰ plainly cannot be read at its full literal width: otherwise the entire Government would be responsible for the most trivial acts of administration going on within a department. It must, at least, be confined to 'action . . . of a major or serious national kind.'[53] Acts within this category of which the Cabinet has no pre-knowledge are naturally rare, and so episodes

75

involving this type of collective responsibility have been few in Britain and, with the exception of the present episode, non-existent in Ireland. Thus there are no precedents to show how serious an action must be to fall within this category. It is, however, hard to imagine a more grave action than that involved in the Arms Crisis. What makes it so peculiarly serious in the present context is that, in contrast to (say) the theft of Government funds for private gain by a minister, it could well have been an act of a Government policy and might have been so understood by interested outsiders. There is, of course, an obvious argument against applying the doctrine of collective responsibility in this case, namely that its operation would be unfair, if it resulted in the punishment of ministers for events of which they were ignorant and which went on outside their bailiwick. In the context of the standards applied in a criminal trial, there would be much to be said for this view. In the present context, however, I consider that the weightier argument was that which was adduced by the Opposition: the knowledge that ministers may be called to account for the fundamental actions of their colleagues will increase both the interest which each minister takes in those actions and the care in the selection of ministers. On this point, it is relevant to mark a provision of the Ministers and Secretaries Act, 1924. This is the Act which divides up government business among the different departments. Yet section 5 of the Act carefully provides that:

Nothing in this Act contained shall derogate from the collective responsibility of the [Government] as provided by the Constitution notwithstanding that members of the [Government] may be appointed individually to be Ministers, heads of particular Departments.

However, notwithstanding these arguments, at the end of the debate following the dismissal of the Ministers, the Government secured its usual majority[54] and won the day, if not the argument. This illustrates, once more, the difficulty of enforcing conventions.

5.5 CONTROL OF DEPARTMENTAL ADMINISTRATION

One of the difficulties in connection with individual ministerial responsibility arises in relation to routine administration going on within a department. Is a minister responsible for all the work being carried out by the hundreds or even thousands of civil servants in his department? Should he resign if one of these civil servants commits an act of maladministration? These questions arose in the context of the scheme created by the Mental Treatment Act, 1945 for the involuntary detention of mental patients. It required the permission of the Minister to be renewed after every six months period of detention. The junior civil servant whose task it was to pass on the applications for permission to the Minister became ill and failed to do his work, with the result that almost three hundred patients were illegally detained. An Opposition deputy said in the Dáil:

[The Minister] is the person whose duty it is to see and to ensure that the Department is administered properly in accordance with the directions given to it by this House from time to time . . . [I]t is the Minister who must stand over the actions of the civil servants under him because they are his and the Government's and not servants of Parliament.[55]

The inference he drew was that the Minister ought to resign. The Minister refused because:

. . . in these matters there must be some realism. It is all very well to say that constitutional theory requires that the Minister should accept full responsibility for everything the department does . . . Am I to accept responsibility for the fact that an officer of my Department suffers a breakdown in health . . .? Is there anything I could possibly have done to ensure that this would not have occurred?[56]

In justifying his refusal the Minister also stressed that the system for dealing with applications was satisfactory in that people at all levels in it were qualified for the work they had to do; that it had never gone wrong before; and that there was no reason to expect it to go wrong in this case. The Minister thus accepted the existence of individual ministerial responsibility but defined its scope differently from the Opposition deputy.

The view deployed by the Opposition deputy in the passage quoted is essentially that of a British former deputy-Premier who said that a minister is responsible 'for every stamp stuck on an envelope'[57] in his department. But it is the alternative view (the minister's view) which has found favour in modern Britain.[58] And it certainly seems unrealistic and dogmatic to expect a minister's head to roll because some routine act of administration is badly executed by one of his civil servants. As explained, the infirmity which afflicts the ministerial responsibility doctrine generally is the way in which it has been swallowed by collective responsibility because of the party system. In addition, in the particular context of civil service maladministration there are special features making the requirement that the minister resign particularly inappropriate. Conspicuous among these is the fact that departments include hundreds of civil servants and it would be artificial to regard one man as responsible for all of their activities. Furthermore, resignation affords no gradation of sanctions to deal with different offences of widely-varying culpability. Finally, resignation would be impossible in a case in which the responsible minister had left the department before the error came to light.

Thus it seems appropriate to take a narrower view of ministerial responsibility so far as it covers the routine activities of civil servants and to say that it means only 'that a Minister alone speaks for his civil servants to the [Dáil] and to his civil servants for the [Dáil].'[59] This idea of the relationship between a minister and his civil servants has also been expressed as follows:

The official knows that the Minister will stand over his action *vis-à-vis* public and parliament if this action is in conformity with the Minister's general views. The Minister knows that the official in taking any action will always be conscious that he may, in relation to the Minister's action, be challenged: that it is his business to have a convincing answer to such a challenge.[60]

The nature of this relationship has naturally led to the tradition that civil servants responsible for an action are not identified in public. Without such a tradition, a minister would be free to say: 'That was Mr X's fault; he is growing old and forgetful.' And the sequel would be that Mr X would want to defend himself and there would be a public dispute. The results would be a lack of clarity as to who was responsible to the Dáil for the acts of the department; and within the department, there would be erosion of discipline. Of course, anonymity of the subordinate *vis-à-vis* third parties is not peculiar to the relationship between ministers and civil servants: something similar exists in most hierarchical organisations.

The rule regarding civil service anonymity has caused some difficulty in the context of inquiries into the running of the departmental machine: how can such inquiries be worth anything if they are barred from exploring the work of the civil servants involved? This problem has predictably caused more difficulty in Britain, with its greater affection for the doctrines of the constitution (an affection which sometimes persists beyond the grave), than in Ireland. Thus in Britain, though not in Ireland, the need to preserve the anonymity of the civil service was regarded by some people as a ground for the non-introduction of the Ombudsman whose duty is to investigate maladministration, often within government departments. In the end the compromise reached was that the British Parliamentary Commissioner for Administration, unlike the Irish Ombudsman, was equipped with an 'M.P. filter'[61] and also a parliamentary select committee to cheer him on. However, even in Ireland this doctrinal difficulty has some force and thus, for instance, select committees of either House are effectively barred from raising policy questions with civil service witnesses.[62]

Devlin proposals: Aireacht and Executive Units The (Devlin) Report of the Public Services Organisation Review Group (1966-69)[63] proposed a change by which the area of activity for which a minister is responsible to the Dáil and to the courts would have been significantly reduced. The chief reason for this departure was that a minister is extremely busy and has insufficient time for what should be his chief function, policy-making. His chief officials are also pre-occupied with administration. The Report analysed the business of government as broadly divisible into two main elements:

(i)   the determination and review of policy and the overall managment of the public service and

(ii)   the execution of the settled policy and the detailed management of executive functions.[64]

The Report proposed, among other things, that in order to lighten a minister's load he should concentrate upon, and only be responsible for, function (i). This function would be discharged by the minister and a relatively few advisers in a unit which would be known as the Aireacht (Ministry) since its chief characteristic would be that its business was the personal responsibility of the minister. Function (ii) would be discharged by specialised executive units. Save where there was a breakdown, these units would be independent of the minister and the Dáil. Instead they would be policed by a sophisticated system of tribunals, overseen by a Commissioner for Administrative Justice who would also act as an Ombudsman.[65]

Obviously this novel idea, imported from Scandinavia, would require radical changes. So, in the mid-1970's, it was tried as an experiment in a few select departments which were physically restructured on Aireacht lines. The results were discouraging because the divorce between policy and administration seemed to be unworkable. Thus, for instance, if the Department of the Environment is considering altering the housing grant schemes, then at present it can draw upon its knowledge of the way the existing system is working. If a policy-maker is untroubled by 'the harassing experiences of everyday'[66] then he loses the opportunity of gaining this type of information at first hand. This proposal was also unpopular with deputies and ministers because removing questions of routine administration from the minister and hence the Dáil, would have robbed deputies of their chance to influence, or appear to influence, issues of moment to the local electorate. The opportunity of greater parliamentary time to focus upon the wider issues of government appeared to be an inadequate compensation.[67]

By mid-1984, reform of the civil service structure was again in vogue and the Minister for the Public Service promised changes which would allow for some form of devolution of responsibility for policy execution from a minister to his civil servants.

5.6 GOVERNMENT CONTROL OVER THE DÁIL[68]

We can sum up the earlier parts of this Chapter by saying that although the Constitution states that the Government is responsible to the Dáil, the reality is usually that the Government controls the Dáil. Even when the Government party(ies) alone cannot command a majority, the Government has often been consistently sustained by deputies who 'though they called themselves "Independents" were rather camp-followers.'[69] In exceptional times when the Government has no dependable majority (of which the period 1981-2 was such a conspicuous example), the beneficiary of its partial loss of control is not the Dail but usually the minority parties or Independents who make up its precarious majority.[70]

This inversion, by which the Government usually controls the Dáil, affects not only the Dáil's power to dismiss the Government and its powers in regard to legislation but also the other functions which the Constitution (or other legislation) has carefuly vested in the Dáil or both Houses of the Oireachtas, for example: war cannot be declared without the assent of the Dáil;[71] 'the right to raise and maintain military or armed forces is vested exclusively in the Oireachtas';[72] a declaration of emergency, under Art. 28.3.3°, consists of parallel resolutions passed by both Houses;[73] the approval of the Dáil is required before the State is 'bound by any international agreement involving a charge upon public funds;[74] many statutory instruments or orders are subject to negative or (rarely) positive resolution, within a specified period, by either House.[75] The chief reason for the Government control of the Dáil is that the Government party(ies) usually has a reliable majority in the Dail. It is theoretically possible that the party could control the Government rather than the other way around. In fact, in Ireland, as in other comparable polities, it is the Government which is top-dog by virtue of its control of the public service machine and because, in a small country, ministers are the chief, and virtually the only, leaders in the Government party. The pre-eminence of the Government over its followers and, thus, over the Dáil does not need labouring but may perhaps be illustrated by one example. In 1979, the family planning Bill caused a certain amount of heart-searching among members of the Government party in the Oireachtas.[76] Yet almost all Government deputies supported it. By contrast, it was made clear, at an early stage, by the responsible minister, that civil servants in the Department of Health who found the measure repugnant to their consciences were not obliged to work on it.

However, this is not the whole story. The price which ministers pay for the support consistently given in public by their back-benchers is the account which is sometimes taken of the views of back-benchers in designing Government policies. Very occasionally, there will even have to be compromise or retreat, following criticism of the Government at the regular, private meetings of the parliamentary party. Usually, this criticism will gather greater force because it is taken to be the articulation of feeling elsewhere in the party and in the country. Examples of cases in which this can be seen to have occurred include: the watering down of the Succession Bill, 1963 and of the wealth tax in 1973; the decision, announced at the Fianna Fáil Árd Fheis in 1979, to exempt sugar-beet from the 2% farm levy; the withdrawal of school-bus fares by the Coalition Government in 1983. Party pressure also forced the withdrawal of the Criminal Justice Bill, 1967, a measure which had a lot in common with the Criminal Justice Bill, 1983. (The clause removing the right to silence, in the 1983 Bill, was omitted from the Bill because of a deal of criticism from back-benchers on all sides of the House. But this criticism was voiced largely during the course of the Dáil debates.)

The peculiar effectiveness of party discipline in Ireland is itself something which calls for explanation. It is not completely explained by the desire for preferment or the possibility of the extreme sanction of withdrawal of the party nomination at a forthcoming election, from a sitting TD. A great part is probably played by factors like tradition and national personality. In addition, the hegemony of Fianna Fáil has meant that its strict party discipline and loyalty has been regarded as setting a headline for other parties.

Secondly, there are numerous features of parliamentary procedure, some of which will be described in Chapter 9, which facilitate the Government's ascendancy: for example, the Government control of the timetable of business, or the extraordinary way in which private members' time was virtually suspended up to 1974.[77] In this context it is important to bear in mind the reform of Dáil procedure including the new group of select committees.[78] If these reforms achieve their full potential, they could have an effect in altering the balance of power between the Government and the Dáil.

Furthermore, it is the Taoiseach who decides when the Dáil is to be summoned or dissolved.[79] Whilst the power to dissolve is obviously a weapon of last resort, it does give the Taoiseach the opportunity of calling an election at a time when he decides he has the best chance of winning.

A further factor is that the Government enjoys the services of civil service experts whilst deputies outside the Government have much more limited access to specialised information. Each deputy is now provided with the services of a full-time secretary and can call on the (limited) research service offered by the Oireachtas library. In addition, public moneys are paid to the leaders of the major parties, to be used for the expenses of their parliamentary parties, including research.[80]But Government spokesmen enjoy a significant information-advantage which means they can usually determine the ground on which the debate proceeds.

Another factor behind the Government's ascendancy over the Dáil is the Irish style of politics in which candidates for the Dáil compete on the basis of what individual services they have performed for their constituents. This tends to reduce a deputy's interest in the business of the Dáil by diverting his attention to the minutiae of Government administration. This situation is largely the product of the single transferable vote and the multi-seat constituencies. For a candidate is usually in the situation of having to compete for a vote against another candidate from his own party since the voter's preference between the parties is more likely to be fixed and beyond the candidate's power to influence. The more efficient way to compete, in these circumstances, is not to be especially for or against the Government since the rival candidate can claim to be equally strong on this ground, but rather to be able to point to services performed for constituents. It will be interesting to see what effect the appointment of an Ombudsman (who started operating on 1 January 1984) will have on this state of affairs.

The question which this review of the Government's control over the Dáil inevitably raises is: what role is left to the Dáil? It has been submitted that the Dáil's ability to control the Government and its influence over legislation are both small. It is sometimes suggested that the Dáil plays a useful part in educating future ministers in public affairs, but, on its own, this would hardly suffice as its *raison d'être*. However, the Dáil would be making a major contribution to the health of the policy if it were to act as the 'Grand Inquest of the Nation' (to use a traditional phrase). What this means is not that the legislature takes decisions but that it investigates, appraises, publicises and even dramatises the Government's decisions and highlights the alternatives. The value of this function would be preventative rather than curative: seldom, if ever, would a Government which had announced a particular course of action feel obliged to beat a retreat before a cogent Opposition argument; but the existence of an effective 'Grand Inquest' would mean that the Government would be less likely, in the first place, to embark on an action which would not bear the light of detailed public scrutiny. Furthermore, a continuous open debate on the Government's performance would help to educate the public for casting its vote at the subsequent election. There is a critical difference between this function and that of legislating or bringing down Governments. It is that a full exercise of this function could never be said to threaten stable government or thwart the passage of necessary Government measures and thus strict party discipline would not be necessary. Yet at the moment, the Dáil is disabled, by the party system, from properly fulfilling even this limited function.

A task usually attributed to Dáil and Senate is that of 'legitimating' the Government's decisions. We may take this rather fluid term to mean a process by which decisions are endowed with a degree of moral authority (so to speak, canonised) and are thus deserving of public respect and obedience. These are essential attributes in a system of government by consent, such as ours. Yet it seems to me that if the decision emerging from the process is to be 'legitimate,' it must be precisely because it has been tested by astringent public debate in a free parliament: if the examination of the decision has been inadequate, the decision cannot be regarded as legitimate and Irish democracy can be regarded as little more than an elected dictatorship.[81]

5.7 PARLIAMENTARY PARTIES

It is evident from what has been said that, although Búnreacht na hÉireann is innocent of any mention of the term 'party' and the word is barely mentioned in statute law,[82] the institution of the party and party discipline play a key role in determining relations between the executive and the legislature. Accordingly, the object of this Section is to sketch the rules of the Parliamentary (or Oireachtas) Party of the three major parties. Each party has a constitution, known, variously, as: *Coru agus Rialacha: Constitution and Rules* (Fianna Fáil; current edition, 1972); *Constitution and Rules* (Fine Gael, 1978); or *Constitution* (Labour, 1978).[83] These instruments have each been adopted by the particular party's annual conference which is, formally, the sovereign body of the party and which is known as the National Conference in the Labour Party and the *Ard Fheis* in the case of the other two parties. These constitutions deal with the structure and duties of the various organs of the parties outside the Oireachtas and the procedure for the selection of party candidates for election to the Dáil. The striking features of these constitutions is that it is only the Fine Gael constitution which contains standing orders for the parliamentary party and even these are by no means complete. For the other two parties, there are only unwritten traditions, the content of which varies with personalities and other circumstances and is likely to be disputed at a time of controversy, the very time when a clear rule is needed. For this reason, the present sketch is bound to be somewhat tentative. The lack of written standing orders is more notable in the case of Fianna Fáil than Labour, since Fianna Fáil has always been the largest party and usually forms the Government. This lack has been variously explained as the consequence of Fianna Fáil's formation, in 1925, as an extra-parliamentary party[84] and as the result of the party's traditional massive unity behind a univerally-respected leader, which persisted until the mid-1960's, and rendered written rules necessary.

Pledge The basis of party discipline in the Dáil is the pledge, a form of which must be signed by parliamentary candidates for each party. It is this which justifies the expulsion of recalcitrant members of the parliamentary party. The wording of the Fianna Fáil pledge is as follows:

Realising the honour conferred on me if selected as a candidate for Fianna Fáil, I undertake to conduct the election campaign in accordance with the instructions of the Director of Elections and to refrain from doing anything inimical to the prestige of the Organisation. I, ..., do hereby signify my consent to stand if selected as a candidate for the Constituency of .... and pledge myself, if elected, to work to the best of my ability for the Aims and Objects of Fianna Fáil, as stated in the Coru, and to abide at all times by majority decisions of the Party or resign my seat as Teachta Dála. I further promise that if called upon by the National Executive, by a two-thirds (⅔) majority of the members present, and voting, at a meeting specially convened for the purpose, to resign my seat as Teachta Dála, I will do so.

Although it has never been invoked, the last sentence of this pledge (of which sentence there is an equivalent in the Labour, but not the Fine Gael, pledge) is notable for its underlying assumption that the seat is, in the final analysis, the property of the party under whose banner the candidate was elected, rather than the deputy himself. The other key feature of the pledge — the promise to abide by majority party decisions — is articulated more precisely in the pledges of the other parties which employ the phraseology, 'to sit, act and vote with [the party]' which was the formula used by Parnell's Irish Party.

The whip The 'whip'[85] is the rather quaint device through which the instructions of the party are conveyed to the members of the parliamentary party. It consists of a weekly letter sent out, during the Oireachtas session, by the officer of the parliamentary party responsible for discipline who is also known, unhelpfully, as the 'whip'. It lists the parliamentary business which is likely to be taken during the following week and the points at which divisions are anticipated. But it gives no instruction as to how the recipient should vote: it is reasonable to expect him to know this for himself.

Breach of party discipline The chief sanction for 'breach of party discipline' — usually, though not exclusively, failure to support the party line in a division — is expulsion from the parliamentary party or, as it is usually put, 'withdrawal of the party whip.' The immediate effects of this sanction are relatively small — merely that the offender may not attend the parliamentary party meetings, does not receive the weekly letter and will not be allowed to use party facilities, such as the party rooms at Leinster House. Its chief significance lies in the possibility that the offender may still be out in the cold at election time, more specifically, at the time when party conventions are held to select the party candidates. It is true that there is a distinction between membership of the party and of the parliamentary party. (Expulsion from the party is a function of the Administrative Council in the Labour Party and of the National Executive in each of the other two parties.)[86] Nevertheless, a party is unlikely to adopt as a candidate for the Dáil a person who has had the whip withdrawn.[87]

A breach of party discipline warranting expulsion may take the form of a public disagreement with party policy (for example, Dr Hugh Byrne, expelled from Fine Gael briefly for a racialist statement in 1979; Mr Desmond O'Malley, Fianna Fáil whip withdrawn for disagreement over the New Ireland Forum in 1984).[88] More usually, it is a failure to support the party line in a vote. A notable example of this was the action of two Fianna Fáil deputies — Messrs Neil Blaney and Paudge Brennan, in November 1971, in abstaining on a censure motion against the (Fianna Fáil) Minister for Defence, arising out of the Arms Crisis. As a result, the whip was withdrawn from these deputies. A year earlier, Mr Kevin Boland, resigned his seat rather than break the pledge by failing to support the Government.[89]

The Fine Gael Constitution (rule 51) deals clearly with the procedure for the withdrawal of the whip: a motion must be passed by a two-thirds majority of those present at a parliamentary party meeting, of which at least one week's notice, specifying that the expulsion is on the agenda, has been given. The member concerned must have had notice of the case against him and the opportunity to make a reply. In the other two parties, the support of a simple majority will suffice. In Fianna Fáil, there is a tradition that the motion for expulsion must be moved by the party leader. As regard re-extension of the whip to a member who has been expelled, in Fine Gael this requires the support of a two-third majority and, in the other parties, a simple majority of the parliamentary party.

Expulsion is, of course, a two-edged weapon which no party could afford to exercise frequently. Often, the situation arising from (say) a statement at odds with party policy has been met by a conversation with the leader followed by a public retraction.[90]

Free vote and conscience exemption The system of party discipline covers almost all issues. In other words, there have been very few free votes, that is, votes in which there is no party decision as to how its members should vote. A rare example was the Labour Party's free vote on the Eighth Amendment of the Constitution Bill, 1982 (the 'pro-life' amendment). Similar to, though less extreme than, the free vote is the 'conscience exemption' by which deputies or senators with conscientious objections to the party line may be allowed to abstain.

Traditionally, Fianna Fáil objects to the conscience objection, on ground of principle, in that it could lead to the complete subversion of party discipline since there is no self-evident demarcation line limiting the issues in respect of which the exception should be allowed.[91] Thus, for instance, in the British Parliamentary Labour Party, up to 1968, a member's conscience, was taken as only being engaged by measures relating to drink, sex, religion or defence, which appears rather arbitrary. Fianna Fáil has allowed occasional exceptions from its doctrine of which the most recent concerned the abstention by the then Minister for Ariculture, Mr Jim Gibbons, on the division on the second reading of the Health (Family Planning) Bill, 1978. His failure to support the measure was retrospectively legitimated by the party leader, Mr Jack Lynch, when a few days after the second reading vote Mr Lynch announced that members with conscientious objections had been free not to support it. This decision stirred up some discontent within Fianna Fáil, both because it broke with a tradition which had served the party well and because certain other members had voted for the measure, with misgivings, but out of loyalty to the party.[92] Fine Gael does allow an abstention on conscientious grounds if, and only if, this has been authorised by a party meeting after taking into account the particular member and the particular issue. There are, however, obvious difficulties where only one of the two major parties allows the conscience exemption on a free vote, and these difficulties materialised when sufficient Fine Gael deputies voted against their own Government's Control of Importation, Sale and Manufacture of Contraceptives Bill, 1974 for the measure to be defeated.[93]

Party meeting A meeting of each of the parliamentary parties (which includes, deputies, senators and MEP's) is held regularly — usually once a week or fortnight during the session. The meeting is convened and chaired by the chairman, who is a senior back-bencher elected annually in Fine Gael and for the period of each Dáil in the other two parties. Theoretically, it is the parliamentary party, together with the other organs of the party, which makes policy. In practice (though to a lesser extent in the Labour Party than the other two parties) the leader commands a great deal of influence simply by virtue of being leader. He also commands considerable powers of patronage: when his party is in government, the appointment of ministers, etc; in opposition, the selection of front bench spokesmen; the distribution of trips abroad and other good things. If the leader cannot get his way in most major matters of policy in the parliamentary party, it is likely that he will, sooner rather than later, resign or be removed. Thus in normal times, the party meeting's chief function is not as a policy-making body, but (as was mentioned in the previous Section) as a means of communication enabling the leadership to explain party policy and to listen, in private, to the frank comments of their supporters, sometimes before a public commitment to a policy.

The election or removal of the leader   The Fianna Fáil and Fine Gael Constitutions each recognise the office of president as chief of the national party. However, although the constitutions do seem to contemplate the election of a president, it is usually assumed that the leader of the parliamentary party will be *ex officio* president in each party.[94] This assumption was demonstrated by the strongly negative reaction which met Mr Haughey's suggestion that he might be dislodged as leader yet continue as president of the party.[95] In the Labour Party, however, the Chairman of the Administrative Council is usually a different person from the parliamentary leader. Of its nature, the Labour Party is less ready to be controlled by a single person.

The role of the parliamentary party in the selection or removal of its leader is thus a most important function. As regards selection, the Fine Gael Constitution provides that:

Whenever the Leader of the Parliamentary Party resigns or dies or, in the opinion of the Parliamentary Party, becomes permanently incapacitated when in office, the Parliamentary Party shall, not sooner than one week or later than one month after such event, meet to elect a new Leader. Each candidate for such election must be duly proposed and seconded. All members of the Parliamentary Party shall be entitled to vote at such election which shall be by the alternative vote (i.e. single transferable) system and shall be by secret ballot.

The other two parties have used an open vote procedure. Since there has never been more than two candidates, it has always been possible for them to use the simple first-past-the-post system. Labour have indicated that if there were more than two candidates, then they would use the single transferable vote, as they do for other elections within the party.

The other function — the removal of a reluctant leader — is likely to prove more difficult. Rules ought to be so designed as to enable party-members to deal with this issue, free of any sort of pressure. On the other hand, party unity requires some limitations on the discussion of such a sensitive topic — perhaps as to how often it may be discussed or as to the amount of support which a motion of no confidence should have before it is debated. Fine Gael appears to have reached a sensible compromise in the following provision:

After each General Election unless the Party is forming or joining in the formation of a Government, the Leader of the Parliamentary Party shall within 2 months after the Election submit himself or herself to a vote of confidence of the Parliamentary Party to be carried out by secret ballot. If he/she fails to secure a majority in such vote of confidence he/she shall resign as Leader of the Party;

The existence of this provision is, at the least, a considerable argument against the raising of the leadership issue at any time other than the period immediately after an election in which the party has been defeated.

The lack of any generally accepted rules of this type for the Fianna Fáil parliamentary party enhanced the difficulties and bitterness when, in 1982-83,[96] three attempts during the course of twelve months were made to unseat a leader (Mr Charles Haughey) who was unpopular with some sections of the party. One question in dispute was whether repeated motions of no confidence could be moved within such a short period. Another was whether there was a right to a secret ballot or whether this procedural issue was a question which should be decided by a majority at the party meetings. Yet a third dispute arose as to whether the party chairman was obliged to convene a meeting to discuss a motion of no confidence in the leader, at the request of a majority of the party.

The nature of these events recalls the contest for the British Conservative Party leadership in 1963 when Sir Alec Douglas-Home 'emerged' from the customary, unwritten 'processes of consultation' by which the leader was traditionally chosen. The controversy generated by the operation of the selection procedure, on this occasion, was so great that it was speedily replaced by a clear-cut and democratic method of selection. Similarly in the case of Fianna Fáil, one of the sequels to the struggle to remove Mr Haughey was the constitution (in early 1983) of a small committee, representative of the various factions in the party, to recommend rules to settle the vital issues mentioned in the previous paragraph. However, it seems unlikely that this committee will ever report.

In Fianna Fáil and Labour, while senators or MEPs speak at party meetings on issues bearing on the leadership, they are barred from voting on this issue. The reason why these two parties (unlike Fine Gael) confine voting rights to Dáil deputies is presumably related to the fact that it is the Dáil which elects, and may remove, a Taoiseach. By an extension of this rule, it was only deputies who were allowed to vote, at the October 1982 Fianna Fáil meeting, on the antecedent procedural question of whether the motion of no confidence in the leader should be a secret ballot. At the January 1983 Fianna Fáil meeeting, it was accepted, without a vote, that the leadership question should be decided by secret ballot.

6

The Place of the Senate[1]

The question to be addressed in this brief Chapter is the *raison d'être* of the Senate. As a preliminary, let us summarise the principal legal powers of the Senate (some of which will be amplified in later Chapters). First of all, the Senate does not appoint — nor can it remove — the Government. Secondly, co-ordinate powers are vested in the two Houses of the Oireachtas in regard to various tasks including for example: the removal of the judges of the superior courts;[2] the declaration of an emergency under Art. 28.3.3° of the Constitution; and the annulment of statutory instruments.[3] Next, in the case of money bills, the Senate's only power is to delay the bill for a period of twenty-one days.[4] Finally, it may delay non-financial legislation for a maximum of ninety days.[5] However, in addition, in the case of non-financial legislation, the Senate can act as a watch-dog by preventing a bill from becoming law until it has been passed either by the people at a referendum or, alternatively, by a Dáil resolution following a dissolution and re-assembly of the Dáil. Before this control can be operated, a petition invoking it must be signed by a majority of senators and one third of the deputies and accepted by the President, acting on his own discretion.[6]

In a federal state, an upper house has an essential and well-defined part to play: it provides a forum in which each of the continental units of the federation may be represented equally within the central legislature. The leading example of this type is the U.S. Senate, which is unique among upper chambers in being the more powerful of the two houses.[7] Again, in certain states, there is an aristocracy of blood which it is thought desirable to recognise in the form of an upper house, and here tradition defines the place of the second chamber. In its original, exclusively hereditary form, the House of Lords was an example of this type of upper house.

Neither of these situations exists in Ireland and it is symptomatic of the lack of consensus regarding the place of, or need for, a Senate that, since 1922, no fewer than six[8] commissions or Oireachtas committees have been set up to examine some aspect of the Senate.

Vocational character   One feature of the Senate which has attracted much attention is the vocational principle which is built into its selection procedure. Out of the sixty senators, forty-nine (all the elected senators) are chosen as the representatives fo some particular group in Irish society, for example, labour or agriculture or university graduates.[9] Vocationalism was a child of its time (the 1920's and 1930's) and an aspect of the enthusiasm for the corporativist idea which was inspired by: the apparently successful model offered by Italian Fascism; the papal encyclical *Quadragesimo Anno*, issued by Pius XI in 1931; and Fabian re-statements of Guild Socialism. The advantages anticipated from vocationalism were not only that such a membership would provide a body of expert legislators but, more fundamentally, that it would resolve conflict between the groups making up the nation. This idea now appears rather simplistic in that true vocationalism would be more likely to emphasise the conflicts between different interest groups than to heal them. But there is no need to dwell on criticism of the theory[10] which was said to underlie the Senate, since this theory is and has always been a long way from the reality, which is that almost all the electors for the panel and vocational seats are politicians, being either members of the Oireachtas or county councillors. The natural result is that nearly all senators are elected, and sit, on a party political basis. This is true even of the nominating bodies' candidates of whom, in any case, the bare statutory minimum is usually elected.[11]

Irish Free State's Senate   A second function which is sometimes attributed to upper chambers is that of acting as a check on the executive. Before pursuing this line of inquiry any further, in relation to the post-1937 Senate, it may be instructive to break off in order to sketch briefly the history of the Irish Free State Senate.[12] The most important feature of this Senate was the system of election to it and, in particular the fact that the term of office was, at first, twelve years[13] and then, following a constitutional amendment in 1928,[14] nine years, with at first a quarter, and, then following the amendment, a third, of the members retiring every three years. The only popular election to the Senate, held in 1925, was a failure due to lack of public interest. As a result of the constitutional amendment, the members of both Houses were substituted as the electorate to the Senate. However, the important point was that the system of staggered elections created a 'time-lag' between the majorities in the two Houses which showed itself when Fianna Fáil took office in 1932. A subsidiary factor which shaped the outlook of the House and made it unpopular, especially with the anti-Treaty Party, was the fact that in the first Senate half the senators were nominated by the Taoiseach and included a number of people with strong connections with the British 'Establishment.' The result of these features was that, after 1932, a lot of the tension in the country surfaced in the form of disputes between the two Houses. Of the ten occasions when the Senate's power to delay non-financial legislation was used, eight occurred after 1932.[15] (Following a second 1928 amendment,[16] the period of delay had been increased from 270 days to twenty months.) Moreover, in many cases the issues involved were regarded as crucial matters of ideology on each side. Thus, for example, in the bill to abolish the parliamentary oath, the Senate inserted a section (which was rejected by the Dáil) to the effect that the bill should not come into effect until an agreement had been reached with the British.[17] There was also some fear that the Senate would interfere with the establishment of Bunreacht na hÉireann.[18] The inevitable result was the abolition of the Senate, on 29 May 1936 (nineteen months before the Irish Free State terminated).

What was more surprising was the inclusion of a senate in the new Constitution. This time, however, amongst other differences in the composition of the new Senate, the Taoiseach has been given the power of nominating eleven senators. In recent years, Taoisigh have included, among their nominees, two or even three respected Independents, often including one or two from the North. This has meant, *on paper* that, when Fianna Fáil is in office, either the Government has a very precarious majority or, alternatively, Independents hold the balance of power. Nevertheless, even in these circumstances, Government defeats have been very few.[19] Thus, for almost all practical circumstances, it can be said that, in contrast with the position in the Irish Free State, Governments have had, and are likely to have, a majority in the Senate. This explains why, with two exceptions, the post-1937 Senate has never exercised its legal powers (listed above) to disagree with the Government majority in the Dáil. The two exceptional cases were each bills which the Senate delayed for ninety days. Of these, one — the Pawnbrokers Bill, 1964 — was comparatively unimportant, whilst the second — the Third Amendment of the Constitution Bill, 1958 — would have been the most significant constitutional measures in the history of the State. It is striking that, although the Senate has never exercised (or come close to doing so) its power under Art. 27 to petition the President for a referendum on a non-constitutional bill, the unprecedented nature of its action over the 1958 bill may have sounded the alarm-bells and tipped the scales of popular support narrowly[20] against the bill at the referendum, and thus had a somewhat similar effect to that intended by Art. 27. Finally, in assessing the almost complete failure of the Senate to thwart the executive, it must be remembered that successive Irish Governments have brought forward few, if any, measures extreme enough to warrant what would be regarded as an extreme remedy. In view of this, the Senate might still be characterised as a watch-dog of some potential importance. On the other hand, Mr Marnane[21] has suggested that since the Senate and the President have similar, though not identical, functions as regards acting as a check on the Government, it would be appropriate to combine all these duties in the office of President, thereby freeing the way for the abolition of the Senate.

A 'revising' chamber Another role which may be canvassed for the Senate is that of a revising chamber for legislation. A number of distinct aspects of this idea are rehearsed in the following extract from the 1967 Report on the Constitution:

... what most countries expect in providing a second house is that they will thereby have a safeguard against ill-considered or hasty action on the part of the first house. A second group of public representatives will have the opportunity of examining legislation and commenting upon it. The first house will thereby be given time for reflection on the utility of the measures which it has proposed. Furthermore, a reasonable opportunity will be given to affected interests to organise public opinion in relation to controversial matters. In addition, important technical matters may receive in the second house more comprehensive treatment than it has been possible to give them in the first house.[22]

The evidence, however, suggests that the Senate makes only a small contribution in this role. During the period, 1971-80, about 300 bills passed the Senate and amendments were made to thirty three of the bills yielding a total of 184 amendments, a very large number of which were drafting points.[23] Moreover, almost all of these amendments were Government amendments (although it should also be noted that Government amendments are sometimes made in response to suggestions made by non-Government or Opposition members). There is no doubt that the Senate sometimes play a useful part in revising legislation, as it did, for example, in amending the Succession Bill, 1965 or the Sale of Goods and Supply of Services Bill, 1978. Again, the Wild Life Bill, 1975 and the Broadcasting Authority (Amendment) Bill, 1975, were each introduced in the Senate, rather than the Dáil, specifically because the responsible ministers wished to be assisted by the higher quality of debate which, it is accepted, prevails in the Senate. But the point under examination here is not the potential of the Senate, but the contribution which it is allowed to make by the Government. And the fact remains that successive Governments have failed to launch bills in the Senate in any numbers[24] so as to avoid the bottle-neck just before the summer or Christmas recess which leaves the Senate with too little time to execute its revising function properly. Nor has any Government sought to enhance the value of the Senate by altering the system of readings in the Senate so that it is not identical with that in the Dáil.

Conclusion   Thus far, our examination of the Senate's role has suggested that its contribution is marginal. Considering the cost of the Senate (in 1983 the cost of both the Houses together was approx £7 million) and considering that before Greece joined the EEC,[25] Ireland had twice as many seats per head of population in the lower House as was the case elsewhere in the EEC, the question must be raised whether Ireland should follow such states as Denmark, Sweden and New Zealand and do away with its upper chamber. Before passing judgment on this question, it may be useful to examine the Senate in the wider perspective of the part which the two Houses of the Oireachtas ought to be playing in our constitutional system. It has already been suggested — at the end of the previous Chapter on the Dáil and the Government — that there is need for an effective 'Grand Inquest of the Nation,' and that the Dáil is failing to discharge this function. It is possible that the Senate could fill at least part of this gap. In a small State in which the Government often has a monopoly of expertise and information and where the level of public debate is often dangerously under-informed, there is a need for a forum for the sort of public-spirited professional man who would have neither time nor inclination to undergo the rigours of election to, and membership of, the Dáil. The fact that genuine ideological differences are few in Ireland would militate in favour of the kind of non-partisan debate which, before the Civil War, was anticipated from the Dáil. A suggestion along these lines was made, in 1969, by Mr Garvin who wrote:

The oddness of [the Senate's] electoral system and the contrast between its pretensions and its actual place in political life ensure its eventual reform or abolition. Its hopes of survival lie, I believe, in its being converted into a small assembly possessing negligible political power, but containing in its ranks administrative, judicial, vocational, academic and political expertise, whether selected through electoral mechanism or otherwise. Such a House would derive its power from the prestige of its members rather than from any legal grant.[26]

It is notable that a similar diagnosis has recently been offered, from the other side of the world, in an article entitled, 'New Zealand's Single Chamber Parliament — An Argument for an Impotent Upper House?'[27] Among other themes relevant to Ireland, this article argues that an upper chamber, which theoretically can exercise control over the lower House-executive, is less likely to be allowed to act as an effective national sounding-board. The reason is that even the bare existence of the possibity of control means that it is in the Government's self-interest to downgrade the upper chamber and not to heed any suggestion it makes.

Yet as the need for the establishment of such bodies as the National Economic and Social Council shows the Senate has not gone far in the direction proposed for it in the passage just quoted. It is true that a few of its members — notably those elected for the university seats — are independent-minded people with special ability and a wide range of contacts. Moreover, the Senate has been either the first or the only House to debate such politically 'risky' subjects as family planning;[28] the removal of the status of illegitimacy and the 'political offence' exemption from extradition. In 1978, a motion calling on the Government to make an order preserving the Viking site at Wood Quay was lost by only one vote.[29] In 1979, Senate standing orders were amended so that a meeting had to be called if thirty senators requested. This power (of which there is no Dáil counterpart) was used, in 1982, to summon a Senate meeting, against the Government's wishes, in order to discuss the economic crisis.[30] The Senate's committee work has been generally praised as thorough and well-informed and before the establishment of the Joint Committee on Legislation, the Senate was the only House to have a committee to scrutinise statutory instruments. Nevertheless, most senators are indistinguishable from the type of career-politician to be found in the Dáil; indeed many are people who are using the Senate to keep themselves in the public eye before capturing, or recapturing, a Dáil seat. The result is that the Senate's performance differs only a degree from that of the Dáil: apart from the few instances noted, the Senate holds under-reported debates on the same motions and measures as the Dáil, by way of a virtually identical procedure. And, if there is a vote, the Government almost always wins. All in all, the case for retaining the Senate, in its present unreformed state, seems to be weak.

7

Legislation

This Chapter is concerned with the process by which acts of the Oireachtas are made and not with the substantive limit on their content, namely that no law may be enacted which is 'in any respect repugnant to [the] Constitution . . .'.[1]

Before a bill is published by being circulated to the members of the House in which it is initiated, it will, if it is a Government bill, have undergone an extensive period of gestation within the Government. Although traditional constitutional doctrine has it that laws are made in public in the Oireachtas,[2] this is only true in the sense that the Oireachtas legitimates bills by conducting a formalised debate on their merits climaxed by a division along predictable, party lines. Because of the Government's majority, Opposition amendments are seldom successful. And if criticism is expressed by a back-bencher, on the Government side, it is usually done privately, in a party meeting or by button-holing a minister. Where amendments are made to a bill as it goes through the Oireachtas, they are often introduced by the minister piloting the bill through the Oireachtas. They may arise from second thoughts within his department, or they may be an attempt to meet criticism of the bill, which may originate either from within or outside the Oireachtas.

Leaving aside an unimportant number of private members' bills,[3] all legislation is drafted and introduced in the Oireachtas by the Government. Frequently, whilst preparing this legislation and before launching it in the Oireachtas, the Government consults relevant interest-groups or independent experts. For example, under the civil service Conciliation and Arbitration Scheme, the Department of the Public Service is obliged to consult the civil service unions about legislation affecting their members. But usually there are no rules or even consistent practices, so that the procedure varies from one minister to another or from department to department. Thus, for instance, the Department of Labour consults trade unions and employers if it is designing legislation in the field of labour law, whereas the Department of Justice is less likely to consult groups interested in its bills. Consultation may be through a minister or a senior civil servant.

A fixed routine is observed in the pre-parliamentary preparation of legislation within the departments and Government. This routine is laid down by the

Government Secretariat in the form of the confidential Government Procedural Instructions. First, the responsible department must consult the Department of Finance, the Department of the Public Service and any departments with a particular interest in that subject-area. Next, a memorandum setting out the proposal together with its cost, and the views of all departments (even if adverse), is submitted to the Government. If the Government agrees in principle, then the responsible department draws up heads of a bill indicating the content of each section. When the heads have been approved by the Government, the embryo bill is sent to the parliamentary draftsmen, who are lawyers specialising in drafting (Government)[4] legislation and working in the Attorney General's Department. At this stage, any legal difficulties will be raised. The draft bill is then sent to the the Government and, if it is approved, it is sent to the Minister for Finance so that he and his advisers can make a more leisurely examination of the financial implications of the bill. If he accepts the measure, the bill is then sent to the Government printer for printing on white paper, the resulting version being known as the 'white print.' Next, the bill goes once more before the Government, for final approval, possibly in an amended form. It is then sent to the Bills Office of the Oireachtas. There it is assigned a number and, after it has been initiated in the House, it is printed on green or yellow paper, according to whether it has been initiated in the Dáil or Senate, respectively.

A bill's priority is indicated by its position in the (confidential) parliamentary programme.[5] This is a schedule of anticipated legislation, together with the projected date when it is expected to be ready. It is prepared by the Chief Whip in the autumn at the start of the session and updated at frequent intervals.

7.2 LEGISLATIVE POWERS OF THE TWO HOUSES

Generally, the Dáil and the Senate have equal, legal power in the process of legislation. Non-financial legislation may be initiated in either House,[6] though in practice most of it is initiated in the Dáil. There are, however, three situations in which the effective, political superiority of the Dáil is reflected in the constitutional provisions regulating legislation. The first of these cases is Art. 23, which provides that, if there is a disagreement between the two Houses, the Dáil can overrule the Senate simply by passing a resolution. This power, which is described more fully below, is more than a mere exception to the general principle: rather, although it is seldom invoked, its very existence helps to tilt the entire relationship between the two Houses in the Dáil's favour. The second type of bill in respect of which the Senate's powers are reduced is a Money Bill,[7] a category which will be covered in more detail below.[8] Finally, Art. 24 enables bills (hereafter called 'Art. 24 bills') which are necessary to deal with an emergency[9] to be passed through the Senate quickly. (The range of emergency contemplated in the Article is wide enough to encompass a nuclear attack or, at the other extreme, an outbreak of smallpox in one town.)

An Art. 24 bill can only remain in force for ninety days from the date of its enactment unless, before the end of this period, each House passes a resolution agreeing to prolong its life for whatever 'longer period' is specified in the resolution (Art. 24 contains no restriction on the duration of the 'longer period'). In view of this restriction and considering how co-operative the Senate has been in passing bills quickly, it is perhaps not surprising that this provision has never been used. According to Art. 24:

If and whenever on the passage by Dáil Éireann of any bill, other than a Bill expressed to be a Bill containing a proposal to amend the Constitution, the Taoiseach certifies by messages in writing addressed to the President and to the Chairman of each House of the Oireachtas that, in the opinion of the Government, the Bill is urgent and immediately necessary for the preservation of the public peace and security, or by reason of the existence of a public emergency, whether domestic or international, the time for the consideration of such Bill by Seanad Éireann shall, if Dáil Éireann so resolves and if the President, after consultation with the Council of State, concurs, be abridged to such period as shall be specified in the resolution.

Thus Art. 24 requires not only the Taoiseach's certificate but also a Dáil resolution to like effect and the concurrence of the President. The effect of the Article (which had no equivalent in the 1922 Constitution) is that, irrespective of what the Senate does, the bill is deemed to have been passed by both Houses at the end of the period specified in the Dáil resolution.

Disagreement Disagreements between the Houses are rare because usually each has the same party in the majority. However, it has happened that a clash has arisen in that one House rejects or refrains from passing a bill passed by the other House or makes amendments which are not acceptable to the other House. Where amendments are involved, disagreements may arise in either of two forms depending on which House the bill was initiated in. First, if the bill was initiated in the Dáil and amended in the Senate, the bill is returned to the Dáil which considers it in committee. If the Dáil disagrees with any of the amendments, the issues are reconsidered by the Senate, which may resolve to 'insist on the amendment.'[10] The second alternative is that the bill was initiated in the Senate but has been amended in the Dáil. The senior position of the Dáil is shown in a rule that, in these circumstances, the bill is to be treated as if it were a bill initiated in the Dáil,[11] thereby putting the onus on the Senate to decide whether to restore its original text. Whether a bill is initiated in the Dáil or Senate, there are two ways of resolving disagreements. The less drastic method is for each House to send representatives to a joint conference which tries to reach an agreement which can be recommended as a solution to each House. This device is not mentioned in the present Constitution (though it was referred to in Art. 38 of the 1922 Constitution) but there is no doubt that a general power exists to send members to a joint conference to make non-binding recommendations A conference has been held on one occasion before, and once since, 1937.[12] In each case, it was recommended that the Senate did not insist upon its amendment, and this advice was accepted.

The alternative method of resolving differences is specified in Art. 23, which applies to all bills apart from money bills or Art. 24 bills. Art. 23 provides that if the Senate rejects a bill within the article or passes it with amendments to which the Dáil does not agree or simply fails to pass it within the stated period, then the Dáil may pass a resolution, as a result of which the bill becomes law on the day of the resolution. The Dáil resolution must be passed within one hundred and eighty days after the expiry of 'the stated period', and 'the stated period' commences on the day when the bill first reaches the Senate and runs for ninety days or whatever longer period is agreed upon by both Houses. Art. 23 has had to be used on only two occasions.[13]

Art. 27 of the Constitution In the context of Art. 23, the existence of Art. 27 must be noted, though, since it has never been used, we may be forgiven for omitting the detailed process for its operation. Art. 27 has been included in the Constitution as a partial compensation for the radical power created by Art. 23, of allowing the Dáil to make law without the consent of the Senate. Art. 27 operates only if Art. 23 has been invoked. (Necessarily, therefore, it does not apply either to money bills or to Art. 24 bills; nor does it apply to bills containing proposals to amend the Constitution, since a referendum must be held, anyway, for such bills.) The first stage in the Art. 27 (coupled with Art. 47.2) procedure is that a majority of senators and at least one third of all deputies must petition[14] the President requesting him to decline to sign the bill. Since Art. 27 (unlike its equivalent, Art. 47, in the 1922 Constitution which was excised in 1928)[15] is confined to bills passed in face of the Senate's disagreement, the requisite number of signatures could well be available. If such a petition is brought to the President, it is up to him to decide, on his own discretion, after consultation with his Council of State, whether the bill 'contains a proposal of such national importance that the will of the people thereon ought to be ascertained.' If the President does decide that the bill falls within this definition, then he must decline to sign it, unless and until either of two events has occurred. The first of these alternatives is that the proposal contained in the bill should be put to the people, at a referendum, within eighteen months from the date of the President's decision. The bill is then said to be vetoed if (both) a majority of votes are cast against it and the votes so cast number at least one third of the voters on the register. Alternatively, a resolution approving of the proposal must be passed by the Dáil, *following a dissolution and re-assembly of the Dáil* and also within eighteen months of the President's decision

7.3 STAGES OF A BILL WITHIN A HOUSE

In principle, a bill is considered at five stages. After a bill has completed all its stages in the House in which it commences the legislative process, it is sent to the other House and there it is exempt from the first stage.[16] The purpose of the different stages may be summarised, as follows. At the first stage, the proposer is authorised to send a copy of the bill to all the members. The second stage is a general debate on the bill set in the context of its subject-matter. The third stage consists of a detailed examination of the bill, clause by clause. At the fourth stage, the amendments made at the third stage are reviewed. The fifth stage provides a final opportunity for a general debate on the bill.

Preliminary collection of views   Before examining the five stages in more detail, it is convenient to pause to notice the power of investigating draft bills which is one[17] of the duties vested in the new Joint Committee on Legislation (described in Chapter 9.4). This power will have to be exercised at a time when the bill is only in memorandum form or between first and second stages, in the first House to hear the bill (usually the Dáil). Where the power is invoked, the Committee (or one of its sub-committees) will be required:

to invite submissions in writing, or orally if considered necessary by the Committee, from interested persons or bodies on bills or other proposals for legislation (other than measures arising out of or relating to the Budget) referred to it by either House on Motion made by, or with the consent of a Member of the Government and to provide a record of same for the information of each House.[18]

The essence of the Committee's task here is neither deliberate not legislative but rather to collect the comments of interested parties. This brings the consultation of interest groups out of the corridors of departments and into the public arena. However, the members of the Committee can effectively contribute their own ideas on the bill through their questions to witnesses or their selection of persons from whom to elicit submissions. It is envisaged that the Committee will make its contribution at an early stage, before the proposals have become 'congealed as a draft bill' and thus at a time when changes would be more readily accepted. It should be emphasised that only three to five bills per year are likely to be referred to the Committees on this basis, but it is anticipated that they will include some of the most significant and controversial meansures: the first bill to be referred was the Independent Local Broadcasting Authority Bill, 1983.

First stage[19]   Bills may be initiated by way of either introduction or presentation. In each case, the title of the bill, together with a short statement of its purpose, appears on the Order Paper. If the bill is being introduced, its proposer moves the House for leave and, if such leave is given, an order is made that the bill be printed and circulated to all members. It also specifies a date for the second stage. Since the House knows very little about the bill, the first stage is usually unopposed and formal and, because of this, standing orders were amended[20] (in 1974, in the Dáil, and, in 1979, in the Senate) to allow for the option of introducing a bill by way of presentation. This means that a bill can be initiated, printed and circulated without obtaining the House's consent. Thus, a bill can be introduced during the recess and, secondly, private members' bills can be sure of reaching second stage and so at least receiving an airing. Initiation by presentation is the method now commonly used. It is a privilege which is confined to ministers; ministers of state; private members nominated by a group of at least seven deputies or five senators; and, in the Senate, the leader of the Senate.[21]

Second stage[22] This is the stage at which the general principles of the bill and even alternative ways of remedying the same 'mischief' are discussed: a member can say what he thinks the bill ought to have contained but he cannot refer to the details of the provision before the House. The motion before the Houses is: 'That the bill be now read a second time.' The way in which opposition is expressed to the bill is almost always by voting against this motion. However, standing orders do allow for another[23] method of opposing a bill, which is less commonly used. This entails deleting the words after 'that' in the original motion and replacing them with a statement of some specific reason against the second reading of the bill. This method was used, occasionally in 1982, when a general election was imminent, as a device by which the Opposition could deploy its alternative policy in relation to a bill. When an amendment of this type is moved, the question proposed from the Chair is 'That the words proposed to be deleted stand.' The point of this arrangement is that it enables all the opponents of the bill to vote against the question, irrespective of whether they support the reasoned amendment. If the question is carried, then the bill is declared to be read a second time with no need for a further question.

Third stage[24] The third stage is the committee stage. At this stage the House's concern is with the detail of the bill and, as it is bound by the principles which are regarded as having been settled at the second stage, the chair has frequently to rule out of order the type of contribution which is sometimes stigmatised as 'second reading speeches.' The rule that an amendment may not introduce a new principle or one which conflicts with existing principles of the bill clearly involves a question of degree, the resolution of which is a matter of judgment for the chair. For example, consider a provision so that the electorate for a quarter of the (Irish Free State) Senate seats was to be the Dáil and Senate voting together. Amendments were put down which sought to confine the members of the Senate who could vote in this election to those who had themselves been directly elected by the people. This amendment was ruled inadmissible because it sought to introduce a principle not to be found elsewhere in the bill, namely, that certain members of the Senate should not have the same rights as others. By contrast, an amendment which would have provided that only the members of the Dáil should be eligible to vote was held to be merely 'an ordinary limitation of the principle' of the bill and, as such, admissible.[25]

Normally, the *modus operandi*, at committee stage, is to work through the bill, section by section, considering any amendments[26] related to the section under consideration. Over the years certain commonsense rules, which elaborate this principle, have evolved or been established by standing order.[27] Thus: sections dealing with the same subject-matter may be discussed together; where similar amendments to the same provision have been put down, the most radical amendment is discussed first;[28] once a section has been agreed — by the passage of a motion: 'That such section (or such section as amended) stand part of the Bill',[29] — the committee cannot return to it. As its penultimate task, the committee must consider the bill's title and preamble. At this point, the committee can see whether any amendment which has been accepted falls outside the bill's title and, if so, 'amend the title accordingly and report the same specially to the [House].'[30] After this the bill is reported to the House, which must then make an order for the report stage.

Which type of committee?   There is, in the Oireachtas, no standing committee system for bills, under which all bills of the same type would be referred to the same committee.[31] The forum in which the committee stage must be heard is determined by an order of the House.[32] Theoretically there are four possibilities: a Committee of the whole House; a Special Committee; the Joint Committee on Legislation; or a Select Committee.[33] In fact, the principal feature which distinguishes a select committee from a special committee[34] — the power to send for persons, papers and records — would seldom be useful in hearing the third stage of bills. Moreover, were the third stage heard by select committee, the fourth stage would have to be re-committed to a Committee of the whole House before its fourth stage could be taken.[35] The result is that only two bills (one in the Dáil and one in the Senate) have been taken in select committee since 1937.[36]

In fact, almost all committee stages are heard by a Committee of the whole House. In the Dáil, during the period 1937-83, only twenty[37] out of almost 1,200 Government-sponsored public bills have been sent to a special committee. The position is similar in the Senate.[38]

One of the chief functions of the new Joint Committee on Legislation[39] (which it may exercise through a sub-committee) is to hear the committee stage of any bill referred to it by either House with the concurrence of the other. The sort of bills allocated to the Joint Committee — technical, detailed measures — are likely to be just the sort of measures which were formerly taken by special committees; thus special committees are now likely to become redundant.

The relative advantages and disadvantages of the smaller committee, as compared with a Committee of the whole House, will be discussed, generally, in the Chapter on Procedure.[40] Here it need only be noted that certain of the difficulties which would otherwise arise from vesting the committee stage of a bill in the Joint Committee have been avoided because the Order of Reference[41] makes the member of the Government in charge of the bill (or a minister of state nominated by him) an *ex officio* committee member. Secondly, any member of the Oireachtas who is not a committee member is given the right to attend and speak, but not to vote, at a committee meeting.

Fourth (report) stage[42] The chief purpose of the fourth stage is not to make a general appraisal of the bill but to review the work done in Committee at the third stage. The examination of a bill in five stages is modelled on the procedure at Westminster where the third stage is usually heard by a small committee. But in Ireland the third stage is usually taken by a Committee of the whole House and as the Government usually initiates the bill and has a majority at all stages, the fourth stage is frequently formal. Apart from minor and drafting amendments[43] the only amendments permitted are those which arise out of proceedings in Committee, whether from an amendment actually made at committee stage; a discussion which did not lead to a decision on an amendment; or an undertaking given by the minister in charge of the bill.[44] No amendment may be moved which is the same as, or similar to, an amendment defeated in a Committee of the whole House.[45] Where an amendment seeks either to make a change which does not arise out of proceedings in Committee or which creates any charge on the public revenue or the people, then the bill must be recommitted *i.e.* sent back to Committee.[46] Where there is a recommital it is the usual practice not to have a separate fourth stage for the amendment made at the recommittal.[47]

Fifth stage The fifth stage may be — and usually is — taken formally, immediately after the fourth stage. In the case of a money bill before the Senate, the motion before the House is: 'That the Bill be returned to the Dáil.' Otherwise, the motion is: 'That the Bill do now pass.'[48] Debate is usually brief, speeches being directed to the merits of the bill's content rather than the need for the bill or provisions which ought to be, but are not, in the Bill. These limitations, which mean that the scope of the discussion is more restricted than at second stage, have had to be pointed out to the House on many occasions by the chair.[49] The only amendments which can be accepted at this stage are those which are 'merely verbal.'[50]

Lapsed bills There is a curious rule regarding bills which have been overtaken by a general election before all their stages in both Houses are complete: provided that a resolution is passed by a House restoring the bill to the Order Paper, it commences in the new House from the stage which it had reached in the outgoing House, without going back to the first stage.[51] By contrast, the Westminster Parliament flies to the other extreme in that all stages of a bill must be passed in the same session (which, in British usage, means just one year); otherwise the bill has to negotiate all its stages again.

101

In the context of legislation, *consolidation* means the re-enactment, as a single measure, of all the statute law on a particular subject. This might be thought to be an especially important task in Ireland because certain pre-1922 statutes are still in force and, as most of these are obsolete in the land of their birth, copies of them are difficult to obtain. The essence of the matter is that the content of the law is not changed, but the law is collected in a more convenient source. In 1946, the Government approved a scheme for consolidating all statute law and a joint Oireachtas committee[52] was set up, as a consequence, to design a special code for considering consolidation bills, which was adapted to their peculiar nature. This code was incorporated in the standing orders of each House.[53] To qualify as a consolidation bill, a bill must meet three conditions: first, its long title must declare that its purposes is to consolidate existing statute law; secondly, the fact that this is its purpose must be certified by the Attorney General in a certificate[54] printed on the Order Paper on which notice of intention to introduce the bill is given; finally, there must be prefixed to it a Memorandum, itemising the enactments repealed by the bill and the sections of the bill in which their content is reproduced.[55]

This special procedure (which has only been employed on three occasions)[56] may be summarised by outlining the four features which distinguish it from the process for ordinary bills. First, minimum time limits between stages (for example, twenty eight days between first and second stages[57]) are laid down — presumably so as to enable members to carry out research. Secondly, the only permissible amendment at second stage is one which states a reason for challenging the Attorney General's Certificate.[58] Thirdly, subject to the concurrence of both Houses, the third stage is heard by the Joint Committee on Legislation (in place of the former Standing Joint Committee on Consolidation Bills). Up to three *ad hoc* members from each House may be added for each bill.[59] The only amendments permitted are those which would remove ambiguities or obsolete machinery or would adapt the bill to conform to existing law and practice. At no stage may substantive amendments to the existing law be made.[60] Finally, the first three stages are waived in the second House to hear the bill.[61]

7.5 PRIVATE MEMBERS' BILLS

Public bills (for private bills, see Section 6) may be divided into two types: Government bills; and private members' bills. The second type of bill is sponsored by a member who is not a member of the Government, minister of state, Attorney General or leader of the House in the Senate. The formal differences between the processes for each type are slight, for instance, in the Dáil: each party may have only one private members' bill before the House at a time;[62] there is a maximum time of six hours for the second stage of a private members' bill;[63] private members' bills must go to a special or select committee for committee stage.[64] The significant difference, however, lies in the fact that the Government will almost always oppose a private members' bill which consequently has small chance of passing even its second stage. Government back-benchers do not initiate bills and there is no tradition in Ireland, as there is in Britain, of Government neutrality towards private members' bills in certain areas, such as family or sexual matters. The result is that very few private members' bills have become law. During the period 1923-37, 694 Government bills were introduced in the Dáil as against fifty private members' bills and, of these fifty, only six became law.[65] And since 1937, only six private members' bills[66] have been enacted. The most recent of these, the Law Reform (Personal Injuries) Bill, 1958, which was promoted by a group of Labour deputies, is of particular interest to lawyers because it laid the doctrine of common employment to rest. As regard private members' legislation initiated in the Senate, since 1937 only one bill (Protection of Animals (Amendment) Bill, 1963) has become law. It has, however, been said that even if the bill does not become law, a bill is a more useful way of focussing public attention on an issue than a motion on the same topic.[67] This now appears to have been recognised in the increased number of private members' bills launched in recent years. One of these, the (Fine Gael) Ombudsman Bill, 1979 acted as a goad which prompted the Government to bring forward its own bill in 1980.

7.6 PRIVATE LEGISLATION[68]

So far all the bills considered (whether they be Government bills or private members' bills) have fallen within the category of public bills, that is, bills which make general law. The antithesis to public bills is private legislation, which Erskine May defines as: 'legislation of a special kind for conferring particular powers or benefits on any person or body of persons — including individuals, local authorities, statutory companies, or private corporations — in excess of or in conflict with the general law.'[69] Private legislation is published separately from the public acts, at the end of the annual volumes of the Acts of the Oireachtas. Recent examples of private bills — the more important of the two types of private legislation — are: the Leopardstown Park Hospital (Trust Deed Amendment) Act, 1974; the Institution of Civil Engineers of Ireland (Charter Amendment) Act, 1969. The procedure by which private legislation becomes law is radically different from that relating to public bills: it is regulated by the joint *Standing Orders of the Dáil and the Seanad relative to Private Business* (current edition: 1939), which are distinct from the standing orders for public business which have been referred to hitherto.

Although the various stages though which a private bill proceeds are modelled on those for an ordinary public bill, they are adapted to take account of the underlying fact that the proceedings on a private bill also partake, to some extent, of a judicial character in that individual rights are directly involved.[70] Whereas a public bill is initiated by a member, a private bill is solicited by the promoters — that is, the persons who are applying for the powers and benefits contained in the bill. The promoters appear as suitors for the bill before the House, whilst any persons who apprehend injury from the bill may be admitted as adverse parties. Each side is usually represented by a parliamentary agent (a solicitor with at least five years experience may be registered as a parliamentary agent) who usually instructs counsel. A private bill has to be introduced in the Senate, not the Dáil, and it can only be introduced, after examination by the Examiner of Private Bills (an officer appointed jointly by the chairmen of both Houses), to ensure compliance with standing orders dealing with advertising and the notification of persons or bodies affected by the bill. After second reading in the Senate, the bill is referred to a joint committee consisting of three members of each House and a chairman nominated jointly by the chairmen of both Houses. (None of the members of the committee may have an interest in the bill.) This is the important stage of the proceedings, since the joint committee is a select committee and it takes evidence, hears counsel on behalf of the promoters and objectors, considers reports from interested departments of state and, eventually, reports with or without amendments, to each House. Next, the fourth stage (where any amendments are considered) and fifth stage are heard in the Senate. Finally, the bill is sent to the Dáil for fourth and fifth stages only, since the first three stages are waived.

It has happened three times,[71] since 1922, that a bill initiated as a public bill has been found to affect private rights in a way analogous to a private bill. Such bills are known as 'hybrid' bills and are subject, partially, to the rules and procedures governing private bills.[72]

Provisional order confirmation bills   Private bills are time-consuming and expensive and have to be promoted by the person or body which benefits from them. In certain circumstances, a device (known as a provisional order) is available for making private legislation, which avoids these disadvantages. Thus, for example, the various City Management Acts provide that extensions to city boundaries may be fixed by provisional order. But an act authorising the provisional order procedure will also state that a provisional order 'shall not have any effect unless or until it is confirmed by Act of the Oireachtas.'[73] Provisional order confirmation bills are introduced into the Senate as public bills, the motion for leave to introduce being moved by the Leas-Cathaoirleach (Deputy Chairman). If leave is given, the bill is ordered to be printed and circulated and then proceeds in substantially the same way as a public bill. However, the bill may be opposed, by way of petition against the order to print, and circulate, and in this case the private bill procedure must be followed. Another opportunity for delaying the bill arises from the rule that where any stage of the bill is opposed, that stage must be postponed to a date which is fixed by the chairman of the House involved rather than by a majority of members.[74]

104

According to Art. 15.1.2.°, 'The Oireachtas shall consist of the President and two Houses . . .'[76] By today, the role of the head of state in law-making is chiefly to give a symbolic blessing to the process, to convert 'the contentious issues of parliamentary strife into binding rules of national authority.'[77] However, (as will be seen) in certain circumstances the President has real powers over a (public or private) bill which he can conveniently exercise as part of the Oireachtas.

As soon as any bill, apart from a bill containing a proposal to amend the Constitution, has been passed, or is deemed to be passed by both Houses, then 'the Taoiseach shall present it to the President for his signature and for promulgation by him as a law . . .'. Then, subject to certain exceptions to be mentioned later, the bill 'shall be signed by the President.'[78] This form of words suggests that, in the unlikely contingency of a private members' bill of which the Government disapproved, the Government could not advise the President to decline to sign. The President signs a bill by affixing his signature to the last page, using the following bilingual formula:

> Ar na shighniú dom do réir an Bhunreachta.
> Signed by me in pursuance of the Constitution.

> Uachtarán na hÉireann.

Dáta:

A bill becomes law on the day on which it is signed. It comes into operation on the same day unless 'the contrary intention appears',[79] as it frequently does where, for example, it is necesary to delay the bill's entry into force until the necessary administrative machinery has been created.

The President is also made responsible for promulgating laws, that is, making them known to the public, which is an essential aspect of the rule of law.[80] He must publish a notice in the *Iris Oifigiúil* (the official gazette) stating that the bill has become law.[81] In addition, the text or texts[82] of the law signed by the President 'shall be enrolled for record in the office of the Registrar of the Supreme Court and the text, or both the texts, so enrolled shall be conclusive evidence of the provisions of such law.'[83] The enrolled text thus constitutes the ultimate authority on the content of the statute. The fact of the signature is recorded in the official Journal of each House of the Oireachtas.

In general, a bill must be signed and promulgated, by the President, 'not earlier than the fifth and not later than the seventh day after the bill shall have been presented to him.'[84] There is, in fact, an exceptional procedure, for bills which the Government wishes to speed into law: 'At the request of the Government, with the prior concurrence of the Seanad Éireann, the

President may sign any Bill the subject of such request on a date which is earlier than the fifth day after [the day the bill is presented to him].'[85] (There is no mention of the Dáil.) Again, naturally, the President must sign an Art. 24 bill on the day the bill is presented to him.[86]

Art. 26 Necessarily, it is after he has received the bill and before he signs it, that the President must consider whether to exercise his discretions under Arts. 26 and 27, since this may require him, at least, to postpone his signature until this procedure has been completed. Art. 27, which provides for the possibility of a referendum on bills passed without the Senate's assent, has already been outlined. Art. 26 is one of the two ways by which the ban on unconstitutional law is implemented (the other method being the invocation of the High Court's power to strike down legislation, in the course of litigation between parties).[87] Under Art. 26, the President, after consultation with the Council of State, may refer any bill to the Supreme Court to consider (in the absence of parties or of a concrete set of facts) whether the bill is unconstitutional. The Court listens to arguments put forward by counsel assigned by the Court to argue against the bill and, on the other side, the Attorney General. The President must make the reference not later than the seventh day after receiving the bill from the Oireachtas, and the Supreme Court (sitting with at least five judges) must pronounce its decision (a single decision with no dissenting or separate judgments)[88] not later than sixty days after the date of the reference.[89] If the Supreme Court's decision is that the bill is unconstitutional, the President must decline to sign it; otherwise he must sign as soon as may be.[90]

Up to early 1984, the Art. 26 procedure had been used on seven occasions. The references have involved: Offences against the State (Amendment) Bill, 1940; Electoral (Amendment) Bill, 1961; Criminal Law (Jurisdiction) Bill, 1975; Emergency Powers Bill, 1976; School Attendance Bill, 1942; Housing (Private Rented Dwellings) Bill, 1981; Electoral (Amendment) Bill, 1983.[91] Of these, only the last three were held to be unconstitutional.[92]

Four of the bills sent to the Supreme Court under the Art. 26 jurisdiction — Offences Against the State (Amendment) Bill; Electoral (Amendment) Bill, 1961; Housing (Private Rented Dwellings) Bill; Electoral (Amendment) Bill, 1983 — were bills which had been passed to replace acts which had been struck down earlier by the High or Supreme Court. In these circumstances, it is often convenient to the Government to have a bill referred to the Supreme Court since this means, at worst, that the bill will be struck down before any reliance has been placed on it. On the other hand, if a bill is pronounced valid on an Art. 26 reference, the Constitution puts it beyond all future challenge before the Courts.[93] If the Government indicates that it wants a bill referred to the Supreme Court, then there is reason to believe that the President is likely to accede to this request. From a more general perspective, there is an obvious advantage in a device which, so to speak, strangles unconstitutional measures before birth.

However, in an outspoken introduction to its decision on the Housing (Private Rented Dwellings) Bill reference, the Supreme Court, speaking through the Chief Justice, pointed out that there are two disadvantages to its Art. 26 jurisdiction. First:

It is to be noted that the Court's function under Art. 26 is to ascertain and declare repugnancy (if such there be) to the Constitution in the referred Bill or in the specified provision or provisions thereof. It is not the function of the Court to impress any part of a referred Bill with a stamp of constitutionality. If the Court finds that *any* provision of the referred Bill or of the referred provisions is repugnant, then the whole Bill fails, for the President is then debarred from signing it, thus preventing it from becoming an Act. There thus may be areas of a referred Bill or of referred provisions of a Bill which may be left untouched by the Court's decision. The authors of the Bill may therefore find the Court's decision less illuminating than they would wish it to be.[94]

Secondly, the Court complained that this jurisdiction obliged it to pass judgment on a law in the abstract, that is, without the advantage of seeing the law in operation in the context of a concrete factual situation. The Chief Justice concluded:

Whether the constitutionality of a legislative measure of that nature which has been passed or is deemed to have been passed by both Houses of the Oireachtas is better determined within a fixed and immutable period of time by means of reference under Art. 26, in which case, if no repugnancy is found, the decision may never be questioned in any court, rather than by means of an action in which specific imputations of unconstitutionality would fall to be determined primarily on proven or admitted facts, is a question on which we refrain from expressing an opinion.[95]

These disadvantages will naturally vary in significance depending on the nature of the case. However, there have been an increased number of constitutional references (five in the last eight years), as the quickening tempo of constitutional review has brought the provisions of the Constitution into sharper focus. It is likely that this increase will continue in the future and possibly that the features of the Art. 26 system to which the Court drew attention will lead to difficulties in particular cases. However, the advantages of the Art. 26 early-warning system have to be weighed against these possible difficulties.

7.8 DELEGATED LEGISLATION

Delegated (or subordinate) legislation is legislation which is made by some body, other than the Oireachtas, to which the Oireachtas has delegated its law-making authority for some strictly limited purpose. In most cases, the purpose of the delegated legislation will be to fill in essential details, and the recipient of the delegation will often be a minister. A typical example of a parent section is the Local Government (Planning and Development) Act, 1963, s.10(1) by which 'The Minister for the Environment may make regulations for prescribing any matter referred to in this Act as prescribed or in relation to any matter referred to in this Act as the subject of regulations.' This section sired the important Local Government (Planning and Development) Regulations[96] which contain detailed procedural rules for planning applications and appeals.

But ministers are certainly not the only ones to whom legislative power has been delegated. One important type of delegated legislation is the Rules of the Superior Court which are made by the Superior Court Rules Committee[97] to regulate the procedure in the High Court and Supreme Court.Again, there are 'bye-laws,' which apply only to a restricted district, premises or undertaking. Typical example of bye-laws are the rules made by local authorities under the power 'to make bye-laws for the good rule and government'[98] of the local authority area.

Constitution, Art. 15.2.1°   Problems of characterisation and classification abound in this area. In the first place, as has been seen,[99] the title 'delegated legislation' may be a misnomer since the existence of delegated legislation can only be reconciled with Art. 15.2.1° on condition that the delegated legislation is 'a mere giving effect to principles and policies which are contained in the statute itself.'[100] The constitutional provision is also relevant in the specialised context of the rarely-used 'Henry VIII clause' which grants an administrative authority the power to amend a statute by way of delegated legislation. An example of such a clause is to be found in the Ministers and Secretaries Act, 1939, s. 6(1) by which the Government is empowered to make 'such adaptation of enactments as shall appear to the Government to be consequential on any thing done under [the delegated legislation powers bestowed by the Act].'[101] It is quite likely that Henry VIII clauses violate Art. 15.2.1° of the Constitution: 'no . . . authority [other than the Oireachtas] has power to make laws for the State'). There is also a common law presumption against Henry VIII clauses.[102]

Statutory Instruments Act, 1947   The need for classification arises, secondly, in connection with the Statutory Instruments Act, 1947,[103] the statute which is designed to provide certain and clear publicity for delegated legislation. The Act commences by defining a 'statutory instrument' widely, as 'an order, regulation, rule, scheme or bye-law made in exercise of a power conferred by statute.' It goes on to distinguish those 'statutory instruments to which the Act primarily applies' from other statutory instruments.[104] To fall within the first category, a statutory instrument must comply with four conditions of which the first is that the statutory instrument must be either 'required by statute to be laid before both or either of the House of the Oireachtas' or (and these two alternatives will frequently overlap) be of 'such a character as affects the public generally or any particular class or classes of the public.' This second alternative is clearly designed to distinguish legislative from administrative instruments.[105] It is worth drawing particular attention to this distinction because it emphasises the very wide range of items encompassed in the term 'statutory instrument', as defined in the 1947 Act. As mentioned, the definition is: '. . . an order, regulation, rule, scheme or bye-law . . .' An order is (or should be)[106] confined to a single exercise of a power in relation to a particular person or situation, e.g. a compulsory purchase order; or an order appointing a person to the board of a State-sponsored body. Plainly an order is administrative, whilst regulations and rules are both legislative, the latter being confined to procedural provisions for courts or tribunals. Bye-laws, which have already been explained, are also legislative. However, bye-laws are excluded from the category of 'statutory instruments to which the Act primarily applies' by the second requirement which refers to the authority which made the instrument. The instrument must have been made by: the President; the Government or any member thereof; any minister of state; any authority having power to make rules of court; or any person or body 'exercising throughout the State any function of government or discharging throughout the State any public duties in relation to public administration.' Thirdly, to fall within this category, the instrument must have been made on or after 1 January 1948. Finally, it must *not* be a statutory instrument which is required by statute to be published in the *Iris Oifigiúil*,[107] presumably because in this case the procedure required in the 1947 Act would be superfluous. The Attorney General's written certificate as to whether a statutory instrument process possesses certain of these characteristics is made conclusive. In addition, the Attorney General is granted the power to exempt statutory instruments from the category of 'statutory instruments to which this Act primarily applies' by reason of their 'merely local or personal application or their temporary operation or their limited application or for any other reason.'[108]

The significance of the category 'statutory instrument to which this Act primarily applies' is that it is only to instruments of this type that the rules regarding publicity, laid down in the 1947 Act, are applied. In the first place, a copy of such an instrument must be sent to ten specified libraries (including the National Library and the Southern Law Association's library, but not the Oireachtas library) within seven days of the making of the instrument. Secondly, each instrument must be printed, as soon as possible after it has been made and notice given, in *Iris Oifigiuil*, of its making and of where copies may be obtained. The statute does not deal with the consequences of failure to publish, save in the case of prosecution for an offence of contravening a statutory instrument. In this case the charge must be dismissed if the prosecutor fails to prove either that notice had been published in *Iris Oifigiúil* or, alternatively, that reasonable steps had been taken to bring the purport of the instrument to the notice of the public.[109]

Parliamentary control The pros and cons of delegated legislation are similar in every country which is both a constitutional democracy and a welfare state.[110] In contrast with the cumbersome process by which bills are

109

transformed into acts, the procedure for making delegated legislation is quick and flexible. Moreover, its subject-matter is often of a technical nature and thus inappropriate for discussion by a chamber largely composed of lay-people. The disadvantage is the lack of adequate opportunity for control or (to be more realistic about the parliamentary process) scrutiny, by the Oireachtas, over the several hundred statutory instruments made each year. Writing in 1930, Donal O'Sullivan[111] painted as alarming a picture of the proliferation of delegated legislation without parliamentary supervision as did his contemporary, Lord Hewart, in Britain. The remedy adopted is to associate the Oireachtas with the making of the delegated legislation. The most common way in which this is done is for the parent statute to provide, typically, that:

Every regulation made under this Act shall be laid before each House of the Oireachtas as soon as may be after it is made and, if a resolution annulling the regulation is passed by either such House within the next twenty one days on which that House has sat after the regulation is laid before it, the regulation shall be annulled accordingly but without prejudice to the validity of anything previously done thereunder.[112]

Very rarely, the technique may be to require a confirmatory act of the Oireachtas to be passed within a certain period of the statutory instrument coming into force (for example Imposition of Duties Act, 1957).[113] Alternatively, and again in rare cases, the parent section may provide that an instrument must be laid, in draft, before each House and may not be made until after a resolution approving of the draft has been passed by each House (e.g. Electoral Act, 1963, s.6(3) and Health Act, 1970, s.4(5)). Parliamentary time is invariably made available to discuss a motion of annulment within the statutory period.[114] However, the Attorney General has opined that failure to observe an obligation to lay does not render a statutory instrument invalid.[115]

Where a statutory instrument 'must be laid before each House . . .', this requirement is fulfilled by copies of the instrument being placed in the library at Leinster House. For the formal controls to have any practical value, there must be some machinery to alert members of the Oireachtas if some statutory instrument is suspect. A watchdog was provided by the creation, in 1948, of the Senate Select Committee on Satutory Rules, Order and Regulations (known from 1951 forward as the Select Committee on Statutory Instruments) which was re-constituted in each subsequent Senate.[116] It issued its last report, covering the period 1978-81, on 8 April 1981. It was never re-constituted but, in 1983, its functions were taken over by the newly formed Joint Committee on Legislation,[117] which, unlike its predecessor, has members from both Dáil and Senate.

Judicial controls   In addition to the restrictions created by the 1947 Act and Art. 15.2.1° of the Constitution, the courts also apply to delegated legislation the same legal controls which cover administrative action generally and which are described below.[118] To anticipate: these controls arise from the

application of the *ultra vires* doctrine to the parent statute so as set some limit
— albeit rather a generous limit — to the wide discretionary power granted
by the statute. *Cassidy v. Min. for Industry*[119] affords a straightforward
example of the *ultra vires* doctrine in operation in regard to a piece of delegated
legislation. Under the Prices Act Acts, 1958-72, the Minister was empowered to
make statutory instruments fixing the maximum prices for, among other things,
intoxicating liquor. He used this power to fix identical prices for lounge and
public bars. The critical fact in the case — of which the court seems to have
taken judicial notice — is that lounge bars offer higher standards of amenity
and service than public bars. In consequence the fixing of the same maxima
for both amounted to an exercise of the Minister's power in an arbitrary, unfair,
and, hence, *ultra vires* way. *Cassidy* is also of note in that it confirmed that
the rules of constitutional justice do not apply to the making of delegated
legislation.

The precise operation of the *ultra vires* rule, in regard to delegated legislation
or any other type of administration action, depends of course on many variables,
including the wording and subject-matter of the parent statute. Thus, for
instance, the terms of the parent statute provide that before any municipal
bye-laws come into force, a copy of them must be affixed to the front door
of the town-hall for forty days. During this period, the Minister for the
Environment is empowered to disallow the bye-laws.[120]

8

Finance

Because of the disparate nature of the material to be covered, it may be helpful to give a preliminary summary of the course of this Chapter. Financial measures are usually cast in the form of bills. However, money bills necessitate modifications of the usual procedure for bills. Section 1 accordingly focuses on the contrasts between Dáil procedure for financial and non-financial legislation, whilst Section 2 provides an account of the major events, relating to finance, in the Dáil year. There has been much criticism of the Dáil's arrangements for scrutinising financial measures, and this criticism has taken on greater significance in view of the substantive economic crisis. The present (1984) Government's commitment to parliamentary reform extends to the financial field, and its proposals are summarised in Section 3. The diminished standing of the Senate in regard to 'money bills' is explained in Section 4. It is paradoxical that, in the area of finance, as elsewhere, the executive has so much more influence than the legislature, yet the published rules as to how this influence should be exercised are very scanty. Section 5 deals with the Department of Finance's powers of control, first, at the pre-parliamentary stage of drawing up estimates and, then, at the subsequent stage of sanctioning expenditure. Section 6 describes briefly the operation of the Central Fund. The final feature of the cycle is the *ex post facto* audit by the Public Accounts Committee of the Dáil, assisted by the Comptroller and Auditor General; this is explained in Section 7.

8.1 PECULIARITIES OF FINANCIAL LEGISLATION IN THE DÁIL

Features which distinguish measures dealing with finance from other types of legislation are as follows:

1. For the purposes of the control of central government expenditure out of the Central Fund, a distinction is drawn between voted and non-voted expenditure. Voted expenditure is the expenditure which is authorised every year, by way of the Appropriation Act, as part of a complicated process which is detailed in Section 2 of this Chapter. The money — 'supply' — is spent on the ordinary services of Government departments which are known as the Supply Services, and the Dáil is thus afforded an annual opportunity to discuss the general work of each department. Where the draftsman wishes to indicate that an item of expenditure is to be paid for out of supply, then the phrase,

'. . . shall be paid out of moneys provided by the Oireachtas' is employed.

By contrast, non-voted expenditure is money which a specified Act has authorised to be paid from the Central Fund (or Exchequer), indefinitely, so that this expenditure does not have to come under the annual review of the Dáil. A statute may authorise a head of expenditure and then go on to provide that it 'shall be charged on the Central Fund,' as is the case with, for example, the salaries of the judges of the Supreme Court, High Court and Circuit Court, and of district justices[1] and the Comptroller and Auditor General.[2] Alternatively, a statute may provide that the money for some specified item 'may be advanced' from the Central Fund, for example, any payments necessitated by the obligations of EEC membership,[3] the payment of development capital to State-sponsored bodies[4] or (by way of the Local Loan Fund) to local authorities.[5] Payments of the first type are in the nature of a first charge on the state; whilst items in the second category are left to the responsible minister's discretion. There is a second type of distinction, between cases where the amount is fixed in the statute (for example, the superior judiciary, etc.) or, at least, the maximum is fixed in the statute (for example, payments to State-sponsored bodies or local authorities) and, on the other hand, where no amount is specified (for example, the national debt).

There are various reasons why expenditure may be made non-voted: first, in the case of the superior judiciary etc., it is regarded as desirable that these matters should not be the subject of annual, political debate. Secondly, in the case of development capital for State-sponsored bodies or local authorities, there is a convention that the statutory maxima are carefully determined to ensure that the amount of capital fixed in the statute is exhausted within three or four years. The result is that, on the one hand, the Oireachtas has a chance to debate the expenditure of a large sum of public money, whilst, on the other hand, the State-sponsored body or local authority has a reasonably long period during which it knows what level of assistance it can rely on from the Central Fund (or Exchequer). Far and away the largest item charged on the Central Fund is the national debt, which is defined, widely, as the principal and interest on any securities issued by the Minister for Finance 'for the purpose of raising money for the Exchequer.'[6] These moneys are charged on the Fund so that lenders (many of whom are foreigners) will have the maximum possible degree of security, since the obligation to repay cannot be interfered with by the executive, but only by an amending act. Furthermore, no limits are fixed to the issue of certificates under this provision. While this carries very obvious dangers, it does improve the security of the loan since there is no danger of an obligation being invalid because some maximum is exceeded (perhaps because of a fluctuation in exchange rates or because of another loan which had been overlooked).

At this point, it may be useful to give a very approximate indication of some of the figures involved. In 1983, voted and non-voted expenditure came to £5.6bn and £2.9bn, respectively. Economists naturally distinguish between current and capital expenditure. Each of the two constitutional categories of expenditure — voted and non-voted — contains elements of both. The current budget is made up of £5bn from the supply services and £1.6bn (of which the interest on the national debt came to £1.5bn) from the Central Fund Services. As regards the Public Capital Programme, that is moneys spend on asset-creating items, £0.3bn came from the supply services (for example, the new home owner grant came out of one of the Department of the Environment Votes) whilst the remaining £1.3bn came partly from the non-voted Central Fund moneys and partly from non-Exchequer funds, namely, moneys generated, sometimes out of revenue or loans, by local authorities or State-sponsored bodies. There is, finally, the Public Sector Borrowing Requirement (£2.3bn in 1983), a measurement used by economists rather than constitutional lawyers. This comprises not only the current budget deficit and capital borrowing by the Exchequer, but also direct borrowing by State-sponsored bodies, which is not financed by way of Exchequer funds, but which is guaranteed by the State so that the State is finally liable for it. (As regards local authority borrowing, all of it, apart from short-term bank overdrafts, comes from the Local Loans Fund and it has thus already been counted as non-voted Exchequer capital funds.) As can be seen, it is the Public Sector Borrowing Requirement, rather than the Public Capital Programme, which encompasses all the money on which the State is finally liable.

2. The committee stage of a bill which imposes 'a charge upon the people' — broadly speaking a taxation measure — cannot be taken until a motion approving the charge has been passed by the Dáil.[7] The motion is a financial resolution, though those introduced immediately after the Budget speech are popularly known as 'Budget resolutions.' The expenditure of 'money proposed for the public service' (that is, voted money) must also be authorised by a motion, in the form of Estimates,[8] the debate on which can range very far. As a result of two changes introduced in 1974, a motion is no longer necessary in the case of non-voted moneys. The former practice, by which financial resolutions or Estimates had to be introduced and debated, not in the Dáil, but in a Committee of the whole House (the 'Committee on Finance'), has also been terminated.[9]

3. A financial resolution or Estimate may only be proposed or initiated by a member of the Government.[10] A bill imposing taxation or appropriating money to the public services must be introduced by the Minister for Finance or another member of the Government acting on his behalf.[11]

4. Where 'the appropriation of revenue or other public money' (that is, expenditure out of the Exchequer, whether voted or non-voted) is involved, any resolution, or the committee stage of any bill, may only be taken after the purpose of the appropriation has been recommended to the Dáil, by a message from the Government, signed by the Taoiseach and printed on the Order Paper.[12] The reason for the restrictions, mentioned in this and the

114

previous paragraph, is the executive's special knowledge and resonsibility as regards the overall balancing of the State's income and expenditure. So far as appropriation measures are concerned, there is also the danger that a private member might be tempted to suggest expenditure which would benefit his own constituency or some other sectional interest.

8.2 FINANCIAL PROCEDURE IN THE DÁIL

Publications[13] and timetable[14] Each year — in preparation for the annual Budget, the Government publishes a number of documents giving information on public expenditure and revenue. The Government discharges its constitutional obligation[15] to lay before the Dáil estimated figures for expenditure and revenue by the publication of the White Paper on Receipts and Expenditure. This shows: the out-turn for the previous year and, in relation to the new year, estimates for the receipts from taxation and other sources (at pre-budget rates — a drawback); Government expenditure (voted and non-voted); and the Exchequer borrowing requirement. This white paper is traditionally published on the week-end before the Budget, in late January — early February. In addition, various other figures — for example, tables showing expenditure over a five-year period classified according to principal services such as Health, Education and Agriculture — (again at pre-budget levels) known as 'Pre-Budget Tables' are circulated on Budget Day, before the Minister's speech. Also published at this time is the Economic Background to the Budget and the Public Capital Programme which lists the Government's proposals for investment in the current year, from whatever source the funds are to come. The most detailed information on expenditure is to be found in the Book of Estimates for the supply services which must be presented to the Dáil and circulated to deputies before 30 January and not less than seven days before the Budget.[16] However, hitherto, the debate on the Estimates has not begun until March or April[17] because, during the intervening period, the Dáil's time is taken up with the Budget and consequential business. The Dáil is usually in recess from July until mid-October. In consequence, even with the latitude conferred by the Central Fund (Permanent Provisions) Act, 1965 (described later in this Section) all the Estimates must be passed by July. This time-pressure means that many of the Estimates have to be passed by agreement and without debate. Usually where this occurs, an undertaking is given that if the Opposition wishes to discuss a particular Estimate, a token supplementary Estimate will be proposed after the summer recess so as to provide an occasion for debating the Estimate. In spite of this relief, much of the House's time before the recess is spent debating the Estimates (about one-sixth of its time over the whole year) and, even then, several Estimates are never debated.

The present Government has announced, in the white paper, *A Better Way to Plan the Nation's Finances*,[18] that it intends to change the Dáil financial timetable so that the Dáil is no longer in the position of debating the

115

expenditure of money *after* the money has been spent. As one of its reforms — for the other reforms, see Section 3 of this Chapter — it intends that Estimates should be published and debated — and the appropriation bill passed — during October-December of the year preceding the year to which they relate. The other publications listed above would also be published towards the end of the preceding year.

Budget-Financial resolutions — Finance Act — Provisional Collection of Taxes Act, 1927 — Imposition of Duties Act 1957 The budget[19] statement includes, first, a general review of the economy, including such topics as unemployment and the balance of payments. Then the Minister for Finance reviews the financial results — both revenue and expenditure — for the previous year. Finally, he discusses the prospects for the current year and the impact of the changes which he proposes to make. After a brief comment from a spokesman for each of the Opposition parties, the Minister introduces the financial resolutions. One of the resolutions is deliberately drafted in the widest possible terms[20-21] so as to afford scope for discussion ranging over the entire area covered by the Minister. It is voted upon after a debate which continues for several days. But each of the remaining resolutions proposes either new taxes or variations in existing taxes. These resolutions are voted upon at the end of the sitting in which the budget speech has been delivered and invariably end with the clause, 'It is hereby declared that it is expedient in the public interest that this Resolution shall have statutory effect under the provisions of the Provisional Collection of Taxes Act, 1927.' The magic of this formula is that if a resolution containing it resolves that a tax be imposed or altered or that a temporary tax in force at the end of the previous financial year (such as income tax) be renewed, then the resolution has statutory effect immediately it is passed.[22] However, the resolution ceases to have effect if any of the following conditions is met: if a finance bill containing provisions to the same effect is not read a second time by the Dáil within the next thirty days after it has been passed; if the provisions to the same effect in the finance bill are rejected by the Dáil; or, in any case, four months after the date when the resolution came into force.[23] (Art. 15.2.1° of the Constitution, which provides that legislation must be by way of act of the Oireachtas,[24] holds good for financial legislation too. However, while there is no authority on the point, it seems probable that the grant of statutory force to the resolutions would be upheld, because the resolutions are passed by the Dáil and because they are in force for such a short time.) Permanent legal force is given to the terms of the financial resolutions by the Finance Act which contains other miscellaneous financial provisions and which usually becomes law in April or May.

At this point, it is convenient to break off to mention the Government's power by order, to impose, vary or terminate any excise duty, customs duty or stamp duty. The power was created (in its present form) by the Imposition of Duties (Confirmation of Orders) Act, 1957,[25] in order to control imports,

116

at a time when the economic policy of the state was protectionist. Unless the order is confirmed by an act of the Oireachtas passed within the period specified in the 1957 Act, the order ceases to have effect at the end of that period.[26] However, the period is rather long: it extends to the end of the year *following* the year in which the order was made. Since the power may be exercised merely by Government order and since orders made under the 1957 Act might easily involve 'more than a mere giving effect to principles and policies which are contained in the [1957] Act itself,'[27] it is likely that such orders break the constitutional rule (mentioned in the last paragraph) that law must be made by Act of the Oireachtas. In addition, running through the Constitution[28] (though nowhere stated explicitly) is the clear assumption that taxation may only be raised with the Dáil's consent.[29]

Central Fund (Permanent Provisions) Act, 1965 The lengthy procedure involved in passing the Estimates (to be described in the next Section) creates a difficulty similar to that already noted in the case of taxation, namely, that at present (the proposed reforms have already been mentioned) it is not until well into the financial year that the Appropriation Act becomes law, yet authorisation for Government expenditure is required from the start of the year. By the Central Fund (Permanent Provisions) Act, 1965, right from the start of the year the Minister for Finance is authorised to issue moneys from the Central Fund and apply them towards making good the supply for a particular service. This authority is subject to three conditions: (i) that the Minister for Finance considers the service necessary; (ii) that he intends to ask the Dáil, during the financial year, to grant supply for the service in question for that year; and (iii) that it is a service for which a sum was appropriated in the previous year's Appropriation Act.[30] It should be noted that under this provision, the maximum amount which may be issued is four fifths of the amount appropriated in the previous year's Appropriation Act. However, *after* the supply for a particular service has been granted and assuming (as is likely these days) that it exceeds four fifths of the sum appropriated for that service in the previous year, then the amount which the Minister is authorised to issue becomes the amount of supply granted by the passing of the relevant vote.[31] Each December, the Minister for Finance must lay before the Dáil a statement of the amount which, as from the start of the next financial year, he will be authorised to issue under the 1965 Act.[32]

Estimates As indicated earlier, the Dáil debates the Estimates over a period of several months, commencing, at present, in March. A separate resolution for supply is moved for each of the fifty or so Estimates. When passed, an Estimate becomes a Vote. As can be seen from the example on the next pages, every Estimate is made up of three Parts. Part I (the ambit) states the service which is covered; the exact amount of money to be voted by the Dáil; and, sometimes, the statutory authority for the establishment of the service. Part II sets out the 'Subheads under which the vote will be accounted for' by the

117

OFFICE OF THE ATTORNEY GENERAL

I. Estimate of the amount required in the year ending 31 December 1983 for the salaries and expenses of the Office of the Attorney General.

Three million one hundred and seventy-eight thousand pounds (£3,178,000)

II. Subheads under which this Vote will be accounted for by the Office of the Attorney General.

	1983 Estimate	1982 Provisional Outturn	Change 1983 over 1982
	£	£	%
A.—SALARIES, WAGES AND ALLOWANCES (a) ...	2,189,000	2,039,000	+7%
B.—TRAVELLING AND INCIDENTAL EXPENSES	100,000	77,000	+30%
C.—POST OFFICE SERVICES	52,000	66,000	−21%
D.—FEES TO COUNSEL	315,000	403,000	−22%
E.—GENERAL LAW EXPENSES	345,000	397,000	−13%
F.—DEFENCE OF PUBLIC SERVANTS ...	7,000	400	—
G.—LAW REFORM COMMISSION (a)	215,000	187,000	+15%
GROSS TOTAL ...£	3,223,000	3,169,400	+2%
Deduct:—			
H.—APPROPRIATIONS IN AID	45,000	56,000	−20%
NET TOTAL ...£	3,178,000	3,113,400	+2%

NET INCREASE £64,600

	1983 Estimate
	£
The total expenditure in connection with this Service is estimated as follows:—	
Gross estimate above	3,223,000
Estimated amounts included in other estimates in connection with this Service:—	
Vote	
9 Public Works and Buildings	161,000
15 Stationery Office	34,400
17 Rates on Government Property	10,400
20 Superannuation and Retired Allowances	135,013
Central Fund—Pensions in respect of former Attorney General and widow of former Attorney General (No. 38 of 1938, etc.)	12,647
TOTAL EXPENDITURE ...£	3,576,460
The receipts in connection with this Service are estimated as follows:—	
Appropriations in aid above ... ... £	45,000

(a) The 1982 column includes a transfer from Vote 51 — Increases in Remuneration and Pensions — see appendix to volume for details.

Extract from *Revised Estimates for Public Services for the year ending 31 December 1983* (Pl. 1407)

III. DETAILS of the foregoing

A.—SALARIES, WAGES AND ALLOWANCES:

Numbers 1982	Numbers 1983		1983 Estimate £	1982 Provisional Outturn £
26	26	Attorney General and staff	395,000	385,000
93	93	Chief State Solicitor and staff	1,017,000	926,500
—	—	32 State Solicitors (Provincial areas) (Part-time)	660,000	654,000
—	—	Proportion of cost of messenger and cleaning services (Attorney General's Office)	62,000	35,000
—	—	Overtime	25,000	16,500
—	—	Social Welfare—Employer's contributions ...	30,000	22,000
119	119	TOTAL ...£	2,189,000	2,039,000

B.—TRAVELLING AND INCIDENTAL EXPENSES:

Travelling and incidental expenses of:—

	1983 Estimate	1982 Provisional Outturn
Attorney General and staff	90,000	67,000
Chief State Solicitor's Office	10,000	10,000
TOTAL ...£	100,000	77,000

C.—POST OFFICE SERVICES:

Postal services, telegrams, telephones and miscellaneous for:—

	1983 Estimate	1982 Provisional Outturn
Attorney General and staff	20,000	24,000
Chief State Solicitor's Office	32,000	42,000
TOTAL ...£	52,000	66,000

D.—FEES TO COUNSEL:

	1983 Estimate	1982 Provisional Outturn
Fees to Counsel engaged on behalf of the Attorney General ... ... £	315,000	403,000

E.—GENERAL LAW EXPENSES:

	1983 Estimate	1982 Provisional Outturn
For various expenses including expenses of juries, payments to witnesses in civil actions, and miscellaneous expenses of State Solicitors, etc. ... ... £	345,000	397,000

F.—DEFENCE OF PUBLIC SERVANTS:

	1983 Estimate	1982 Provisional Outturn
Expenses in actions taken against public servants, including members of the Garda Síochána, in respect of acts done by them in the execution of their duty ... £	7,000	400

G.—LAW REFORM COMMISSION:

Grant under Section 8 of the Law Reform Commission Act, 1975 (No. 3 of 1975) to enable the Commission to perform its functions:

	1983 Estimate	1982 Provisional Outturn
Remuneration of members of the Commission, other than a Commissioner who holds judicial office (Section 3 (11) of No. 3 of 1975)	40,000	40,000
Other remuneration, including salaries of staff of Commission	109,000	113,400
Other expenses	66,000	33,600
TOTAL ...£	215,000	187,000

H.—APPROPRIATIONS IN AID:

	1983 Estimate	1982 Provisional Outturn
1. Costs and fees recovered by the Chief State Solicitor, etc.	43,000	54,000
2. Receipts from the Department of Posts and Telegraphs.	2,000	2,000
TOTAL ...£	45,000	56,000

Extract from *Revised Estimates for Public Services for the year ending 31 December 1983* (Pl. 1407) department administering it. The sub-heads form the basis both of the Appropriation Accounts, which are used to account to the Dáil for moneys spent and, also, of the controls exercised by the Department of Finance and Comptroller and Auditor General.[33] It is notable, however, that it is only Part I which is given statutory effect, by inclusion in the Schedule to the Appropriation Act. This is significant because it leaves the Department of Finance with the discretion to permit *virement* (from the French nautical term, *virer* = to tack, change course or transfer), that is, the transfer of money between sub-heads, though not between Votes.

Finally, Part III goes into further detail about the sub-heads listed in Part II. Its value is partly explanatory and partly as the framework for departmental internal accounting. So far as Dáil debate is concerned, an Estimate is taken to afford an opportunity for a prolonged discussion over a department's entire range of activities, since almost all of these entail expenditure.

Under the present timetable, the Appropriation Bill is introduced and passed in December, right at the end of the year to which it relates. It is a short bill with a lengthy schedule in which are listed the particular services for which the amounts specified have been granted.

Grants-in-aid, bulk grants and appropriation-in-aid As well as providing funds for the ordinary services administered by a department itself, a Vote may make provisions to enable the department to make a grant to an outside body. These grants may be presented as either a bulk grant (for example, to a local authority or health board) or, alternatively, a grant-in-aid — which was devised originally to make a contribution to a charity and is now also used to finance non-commercial State-sponsored bodies. The distinctive feature of a grant-in-aid is that it is exempt from the normal rule that any monies issued from the Exchequer must either be spent within the financial year or returned to the Exchequer. What is more significant, considering the amounts involved, is that, in the case of grants-in-aid and most bulk grants, no extra detail is supplied in Part III of the Estimate so that adequate information is not available when the Estimates are being debated.[34] However, there is an *ex post facto* check in that all bulk grants have to be accounted for to the Comptroller and Auditor General and the appropriate Estimate now[35] always indicates that the CAG must audit any grant-in-aid or, at least, inspect the books and accounts of the grantees.

Another item which occasionally features in the Estimate and Appropriation Account is an appropriation-in-aid. This is an incidental item of revenue, which has been generated by the activities associated with the Vote. It is, therefore, not paid into the Exchequer[36] but included in the Vote and is set off against the items of expenditure so that the final total amount is a net figure.

Supplementary Estimate, Excess Vote A Supplementary Estimate is an estimate modifying the original Estimates which is presented to the Dáil during the currency of a financial year. It may be necessary, for instance, because expenditure is greater than anticipated or because of the creation of a new service. A Supplementary Estimate is introduced and adopted in substantially the same way as the original Estimates, and it becomes law either by inclusion in the Appropriation Act for the current year (which is not enacted until December) or the Appropriation Act for the following year. Supplementary Estimates are unwelcome because they throw out the balance between expenditure and revenue which has been struck in the Budget. Nevertheless, in recent years, sizeable numbers have been necessary, for instance in 1981 their aggregate amount was £600 million, the equivalent of a seventh of the amount voted in the Estimates.

Whereas a Supplementary Estimate is undesirable, an 'Excess Vote' is lamentable, for it is the outcome of a situation which it is the whole purpose of the Dáil's control of expenditure to prevent. An Excess Vote is necessary where the shortfall between expenditure and the amount allocated in the Estimate is not discovered *until a later financial year*. In that event, the Public Accounts Committee examines the matter as its first business and then issues an interim report stating (if this be the case) that it has no objection to an Excess Vote. The Minister for Finance then decides whether an Excess Vote (which follows the same procedure as a Supplementary Estimate) should be put to the Dáil. If there were no Excess Vote, then the accounting officer responsible would be personally liable for the expenditure.

8.3 REFORMS IN THE DÁIL

In addition to the changes in the timetable already noted in Section 2, the present (1984) Government has mooted the following reforms[37] which have reached varying stages of completion.

1. Comprehensive Public Expenditure Programmes In the design created for their original purpose, as the basis for appropriation accounts, the Estimates volumes do not fulfil the distinct task of supplying, in a comprehensive form, information suitable for policy discussion. In addition, the Estimates exclude non-voted expenditure and, even in regard to voted expenditure, there is little information about the way in which the grants made to the major agencies are used. To meet these difficulties, a new method of presentation is to be adopted, the Comprehensive Public Expenditure Programmes, of which a pilot version has recently been published.[38] In these Programmes expenditure is categorised according to the programme on which it is spent, rather than by department, and there is a multi-annual focus compared with the exclusive concentration on the current year, in the Estimates. Finally, whilst the Estimates consist of a list of the bare components of expenditure (for example, Salaries, Wages and Allowances), by contrast in the Programmes there is, for each area, a policy statement and a summary of the total costs. Ultimately, there will also be appropriate yard-sticks to enable the effectiveness of a programme to be assessed. (It is undecided as yet whether the Programmes and the Estimates volumes will continue an independent existence or whether they will be integrated.)

2. Estimates debate At present, the minister responsible for the department whose vote is under examination speaks only twice:[39] once at the start of the debate to propose the motion and again — it may be weeks later — to close the debate. Other members may only speak once, for up to one hour.[40] The result is a series of long, general speeches with no possibility of dialogue between a deputy and the minister on particular items in the Estimate. Under the new regime, a new commttee-style format is envisaged to as to allow a more effective scrutiny of individual items within an Estimate, in place of the present general debates. Special rules of debate will allow multiple (possibly up to fifteen per deputy) brief interventions, with no limit on the number of times the minister may speak.

3. Balancing the books At the same time as the Dáil is debating the Estimates, it will be given some indication of the taxation and borrowing needed to finance that expenditure. This would necessarily have to be in broad outline so as not to confine the Government's decision to introduce revenue measures in the Budget. Such development would also have the effect of tending to reduce the rather unhelpful mystique which presently attends the budget statement.[41]

4. Public Capital Programme debate The Public Capital Programme will be modified so as to indicate whether each capital subject will yield a direct financial return. Coupled with this there will be a debate on the Programme and on the Government's overall borrowing, giving deputies an opportunity to discuss the priority of capital projects. Hitherto there has been no debate on the entire Programme, though it sometimes happens that isolated elements from it have come before the House as 'Voted Capital Services.'

5. Public Expenditure Committee Whereas the Public Accounts Committee (which is described in Section 4 of this Chapter) is austerely confined to such questions as whether expenditure has been properly authorised or is indisputably wasteful, the newly-constituted Public Expenditure Committee will address the broader question of whether expenditure is effective in the light of the purposes for which it was authorised. It may go as far in the direction of policy-review as is necessary in order

to review the justification for and effectiveness of on-going expenditure of Government Departments and Offices and of [non-commercial] State-sponsored Bodies . . . in such areas as it may select and to report thereon to the House recommending cost effective alternatives and/or the elimination of wasteful or obsolete programmes, where desirable.[42]

Its object of interest is the expenditure in a particular field, for example, health services, over a number of years, rather than concentration on a single year, as is the case with the Public Accounts Committee. The new Committee's importance is emphasised by an order that each of its reports must be debated (for three hours) within twelve sitting days after it has been laid before the Dáil.

8.4 THE SENATE'S INFERIOR STATUS: THE IMPORTANCE OF BEING A 'MONEY BILL'

Roughly speaking, a 'money bill' is a bill imposing a charge upon public funds or a tax. The category of money bills is of importance at three points in the Constitution. Such bills are excluded from the scope of both Art. 26 (reference of bills to the Supreme Court to test their constitutionality)[43] and Art. 27 (references to the People of bills with which the Senate has not agreed).[44] The reason presumably is the need to avoid delaying money bills. Thirdly, flowing from the history of the development of the House of Commons in the thirteenth and fourteenth centuries, as the representatives of the classes with ready money, and due to the central part played by finance in the functioning of the Government, the ascendancy of the lower House *vis-à-vis* the upper House is especially marked in the field of finance.[45] Thus, in Ireland, money bills must be initiated in the Dáil. More important, the Senate may only make recommendations and has only twenty-one days in which to do so. (Each day, whether sitting or not, counts for this period and there are no *dies non*. Even if the Senate fails to consider the bill within the time limit or if it makes recommendations which the Dáil chooses not to accept, then the bill is anyway deemed to have been passed by both Houses at the expiry of the twenty-one-day period.[46] During the period 1938-82 the Senate accepted about four hundred bills without recommending any amendments; recommendations were made in respect of seven bills and, in consequence, six of the bills were amended by the Dáil.[47]

There are no Estimates or financial resolutions in the Senate. There are only two major financial debates: in or about May, on the Finance Bill, and in December, on the Appropriation Bill. In each case, the debate is formally divided into stages, in the usual way.

Definition The Constitution provides both a definition of a money bill and machinery for applying the definition, contained in Art. 22.1, which reads as follows:

A Money Bill means a Bill which contains only provisions dealing with all or any of the following matters, namely, the imposition, repeal, remission, alteration or regulation of taxation; the imposition for the payment of debt or other financial purposes of charges on public moneys or the variation repeal of any such charges; supply; the appropriation, receipt, custody, issue or audit of accounts of public money; the raising or guarantee

123

of any loan or the repayment thereof; matters subordinate and incidental to these matters or any of them.

In this definition the expressions 'taxation,' 'public money' and 'loan' respectively do not include any taxation, money or loan raised by local authorities or bodies for local purposes.

The definition uses the word 'only' thereby excluding the device of 'tacking' on to a money bill provisions dealing with 'non-money' matters, a device used at various times in British constitutional history. This means that laws and institutions which do not fall exactly within the definition are excluded. Thus a clause had to be excised from the Finance Bill, 1976 because it dealt with the recording, by order of the Revenue Commissioners, of exports leaving the country and such recording has other uses apart from those related to taxation.[48] Again, Social Welfare bills are usually excluded from the category of 'money bill' because they contain provisions regarding employers' and employees' contributions.

In 1935, a Committee of Privileges (on which see next Section) was constituted to consider whether the Land Purchase (Guarantee Fund) Bill was a money bill.[49] The bill's essential objective was to provide that where there had been a default in the payment of land annuities, the deficit was to be charged on the Guarantee Fund. Indisputably, if the bill fell within the definition at all, it must have come within the head, 'the imposition . . . of charges on public moneys or the variation or repeal of any such charges.' Now the principal elements of the Guarantee Fund were the Estate Duty Grant and the Agricultural Grant, which were moneys made available by specific acts or appropriation acts for distribution among local authorities. Plainly, the exemption contained in the equivalent of Art. 22.1.2° was not relevant since the money had not been 'raised by local authorities or bodies for local purposes.' Rather, the principal argument against the bill being a money bill was that money contained in either Grant ceased to be 'public moneys' and became the property of the local authority, once it was voted to the authority.[50] The other side of the argument (put by the Government supporters on the Committee) took a wider view of the phrase 'public money', holding that the term caught any funds 'in the nature of public funds [that is, local authority moneys] under the control of Parliament.'[51] Alternatively, Government supporters asserted, the underlying objective of the bill (to protect the Exchequer in the case of default in the payment of land annuities) was analogous to the matters contained in the definition of a money bill. Although the chairman (the Chief Justice) confessed that he was 'a good deal shaken' by the arguments to the contrary, he exercised his casting vote to decide that the bill was a money bill, holding also that he was not required to give his reasons for the decision.

Procedure The Constitution[52] lays it down that the question of whether the bill is a money bill must be determined, in the first instances, by the certificate of the Ceann Comhairle. However, unlike the certificate of the Speaker at Westminister in similar circumstances,[53] this certificate is not conclusive. The Ceann Comhairle's certificate may be challenged if the Senate, at a sitting attended by at least thirty members, requests the President to refer the question of whether a bill is a money bill to a 'Committee of Privileges.' Next, the President, after consultation with the Council of State, decides whether to accede to this request. If he does so, he appoints (again after consulting his Council of State) an equal number of deputies and of senators, under the chairmanship of a High Court or Supreme Court judge, who, however, has only a casting vote. The Committee's decision shall be 'final and conclusive.' Alternatively, if there is no Senate resolution or if the President decides not to set up a Committee or if the Committee fails to report within the specified time, then the Ceann Comhairle's original decision remains 'final and conclusive.' In any event, no court of law can be asked to review the question. As a matter of history, the only occasion when the Committee of Privileges has had to be constituted arose from the Land Purchase (Guarantee Fund) Bill, mentioned in the previous Section, when the similar, though not identical, machinery created by the 1922 Constitution (Art. 35) was invoked.

8.5   CONTROL BY THE MINISTER FOR FINANCE

Before focussing on the Department of Finance's control of expenditure, it may be worth giving a summary of the full range of the work done in what is, leaving aside the Department of the Taoiseach, the premier department of state. (This ascendancy is reflected in the fact that there are special Finance salary scales, now shared by civil servants in the Department of the Taoiseach, which are above those paid in other departments.) The statutory authority for the Department's work is contained in the Ministers and Secretaries Act, 1924 s.1(ii) quoted above.[55]

As an administrative arrangement, the Department is now divided into three divisions, each of which is under the control of a second secretary, a grade peculiar to the Department. The first of these divisions, the *Finance Division* covers: banking; insurance; exchange control; the state borrowing programme, including the control of the gilt-edged market; and monetary policy, generally. It also deals with the international economic dimension arising from Ireland's membership of the European Economic Community; European Monetary System; European Investment Bank; and the International Monetary Fund. The work of the second division, the *Budget and Planning Division* (the planning side of which was housed in the Department of Economic Planning and Development between 1977-80), stems from the idea that a Government must not only control its own finances but also try to promote the health of the entire national economy. This division, thus, bears responsibility for the preparation of the Budget and for fiscal and economic policy generally. Thirdly, the *Public Expenditure Division* deals with the Public Capital Programme, the

Book of Estimates and finally, the control of individual items of current and capital expenditure, a matter to which we shall return in the next few paragraphs. In addition, various 'branches and offices of the public service' (to quote the Schedule to the Ministers and Secretaries Act, 1924) fall under the overall control of the Minister for Finance. These include the Revenue Commissioners; the Paymaster General's Office; and the Office of Public Works. There are also certain State-sponsored bodies, for example, the Central Bank of Ireland,[56] which report to the Minister.

The need for the ascendancy[57] of the Minister for Finance and his Department arises from the fact that one of their most important duties is the control of the expenditure of the other departments, the so-called 'spending departments.' The Minister for Finance bears the frequently unpopular duty of ordering priorities and, often, rejecting cherished proposals out of hand:

In the division of government functions, it is the job of other departments to formulate proposals for carrying out the functions entrusted to them . . . and it is the job of the Department of Finance to give a dispassionate hearing to the proposals of the others, criticising them patiently and intelligently. It is all part of a system of checks and balances . . .[58]

Each draft Estimate receives a detailed scrutiny by officers of the Public Expenditure Division and must, finally, be approved by the Minister for Finance. Sometimes, where large amounts are involved, negotiations between the Minister and the minister of the relevant spending department are necessary in order to reach agreement. The Estimates campaign goes on over several months from the spring to the autumn. In the end, if all else fails, a dispute may have to be settled by the Government, whose authority is underlined by the constitutional rule[59] that the Dáil may not pass any vote or resolution or law to appropriate public money unless the purpose of the appropriation has been recommended by a message from the Government signed by the Taoiseach.

The next stage, already described in Sections 1 and 2, is that the Oireachtas' approval is granted, in the case of the supply services, by way of the Estimates and Appropriation Act or, in the case of non-voted moneys, by a specific substantive act. However, this merely fixes maximum amounts for expenditure. The Minister for Finance retains a detailed power of surveillance over the spending departments to ensure, before money is spent, that it is being spent economically and within the amounts fixed by the Oireachtas and in accordance with the intention of the Oireachtas, taking account of changing circumstances. The Minister for Finance's sanction, which is granted by the Public Expenditure Division, may impose conditions additional to those fixed by the Estimates. The form of the permission is usually a departmental minute.

This type of control is most likely to be stringently exercised, for example: if the expenditure is unexpected; or where *virement*[60] between two sub-heads is involved; or, in the case of a grant, if the conditions for its award have been changed. But the Minister for Finance's sanction is frequently delegated so that departments do not need to have recourse to the Minister, in certain clearly-defined cases, up to a monetary maximum. The statutory authority for Finance's control is as follows. In general, where voted moneys are to be expended, the expenditure will be authorised by some substantive, specialist statute as distinct from the Appropriation Act and that statute will make the sanction of the Minister for Finance a condition for the payment of the moneys. For example, where the expenses of administering a department are involved, the Ministers and Secretaries Act, 1924 provides that 'The expenses of each of the Departments of State established under this Act, to such amount as may be sanctioned by the Minister for Finance, shall be paid out of moneys provided by the Oireachtas.'[61] Secondly, for better assurance, the (British) Exchequer and Audit Departments Act 1921 provides, with reference to all types of expenditure in an appropriation account, that unless it is authorised by the Minister for Finance, it must 'be regarded as not being properly chargeable to a Parliamentary grant, and shall be so reported to the [Dáil].'

8.6 CENTRAL FUND

Before 1787, British government finances existed as an irregular system of *ad hoc* accounts and funds, each intended for a different purpose and fed from an individual head of taxation. The result was that parliamentary control was virtually inoperative and great opportunities existed (and were seized) for misappropriation. Pitt's reform of 1787 established a single fund, under the surveillance of an independent officer (now the Comptroller and Auditor General) appointed by Parliament. This simplification made it easier to obtain a comprehensive view of the state of government finances and to implement effective parliamentary control. The same principle is established in Ireland by the Constitution, Art. 11 of which provides that 'All revenues of the State from whatever source arising shall, subject to such exceptions as may be provided by law, form one fund . . .'[62] This fund is known as the 'Central Fund'[63] and its existence has been judicially regarded as evidence of the fact that the State is a juristic person capable of holding property.[64]

The banking transactions of the Central Fund are effected though the Exchequer Account, which must be kept at the Central Bank.[65] State revenues are collected, first, in the particular intermediate account (for example, Revenue Commissioners' account) and then transferred on to the Exchequer. As regards expenditure of voted moneys, the stages by which money is released from the Exchequer (known as the 'Course of the Exchequer') may be briefly summarised as follows. First, the Minister for Finance requests (usually each quarter, in the case of supply) the Comptroller and Auditor General to grant a credit for a specified amount on the Exchequer. This is necessary because the Comptroller and Auditor General, in his role as Comptroller, bears the duty of 'control[ling] on behalf of the State all disbursements of moneys administered by or under the authority of the State.'[66] The Comptroller must thus decide whether the sum requested falls within the amounts prescribed by statute. If the Comptroller General is satisfied on this point, he informs the Central Bank that he has granted the credits sought and the money is transferred from the Central Fund, to the Paymaster-General's Supply Account. The Paymaster General is an office attached to the Department of Finance which acts as banker to most of the departments of state. Once the CAG's sanction has been obtained, money can be transferred as needed by the spending departments. The *modus operandi* is that the spending department contacts the Department of Finance which issues instructions to the PG, as a result of which the amount is transferred to the particular spending department's vote account with the PG. It is then available to meet payable orders drawn by the departments in the same way as orders drawn on a bank.[67]

8.7 AUDIT OF PUBLIC ACCOUNTS

Comptroller and Auditor General The Comptroller and Auditor General is a vital element in the field of state finances. According to the Constitution (Art. 33.1), his duty is: 'to control . . . all disbursements and to audit all accounts of moneys administered by or under the authority of the Oireachtas.' The importance of the office is reflected in the fact that it is established by the Constitution and its independence from political pressure is maintained by a similar regime to that which sustain the higher judiciary. The CAG is conventionally regarded as an officer of the Dáil, since he is appointed, by the President, on the nomination of the Dáil and he reports to the Dáil;[68] he is barred from membership of either House; and he may only be removed from office for stated misbehaviour or incapacity as established by a resolution of each House.[69]

The title of the office reflects the fact that, in Britain, there were, until 1866, two separate offices, that is, Comptroller General of the Exchequer and the Commissioners for auditing the Public Accounts. And true to this history, the CAG has two principal functions. His first function, as Comptroller General, has already been described in Section 6. His other duty, as Auditor General, is chiefly, to audit the appropriation accounts (a term which is explained in the next Section), in three different ways. First, he carries out an accountancy audit, that is, he examines the soundness of the department's accounting method by performing a detailed audit of a sample of transactions; he need not audit all the transactions if he is satisfied with the sample. Secondly, he makes an administrative audit to ascertain whether the general or specific sanction of the Department of Finance — mentioned in Section 5 — has been obtained for all expenditures. His final and principal function is the appropriation audit (the scope of which is wider than that of a commercial auditor) in which he ensures that the supply grant authorised in the relevant Vote has not been exceeded, that money was spent for the purpose intended by the Dáil and that there has been no waste or administrative inefficiency. He has no function in regard to policy, although he may examine the implementation of policy in the course of investigating waste.[70] Points to which the CAG has drawn attention in recent years include: failure or delay by employers in paying tax deducted from their employees' wages to the Revenue Commissioners;[71] the Department of the Environment's procedure for verifying that applicants for housing grants fulfil the requirement of being a *first-time* home-owner;[72] the unnecessarily large accommodation provided for the incoming Bord Telecom's skeleton staff.[73]

To assist investigation, the CAG has 'free access, at all convenient times, to the books of account and other documents relating to the accounts of . . . departments.'[74] In 1967, a dispute arose as to the extent of his powers of investigation when the accounting officer in the Department of Justice refused him access to certain files, dealing with Garda travelling expenses and accounting procedures for the payment of witnesses' expenses, on the grounds that these files related to administrative discretions of a policy character. The dispute was resolved in the CAG's favour and, since it was regarded as undesirable that the CAG's access to documents should become a matter of strict legal definition, a Department of Finance circular was issued which provides as follows:

. . . the Comptroller and Auditor General should be given access to any document or file of documents which he states that he requires for the purpose of his audit, unless it is considered to be of exceptional secrecy when it should be shown to him, personally, in confidence. In the rare event that a requisitioned document or file is of such a secret nature that, in the opinion of a Minister, it would not be in the public interest to show it even to the Comptroller and Auditor General personally, this should be explained to him and every possible effort should be made to satisfy him in some other manner. If not satisfied, he may report the matter to the Dáil.[75]

The classic method by which financial responsibility to the Dáil is maintained is the appropriation account which is prepared at the end of the year for each supply grant administered by a department.[76] The design and lay-out of each account[77] and the information which it must contain is under the control of the Department of Finance.[78] In fact, each account follows closely Parts I and II of the corresponding Estimate so that it is easy to compare the intentions of the Dáil with the way in which they have been executed. Copies of all the accounts are transmitted to both the Auditor General and the Department of Finance and, when they have been examined and certified by the Attorney General, all the accounts are printed in a single volume and laid before the Dáil.[79]

It is the accounting officer who signs the accounts and who is, therefore, responsible to the Dáil for the proper expenditure of money from that Vote. His functions are not defined in any statute but, from his general brief and the comments made by the PAC, it is clear that his approach must be similar to that of the PAC. He must not only ensure that all expenditure is duly

129

authorised in the Vote and that a regular and proper procedure for all financial transactions is followed, but also that, in all policy decisions, financial considerations are taken into account. Accounting officers are selected and appointed by the Minister for Finance. In practice, the accounting officer is almost always the secretary of the department or office since he is the only person with sufficient authority for the task. Where an office or branch is not under the immediate administrative control of a secretary, the accounting officer is the head of that office, (e.g. the chairman of the Revenue Commissioners).

An accounting officer's responsibility is personal. In a few extreme cases in the early years of the state, the Public Accounts Committee has recommended the ultimate sanction, that is, that an item of expenditure be disallowed and no supplementary estimate made, so that the accounting officer has to bear the expenditure himself. More usually, the Committee will content itself with recording (in a published report) its disapproval. Because of an accounting officer's personal responsibility, his relationship with the minister of his department in regard to this matter is different from that which otherwise exists between a secretary and his minister. To take the extreme case, if a minister directs that a payment be made which the accounting officer regards as unauthorised, the accounting officer's duty is to protest in writing and to obey the minister if, and only if, the instruction is repeated in writing. In such a case, all the papers would be shown to the Comptroller and Auditor General and the Department of Finance.

In addition to the appropriation accounts, the CAG also audits: the accounts of certain State-sponsored bodies; all issues from the Central Fund (including interest on the public debt; salaries of judges, etc.);[80] the receipts of revenue which is payable into the Central Fund;[81] and, if required by the Minister for Finance to do so (as he is), the accounts of the Paymaster General and the Revenue Commissioners.[82] The CAG must also examine departmental stock and store accounts.[83]

Most of these additional heads of jurisdiction have been granted by various statutes. So far as the Constitution is concerned, the CAG's only mandate is to scrutinise 'moneys administered by or under the authority of the Oireachtas' (Art. 33.1). Certain State-sponsored bodies (chiefly commercial State-sponsored bodies) prefer their accounts to be audited by a private auditor whose checks are less wide-ranging than those of the CAG.

As a result, there has been some discussion in the Public Accounts Committee,[84] of the limits of the CAG's general jurisdiction, under Art. 33.1. The occasion for the discussion was the question of whether the accounts of certain State-sponsored bodies fell within the CAG's bailiwick. The CAG argued that where the entire share capital of a company was provided from the Central Fund by act of the Oireachtas, and all the shares were held by a minister responsible to the Oireachtas, then the accounts of the company fell within the constitutional definition and, consequently, were subject to the scrutiny of the CAG. However, Counsel's opinion was obtained and was to the effect that, legally, the minister holding the shares was a mere shareholder and the company was a distinct entity whose capital did not have the character of moneys 'administered by or under the authority of the Oireachtas.' This opinion was accepted by the Committee.

Public Accounts Committee   The most respected of the Dáil's select committees is the Public Accounts Committee. Traditionally, it consists of equal members from Government and Opposition parties and the chairman is a senior member of the Opposition. None of its members may be a member of the Government or a minister of state. According to Dáil Standing Order 126, the Committee must be appointed, as soon as possible after the beginning of the financial year and its brief is:

. . . to examine and report to the Dáil upon the accounts showing the appropriation of the sums granted by the Dáil to meet the public expenditure, and to suggest alterations and improvements in the form of the Estimates submitted to the Dáil.

The Committee is assisted in the task of scrutinising the appropriation accounts, by the Comptroller and Auditor General. His report, which is published with the appropriation accounts on which he is reporting, is the basis of the Committee's examinations and he is permanently in attendance at its meetings. In practice, its investigations, which are not usually held in public, are directed largely to points selected from those raised by the CAG. The Committee has before it, as a witness, the accounting officer for the Vote under investigation. In addition, officers from the Departments of Finance and of the Public Service are always present. Thus the Committee is equipped to probe a point further than the CAG and, since it is a political body, its findings are likely to attract more publicity.

The Committee's inquiry is on the financial, rather than the political plane. Consonant with the attitude of the CAG and the accounting officers, it asks whether a certain item of expenditure was unwise or extravagant,[85] or whether a scheme was badly administered, but not whether the scheme's objective was ill-conceived. This approach accords with the idea (which was the conventional wisdom when the Committee was first established), that policy is a matter for the Dáil as a whole since it is to the Dáil that a minister is responsible for the policy of his department.[86] It should be noted that the narrowness of the brief allocated to the PAC has now led to the constitution of the Public Expenditure Committee, already described in Section 3.

A specific reply to the recommendations in the PAC's reports is prepared by the Department of Finance in consultation with the other departments concerned and published in the form of a minute, which is appended to the Committee's report for the following year. If the response is not satisfactory, the Committee appointed to examine the following year's accounts may return to the matter in its report.

Neither the Comptroller and Auditor General nor the PAC has any executive power. The CAG simply reports the facts and figures as he finds them. The Committee's only power is the power to recommend, supported by the publicity which its reports generate (though its reports have not been debated in the House since the days of the Free State). If the Minister for Finance (who would be involved, in most cases, in executing the recommendation) does not concur in the recommendation, he is obliged to state the reasons for his dissent in the Minute in which he replies to the Committee. If agreement cannot be reached and the matter is important, the Minister is answerable to the Dáil, which must be specifically notified of the disagreement.[87] Furthermore, there is considerable delay between the actual expenditure by a government department and the publication of the Committee's report. The CAG is supposed to complete his examination of the appropriation accounts by 15 October of the year after the financial year to which the accounts relate.[88] The PAC then takes a further year for its review.[89] Nevertheless, the mere existence of the Committee — and its power to cross-examine accounting officers — tend to ensure that the various laws and Department for Finance standing controls in the field of financial procedure are properly observed.

9

Procedure in the Houses of the Oireachtas

There are five sources of procedure.

1. Standing orders   In Ireland, unlike the U.K,, the bulk of parliamentary procedure is codified in the form of a set of Standing Orders relative to Public Business. There are separate, though similar, sets for each House. On its second sitting day, the Third Dáil constituted a committee to draw up, as a matter of urgency, draft standing orders of its own.[1] These standing orders, which were modelled fairly closely on procedure at Westminster, were adopted a few days later.[2] In the light of experience, these were repealed and replaced in 1926.[3] In 1938, these standing orders were slightly amended.[4] It has been held that this amendment meant that the new Dáil had complied (albeit with a 'taciturnity uncharacteristic of parliaments')[5] with the requirement of the new Constitution that 'Each House shall makes its own rules and standing orders . . .'.[6]

The amendment, repeal or adoption of standing orders can be made by way of an ordinary resolution.[7] The only special element in the procedure is that 'any additions or amendments' must be recommended by the Committee on Procedure and Privileges.[8] In fact, the last major revision of Dáil standing orders was carried out by an informal Oireachtas committee.[9] Its report was considered by the CPP, which adopted most of its submissions, together with others suggested by the Ceann Comhairle and his staff. The CPP's report was then adopted by the Dáil and incorporated in the current (1974) edition of the Dáil Standing Orders.[10] Appended to the Dáil (though not to the Senate)[11] Standing Orders is a list of the various editions of the standing orders and a history of the amendments to each individual standing order.

2. Sessional orders   Standing orders are indefinite in duration.[12] However, sometimes procedural rules are made in the form of Sessional Orders, which are stated to last only for the length of the session, 'sessional' here being used to mean the length of a Parliament. One context in which this device is employed is where the House wishes to experiment to see how a rule works in practice: if it is a success, it can be adopted later as a standing order. If not, then it automatically falls out of use at the end of the session. The rules regulating times of sitting and the systems for questions are examples of sessional orders in the Dáil.

3. Rulings from the Chair The Chairman, whether in the Dáil or Senate, bears the authority and duty not only to intercept standing orders and apply them to situations as they arise, but also to rule on other matters not specifically covered in standing orders. This has been said to follow from the fact that he is made 'the [sole] judge of order in the House.'[13]

An episode which illustrates this residual discretion of the Chair in use in a broad constitutional context arose out of the submission of the Land Purchase (Guarantee Fund) Bill, 1935 to the Committee of Privileges in order to determine whether it was a 'money bill.' (The substance of this submission is recounted in Chapter 8.4.) During the period when the signatures of sufficient deputies to send a bill to a Committee were being collected, an attempt was made to rush the bill through all its stages in the Senate, in one day. There was nothing in Senate standing orders to cover this contingency and so the Cathaoirleach invoked his residual discretion to rule that the bill could not be heard until the time within which the necessary signatures had to be collected had elapsed or, if a Committee were set up, until it had completed its deliberations. His reason was that if a vote had been taken on the bill in the Senate and it had gone against the bill, the Committee of Privileges (assuming there were one) would have been prejudiced by the knowledge that a decision that the bill was not a money bill would have the effect of killing the bill. This decision of the Cathaoirleach's was subsequently approved by the Senate Committee on Procedure and Privilege.[14]

Analogies have sometimes been drawn between the Chair and the position of a judge. who is responsible both for interpreting statutes and for 'declaring' the common law in areas not covered by statute law. Such analogies raise the question of whether the Chair is bound by previous rulings in the same way as a court is bound by precedent. The answer is a qualified 'no.' The principal and long-established rule is that the Chair's ruling should not be challenged or commented upon[15] and citing precedents or giving explanations might, in certain circumstances, undermine the Chair's authority or lead to a prolonged procedural wrangle. Moreover, consistency between similar cases may sometims be purchased at too high a price since it may overlook such factors as 'the mood of the House'; a member's tone of voice; or the need for a Chairman to bend over backwards to be fair to the political party of which he is not a member. On the other hand, a *verbatim* record of all past decisions is available to everyone in the form of the *Dáil Debates* and *Seanad Debates*, and officials of the House keep classified records of decisions on procedural points. The best way for the Chair to avoid suspicions of arbitrariness is to maintain consistency with past decisions and this in fact is what occurs. Moreover, in some cases (two examples of which are given below)[16] the Chair and/or members do refer to precedents. The ultimate sanction if the House regards the Chair's rulings as unfair or inconsistent is a motion of censure.

4. The Constitution According to the Constitution (Art. 15.10): 'Each House shall make its own rules and standing orders, with power to attach penalties for their infringment . . .'. Does it follow from this that matters bearing on a House's procedure may only be regulated by 'rules and standing orders' and not by statute? Support for this argument is provided by the following statement made by the then Minister for the Public Service in the Dáil:

It has been argued that since the Constitution provides that each House may make its own rules and Standing Orders, section 8 of the Ministers and Secretaries (Amendment) Act, 1939 which purported to give a Parliamentary Secretary a right of audience in the House of which he was not a member was in conflict with the Constitution since it would interfere with the right of that House to makes its own rules and Standing Orders on the matter as provided in Art. 15 of the Constitution.[17]

A less extreme version of this argument suggests that if an act of the Oireachtas and a standing order conflict, the standing order must prevail. Admittedly, the practical significance of these questions is undermined by the consideration that a side which has a majority in the Houses of the Oireachtas for legislation will also have a majority in either House to amend standing orders.

There is a second consequence which may flow from the mention of 'standing orders' in the Constitution. Assuming that 'standing orders' is a term of art with certain well-established characteristics, including respect for the right of minorities (an assumption which is supported by the democratic principles running through the Constitution), does it not follow that 'standing orders' which lack any of these characteristics would be unconstitutional and invalid? Of some relevance in showing that the term 'standing orders' has a definite core of meaning, was the Senate's refusal, in 1925, to amend its standing orders to exclude private divorce bills. The reason given, by the Cathaoirleach, for this refusal was the fundamental distinction, between a Parliament's competence (the range of subject-matter which it may treat) and its procedure (the methods and forms through which it expresses itself). It is the latter and only the latter, which may be regulated, by way of standing orders.[18]

5. Acts of the Oireachtas There have been a few acts of Parliament which bear on preliminary procedure. In regard to the argument mentioned in the last Section — that the Constitution forbids statute law in the area usually covered by standing orders — it may be that this area does not extend rules involving third parties, that is, non-members of the Oireachtas as, for instance, the Oireachtas Witnesses Act, 1924.

9.2 ARRANGEMENT OF BUSINESS

Timetable During the most recent period for which figures are available (1977-81), the Dáil sat for an average of eighty days (usually Tuesday, Wednesday and Thursday) in each session[19] and for an average of nearly eight hours each sitting.[20] The Dáil is in recess at Christmas, Easter and between July and October. Currently about one sixth of its time is taken up with estimates, financial resolutions and consequential legislation. During the decade 1969-78, the Senate met an average of thirty-five times each year for an average of six and a half hours each sitting.[21] The time the Senate spends on financial matters is much less than the Dáil and there is no question time. Its timetable is distorted by the fact that most bills are initiated in the Dáil. This means that, during the greater part of the year, the Senate has little work to do, whilst just before the summer and Christmas recesses it receives a number of bills and is required to hold prolonged sittings in order to rush them through before the recess. Naturally this bottleneck has given rise to criticism.[22]

Dáil: Order papers and sequence of business For each sitting of the Dáil, the Ceann Comhairle prepares a printed Order Paper a copy of which is distributed to each member.[23] The order paper lists the business pending before the House (including questions), giving notice of the motions which require notice and indicating the stage which bills have reached.[24] It also lists the documents which have been laid before the House, whether or not there is a statutory duty that they should be so laid, and includes such matters as notices from the Government for the purposes of Art. 17.2. The format of the order paper follows the model laid down by Dáil S.O. 26, which is as follows:

1. Questions [Subject to the provisions of Standing Order 34]

2. Private Business.

3. Public Business.
   - (i) At the commencement of Public Business —
     - (a) Reports from committees
     - (b) Messages from the Seanad
     - (c) Bills from the Seanad
     - (d) Initiation of Bills
     - (e) *Notices of Motions*
   - (ii) *Orders of the Day.*[25] *(my italics)*

Apart from Questions, Private Members' Time and the half-hour Adjournment Debates, each of which is covered below, almost the entire sitting is occupied with Government business, which thus takes up about two-thirds of the time available in the Dáil chamber. Sometimes — more frequently than used to be the case — the Government will heed the urgings of the Opposition and allow a motion of confidence to be debated in Government time.

The sequence of Government business in the Dáil is settled by the Taoiseach.[26] Each day, the Taoiseach (or, in his absence, the Tanaiste) announces by reference to the number of each item on the order paper, what items of Government business are to be taken that day and the sequence in which they are to be taken. In fact, an attempt is made — usually successfully

— to take Government business in an order which is agreeable to all three of the major parties. The Government, of course, is not bound to do this,[27] but it usually does so, not only because this is accepted as the proper way to behave but also because, if it is not done, the Opposition parties may obstruct the Government's business.[28] Agreement between the parties may be reached 'through the usually channels,' that is, the three chief whips (or two where Fine Gael and Labour form a Coalition Government), who meet every Thursday, during the Dáil session, to discuss the coming week's business. The Taoiseach's announcement is made at the commencement of public business and it is usual to take brief matters — such as, messages from the Senate or orders for printing committee reports — immediately after the Order of Business announcement. Ministerial statements[29] are also normally heard at this time. Thereafter, the House goes on to consider lengthier matters, namely substantive motions or the second to fifth stages of bills.

There will often be some dispute as to whether a matter can properly be regarded as 'arising on the Order of Business.' It frequently happens that an Opposition deputy wishes to bring some burning issue of the day before the House. Yet, because the Government controls most of the House's time; because of the need for notice, and because of the delay before Question Time comes round to the minister to whom a question is addressed, there will often be no procedural device by which the deputy can raise the matter, while it is still a live issue. In these circumstances, the Order of Business, with the Taoiseach present and the Houses and press gallery full, may constitute a temptation which is too much for political flesh and blood to resist. The upshot may be that the deputy attempts to raise the matter on the Order of Business, and the Ceann Comhairle, anxious to confine the proceedings to orderly debate on topics of which adequate notice has been given, rules out of order 'this sort of impromptu or instant Question Time.'[30] The Ceann Comhairle has recently ruled — in line with earlier precedents — that, on the Order of Business:

There is no motion before the House and no room for debate . . . the only questions which may be permitted must relate, first, to the business of the day, secondly, to the taking of other business on the Order Paper and thirdly, the taking of business which has been promised and which therefore can be anticipated, and fourthly, arrangements for sittings.[31]

Senate: Order paper   Compared with the Dáil, there are, in the Senate, various differences of detail, in the layout of the order paper and the arrangement of business. The only difference of principle is that in the Senate 'The business shall be dealt with in order as printed [*sc.* on the order paper] unless the Seanad shall otherwise order.'[32] The result of this is that, whilst the business is arranged on the order paper in the sequence suggested by the leader of the House (a senator appointed by the Government to manage its business in the Senate), it is open to a majority of the House to make an order varying this sequence; by contrast, in the Dáil the sequence of business is settled by the Taoiseach. There are thus frequent short debates and occasional divisions on the order of business in the Senate.

Private members' business As already mentioned, the lion's share of parliamentary time, in both Houses, in consumed by the Government. Apart from half-hour adjournment debates, the only periods regularly available to debate business not introduced by the Government is 'Private Members' Time.' The use to be made of private members' time, both as to the items covered and the order of priority, is determined by agreement[33] between the party whips rather than by individual private members. However, in reaching their agreement the whips take account of the views of their back-benchers.

In the Dáil, in order to count as a party for the purposes of private members' time, that is, to present a bill or to move a motion, a party must have at least seven deputies. In addition, all the remaining deputies (whether independents or members of small parties) will be treated as a party for this purpose if they number at least seven.[34] Until the revision of Dáil standing orders in 1974, in practice, private members' time in the Dáil was confined to the period between Christmas and Easter when there were no Estimates before the House. The result was that during the period 1951-72, private members' time was assigned an average of 3.5% of total Dáil time (less than an hour each week). Since 1974, private members' time has been available for one and a half hours each Tuesday and Wednesday that the Dáil sits.[35] A minister may move a motion that private members' business be cancelled on any particular day so as to continue with specified Government or private business, but this power has been used sparingly.[36] So as to make the most of the precious time available, there are time limits in relation to private members' business. Debates must not exceed a total of three hours in the case of a motion not relating to a bill and six hours for the second reading of a bill; the member proposing the motion is confined to forty minutes; the speaker 'in reply' at the end of the debate is entitled to at least fifteen minutes; and all other speeches must not exceed thirty minutes.[37] Usually, the Government party does not take its turn in private members' time.

In the Senate, standing orders do not provide for private members' time, but, in practice, similar arrangements to those prevailing in the Dáil have been agreed between the parties.

Adjournment debates Generally speaking, a motion can only be moved in Government or in private members' time. It will thus only be actually debated if it is moved or at least approved, by the Government or the leaders of the Opposition. There are available, in each House, two other procedural devices — the half-hour *adjournment debate* and (less important) the adjournment debate on a matter requiring urgent *consideration* — which do not suffer from these infirmities, although they do suffer from limitations of their own.

138

Half-hour adjournment debate[38] After the previous business has been concluded or interrupted, any member may initiate a half-hour debate, as the last item before the adjournment. The member customarily has twenty minutes to outline the issue and the responsible minister replies in the remaining ten minutes. There are no other speeches and no vote. In the Dáil, adjournment debates are held every sitting day; whilst in the Senate they are held on approximately half the days.

The purpose of this debate is to enable a member to agitate some matter of administration, which will often be a matter of local interest. In the Dáil, an adjournment debate may arise out of a member's dissatisfaction with some answer given at question time. A topic may not be raised if its breadth means that it would be more suitable for a substantive motion: thus the closure of a particular school would be a suitable topic; the entire question of comprehensive education would not. Otherwise the exclusionary rules are similar to those for questions.[39] For instance, the subject must fall within the minister's field of responsibility and this rule is more strictly applied than it is in the context of questions.

Adjournment debate on a matter requiring urgent consideration[40] Only a few hours notice need be given for a half-hour adjournment debate, which means that the minister and his civil servants have little time to prepare. But the effects of this are mitigated because no vote is taken and because the subject-area is narrow. Issues will occasionally arise which require the House's urgent attention, yet which do not fit within the relatively narrow ambit of the adjournment debate, for instance because several members wish to speak or because it is desired to take a vote. Standing orders in each House had always provided for an emergency debate in these circumstances. However, successive chairmen had built up a series of restrictive precedents regarding the situations which fell within this category and the result was that there had not been a single debate of this type in the Dáil between 1947 to 1972. To ameliorate this situation, the Informal Committee[41] made a proposal, which was accepted, that a new form of words be inserted in the relevant standing order so that the chain of precedents would be broken and the Chair would no longer be bound by existing precedents. The standing orders of Dáil and Senate now contemplate the existence of 'a specific and important matter of public interest requiring urgent consideration' (instead of, as previously, 'a definite matter of urgent public importance'). Notwithstanding the change, a handful of requests for a debate have been granted in either House and a number have been refused by the Chair. Frequently, the ground for the refusal has been that, though the issue is urgent, it has not arisen suddenly. (Although there is no mention of it in standing orders, the Informal Committee plainly envisaged that the matter should have arisen suddenly.) A request for an emergency debate (which lasts one and a half hours) must be supported by twelve members in the Dáil or five in the Senate.

The code   The forms and terminology through which the Houses express themselves constitute an elaborate code which has evolved over several centuries, mostly in the Westminster Parliament. Some of its elements can be traced even further back to the mediaeval courts and the councils of the Church. The resultant form of debate has been summarised in Britain in the observation that 'Every matter is determined in both Houses upon questions put from the chair upon a motion made by a Member and resolved in the affirmative or negative as the case may be.'[42] The importance of the motion is that it provides some clear, central proposition to which all speakers can address their remarks. The motion may be one which marks the passage of a bill through its various stages, for example, *'that the Bill be now read a second time.'*[43] Alternatively, it may be the type of motion which, if it is passed, takes the form of either an *order* or a *resolution*. Which form it takes is indicated in the Journal (or *Imeachta*).[44] There is no necessary difference in the debate on a motion leading to an order, rather than a resolution, though in practice it often happens that a motion leading to an order does not have to be debated or voted upon because there is no opposition to it. Very roughly speaking, the basis of the distinction between an order and a resolution is that orders deal with questions of procedure, for example, an order fixing a time-limit within which a debate must conclude; whilst resolutions cover substantive matters, for instance, resolutions of no confidence in the Government. However, there are numerous exceptions to this demarcation line: for example, amendments to standing orders or the appointment of the Chairman are regarded as sufficiently important to be couched in the form of resolutions.

Standing orders[45] lay down rules regarding the notice which is required for motions leading to an order or resolution. The motion must appear on the order paper (as a 'notice of motion') for four days before it is eligible to be moved (though it will not necessarily be moved at this point). Members are thus given sufficient warning to prepare speeches etc. However, the Chair has a discretion to allow shorter notice and, in practice, these requirements are frequently waived (wholly or partially) by agreement between the Government and Opposition whips. Where any business which has already been before the House is concerned, an Order of the House fixes the earliest date when the item of business may be taken and this item then appears on the order paper as an 'order of the day.' The principal example would be a stage of a bill and thus, for instance, at the end of second stage, the House will fix the earliest day for the third stage. As can be seen, an order of the day and a notice of motion constitute alternative devices for alerting the House as to when a particular piece of business may be taken.

Amendments   Members may, and frequently do, move an amendment to a motion. Every amendment to a motion must be relevant to it and must be directed to deleting, adding or substituting words: it must not be equivalent

140

to a direct negative:[46] otherwise the proposers might just as well vote against the motion. (The specialised rules regarding amendments to bills at each stage are described in Chapter 7.3.) It is the practice to move an amendment immediately after the motion has been proposed and, in the Senate, seconded. (In the Dáil, no seconder is required.) The subsequent debate can then range over the entire subject-matter comprised in both motion and amendment. At the end of the debate, the question on any amendment(s)[47] is put immediately before the question on the main motion.

Speeches The proposer of a motion or bill speaks first. In the Senate, the requirement that the proposer or seconder must be a senator, whilst the minister responsible for a Government bill or motion is almost always a deputy, means that the motion is usually moved formally by a senator and the minister speaks next. The seconder is then free to reserve his speech until a later stage.[48] At the end of the debate, the proposer has the right to make a concluding speech replying to the debate: apart from committees, this is the only occasion on which a member may speak more than once.[49] For the first 'round', after the opening speakers, the sequence of speeches is: Government party(ies); main Opposition party; and (if the Labour Party is in opposition) Labour Party. Subsequently, speeches alternate to and fro between the Government party(ies) and Opposition party(ies). Speakers speak by standing up.[50] In selecting speakers, the Chair takes care — as Mr Paddy Hogan was wont to say when he was Ceann Comhairle — 'to interlard the debate,' that is, to ensure that every viewpoint is represented.[51] The Chair will take it into account that a member who wishes to speak is, for example: a former Taoiseach; an expert on the subject under discussion; or a representative of a constituency which is peculiarly affected by the outcome of the debate. In any case, the Chair's rulings in this area usually determine only the sequence of speeches since the Houses are small enough for every interested member to have his say on Government business (though not always during the brief private members' time).

Save in private members' time in the Dáil[52] there is no limit to the length of a speech, which may not, however, be read *verbatim*. If any member persists in irrelevance or repetition or is, in the Chair's opinion, speaking in order to obstruct business, then he may be directed to discontinue his speech by the Chair. Before this is done, the Chair must draw the attention of the member and the House to this misbehaviour.[53] Whatever the temptations, members may not read books, write letters or smoke in the chamber.

Rules of debate The rules of debate, which are designed to maintain decorous debate, are legion. Successive chairmen have ruled that a speaker may not refer to another members as (*inter alia*): a liar, drunk, traitor; rat; or 'briefless lawyer.' However, political charges may be made against a member and it is well established that statements may be made about a policy or a party, which would not be permitted about an individual, for example, that

141

a party was guilty of 'bribery, corruption, intimidation and all shapes of Tammany Hall and Castle Hack.'[54]

Speakers must refer to other members in a respectful manner by reference to the ministerial office which he holds or as Deputy — or Mr —. Speeches may not refer to the President. If at all possible, reference to officials or to persons or bodies outside the House ought not to identify the person concerned, whether to praise or blame them. In this way, the House is careful not to abuse the rules of parliamentary immunity from defamation actions; indeed, the rules of debate go very much further than the law of defamation: for example, derogatory references to the dead are excluded.

Among the most commonly invoked of the exclusionary rules is the rule that the conduct of a judge may only be discussed on a substantive motion for his removal, of which there has never been an example in Ireland. (There is a distinct rule banning discussion of a court case which is *sub judice*.) This first rule came to public attention[55] following a criminal case in which a short suspended sentence was imposed for a very serious crime. Because of the degree of public concern about this leniency, this case was debated in the Dáil, the exclusionary rule being avoided (or evaded) by casting the discussion in the form of a general motion calling for legislation to ensure uniformity in sentencing, in which context the criminal case could be discussed as an example

Voting   When a question is to be put to the House or a Committee of the whole House, the Chair rises and announces: 'The question is that . . .' with the remainder of the question being framed in the same terms as the motion. The Chair requires that 'as many as are of that opinion shall say 'Tá' [Yes], and as many as are of contrary opinion shall say 'Níl' [No]. The Chair then gives his opinion as to which side has won, basing himself not on the levels of noise on each side, but rather on which side (usually the Government) he expects to be in a majority. If, as frequently happens, the Chair's guestimate is challenged by any member, the the House proceeds to a division.[56]

Adjournment and closure   Normally, no limits are imposed on the length of time for which Government, as contrasted with private members', business may be debated. The times at which the House must adjourn have already been mentioned. Where an item of business has not been completed by the time of the adjournment, it is automatically placed on the order paper for the next sitting, unless the House orders to the contrary.[57]

Fairly frequently, Government and Opposition whips reach an agreement that particular business will be completed within a specified time (sometimes accompanied by an agreement as to the maximum length for each speech). Sometimes these voluntary arrangements are formally implemented by a procedural order of the House. More often, they remain informal agreements of which the Chair is notified and which he is supposed to have in mind in ordering business. However, if there be any objection to these informal limits, they cannot be enforced.

142

Very rarely, agreement is not possible and the Government sometimes uses its majority to make an order, known as a *guillotine*, by which the time to be spent on a motion or a stage of a bill or even a particular clause is limited in advance and thus filibustering is prevented. Filibustering means that the Opposition, (usually because they particularly object to the specific business but sometimes out of a general desire to hamstring the Government) seizes every opportunity for delay, insisting on debating every last sub-section of every bill and every sub-head of the Estimates. A guillotine is made at the same time as the order for the next reading and takes the form of instructions to the Chair to put, at the expiry of the limit, the question which is necessary to bring the proceedings to a close.[58]

The *closure* is a second device which can be used to control the time spent on business. There was no provision for a closure in the Westminster Parliament until the late nineteenth century. At that time — to quote Sir Ivor Jennings:

. . . the Irish [Party] began . . . to obstruct all legislation that did not apply to Ireland because they wanted legislation for Ireland, and all legislation that related to Ireland because they did not like it . . . The Irish Nationalists finally broke down the notion that the House could do its business even when every member had the right to talk at any length on any subject.[59]

The final straw was the proceedings on the Coercion Bill, 1881, debate on which occupied fourteen sittings, culminating in a sitting of forty-one hours, before the closure was imposed by the Speaker on his own responsibility. The sequel was the introduction of a standing order in similar terms to that which exists in the present-day Dáil or Senate standing orders.[60] Under this order, a motion may be initiated for the closure of a debate on a motion or a stage of bill. The Chairman has a discretion not to put the motion 'if it shall appear to the [Chair] that such a motion is an infringement of the rights of minority, or that the question has not been adequately discussed, or that the motion is otherwise an abuse of these standing orders . . .' But if he decides in favour, the motion 'That the question be now put' must be decided immediately without debate. Because of the importance attached to this discretion, a closure motion may only be moved when the Ceann Comhairle or Cathoirleach is in the Chair, and such motions are recorded in a special section of the returns of other business. There have only been Dáil closure motions in the case of twelve measures during 1937-81 (though the closure has been applied several times over a single measure — for example, fourteen times over the Livestock Marts Bill, 1967). The closure is used even more seldom in the Senate. Though they are rarely used, the very existence of the guillotine and the closure constitutes a cane in the cupboard and helps to fix the framework of the Government-Opposition relationship in the Oireachtas.

In 1981, the short-lived Coalition Government created the new post of Leader of the House with the task of implementing its proposals for Dáil reform.[61] The post was re-constituted by the 1982 Coalition and, early in 1983, an eighteen-hour debate on general Dáil reform was held.[62] The specific reform measures which are presently either under consideration or being implemented include the reform of financial procedure,[63] the broadcasting of Oireachtas proceedings, probably in an edited form; and the new committee system, which will be discussed later in this Section and which was introduced in mid-1983.

Lest anyone should become trapped in the procedural details of reform, rehearsed here, it must be emphasised that the impact which the reforms make, depends ultimately upon a fundamental political question — the effect which the reforms have on the balance of power between the Government and the legislature. At one extreme was the view of the Leader of the Opposition (Mr Haughey): '. . . the running of the country, particularly the running of the economy, is a matter for clear, hard decisions by the Government.'[64] On the other hand, the Leader of the House, Mr John Bruton, said: 'The central objective of the reform of the Dáil is to enable this House to take the leadership in public affairs [which] it should be capable of doing as the elected assembly of the people.'[65] Three observations may be made. First, the success of the sort of change Mr Bruton appears to be contemplating turns, *inter alia*, upon the calibre, enthusiasm and sense of responsibility of deputies. Second, it may be said that such a change is against the Government's interest, just as it is in the Opposition's interest, since it means better opportunities for seeming to score off the Government. (This is true at least in the short term. In the long term, if the reforms succeed, such a matter as the Government accepting an amendment to a bill or not voting down a private member's bill may no longer be perceived as a loss of face for the Government.) Finally, the reforms require all-party co-operation to have any chance of success. In fact, the new committees are based on all party agreement and, indeed, the Select Committee on Crime, Lawlessness and Vandalism was constituted at the suggestion of the Opposition (Fianna Fáil). Fianna Fáil have also given their chief whip the title of 'Shadow Leader of the House.' Five of the committees dealing with policy and policy-related issues are chaired by Fianna Fáil members whilst Fine Gael and Labour members chair five and two, respectively, of such committees.

Committees Even under the new system, committees will not take final decisions and the main forum for business will remain the floor of the House. There are three types of committee. The first is the Committee of the whole House which undertakes the third (committee) stage of most bills. Secondly, there are the special committees to which the third stage of (in practice) all the bills not committed to the whole House used to be sent. It is likely that, with the advent of the Joint Committee on Legislation, it will take over the special committee's work.[66] The remaining committees are all select committees. The 'primary purpose [of a select committee] is to consider the matter and to report its opinion thereon for the information and assistance of the House.'[67] The distinguishing feature of a select committee is that a House may, in the order of reference setting it up, empower it 'to send for persons, paper and records.'[68] It seems, in the wake of *In re Haughey*,[69] that there is *normally*[70] no legal obligation on a witness to obey such a summons or, if he attends, to answer questions.

At this point, it may be appropriate to mention a point regarding the procedure of a select committee hearing evidence. It was held, in *In re Haughey*, that where evidence is given before a select committee which impugns a person's good name, then, as a matter of constitutional justice,[70a] that person is entitled to be given a copy of the evidence; to be allowed to cross-examine (by counsel, if he wishes) his 'accuser'; to call rebutting evidence; and to address the committee in his own defence. Following the decision in *In re Haughey*, the Committee of Public Accounts investigating the expenditure of the grant-in-aid for Northern Ireland Relief adapted its procedure to accommodate these rights.[70b] Two points of elaboration should be made: first, presumably, the person enjoying these rights of self-defence need not necessarily himself be a witness (although this was the case in *In re Haughey*). Secondly, these rights will only arise in extreme cases. In *In re Haughey*, for instance, it was said that 'Mr Haughey's conduct is the very subject matter of the Committee's examination and is to be the subject matter of the Committee's report.'[71]

There are four committees which deal with different aspects of the running of the House. Two of these — the Committee of Selection and the Committee on Procedure and Privileges — are select committees which the standing orders of each House require should be constituted at the start of each new session. The Committee of Selection[72] is the lynch-pin of the entire system since its functions are to nominate members to serve on select or special committees; to discharge committee members, either for non-attendance or at their own request, and to appoint replacements. Whilst, theoretically, the Dáil Committee has eleven members, in fact it usually consists of a conversation between the Government and Opposition chief whips.

The other sessional committee is the Committee on Procedure and Privileges which is chaired by the Ceann Comhairle in the case of the Dáil Committee and by the Cathaoirleach in the case of the Senate Committee. It has three major functions. First, it must keep an eye on procedure generally and its recommendation is necessary before standing orders can be amended. Secondly, it investigates alleged breaches of privilege. Finally, the Committee may consider 'any matter relating to the conditions or premises in which members carry out their duties and which are not specifically referred to any other committee.'[73] Under this head it has considered for instance: members' salaries and expenses; physical security at Leinster House; the proper role of the Leas-Cheann Comhairle and in particular its reconciliation with his duties as a TD; and the wearing of gowns by the Ceann Comhairle and the Leas-Ceann Comhairle.[74]

There are two other committees which are formed by joining select committees from each House to form a single committee, namely, the Joint Committee on Standing Orders (Private Business);[75] and the Joint Services Committee which directs the Oireachtas restaurant and library, the research service for members and the information service for the public and media.[76]

New investigative committee system By way of a preliminary to a description of what is known as the 'new committee system,' it should be emphasised that whilst this is a convenient phrase, there have always been investigative, select committees and the principal change has been a substantial increase in the number of such committees. The terms of reference and, it is likely, the *modus operandi* of the new committees will follow the experience of existing committees; for example, the Joint Committee of European Community Secondary Legislation pioneered the provision,[77] now included in the order setting up each committee, by which permission is given in advance for the committee report to be published; the previous practice was that a committee had to go to the House for a separate order for publication.

In designing the new committee system it was suggested that the subject-areas of the committees should be designed to match the areas covered by particular departments of state. This suggestion was rejected because of the danger that such a committee might simply become a pressure group in favour of the activity it was supposed to be investigating. For example, Mr Bruton said:

. . . [an] Agricultural Committee would become an extension of the Department of Agriculture exercising pressure on the Government to get more money for agriculture. The type of people who would go on the Agricultural Committee — farmers — would want to express that point of view anyway . . . . In effect, instead of this House becoming an assembly which presides over and rises above pressure group politics, we would turn this House into an extension of pressure group politics.[78]

Instead, following the recent changes, there are now three types of investigative committee. The functions of the Joint Committee on Legislation[79] (which may act through sub-committees) are dealt with in the Chapter on legislation. Here they may be summarised as being: to receive submissions from the public on draft legislation referred to it;[80] to act as Standing Joint Committee on Consolidation Bills;[81] to examine the reports of the Law Reform Commission and to keep the law under review; to hear the committee stage of bills referred to it; and to discharge a widened version of the functions formerly vested in the Senate Committee on Statutory Instruments.[82] Secondly, a new Dáil committee, the Public Expenditure Committee,[83] is constituted to work alongside the traditional Public Accounts Committee.[84] The duties of both these committees are explained in the Chapter on finance.[85-86] Finally, there are a number of committees set up to investigate some narrow, topical problem-area. In the past decades *ad hoc* select committees have been set up occasionally to inquire into a single issue, for example: the Joint Committee on Electoral

Law;[87] or the Dáil Committee on Health Services, which has been set up on many occasions.[88] But, in 1983, a series of joint select committees, was constituted to consider: the price and supply of building land;[89] small businesses;[90] women's rights;[91] and marriage breakdown.[92] A Dáil select committee on crime, lawlessness and vandalism was also set up.[93] In addition, joint committees maintaining a continuing surveillance over the Secondary Legislation of the European Communities, Commercial State-sponsored Bodies, and Co-operation with Developing Countries[94] were established before the present reforms and have been re-established (in substantially the same form) in 1983.

Advantages and disadvantages of committees The first advanatage is that (although the procedural rules are largely the same in committees as in the House)[95] in a smaller group a more relaxed atmosphere will prevail and a detailed discussion, with some give and take, is likely to result. Moreover, much of the business transacted in the House is heard by a virtually empty chamber. By contrast the very fact that there are relatively small numbers on a committee creates pressure on members to attend meetings and also means that there are greater opportunities for them to contribute. Again, in a committee room the expert advice which civil service advisers supply to any minister on the committee can be heard by the other committee members and thus it enriches the discussion. There is even at least one case of a civil servant speaking directly to the committee.[96] The fact that the committee has no other business pressing upon it means that complicated legislation can receive a more leisurely and minute scrutiny than might be feasible in the House. It is significant, in this context, that the Dáil (though not the Senate) is obliged, by standing orders, to send a private member's bill to a committee.[97] The reason for this is that a private members' bill may be inadequately prepared before it reaches the Oireachtas and it will probably receive a better examination in a special committee than in a Committee of the whole House.

A further advantage which has been claimed for committees it that, away from the gladiatorial associations of the chamber, there is a better chance that areas of consensus between the parties will emerge.[98] This view especially underlies the establishment of the committees on building land[99] and marriage breakdown.[101] It seems to be a realistic expectation in a polity, like Ireland, in which disagreement between parties are duties imposed by the political culture, rather than necessities required by any major differences of policy betwen the two larger parties. Finally, it is said that the committee system will give members of the public a channel by which they may be able to influence policy-making in that they will be able to give evidence before a committee. As the leader of the House said:

. . . there will be an alternative focus for public concern here in the House, broadly speaking working in public in addition to the existing focus of governmental discussion through the civil service which in most cases takes place in a private arena . . . [This will also] strengthen the role of this House in national policy-making.[102]

As against these advantages, there are some practical doubts and difficulties. The first of these is the increased demands on the time of members and Oireachtas staff. Leaving aside the committees which meet less regularly and generate less work (Committees of Selection, Committees on Procedure and Privileges, Joint Services Committee and Joint Committee on Standing Orders (Private Business)), one hundred and forty deputies and fifty two senators are necessary to man the remaining committees. Since ministers of the Government, ministers of state and the chairmen of the Houses are excluded from most, though not all, committees, this means that every member must serve on one or (in the case of some Government back-benchers in the Dáil) two committees. Meetings are held (depending on the particular committee) each week, each fortnight or each month and take two or three hours plus (ideally) several hours' preparation. Whilst too much should not be made of this point, clearly committee duties will have to compete for priority against the constituency work to which members (especially deputies) assign so much of their time.

Another difficulty concerns the provision of staff for committees. Their importance to fact-finding is obvious, as is the danger that, in certain subject-areas, the executive might prefer that the fact-finding should be of the less rigorous kind. More legitimately, there is, at this time of increase in the number of committees, a policy of reduction of staff throughout the public sector. In the past, there have been frequent complaints about staffing as, for example that the Senate Committee on Statutory Instruments, with its vast and important work-load, was staffed by a single (part-time) higher executive officer.[103] As regards the provision of professional expertise, the order of reference for a committee typically deals with the matter thus: 'That the Committee shall, subject to the consent of the Minister for the Public Service, have power to engage the services of persons with specialist or technical knowledge to assist it for the purpose of particular enquiries.' The report of the Public Accounts Committee investigation into the expenditure of the Grant-in-Aid for Northern Ireland Relief recorded that it found 'onerous and unsatisfactory' the need to seek the sanction of the Minister for Finance (this was before the Minister for the Public Service was constituted) every time it required legal advice and that its requests were not always granted in full.[104] In 1983, the Committee on Building Land was delayed for four months, waiting for the Attorney General's advice on various points on the Constitutional right to property, only to be told, finally, that the Attorney General could not assist the Oireachtas since he is the *Government's* chief legal adviser. Anomalously, the Committee was then granted the advice of the legal officer at the Department of the Environment.[105] However, the Committee on State-sponsored Bodies has been able to retain the full-time services of an economist.

The impact which the communications media make on the business of each House is immense[106] and is often neglected by academic commentators. In the past the media chose to pay very little attention to committee work because

148

it lacks the colour of (say) a good row in the Dáil on the order of business.[107] The result is that the conventional wisdom at Leinster House (as it was put at a meeting of the special committee on the Corporation Tax Bill, 1975) is that: '. . . service on a committee such as this, from a political point of view, no matter what work is put into it, is of absolutely no value.'[108] The consequential danger, that members may not attend committee meetings, remains a real one. In fact, since the establishment of the new committee system, the committees have been well-reported and — it is not cynical to say — consequently well-attended.

By convention,[109] the composition of these committees has to be proportional to party strengths in the House. This is subject to the rule that where a committee has an odd number of members (as is usually the case with committees hearing contentious business) it is customary that the Government should have a majority.[110] However, this will often be a majority of only one, which poses difficulties for the Government whip. The position is ameliorated by the fact that the standing orders which apply to the Joint Committees on Legislation, when it is hearing the committee stage of a bill, provide that if a committee member is absent his place may be taken by another member of the House nominated by the absent member's party.[111] Orders constituting certain of the other committees, for instance the Joint Committees on Secondary Legislation of the European Communities and on Co-operation with Developing Countries also allow for an alternate. Nevertheless, it is likely that this factor will still loom large in the minds of the Government's business managers. Moreover, there is also a rule (which will usually profit the Opposition) that, on a tied vote, the Chairman has no casting vote and the question must be decided in the negative.[112]

Adverse comment has often been made on the fact that, in the past, committee reports have seldom been discussed (on a 'take note' motion) by the chamber of either House. Thus, in recent years the work of the Senate Committee on Statutory Instruments has only once been celebrated by a debate.[113] Notwithstanding the peculiar importance of keeping EEC instruments under parliamentary scrutiny,[114] the first time a report from the Joint Committee of Secondary Legislation of the European Communities was debated occurred in the Senate five years after the inception of the Committee.[115] This came about because of a Senate motion (which has been renewed in subsequent years) providing that where the Committee has laid a report before the Senate requesting a debate, the Senate would hold a rebate within a specified time period.[116] There is also now an order providing that the Dáil must hold a three-hour debate on all reports of the recently-established Public Expenditure Committee.[117]

There are other ways in which a committee's work can have an effect. Thus the Joint Committee on Secondary Legislation of the European Communities has had an influence on the drafting of domestic statutory instruments,[118] and the Joint Committee on Commercial State-sponsored Bodies has issued a number of reports which have been fairly well-reported, especially in the specialist press, and have focussed public attention on the problems and defects of these bodies.[119]

Finally, mention should be made of a constitutional distinction which was regarded as significant at the time when the Committee on Commercial State-sponsored Bodies was being launched.[120] It is that if the Committee were authorised to investigate policy matters, there would be a danger of subverting the responsibility of the State-sponsored body to the responsible minister and of the minister to the *entire* Dáil. There is obviously a practical difficulty in distinguishing policy from the matters which the Committee was empowered to consider, namely reports, accounts and over-all operational results. However, it seems likely that the Committee did consider certain matters which might be regarded as policy, without any adverse consequences ensuing. What is even more significant is that the new generation of committees includes some committees — for example, the committees on building land and marriage breakdown — whose terms of reference direct them squarely to confront policy questions. The implications of the doctrine of ministerial responsibility to the Dáil also arise in regard to civil servants giving evidence before committees: a Department of the Public Service circular has been issued advising them not to answer policy questions.

Joint Committee on Commercial State-sponsored Bodies　　In order to illustrate some of the features which have been mentioned and to give some idea of the sort of work a committee does, it might be useful, first, to quote a typical Order of Reference for a committee and then to list some of the recommendations made by it. The (Dáil) Order of Reference for the Joint Committee on Commercial State-sponsored Bodies is as follows:

1. That a Select Committee consisting of 7 members of Dáil Éireann (none of whom shall be a member of the Government or a Minister of State) be appointed to be joined with a Select Committee to be appointed by Seanad Éireann [consisting on four members] to form a Joint Committee (which shall be called the Joint Committee on Commercial State-sponsored Bodies) to examine the Reports and Accounts and overall operational results of State-sponsored Bodies engaged in trading or commercial activities referred to in the Schedule hereto and to report thereon to both Houses of the Oireachtas and to make recommendations where appropriate.

2. That, after consultation with the Joint Committee, the Minister for the Public Service with the agreement of the Minister for Finance may include from time to time the names of further State-sponsored Bodies in the Schedule and, with the consent of the Joint Committee and the Minister for Finance, may delete from the Schedule the names of any bodies.

3. That, if so requested by a State-sponsored Body, the Joint Committee shall refrain from publishing confidential information regarding the Body's activities and plans.

4. That the Joint Committee shall have power to send for persons, papers and records and, subject to the consent of the Minister for the Public Service, to engage the services of persons with specialist or technical knowledge to assist it for the purpose of particular enquiries.

150

5. That the Joint Committee, previous to the commencement of business, shall elect one of its members to be Chairman, who shall have only one vote.

6. That all questions in the Joint Committee shall be determined by a majority of votes of the members present and voting and in the event of there being an equality of votes the question shall be decided in the negative.

7. That the Joint Committee shall have power to print and publish from time to time minutes of evidence taken before it together with such related documents as it thinks fit.

8. That every report which the Joint Committee proposes to make shall on adoption by the Joint Committee be laid before both Houses of the Oireachtas forthwith whereupon the Joint Committee shall be empowered to print and publish such report together with such related documents as it thinks fit.

9. That 4 members of the Joint Committee shall form a quorum of whom at least 1 shall be a member of Dáil Éireann and at least 1 shall be a member of Seanad Éireann.

[The Schedule includes all commercial State-sponsored bodies plus Udárás na Gaeltachta.]

Here are three specimen recommendations made by the Joint Committee on Commercial State-sponsored Bodies:

The British and Irish Steam Packet Company Limited in its evidence accepted the broad responses which the Department of Tourism and Transport has made with regard to the overall operations of the group. Notwithstanding the disciplines which this necessitates at times, the Company felt that by putting forward rational cases for further action, intelligent and reasonable responses were forthcoming. The Joint Committee believes that any uncertainties that might arise in the future as between the parent department and the Company could be dispelled by having a sufficiently long term policy framework for transport.[121]

Up to and including 1975/76, the Revenue Account (for Bord na Móna) distinguished among the four products [sod peat, milled peat, briquettes, and moss peat] and so the reader was able to see the extent to which each product contributed to the overall financial performance. Since then this Account has shown only aggregate results. It is recommended that the former practice be restored. It is also recommended that the Revenue Account give more information regarding costs and, in particular, identify wages and salaries as a separate item. Aggregate labour costs are shown at present in a separate table, but this should be disaggregated by product in the revised Revenue Account, thus permitting the identification of the important matter of unit labour costs by product.[122]

[The Joint Committee] is of the opinion that further State investment in [Ceimici Teoranta] should not be made without a fundamental reappraisal of the company's role. The Joint Committee recommends that such a reappraisal be undertaken by the Department of Industry, Commerce and Energy as a matter of urgency. The Joint Committee proposes to have another look at the company within the next twelve months.[123]

A question to a minister about his own or his department's policy or performance is the most frequently used element of the Dáil's formal control over the executive. There is no equivalent in the Senate (in contrast to the House of Lords).

Subject-matter Questions may be divided into three major classes. First, there are those which seek information. For example: 'To ask the Taoiseach if he will outline the changes made since July, 1977 in the compilation of the Live Register for the unemployed; and the figure which the Live Register would have been for the end of January, 1981 had these changes not been made — Jim Mitchell.' Secondly, a question may seek to explore some administrative departmental action which has affected some individual, from a constituent of the questioner. Usually, as in the following example, the identity of the individual involved is not made public: 'To ask the Mnister for the Environment when a house improvement grant will be paid to a person (details supplied) in the South County Dublin area — Barry Desmond.' Finally, a question may bear upon the Minister's future policy or past decision in regard to some issue. Often the question will indicate the questioner's own preferred policy, for example: 'To ask the Minister for Industry, Commerce and Tourism if he will give an assurance that the decision to close the Ceimici Teo glucose plant at Corroy, County Mayo will be rescinded — Paddy O'Toole.'[124]

Especially in the case of questions on more contentious subjects, the minister's reply will have been carefully crafted by his civil servants, to present a smooth surface and to leave as little scope as possible for supplementary questions. On the other side of the hill, the questioner will want to put supplementary questions in order to extract information which he wishes to be made public. The minister is armoured against this cross-examination by a file of answers to anticipated supplementaries. In addition, Dáil Standing Order 37 provides that supplementaries may be put 'only for the further elucidation of the information requested, and shall be subject to the ruling of the Ceann Comhairle both as to relevance and as to number.'

In addition to the general exclusionary principles (e.g. in regard to criticising a judge) which apply to all parliamentary business, there is a fairly complicated catalogue of rules, drawn from standing orders, past practice and general constitutional notions, which determine whether a question is admissible. One of the principal rules is enunciated (in Dáil Standing Order 32) as follows: 'Questions addressed to a member of the Government must relate to public affairs connected with his Department, or to matters of administration for which he is officially responsible.' Where there is clearly no official responsibility — for instance as regards comparable situations in other EEC Member States — information has sometimes been given by ministers as a courtesy. Generally, however, questions will not be answered in respect of activities for which responsibility is vested outside Government departments

— for example, those performed by the Director of Public Prosecutions or involving the Houses of the Oireachtas themselves. The exclusion also extends to decisions taken by the President, on his own discretion. Because of the Taoiseach's residual responsibility for public business covered by the Ministers and Secretaries Act, 1924, which is not vested in any department of state, questions about the Attorney General's functions, including individual prosecutions, are answered by the Taoiseach.[125] State-sponsored bodies and commissions are in this context, as in others, a border-line case: the usual convention in relation to a minister's jurisdiction over a State-sponsored body which is related to his department is that the minister is responsible only for policy, so that it remains independent so far as its day-to-day running is concerned. Thus questions may not usually be addressed in regard to such day-to-day matters. However, this rule is not applied rigorously in relation to all the State-sponsored bodies and commissions. Thus, for instance, for whatever reason of party advantage or desire to inform the public, the Minister for Agriculture usually announces, in reply to a question, the number of acres of sugar beet which Comhlucht Siúicre Éireann intends to buy in the following year.

There are also rules which are designed to prevent duplication and possible conflict. Questions may not be asked on the interpretation of the law lest there be a conflict between the minister's view and that of a court. Questions are not allowed which call for a change in the law, since such a question would be tantamount to a debate on a bill outside the proper procedural forms. Moreover, a question may not be put on the same subject as a motion or bill which is to be discussed within a reasonable time nor go over ground already covered by a bill or motion within the previous six months (assuming, in each case, that there has been no change in circumstances). Again, a question will be disallowed if it proposes a change which would require some public expenditure which could not be accommodated within the scope of some existing estimate. However, there is no rule, as there is at Westminster, that a TD may not ask for information which is readily available from some published source.

Finally, questions should be brief and not amount to a short speech. Whilst they may propose an alternative policy to the minister's, they may not contain argument supporting that policy or damning the minister's policy. A question must not be frivolous. (A question as to the size of the Irish rat population has been disallowed.) It must not contain personal imputation or be designed solely to cause embarrassment, as by raking up some spectacular departmental failure which bears no contemporary significance.[126] Questions which seek the minister's opinion on some hypothetical matter are disallowed. So, too, are questions which seek to expose or create disagreements between minsters since these would threaten the doctrine of collective responsibility by which ministers speak with one voice in public.[127] And questions concerning the internal affairs of Government — for instance the existence of Cabinet committees — have been turned away because they would violate Cabinet confidentiality.

Procedure Normally, a question must be submitted in writing to the Clerk not later than 11 a.m. on the third day (not counting a Saturday, Sunday or public holiday) preceeding the day on which they are to be asked.[128] To cater for more urgent matters and to avoid a delay which might otherwise be of several weeks' duration, the device of the 'private notice questions' has been created by which 'matters of urgent public importance may, by permission of the Ceann Comhairle, be asked on private notice.'[129] It is the practice to give notice of such questions, both to the Chair and the minister concerned, before the sitting commences.

Normally, one hour — commencing at 3 p.m. on Tuesdays and Wednesdays and at 2.30 p.m. on Thursdays — is devoted to questions each day. Some 150-200 questions are usually answered each week, not including any supplementary questions. In order to save time, a question is not read out in the chamber.[130] Instead the deputy rises and states the number of the question on the order paper.[131] A written answer may be given in the Official Report of the Debates if the deputy so desires or if the minister so requests because the question requires a lengthy reply or a reply in the form of a table.[132]

Questions are taken in the order of seniority of the minister to whom they are addressed. If, for instance, at the end of the Wednesday's Question Time, the Minister for Happiness is answering, he will complete his answers at the start of Thursday's Question Time and then the minister next in order of seniority will reply to his questions. The sequence continues until all members of the Government have replied, when the cycle starts again. The only exception are the questions to the Taoiseach which are always taken first on a Tuesday and Wednesday.[133]

There is no express rule compelling a minister to answer a question. If a reply is refused, the disappointed deputy may raise the matter in an adjournment debate. The real sanction, of course, would be a motion of no confidence in the minister. However, there is probably a custom that such a motion should not be brought in this situation. Moreover, if there was a vote, the result would be a foregone conclusion. Nevertheless, the fact is that, for whatever reason of habit or convention, minsters usually do answer and that, if they do refuse, they usually offer a reason based on a limited number of well-established grounds, for instance the danger to security, reluctance to embarrass some private person or, more widely, that an answer would not be in the 'public interest.' Where the Ceann Comhairle is in doubt as to whether a question falls within a minister's bailiwick — for instance because it seems close to the line marking off the day-to-day running of a State-sponsored body — then his practice is to consult the minister and accept his judgment on the point.

Appraisal In spite of the number of questions put down, many of the questions (whose estimated average cost is £70-£80)[134] could be answered by a simply phone call to the relevant department.[135] The objective of a question is not usualy to inform the questioner, as can be seen from the fact that so few questions emanate from the Government side. Rather it may be: to discomfit the Government; to promote the questioner's policy; to probe some act of alleged maladministration (though the extent to which the random incidence of questions acts as an effective, general discipline on the civil service may be questioned);[136] if it is an 'inspired' question from a friend of the Government, to enable a minister to publicise some policy or achievement of which he is proud; or to demonstrate to the deputy's constituents that he is straining every sinew on their behalf. Each of these purposes relies upon the fact that this is the most exciting, the best attended and the best publicised hour in the parliamentary day. It is held at a time when it is likely to receive maximum coverage on radio and television and in newspapers, and it retains this position even on the days of the week when business commences in the morning. It is, noticeably, the only part of the Dáil's business for which the press gallery and the chamber are crowded.

It seems that question time is peculiarly afflicted by the malady which affects the Dáil generally, that is the time which is spent on constituents' personal minutiae, to the detriment of discussion of policy issues. (A half of all questions to the Minister for the Environment deal with individual constituent's problems; more than half in the case of the Minister for Social Welfare.)[137] One remedy which has been suggested[138] would be what might be called the 'Devlinisation' of question time. This would involve hiving off questions of exclusively individual or local interest to be answered by officials from the relevant department, in public, in a committee room in Leinster House. The Minister would then be left to answer, at greater length than at present, the more political questions.

9.6 CHAIRMAN AND ADMINISTRATION[139]

Chairman   Clearly it is essential that the Chairman — the Ceann Comhairle in the Dáil and the Cathaoirleach in the Senate — should both be, and be seen to be, neutral beteen the contending parties in the House. The difficulty in achieving this goal arises from the fact that the Chairman himself will usually have been elected to the House as a candidate of one political party. Certain rules exist which are designed to contribute to the success of the metamorphosis from partisan to neutral. First, whilst the Chairman must be a member of the House, he may not be a minister or a minister of state,[140] though he may be a former minister. Secondly, subject to certain exceptions,[141] his period of office is the term of the House existing at the time of appointment, and he may be removed only by special resolution (of which, in the case of the Cathaoirleach, seven clear days' notice has been given).[142] In each House, removal must be by way of a substantive motion dealing exclusively and explicitly with the Chairman. No such motion has ever been successful. The same person may be re-elected as Chairman for any number of reasons. Indeed in the case of the Dáil only, the outgoing Ceann Comhairle is deemed to be re-elected to the new House without an actual election.[143] The object of this rule, it was said when it was introduced in 1927, is to free the Ceann Comhairle from having to fight a re-election campaign, at which he would be at a disadvantage by virtue of having been out of active politics for a period of years and, secondly, after the election, to provide an experienced candidate for the office who has not recently undergone a partisan re-election campaign.[144] Up until 1973, there had been only four incumbents[145] of the office of Ceann Comhairle since Independence. However, since 1973, each incoming Government has nominated one of its own supporters, (save that in 1981 and March 1982, the exigencies arising from the Government's narrow majority forced the election of an Independent. There has been no discernible pattern regarding the party of the Leas-Cheann Comhairle. Since 1937, the Government party has always had its own nominee elected Cathaoirleach, with the Leas-Cathaoirleach coming from the Opposition parties, save during 1973-77, when the Fine Gael and Labour Parties took both posts.

One incident of the Chair's neutrality is that he may neither make a speech nor cast a deliberative vote. However in the event of a tie, he has the casting vote.[146] Various guidelines have been adopted by chairmen to enable them to exercise the casting vote without having to rely upon their own view of the merits of the issue. If possible, they should vote in such a way as to ensure that the House will have an opportunity later to review the decision, as for example by voting for an amendment to a bill at third (committee) stage in order to give the House a further opportunity to consider the amendment at fourth (report) stage.[147]

The Chairman also votes so as to preserve the *status quo*, for instance, by voting against a motion of no confidence in the Government (as in 1927).[148] In addition, he votes against motions involving the expenditure of public funds.[149] Sometimes, neither of these guidelines will meet the occasion and the Chairman has to decide for himself. Thus, for instance, in 1981, the Ceann Comhairle voted for an Opposition TD, as Leas-Cheann Comhairle, on the ground that he had, himself, been nominated by the Government.[150] It is customary, when the Chairman exercises his casting vote, for him to state the reasons for his choice.

The Chairman has the responsibility of maintaining orderly behaviour, and if necessary, of imposing the punishments envisaged by the Constitution (Art. 15.10) and provided for by standing orders. He must 'order a member whose conduct is grossly disorderly to withdraw immediately from the [House] for the remainder of that day's sitting.'[151] Alternatively, with a more serious breach, the Chairman may 'name [the] member for misconduct' and then the House immediately votes upon the motion 'that . . . (*naming the member*) be suspended from the service of the House.' If the motion is passed, then the sentence is fixed according to whether the member has any previous 'convictions' in the same session. In the case of a first offence, the member is suspended until the fourth sitting day reckoning the day on which he is suspended as the first day, unless he earlier makes a written apology to the Chair.[152] Each of the two sanctions is peremptory so that the member being punished has no opportunity 'to put his case'[153] before he must 'forthwith withdraw from the precincts of the [House].'[154] Whilst the member may neither speak nor vote in the chamber, he does retain the right to serve on a select committee[155] and to draw his salary.

The power of naming a member for misconduct so that he is suspended (though not the power of ordering a member to withdraw) is regarded as so grave that it may only be exercised by the Chairman himself.[156] Normally, the Chairman and his deputy take turns in chairing the proceedings in each House, alternating after each hour. However, if the deputy is in the chair when the disorder occurs, the proceedings have had to be adjourned until the Chairman can be called to the chamber.

In the case of 'great disorder,' the Chairman or deputy chairman may either himself adjourn the House without putting the question to the House or suspend the sitting for a specified time.[157]

The Clerk and his staff The Houses are assisted in their work by the staff of the Houses of the Oireachtas, who include about thirty clerks plus ancillary staff. At the head of the staff, in each House, are the Clerk and his deputy, the Clerk-Assistant. In addition, there is the Captain of the Guard, who is in charge of the ushers and is responsible for maintaining order, including the eviction (on the instructions of the Chairman) of recalcitrant members. Above the Captain is the Superintendent, Houses of the Oireachtas, who deals generally with security and with the upkeep of the Leinster House premises. These six — the Clerk and Clerk-Assistant of each House, Captain of the Guard and Superintendent — are classified as 'officers of the Houses of the Oireachtas.' The rest of the staff comprise the 'joint staff of the Houses of the Oireachtas.' Unlike the officers, their functions are not defined by statute and they can be allocated to any duty in either House. One member of the joint staff is allocated to the non-statutory post of Clerk Administrator which deals with non-operational matters like personnel, translation and inter-parliamentary liaison.

All members of staff are civil servants of the state rather than of the Government.[158] Their employment régime is determined by the Staff of the Houses of the Oireachtas Act, 1959, which, broadly speaking, imports the Civil Service Commissioners Act, 1956 and the Civil Service Regulation Act, 1956, but makes certain adaptations to reflect the special status of the Oireachtas and the special position of the officers.

The standing orders of each House provide, identically, that: '[T]he Clerk shall have the direction of and control over all the officers and joint staff, subject to such orders as he may, from time to time, receive from the [Chairman] of the [House].'[159] Since this provision is found in the standing orders of each House, it leaves open the possibility of a disagreement in an area which impinges on both Houses and for the resolution of which no machinery is explicitly provided. An episode of this nature arose in 1934 when each House had different parties in the majority. The Cathaoirleach gave an order to the Superintendent to admit to Leinster House two visitors wearing blue uniforms. The Clerk of the Dáil instructed the Superintendent not to allow in any blueshirts, even if they had cards of admission to the Senate.[160] This dispute was not resolved. However if a similar event were to arise today, it might be resolved in the Dáil's favour on the ground that the 1959 Act appears to make the Ceann Comhairle head of the Oireachtas Staff including the Superintendent.[161]

In many areas, the Clerk bears the same relation to the Chairman of the House as does a secretary of a department to the minister and many functions which are formally vested in the Chair are largely the responsibility of the Clerk of each House. In the chamber, the Clerk or Clerk-Assistant sits near the Chair to advise him; the order paper is drawn up by, or on the instruction of, the Clerk. In addition certain functions are vested (usually by standing orders) specifically in the Clerk or, in his absence, in the Clerk-Assistant.[162] In the first place, he has various functions in regard to elections and bye-elections: as will be explained later, the Clerk of the Senate is *ex-officio* returning officer for the general election or a bye-election to the panel-seats, whilst the Clerk of the Dáil issues and receives writs for general or bye-elections.[163] In each House, the Clerk keeps the Roll of Members which each member must sign in his presence before taking his seat. To qualify for allowances etc., as from the date of election or nomination, the Roll must be signed within thirty days after the member was elected or nominated.[164] At a meeting of the new Dáil or Senate, the Clerk reads out a list of the members and acts as chairman until the Chairman is elected.[165] However, the bulk of the work of the Clerk and his staff arises from the fact that they perform all the administrative and clerical duties arising from the business of the Houses and their committees.[166]

Minutes and Journal According to Standing Orders:

All proceedings of the [House], or of the Committee of the whole [House], shall be noted by the Clerk, and the minutes of proceedings after being perused and signed by the [Chair] shall be printed and shall constitute the *Journal of the Proceedings of the* [House].[167]

As well as times of sitting, business transacted, and documents laid before the House, certain other matters, for example an expression of regret received from a member who had been suspended,[168] must also be recorded in the Journal (which is often referred to by its Irish title, *Imeachtaí*). The Journal constitutes the official record which is accepted in all courts as *prima facie* evidence of what has been done in that House.[169] Whereas the Journals provide a record of the decisions, the Official Reports of Parliamentary Debates (usually known as the *Dáil Debates* or *Seanad Debates*) constitute a *verbatim* record of what is said in the chamber. (The transactions of select or special committees are published separately.) Speeches made in the House (as recorded in the Official Reports) have recently been accepted as good evidence of that elusive quality, 'the intention of the legislature', which has to be discerned when a court is interpreting a doubtful point in an act of Parliament.[170]

10

Parliamentary Privilege

10.1 GENERAL

The best starting point for a description of parliamentary privilege[1] is Erskine May's definition of it as 'the sum of the peculiar rights enjoyed by each House collectively . . . and by members of each House individually, without which they could not discharge their functions, and which exceed those possessed by other bodies or individuals.'[2] This definition draws attention to the chief feature of parliamentary privilege — that it consists of exceptional rights, some bestowed upon individuals and some upon the Houses as entities, so as to enable them to discharge their functions more effectively.

But more detailed analogies with British parliamentary privilege would be and, sometimes have been, misleading. Westminster's privileges still bear the mark of the historical times in which they developed. They are the product of six centuries of precedents in Parliament and the courts. One structural peculiarity arises because of the evolution of the Westminster Parliament from an amphibious body, the *Curia Regis*, which acted not only as a parliament, but also as a court. Thus the British Parliament claims the right — which is disputed by the courts — to determine the extent of its own privileges, even where a point of parliamentary privilege arises in court. Its privileges also include the power to regulate its own composition.[3] The Oireachtas does not possess either of these privileges. Rather, in Ireland, parliamentary privilege is relatively undeveloped, comprising, almost exclusively, rights of a functional nature which are bestowed by the Constitution. Whilst there is little authority on the point, my view is that privileges whose source is pre-Independence common law or statute no longer exist in Ireland, even if they were in force before Independence. The reason for this submission is that pre-Independence law 'came over' only so far as it was not inconsistent with the 1922 Constitution and, now, the 1937 Constitution.[4] Parliamentary privilege is covered in three special sections of the Constitution (in Art. 15). These sections strike a balance between the need for free speech and conflicting claims, such as the citizen's right to his good name (in Art. 40.3.2°). Furthermore Art. 34.3.1° grants the High Court 'full original jurisdiction in all matter [of] law or fact' by contrast with which the various aspects of British parliamentary privilege vest exclusive jurisdiction in certain matters in the Houses of Parliament. It is unlikely that it was intended that the balanced arrangements which were deliberately established in the Constitution could be disturbed by the eccentric relics of British constitutional history, whether these are expressed through the common law or statute.[5] Moreover, the most important of these possible pre-Independence sources of privilege — the Bill of Rights, 1688 — was probably not part of even pre-Independence Irish law.[6]

In Ireland, parliamentary privilege has been considered in only about a dozen cases in the Houses of the Oireachtas (almost exclusively in the Dáil) and in one major case before the courts, in *In re Haughey*.[7] Little has emerged from these cases which is of help in interpreting the extent of the privileges so that what is said in this Chapter is, in places, rather speculative.

In the context of both the constitutional setting of Irish parliamentary privilege and its relatively limited nature, the *Haughey* case is instructive, even though it is possible that the substantive issue involved — the power of sub-poena — will soon be regulated by statute (as will be explained in Section 3 of this Chapter). The case arose from the investigation into the improper use of Government funds to purchase arms for the defence of the Northern minority in 1970 (the so-called 'Arms Crisis'). The medium chosen for the investigation was the Dáil Public Accounts Committee, which at its first meeting discussed the difficulties arising from, first, doubt as to whether parliamentary privilege against defamation extended to the Committee's activities and, secondly, the absence of any power to sub-poena witnesses. An interim report to the Dáil[8] requested the passage of legislation to meet both difficulties in regard to the investigation before it. The response took the form of the Committee of Public Accounts of Dáil Éireann (Privilege and Procedure) Act, 1970.[9] This Act extended privilege to the utterances of both members and witnesses.[10] In addition, by s. 3(4) of the Act:

If any person—

(b) being in attendance as a witness before the committee refuses . . . to answer any question to which the committee may legally require an answer . . . the committee may certify the offence of that person under the hand of the chairman of the committee to the High Court and the High Court may, after such inquiry as it thinks proper to make, punish or take steps for the punishment of that person in like manner as if he had been guilty of contempt of the High Court.

Under this procedure, H. was convicted in the High Court, but this conviction was reversed in the Supreme Court. The important point, for present purposes, is Chief Justice Ó Dálaigh's finding that any provision which authorised a Committee of a House to convict a recalcitrant witness would fall foul of Art. 34.1 in that it would constitute an administration of justice by a body which was not a court of law.[11] In the light of this finding, the Chief Justice considered that, in the case of the particular provision before him, he could apply the presumption of constitutionality so as to hold that the Committee was not itself convicting a reluctant witness and handing him over to the High Court for punishment: it was, rather, taking a step which was only a preliminary to a High Court trial. Nevertheless, the provision was still held to be unconstitutional principally because it entailed the trial of a non-minor offence without a jury and because the accused was not allowed an opportunity to cross-examine the witnesses against him. This decision deprived the Committee of any effective sanction if a witness refused to attend, to produce documents or to answer questions. The Committee rejected a proposal to seek amendment of the Act so as to grant to the Committee the power of certification to the Courts in respect of a recalcitrant witness.[12] As a result, a number of key witnesses were not examined and the evidence heard by the Committee was incomplete.

(Legislation which the Government was contemplating in mid-1984, in the context of a select committee investigation into the affairs of Údarás na Gaeltachta, would make it an offence triable before the courts in the ordinary way for a witness to refuse to appear before a committee, or to answer its questions, provided that the House constituting the committee had passed the necessary resolution. However, there is a school of thought which holds that the grant of such powers to committees made up of partisan politicians is undesirable.)

In re Haughey is authority for the proposition that, in addition to the Dáil's different historical origin from the House of Commons, there is a positive bar in Art. 34.1 of the Constitution, which prevents legislation from being enacted to grant a House of the Oireachtas the power to sub-poena witnesses and itself to try and punish witnesss who fail to attend.[13]

10.2 FREEDOM OF SPEECH

The essential condition of an effective parliament is that its members should have untrammelled power to speak their minds on any matter of public concern. Thus the most important of the privileges of the Oireachtas and the one which has received most attention is the privilege of free speech. The Constitution takes three provisions to deal with it — Art. 15.10, 15.12, and 15.13.[14] Art. 15.13 reads as follows:

The members of each House of the Oireachtas . . . shall not, in respect of any utterance in either House be amenable to any court or any authority other than the House itself.

Evidently this provision affords to members of either House complete protection against civil proceedings (most obviously, defamation)[15] or criminal prosecution (for example, under the Offical Secrets Act, 1963) or the control of any other authority external to the House (for example, discipline by any professional body to which a member might belong). However, the provision leaves it open to each House itself to discipline its members for (say) the use of unparliamentary expressions.

Some questions involving Art. 15.13 were raised, though not finally answered, in a recent Tribunal of Inquiry[16] which was set up under the pre-Independence Tribunals of Inquiry Act 1921 to investigate allegations made in the Dáil, by two deputies, against the then Minister for Local Government, concerning planning appeal decisions.

At the Tribunal of Inquiry, the deputies took two points founded upon Art. 15.13. The first of their submissions was that the Tribunal could not subpoena them to give evidence before it. The Tribunal found that the deputies' evidence was not necessary to its investigation and so explicitly refrained from ruling on this point.

The deputies' second submission was that the Tribunal was not competent to examine the allegations because it was 'an authority other than the House itself' which was purporting to investigate an 'utterance in a House.'

The Tribunal assumed, without argument,[17] that Art. 15.13 was relevant but then went on to hold that, in this particular case, the privilege was excluded. The more cogent of the two reasons given for this was that, under the 1921 Act, a tribunal of inquiry can only be set up following the passage of a resolution authorising its establishment by each House and this procedure had been followed in the instant case. Thus the tribunal was not 'an intrusion into the affairs of parliament [but rather] the instrument chosen by parliament itself to make the inquiry.'[18]

The second constitutional provision which is relevant to the privilege of freedom of speech is Art. 15.12:

All official reports and publications of the Oireachtas or of either House thereof and utterances made in either House whenever published shall be privileged.

This Section states that certain matters, the identity of which will be considered in the next paragraph, 'shall be privileged.' This phrase is usually used in the context of defamation, and this suggests that the protection given by Art. 15.12, in contrast to that afforded by Art. 15.13, is confined to defamation proceedings. This means that a printer who published the report of a speech which broke the Official Secrets Act, 1963 could be prosecuted, whilst, as a result of Art. 15.13, the member who made the speech would be free. It seems likely that the privilege bestowed by the section is absolute, rather than qualified, because it is not stated to be qualified and, more important, because of the wording of the Irish text ('táid saor ar chúrsaí dlí').

The first part of the section states that its protection extends to 'all official reports and publications of the Oireachtas.' Evidently, this means reports or other publications, published in accordance with the order of a House, for instance the report of a select committee.[19] It would probably, however, not cover annual reports of non-parliamentary bodies, such as departments of state or State-sponsored bodies, which are laid before each House. So much is clear. What is opaque is the phrase 'utterances[20] made in either House wherever published.' This appears to mean publication which is distinct from the utterance, in other words, an utterance in either House followed by a later publication, which will usually (but not necessarily) be in a newspaper or a radio or television broadcast. Read literally, it could be said that the section bestows privileges only on the utterance itself and not on the later publication. But members make most of the utterances and they are already protected by Art. 15.13. And, considering that the first part of Art. 15.12 ('official reports and publications') is plainly designed to protect publications and that the first and second parts of the section are linked by the phrase 'wherever published,' it seems likely that the purpose of the entire section is to protect publication. Thus the publication of utterances made in either House is probably privileged.[21] Presumably the publication does not have to be *verbatim*: any fair and accurate report would suffice, but not a selective account.[22]

A further difficulty in regard to the scope of Art. 15.12 concerns a case in which the defendant (the speaker making the utterance) is not a member of the House. One example would be a case in which the utterance were made by a witness before a select committee.[23] Assuming that the protection given by the Constitution extends to committees (a point which will be agitated in the next paragraph), it is possible that, in such a case, the section would be interpreted to protect the speaker, since, as already mentioned in the last paragraph, on a literal reading of the section, the utterance would be privileged. Any other interpretation would have the unfair result that the publisher would be absolutely privileged whilst the speaker would be responsible for all the damages to the plaintiff resulting from mass publication. However as against this, it might be argued that Art. 15.13 is exclusively concerned with publication as distinct from utterance.

The next point which requires attention is the extent to which the proceedings of a committee can be regarded as coming within the protection conferred by Art. 15.12 and 13. So far as members of the Houses of the Oireachtas are concerned, all doubts have been set at rest by s. 2 of the Committees of the Houses of the Oireachtas (Privilege and Procedure) Act, 1976 by which protection, in the same terms as Art. 15.13, is extended to the utterances of members, advisers, officials and agents of the committee. The same section also extends privilege to the documents of a committee and all official resports and publications of a committee. But the Act does not extend to witnesses.[24] However, the better view is probably that since a committee is set up by, and composed of, members of a House in order to assist the House, the committee may be regarded as the *alter ego* of a House and thus the House's constitutional privilege also avails the committee.[25] Hence Art. 15.12 would afford protection in respect of both the publication of what a witness says and (assuming that the submission made in the last paragraph is correct) the actual utterance itself.

(However, it is possible that most of the difficulties canvassed in the last few paragraphs will soon be settled. Inspired by the need to facilitate a select committee investigation into the affairs of Údarás na Gaeltachta, the Government was, in mid-1984, contemplating the introduction of legislation which would extend qualified privilege to witnesses before all select committees and to reports of what they say.[26] In addition, where a specified resolution had been passed by the House constituting the committee, then the privilege would be absolute.)

The protection afforded by Arts. 15.12 and 13 is confined to utterances which are made 'in either House.' The type of doubt which this phrase creates may be illustrated by reference to the British *Strauss* case[27] in which a third party claimed to have been libelled in a letter written on constituency business by an MP to a minister. The British House of Commons decided, on a free vote (by a margin of only 218 to 213), that this letter did not fall within the category of 'proceedings in parliament', which is the phrase used in the British Bill of Rights, 1688. Almost certainly an Irish court would also reach this result by giving 'in either House' a narrow construction. The reason for this submission is that Art. 15.13 uses the phrase 'the precincts of either House' when it intends to refer to the House as a physical place. This suggests that, by contrast, 'in either House' is intended to be confined to utterances made during formal Oireachtas proceedings.

Apart from any question of parliamentary privilege, statements made during the course of a member's official business, even outside the house, probably enjoy qualified privilege as being made during the performance of a duty. Thus in a British case[28] a letter written by a constituent to his MP alleging dishonesty against a policeman was held to be protected by qualified privilege, even though the action was brought against the constituent. It is likely that the same result would obtain in Ireland, and there is authority[29] for saying that qualified privilege protects members of the Oireachtas, MEPs or councillors making public statements on matters of concern to their constituents.

The third section of the Constitution which bears on freedom of speech is Art. 15.10 which provides that each House 'shall have power to ensure freedom of debate.' In contrast to the other sections, this provision does not deal with a privilege of exclusion from the courts' jurisdiction but rather with the Oireachtas' (limited) positive powers of enforcement, which are dealt with in the next section. The word 'debate' probably embraces, but is wider than, freedom of speech, in that it might also include the right of a minority to have a fair chance to put its case: if it does bear such an interpretation then this could have an impact on the content of standing orders.[30]

10.3 ART. 15.10

The privilege of free speech will usually be invoked in the context of a court case, but, of their nature, the privileges created by Art. 15.10 will be implemented (so far as they can be implemented: see below) principally by the House itself, as distinct, be it noted, from the Oireachtas acting, as a whole, by way of statute. Art. 15.10 provides as follows:

Each House shall make its own rules and standing orders, with power to attach penalties for their infringement, / and shall have power to ensure freedom of debate, to protect its official documents and the private papers of its members, and to protect itself and its members against any person or persons interfering with, molesting or attempting to corrupt its members in the exercise of their duties. [For descriptive purposes, this section has been divided into two parts, 'the first part' and 'the second part,' by the stroke which I have inserted].

As the All-Party Report of the Committee on the Constitution observes mildly: 'The wording of this provision presents some difficulties.'[31] It is important, in analysing the provision, to notice the distinctions between the first and second parts. The first part uses the phrase 'its own rules and standing orders' and so seems to be directed at rules controlling a House's own internal procedure, as opposed to matters of privilege which protect the House from interference with its deliberations, whether by either outsiders or members. It is the second part which covers matters of privilege and which, in contrast to the first part of the section, does not bestow any power 'to attach penalties.' This suggests that the Houses of the Oireachtas have not been given the capacity to punish those who breach their privileges. This negative result immediately leads to the question (to which no completely satisfactory answer is offered here) of what practical application is to be given to 'the power', presumably exercisable by resolution of the House, bestowed by the second part of the section, 'to ensure freedom of debate' etc. It has been suggested that, if it wished to punish someone, a House might apply some 'indirect sanction', for example, in the case of a newspaper, by excluding its representatives from the Oireachtas Press Gallery.[32] If justification were required for this discrimination, it might be found in 'the power' to protect against interference. Again 'the power' might be applied in a case in which an usher had to use force to expel a protestor who was attempting to shout down a debate. The power could then be used to provide a defence to a civil claim or criminal prosecution arising out of the usher's action.

Amidst all the uncertainty and lacunae, what does seem definite is that the present situation is unsatisfactory, if only because Art. 15.10 seems to create privileges with no effective sanctions to enforce them. The All-Party Report recommended,[32] very reasonably, that, as with certain foreign parliaments, legislation should be enacted making certain types of interference with Parliament an offence which would be prosecuted before the ordinary courts.[33]

Protection of documents We have dealt, rather tentatively, with the type of power created by Art. 15.10. The other question is the type of privileges which this power may be used to protect. The first of these is the freedom of debate, already mentioned briefly at the end of section 2. Secondly, each House has the power to 'protect its official documents and the private papers of its members . . .'. This would probably enable the Oireachtas to resist the normal police powers of search or a court order in respect of documents and papers. This privilege came before the Committee on Procedure and Privileges in a case[34] in which a report of the Select Commitee on Judicial Salaries, Expenses Allowances and Pensions was published in the British newspaper, the *Sunday Express*. At that time, select committees sat in private and their reports were published only after an order of the House. This newspaper report was published before any order was made. In this case, the editor of the paper apologised and the apology was accepted, so relieving the Committee of the difficulty of deciding what action to recommend where the culprit was outside the Republic.

Freedom from 'interference' etc. The remaining part of the section bestows:

... the power ... to protect [each House] and its members against any person or persons interfering with, molesting or attempting to corrupt its members in the exercise of their duties.

'Corruption'[35] is clear enough, and 'molestation' presumably refers to physical interference with a member (or his transport to the House) or the threat thereof. Phone tapping would fall either within 'molestation' or the wider term 'interference.' In connection with interference, it is useful to mention the distinction, drawn in Britain, between breaches of well-established, named 'privileges' and, on the other hand, 'contempts' which refer to a wide category of acts which offend against the authority and dignity of the House and for which the House may, in its discretion, punish the offender. It seems likely that the sort of incidents classified as contempts in Britain should be put under the umbrella heading of 'interference.' Sometimes, however, even in Ireland, the label 'contempt' has been used in the same sense as in Britain, in spite of the fact that the Irish Houses have never been courts. Whatever the nomenclature, cases in which the Houses' jurisdiction to protect against interference has been invoked have been few and have usually fallen into the categories of: violence in the precincts of the House;[36] casting aspirations on the personal honour of a member;[37] criticisms of a House.[38] It is at least qestionable whether this last should be regarded as capable of being an interference with an assembly of well-tempered men of affairs used to public controversy. As a contempt in the Westminster Parliament, it is an inheritance from earlier centuries in Britain when the limits on free speech were narrower than in contemporary Ireland. Its existence would probably be a violation of the constitutional freedom of speech (Art. 40.6.1°.i) and would certainly breach the rule of the wider, unwritten constitution that a reasonable quantum of free speech is essential in a functioning democracy.

There is another act which is often stigmatised as a breach of privilege and which, if it exists as such, must be located under the head of an offence against the authority and dignity of the House. It consists of the publication of the text of a bill outside the Oireachtas before the first stage, at which the House orders it to be printed and circulated to members. Because of the supposed rule banning such publication, when the Minister for Justice showed the Fine Gael version of the (pro-life) Eighth Amendment of the Constitution Bill, 1983 to the Hierarchy of Bishops, he showed only 'words and phrases' rather than the entire text.[39] Again, when the Department of the Public Service honours its obligation under the Conciliation and Arbitration Scheme, to consult the civil service unions about legislation affecting their members, it does so *after* the bill has been initiated.

Finally, in the present context, it is relevant to note that by Art 15.13 members are 'privileged from arrest in going to and coming from, and while within the precincts of, either House.' In bygone centuries, this privilege was of some importance because the King was prepared to use imprisonment as a weapon in his duel with the Commons. But by today, this freedom of arrest is of slight importance, especially since it applies only to misdemeanours, most of which, anyway, are initiated by summons rather than arrest.

10.4 PROCEDURE IN THE DÁIL

Where the Dáil (the Senate has seldom exercised its privileges) is enforcing its privileges, the first stage is usually[40] that a member refers the matter to the Ceann Comhairle. He considers, in the light of any precedents, whether there is a *prima facie* breach and, if so, an order is made referring the matter to the Committee on Procedure and Privileges.[41]

As indicated already, the rules regarding privileges are frequently unclear and precedents are scanty. No tradition of non-partisan voting in privilege cases has developed and divisions are usually along party lines. A report is prepared which concludes with a recommendation as to whether a breach has occurred and, if so, what course of action should be followed.

A motion is then put down on the order paper ordering that the report be printed and adopting its recommendations. This motion is often passed formally, by the Dáil, without a debate or division, partly because members may consider that sufficient time has already been spent on the matter and partly because they may be reluctant to bruit it forth to the public that members enjoy 'privileges.'

Where an apology to the House by a member is recommended, this is usually tendered to the Chair at the commencement of public business. Thus far, when a House has commanded an offender to apologise, he has always done so and, consequently, there has been no need for the House to explore the thorny question (briefly raised *supra*) of how it should exercise the power of enforcement created by Art. 15.10, in the case of an unrepentant offender.

10.5 APPRAISAL

It is difficult to escape the feeling that the scale of Irish parliamentary privilege is the product of a semi-conscious hankering after the Westminster model. The result is that the law contains several defects of which the worst is the unclearness of all three constitutional sections. This makes them something of a blunderbuss — as likely to embarrass the legislature as to protect it.

Two comparisons seem apt. First, there is a strange contrast between the care taken to remove certain types of threat to free debate and the more real and effective constraints which remain to limit what members say in public. These constraints include: party discipline; the need to maintain popularity with the electorate; the fear of crossing the Church; and the exclusionary rule of debate in the House. These factors may be no reason for making matters worse by sweeping parliamentary privilege away; but they do set its value in perspective. Secondly, consider the other public bodies whose unfettered discourse is necessary to the good of the polity: apart from the Senate and the Dáil, there is the cabinet; the courts; and local councils. The courts, certainly, and the cabinet, probably, enjoy absolute privilege, at common law, for their deliberations.[42] But only one organ, the Oireachtas, is singled out to be given its own peculiar, Constitutional régime. Would it not be more appropriate and more useful (because of the common case law which would be produced) to have a single law creating a common set of privileges for all public bodies which warrant these special protections from the general law?

11

Dáil and Senate Elections

As befits a matter of capital importance in a parliamentary democracy, the principles regarding election to the Dáil are laid down in the Constitution. The chief organic law is the Electoral Act, 1963[2] which was based upon the recommendations of a Joint Oireachtas Select Committee set up to suggest amendments in electoral law.[3] (In addition to Dáil elections, the 1963 Act also deals with Presidential elections, referenda and local elections.) The 1963 Act repealed many older statutes, but one has still to go to the Electoral Act, 1923 for parts of many procedures, which inconveniently straddle the two Acts, and to specialised acts like the much amended Prevention of Electoral Abuses Act, 1923 for electoral offences. Constituency boundaries are frequently amended by an Electoral (Amendment) Act. For the rules regulating election petitions which are heard by two High Court judges, one has to quarry the British legislation of the nineteenth century.[4] In truth, the sources of electoral law are something of a jungle with the Department of the Environment, which is responsible for elections, promoting legislation on the subject, almost every year. However, since much of the procedural detail is contained in schedules to the Acts, there are only four major statutory instruments, dealing with election forms,[5] registration of electors,[6] polling schemes[7] and free postage,[8] respectively.

As a matter of history, it is worth noticing that the Irish proportional representation system was first established by the (British) Government of Ireland Act of 1920 which had such a brief career in 'Southern Ireland.'[9] This feature of the Act had the support of Arthur Griffith and the other leaders of Sinn Féin.

11.2 'ONE MAN, ONE VALUE'

Art. 16.2.2° of the Constitution provides that the total number of Dáil deputies shall be fixed by law, but must be such that there is at least one member for each thirty thousand of the population and not more than one member for each twenty thousand of the population.[10]

Since democracy means not merely that each person has the same number of votes but that each vote carries the same weight, the key provision in this area is Art. 16.2.3°, which enshrines the principle of one vote one value as follows:

s110 The ratio between the number of members to be elected at any time for each constituency and the population of each constituency, as ascertained at the last preceding census, shall, so far as is practicable, be *the same throughout the country* [my italics].

As a preliminary, it should be noted that in each of these constitutional provisions, it is the 'population' and not the electors in a constituency which is the key factor. This is a significant distinction since, for example, at the time of the 1977 general election, the number of inhabitants per deputy varied between 19,149 and 21,119, throughout the country, whereas the number of electors varied from 11,950 to 18,315. Again, the percentage of the population which may vote varied from 61% in one constituency to 90% in another. The idea that the population ought to be taken as a national figure derived by deduction from the number of voters on the electoral register has been rejected by the Supreme Court.[11] Thus the Constitutional rule seems to be based on the idea that a deputy represents all the people in the constituency and not only the voters.

Art. 16.2.3° was applied with considerable effect in *O'Donovan v. Attorney General*,[12] which has some claims to be regarded as the first judicial incursion into a highly-charged political area, indeed arguably into the most political area of all. The Electoral (Amendment) Act, 1959[13] was impugned for violating Art. 16.2.3° The plaintiff (who happened to be a Fine Gael senator) relied on the facts that certain of the rural constituencies where the Government party, Fianna Fáil, were strong had too many, and certain of the urban constituencies had too few, members per head of population, by comparison with the national average. The variations from the national average (= 100%) ranged from +14.9% in South Galway to −17.6% in Dublin South (West). (In contrast, in *R. v. Boundary Commission ex p. Foot*[14] the Court of Appeal held that, in English law, there was nothing to prevent divergencies as large as +26% or −44% from the national average.) The chief dispute is applying the provision was in regard to the factors to be taken into account in deciding what was 'practicable.' In defending the constitutionality of the Act, the Attorney General relied heavily on the fact that in a sparse constituency, like Galway South, a deputy would have to spend more time in servicing each constituent than would be the case in Dublin South (West) and hence a greater number of deputies would be required. Budd J rejected this argument because he found that 'the Constitution does not anywhere in the Articles relating to the functions of deputies recognise or sanction their intervention in administrative affairs',[15] a view which has been characterised as 'formalistic' and taking 'little account of the realities of Irish parliamentary life.'[16]

Because the twelve-year period within which a revision has to be made[17] had been exceeded, and because the 1961 election was looming, there was no appeal from the High Court decision in *O'Donovan*. Instead, a substitute law, the Electoral (Amendment) Bill, 1961 was enacted. Because of the fate of its predecessor, the President referred this bill to the Supreme Court under his Art. 26 power and its constitutionality was upheld.[18]

171

Although the High Court, in *O'Donovan* rejected the view that the Constitution required 'an all but mathematical parity of ratio,'[19] it did hold that the only factors which could be taken into account in deciding what was 'practicable' (in the language of Art. 16.2.3°) were those dictated by the administrative machinery necessary to hold an election. According to Budd J, 'an adjustment of constituency boundaries by the process of adding and shedding of district electoral divisions would enable a reasonably close approximation of ratio of deputies to population throughout the country to be obtained.'[20] Since district electoral divisions have a population of about one thousand, this was taken to mean that the permissible tolerance could only by a maximum of one thousand population per deputy (equivalent to about 5%) above or below the average throughout the country. In addition, the High Court held that a desire to follow county boundaries in drawing boundaries would not justify the breach of these limits.[21] The Electoral (Amendment) Acts of 1961, 1969 and 1974 all adhered to these limits, frequently at the cost of crossing county boundaries.[22]

In the case of the 1969 and 1974 Acts, this adherence is surprising, considering that in the 1961 Reference, the Supreme Court had differed from the High Court on these points. And in 1980, the Dáil Éireann Constituency Commission, chaired by Mr Justice Walsh, approved the Supreme Court judgment. The Commission's terms of reference included the injunction to take into account county boundaries and 'clearly-defined natural features' and to ensure that 'larger-seat constituencies should preferably be situated in areas of greater population density.' The Commission indicated that it considered these terms of reference constitutional. It also stated that 'there is no rigid tolerance level' and the constituencies which it recommended involved deviations in the member/population ratio ranging from 6.3% above to 6.4% below, the national average.[23]

As time passes, people die or move, thereby disturbing what was initially a uniform deputy/population ratio throughout the country. The Constitution meets this difficulty in two ways. First, Art. 16.2.4° provides that 'The Oireachtas shall revise the constituencies at least once in every twelve years with due regard to changes in distribution of the population . . .'. The subsidiary ground on which the plaintiff succeeded in *O'Donovan's* case was that the Electoral (Amendment) Act, 1959 disclosed a failure to pay due regard to these changes.[24] Secondly, Art. 16.2.3° (already quoted in full) probably imposes a potentially more stringent standard in that it provides that there must be uniformity throughout the country in 'The ratio between the number of members to be elected *at any time* for each constituency and the population of each constituency *as ascertained at the last preceding census* . . .'. This requirement is qualified by the words 'as far as practicable.' Successive Governments seem, however, to have accepted that there is an obligation to redraw constituencies within a short period of the publication of the results of a census.[25] For the last four Electoral (Amendment) Acts have been passed in the years shown, whilst censuses have been held on the dates shown in

172

square brackets: [1966]; 1969; [1971]; 1974; [1979]; 1980; [1981]; 1984. The date when a census is to be held is not fixed by the Constitution but by order made by the Minister for the Environment under the Statistics Act, 1926; thus the system could be subject to political abuse. There is, however, pressure from the EEC to hold censuses uniformly with other member states.

The Constituency Commission Art. 16.2.3° and 4° and the two court decisions interpreting these sub-sections have ensured that, since 1961, there has been a fairly uniform member/ population ratio throughout the country. The need for this uniformity makes more difficult, but does not altogether exclude, the possibility of drawing the boundaries of a constituency and/or fixing the number of deputies it returns, so as to give one party an unfair advantage. Art. 16.2.1° and 4° provide that the Oireachtas, itself, must revise the constituencies by way of an act of the Oireachtas. And up until 1980, there were frequent allegations that the Government was using its majority in the Oireachtas to design the constituencies so as to give it an advantage.[26]

In 1977 the Government set up the state's first constituency commission to draw up constituencies for the European Assembly elections held in 1979. Honouring an election commitment made in the 1977 election, the Government constituted a similar commission for the Dáil, the *Dáil Éireann Constituency Commission*.[27] Because of the constitutional requirement that the Oireachtas shall revise the constituencies, the Commission's status was only advisory. However, the Commission's recommendations were enacted without modification and the Electoral (Amendment) Bill, 1980 was passed with a great measure of agreement on all sides.[28] The Commission was an *ad hoc* body making recommendations for one revision only and set up informally by the Government, rather than by an act or Oireactas resolution. Nevertheless, similar commissions were set up in 1982[29] and next in 1983, and it seems likely that these precedents will be followed in the future. So far, the Commissions have been chaired by Mr Justice Walsh, a Supreme Court judge who was not a public supporter of any political party even before his elevation to the bench. The other two members were the Secretary of the Department of the Environment and the Clerk of the Dáil.

11.3 SINGLE TRANSFERABLE VOTE[30]

The alternatives The system of voting which is used for Dáil elections is proportional representation by means of the single transferable vote[31] in multi-seat constituencies. The merit which this system carries, by comparison with the list system[32] of proportional representation, is that it does not require such huge constituencies and so allows for a closer link between the members and their constituencies. However, even with a single transferable vote, the quality of proportionality between seats and votes tends to be weakened as constituencies become smaller, and it is for this reason that the

173

Constitution bars constituencies with fewer than three members.[33] One feature of the Irish electoral system is that, in the case of the two major parties, more than one candidate from the same party is put up and the voter is able to indicate which party candidate he prefers. Thus an element of the U.S. party-primary elections is built into the system. This is some counterweight against the fact that there is no legal control over the way in which a party chooses its candidates.

The chief merit which proportional representation systems of election share is that they come closer to ensuring that each vote weighs equally in the election of a member than does the straight vote system. Under the straight vote system used, for instance, in Britain, the candidate who tops the poll is the only one to be elected for that constituency and all the votes expended on the other candidates go for nought. One striking example of the straight vote system in operation was the British General Election of 1983 when the Liberal-SDP Alliance won 27% of the popular vote and fewer than 5% of the seats; by contrast the Irish Labour Party often wins approximately 10% of the vote and 10% of the seats. Supporters of the straight vote system turn this argument on its head by urging that it is just because the straight vote system is not precisely democratic, that the result is weighted in favour of the party which wins most votes, and the emergence of a Government formed by a single party and with a stable majority is encouraged. The outcomes of the 1981 and February, 1982 Irish General Elections illustrate the weakness of proportional representation in this respect.

On two occasions — in 1968 and 1959 — constitutional amendments have been proposed which would have substituted the straight vote system in place of the present system of proportional representation.[34] These were rejected at referenda. The key difference between the operation of the straight vote system in Britain and in Ireland would be that in Britain each of the two major parties has taken it in turns to benefit from the uncovenanted bonus bestowed by the electoral system, whereas in Ireland, since 1932, the largest party has always been Fianna Fáil, which would thus have monopolised the bonus for itself and, in all probability, formed the permanent Government of the country.

Single transferable vote   The expression 'transferable vote' is defined in the Electoral Act, 1923.[35] Essentially, it means a vote which can be transferred to the candidate of the voter's (expressed) second preference if it is not used to elect the candidate of his first preference; if the vote is not used to elect the second preference candidate, then it is transferred to the voter's third preference; and so on. The object of these transfers is to ensure that the elector's vote is not wasted but is used in the election of some candidate even if this cannot be his first preference.

Let us consider the counting system in more detail. The key to it is the quota, which is the smallest number of votes which will be certain to secure the election of a candidate in that constituency. The quota is calculated, after the first count, by dividing the total number of valid votes by the number of seats plus one and then adding one to the result.[36] At the first count, the returning officer's staff also allocate all votes according to the first preference of the voters. Assume that candidate A's vote exceeds the quota. He is declared elected. Before the second count A's votes are divided into parcels — for candidate B, C, D . . . — according to the second preference of the voters. (Some voters will have expressed no second preference and their votes are 'non-transferable.') It is important to note, though, that it is not all the votes of B's parcel which will transfer to B. Rather, if there are Y votes in that parcel, B will receive:

$$\frac{A's\ surplus}{A's\ total\ transferable\ vote}\ x\quad Y\ transfers$$

This number of votes is taken, at random, from B's parcel. Assume that the result of the re-distribution of A's surplus is to push candidate B's total above the quota. Thus B is elected on the second count and, at the third count, his surplus is transferred. It should be emphasised that B's original votes, that is, the votes of those electors for whom B was the first preference, are not touched. The votes transferred on from B to C, D, E . . . are drawn only from those which were transmitted to him at the final count before he exceeded the quota.[37] Assume that, following the third count, no additional candidate has been elected. In this case, the lowest of the remaining candidates is eliminated and his votes — all his votes — are transferred according to the next preference indicated.[38] It may happen, and it becomes increasingly likely as the counts continue, that a voter's next preference is for a candidate who has been elected or eliminated: in that case the vote transfers to the next-but-one-preference. Counting continues until all the seats have been filled. Frequently, because of the failure of some electors to indicate their preferences right down to the end of the field, the last remaining candidate will be elected without reaching the quota.[39]

11.4 FRANCHISE AND REGISTRATION

Under the Constitution as recently amended:

(i) All citizens, and
(ii) such other persons in the State as may be determined by law, without distinction of sex who have reached the age of eighteen years who are not disqualified by law and comply with the provisions of the law relating to the election of members of Dáil Éireann

shall have the right to vote at an election of members of Dáil Éireann.[40]

Thus, under paragraph (i) of this provision, Irish citizens, aged eighteen or more, have the right to vote in Dáil elections. The provenance of paragraph (ii) of this provision is as follows. First, the Supreme Court decided[41] that

175

the Electoral (Amendment) Bill, 1983, which would have extended the franchise to British citizens over the age of eighteen, was in conflict with the Constitution in its original form on the principal ground that Art. 16 of the Constitution provides a comprehensive code for the holding of Dáil elections and that it does not contemplate the extension of the franchise to non-citizens. In response to this decision the Constitution was amended by the Ninth Amendment of the Constitution Act, 1984, to enable the Oireachtas to widen the franchise to include non-citizens.

The Constitutional provision quoted in the previous paragraph contains the words '. . . and complies with the provisions of the law relating to the election of members of Dáil Éireann . . .'. This suggestion is accepted by the Electoral Act, 1963, which creates a registration system and lays it down that before a person may vote, first, he must be entitled to be registered and, secondly, his name must appear on the register.[42] (The possession of a voting card is of no consequence.) To be entitled to be registered a person must have reached the age of eighteen years on 15 April and, in addition, be 'ordinarily resident' in the constituency, on 15 September of the preceding year.[43] This last requirement is relevant to the question of whether a student may vote in the constituency of his university or college, even though he lives, during the vacation, in another constituency. It has been held by the Circuit Court that he may do so.[44] However, these are clearly deep waters and it should be noted that the Circuit Court relied on an English authority,[45] although in British law the requirement is 'residen[cy]' *simpliciter* and the better view is that 'ordinary residence' is a narrower concept than residence.[46]

Before a person may vote, he must be not only entitled to be registered but actually be registered as well. A register is prepared for each administrative county or county borough by the county council or county borough corporation respectively. A draft register is published on 1 December each year[47] and displayed in post offices and libraries. Claims for, or objections to, the entry of names in this draft must be made before 15 January in the subsequent year, to the county registrar,[48] who is a legally-qualified official of the Court, with appeal lying to the Circuit Court and thence, on a point of law only, to the Supreme Court.[49] The register remains in force for one year from 15 April. Because of the delay between the preparation of a register and the end of its life, there will be an increasing discrepancy between those who are entitled to be registered and those who are actually registered, a feature which is reflected by referring to an election held towards the end of the register's year as being held on a 'dead register.' (It may be noted, though, that if an elector moves away from the constituency in which he is registered, it would still be lawful for him to vote in his former constituency.) The discrepancy created by the 'dead register' is one instance of the tension between the abstract right to vote and the need for an orderly registering and voting system. *Reynolds v. Attorney General*[50] is a case which illustrates this tension. About 140,000 young people, including the plaintiff, were affected by the fact that the 1973 General Election was held after the Constitution had been amended to reduce the voting age to eighteen but before the Electoral Act, 1963 had been altered to reflect this change. The High Court held that, although the reference to twenty-one was plainly unconstitutional, Mr Reynolds did not have the constitutional right to vote because that right only arises if, as the Constitution says, a person has compiled with 'the law relating to the election of members . . .' including the law relating to registration: to hold that Mr Reynold's had the right to vote just because he was over eighteen would mean that anyone who attained that age on the day before a general election could vote and that would make the compilation of a register impossible. It is, nevertheless, implicit in the case, and indeed in the creation of a constitutional right to vote, that any law qualifying the right to vote must be reasonably necessary to the holding of an election.

The task of reconciling the right to vote with the need for an orderly registrations system recently came before the Supreme Court again, in *Draper v. A.G.*[51] By way of background to *Draper* it should be said that, as the law stands at present, the right to a postal vote is confined, narrowly,[52] to the Defence Forces and the Garda Síochána, excluding, for example, prisoners or Irish diplomats posted overseas. In *Draper v. A.G.* the plaintiff claimed that postal voting should be extended to persons who are too handicapped to attend a polling station. The Supreme Court rejected this argument because it held that a wide extension of postal voting to persons who declare an inability to attend a polling station would carry a high risk of abuse, which could only be met by extraordinary safeguards.

The other exception to the right to vote authorised by the Constitution are those persons who are 'disqualified by law.' At present[53] no law passed under this dispensation is in force. And so it will be sufficient to submit, briefly, that the scope of this exception must be regarded as circumscribed by: the need not to make a mockery of the right to vote; the requirement that the exception be relevant to the duty of voting and the general right to equal laws contained in Art. 40.1. The exception would, thus, not allow the exclusion from the franchise of (say) persons who had not received secondary education or those who could not prove that they were up to date in paying their taxes.

11.5 MEMBERS

The rules regarding the number and distribution of seats have already been examined in Section 2.

As regards qualifications for membership of the Dáil the Constitution provides that:

Every citizen without distinction of sex who has reached the age of twenty-one and who is not placed under disability or incapacity by this Constitution or by law shall be eligible for membership of Dáil Éireann.[54]

The distinction between 'disability' and 'incapacity' which is only of verbal significance is that incapacity refers to cases in which a person, otherwise qualified, under the Constitution is not eligible because of his office or occupation, whereas disability applies to some quality or behaviour of the person himself. A person is disabled[55] from being elected or sitting as a member or, if he is already a member, from continuing as such if he is or becomes: a person serving a prison sentence longer than six months; a mentally-handicapped person; or an undischarged bankrupt.[56] Persons who commit any offence which is a corrupt practice are no longer disqualified.[57]

The Constitution itself renders the incumbents of certain offices incapable of being a member: the president;[58] the Comptroller and Auditor General,[59] and the judges, including the Circuit Court judges and district justices.[60] Several acts of the Oireachtas create further incapacities, but there is, unfortunately, no single, comprehensive statutory list of incapacities. Civil servants (whether temporary or permanent) and members of the defence, reserve defence or police forces may not be elected or sit as a TD, nor may a TD continue as such if he joins any of these bodies.[61] The members and staff of state-sponsored bodies are invariably incapable of being members of the Oireachtas. Up to 1942,[62] the way in which this result was achieved was for the constitutional statute setting up the body to declare that such people were incapable of being members of the Oireachtas. Since that date, the usual style has been to provide that a member of the Oireachtas is incapacitated from being a board member, and that a person ceases to be a board member if he accepts nomination as a senator or for election to either House.[63] The substance is the same but the new form is based on the principle 'that the Oireachtas has the prior claim to the person's services.'[64] Whilst members of the Oireachtas are barred from being staff-members of State-sponsored bodies, the normal practice now is to provide that, if a staff-member becomes a member of the Oireachtas, he may be seconded from his post.[65] In a recommendation that was not implemented,[66] the Joint Committee on Electoral Law suggested that the same dispensation should be granted to civil servants in the manipulative grades in the former Department of Posts and Telegraphs (who were until 1984 civil servants) and to corresponding grades in other departments. It seems likely that the failure to implement this proposal violates the European Convention on Human Rights, Art. 23 ('Right to Participate in Government').[67] The position regarding civil servants remains that there is a complete ban on civil servants standing for election to either House, but industrial civil servants and most clerical workers may engage in other forms of political activity, including standing for election to local authorities.[68]

11.6 ELECTORAL PROCESS

Timing The maximum length of a Dáil has been fixed at five years, from the date of its first meeting, by the Electoral Act, 1963.[69] Subject to the

President's power, under Art. 13.2.2° to refuse a dissolution to a Taoiseach who has ceased to retain the support of a Dáil majority, the Dáil may be dissolved by the President, on the Taoiseach's advice, at any time within this period. The Proclamation, the instrument which fixes the date of dissolution, also sets the date on which the new Dáil is to meet.[70]

The first stage of the election process is that, immediately after the issue of the proclamation, the Clerk of the Dáil issues a writ to the returning officer who is the city or county sheriff in Dublin or Cork City or County and, elsewhere, the county registrar.[71] The writ is a document instructing the returning officer to hold an election in his constituency and, thereafter, to endorse on the writ the names of the members to serve in the Dáil and return to the writ to the Clerk.[72] The returning officer is responsible for the conduct of the election in his constituency and in carrying out his duties, within the law, he is not subject to any direction from, for instance, the Minister for the Environment.

The Constitution provides that a general election must take place not later than thirty days after the dissolution and that the new Dáil must meet within thirty days of polling day.[73] The precise date of polling day (traditionally a Tuesday, Wednesday or Thursday) is fixed by the Minister for the Environment and published in *Iris Oifigiúil*: it must fall during the period between the seventeenth and twenty-sixth day after the writs were issued[74] (disregarding any 'excluded days,' that is, Sundays and public or bank holidays).[75] The date on which the new Dáil is to meet is usually about two weeks after polling day in order to allow time for negotiations regarding the formation of the new Government.

Nomination   In order to be listed on the ballot, a candidate must be nominated in the specified form. A candidate may either nominate himself or be nominated by another person, who must be a voter in the constituency.[76] To be nominated a candidate must make a deposit of £100 (as it has been since the commencement of the State) and this will be returned unless the candidate's total votes (at their highest figure) is less than one third of the quota.[77] Nominations are received by the returning officer usually on the eighth or ninth day (disregarding any excluded day) next following day on which the writs for the election are issued.[78] He must rule on the validity of a nomination paper within one hour of receiving it and he may rule that it is invalid, if, and only if, he considers that it is 'not properly made out or subscribed.' His decision is final if it rules that a nomination paper is valid, but subject to reversal on an election petition if it rules that the nomination paper is invalid.[79]

Political party on ballot paper   The returning officer may, if 'he is satisfied that it is appropriate to do so in relation to the candidate,' allow a candidate to have included on the ballot paper the name of his political party. However, the discretion which this formula leaves to the returning officer would of course have to be exercised reasonably. In addition, the name of a political party can only be included if that party is registered on the Register of Political Parties and if the nomination paper is accompanied by a certificate signed by the officer(s) of such party who are authorised to sign certificates authenticating party candidates.[80] These latter requirements are a device to ensure that only the genuine candidates of genuine parties enjoy the advantage of running in party colours. If a candidate has no political party after his name he is entitled to have 'Non-Party' printed there instead.[80] The Clerk of the Dáil is *ex officio* the Registrar responsible for the Register of Political Parties and he must decide whether any party which applies for registration is 'in his opinion (i) a genuine political party and (ii) is organised to contest a Dáil election or a local election.'[81]

In 1965, the Christian Democrat Party of Ireland was refused registration by the Registrar and, on appeal, by the appeal board, which consists of a judge of the High Court, as chairman, together with the Ceann Comhairle and the Cathaoirleach.[82] Thereafter, it challenged the constitutionality of the registration system unsuccessfully, in both the High and Supreme Courts, in the case of *Loftus v. Attorney General*.[83] The plaintiff's first argument was that the system interfered with his freedom of association under Art. 40.6.1° (iii) The Court, however, held that rules which prevented 'the proliferation of bogus front organisations calling themselves political parties but with aims and objects far removed from the political sphere'[84] were beneficial to genuine political activity and, as such, within the public interest exception to this constitutional right. The second argument was directed towards the rule that all parties which were represented in the Dáil (even by one seat) at the time when the register was set up (9 December 1963) were to be automatically registered.[85] It was submitted that this violated the equality provision (Art. 40.1). The Court held that the discrimination was legitimate because 'The very fact of being represented in the Dáil satisfied in respect of each such party the statutory requirements that the party be genuinely political and that it be organised to contest elections.'[86] Undoubtedly, this is an important factor, but it might be questioned whether it would in every case be conclusive. In this regard, a lacuna in the system not mentioned in the case ought to be emphasised: there is no provision for removing a party once it has been registered.[87] Thus, a party formerly represented in the Dáil by a few members which then lost these seats and withered away, so that it ceased to be a 'genuine political party,' would remain on the register.[88]

However, the second part of *Loftus*[89] was as important as the earlier part. For the Court went on to consider whether, given the constitutionality of the registration system, the appeal board's refusal to register the Christian Democratic Party of Ireland was based on wrong principles. The board had three grounds to its refusal. First, it held that to be 'a genuine political party' (in the words of the statutory test) a party must have 'a sizeable public image' and 'a viable organisation.' The Supreme Court regarded these factors, on their own, as irrelevant, holding, instead, that:

180

[A party] must be judged to be a 'genuine political party' if it is bound together by the cohesion of common political beliefs or aims and by being organised for electoral purposes into an entity to such an extent and with such distinctiveness as to justify its claims to be truly a political party in its own right.[89]

Secondly, the board had held that the party lacked the 'degree of organisation . . . which is usual for contesting a Dáil election.' This was regarded by the Court as too high a standard. Finally, the board found that the party existed only in Dublin city and yet failed to make this clear in its title. However, the Supreme Court classified the party as one with national aims and objectives but which because of its actual strength was confined to a single area. However, in spite of these decisions, in the instant case, the Court refused to grant an order because the plaintiff's delay before taking action — thirteen years — was excessive.

Campaigning   The 1963 Electoral Act[90] removed the former limits on the expenses and resources which a Dáil candidate could spend on the campaign in his constituency. This change was based on the view of the Joint Committee on Electoral Law[91] that such limitations are out-dated now that a general election is no longer a collection of unrelated constituency campaigns and expenditure on political promotion is not yet confined to a few weeks before polling day. Moreover there is no national limitation on expenditure on political campaigning.

Political parties do not have to publish accounts, so that the exact amounts spent may never be known. And there is no requirement that private companies disclose the amount paid to the parties.[92] Most party funds go on posters, newspaper advertising and nation-wide transport for their leaders. Candidates continue to receive substantial assistance in that each is allowed to send one 'postal communication,' free of postal charge, to every registered person in the constituency for which he is standing. However, candidates from the same party are normally treated as joint candidates who are therefore only entitled to a joint communication.[93]

In *Dillon v. Minister for Posts*[94] the plaintiff was a candidate, yet the Minister refused to allow his brochure to be circulated free of charge. The plaintiff successfully challenged this refusal which was based on two grounds of which only one was specifically related to electoral law. This ground was founded on the statutory requirement that the letter should 'contain . . . matter relating to the election only,' whereas the plaintiff's brochure including a list of ten proposals for legislation and asked the recipient to write to him arranging these in order of importance. It was argued for the Minister that this went beyond electioneering and might even result in replies which arrived after the date of the election. The Supreme Court, however, held that the plaintiff was merely attempting to show that he was the type of candidate who regarded the views of his putative constituents as important. Moreover:

. . . the expression 'matter relating to the election only' should be liberally construed. This is particularly so when, as in this case, the person seeking to block the free postal circulation of the plaintiff's election brochure is a member of the Dáil and whose party leader is seeking re-election to the Dáil in the same constituency as the plaintiff has chosen to contest.[95]

This passage, of course, suggests a question which was not directly considered by the Court, namely whether the fact that the decision regarding post-free literature has to be taken by a politician, who may be partisan, renders the provision unconstitutional for breach of the rules of constitutional justice.

Television or radio advertising is forbidden.[96] However, the major parties do enjoy the priceless authority of party political broadcasts.[97] Obviously the way in which this is distributed among the parties is crucial. For all elections, bye-elections and referenda, RTE negotiates an *ad hoc* arrangement with the political parties regarding the number and duration of such broadcasts to be made during the specific campaign in question. The contact point for discussion with the bigger parties is the whip and, with smaller groups, accreditied liaison officers. Sometimes, as during the 1981 election when a number of H-Block candidates were put forward, RTE deals with a representative committee. RTE believes (correctly, in my view) that, failing agreement between the parties on the allocation of party political broadcasts, RTE would be free to impose its own distribution, providing that in the net result, it adhered to its overriding duty of being 'objective . . . and impartial . . .'.[98]

In *The State (Lynch) v. Cooney*,[99] the statutory ban on the broadcasting, by RTE, of any matter which would promote crime or undermine the activity of the State was examined in the context of an order prohibiting, *inter alia*, a party political broadcast on behalf of Provisional Sinn Féin in the February 1982 election. The Supreme Court held that the words of the statutory provision could be read, in the light of the presumption of constitutionality, as creating an objective test to be applied by the Minister for Posts and Telegraphs (as he then was) and, thus, as being in accord with Art. 40.6.1(i) of the Constitution (the right to free speech).

The poll Each county council or county borough council is responsible, after consultation with the appropriate returning officer, for making a scheme (which is subject to the approval of the Minister for the Environment) dividing the area into polling districts and appointing a polling place for each polling district.[100] Usually these arrangements are such that electors do not have to travel more than three miles to vote. The returning officer must send a card to each elector giving him his electoral register number and informing him where his polling place is.[101]

The returning officer appoints a presiding officer for each polling place.[102] His duty is to preside at the polling place, giving each voter a ballot paper,[103] preventing any interference with a voter or personation and delivering all the sealed ballot boxes to the returning officer.[104] The presiding officer must maintain order at the polling station and regulate the number of electors admitted at the same time and exclude every one else apart from his clerk(s), the companions of electors who need assistance and the agents of candidates whose task is to guard against personation.[105] The presiding officer (or returning officer) may or, if so requested on behalf of a candidate, must require a person who has asked for a ballot paper to take an oath and/or answer specified questions, concerning his right to vote. A failure to take the oath to give the required answers would mean that the person would not be allowed to vote. The procedure acts as a deterrent to a would-be offender and may also serve to provide unambiguous evidence that an offence has been committed. Apart from this procedure, no questions may be put, at the time of the poll, as to the right of any person to vote.[106]

The poll must be held, at the same time and day in each constituency, over a period of twelve hours within the period 8.30 a.m. — 10.30 p.m. as determined by the Minster for the Environment.[107]

Secrecy   One feature of the voting procedure to which attention ought to be drawn is its secrecy. Until the Ballot Act was passed, as recently as 1872, voting at elections was by show of hands. The frequent sequel was episodes which have transmitted 'bitter memories'[108] to the present-day. To prevent any recurrence of such episodes Art. 16.1.4° provides that 'voting shall be by secret ballot.' The centenary of the Ballot Act was celebrated by the reporting of the case of *McMahon v. Attorney General*[108] in which the plaintiff impugned the system by which both the ballot paper and the counterfoil were marked with the same serial number whilst the elector's number in the register of electors was marked on the counterfoil. The result of this system was that it would have been possible to discover the way in which a person voted. This could only have been done lawfully, under an order of the Dáil or of the High Court, to be granted by such court on being satisfied that inspection of the vote was necessary to prosecute for an offence in relation to ballot papers, like impersonation, or for the purpose of an election petition. Nevertheless, the Supreme Court, by a majority of three to two, held that the right to secrecy was absolute and so the system of identification was unconstitutional. The law was changed to accord with the ruling in *McMahon*, by the Electoral (Amendment) Act, 1972.[109] The only exceptions allowed by the court to the principle of secrecy were in the cases of blind, incapacitated or illiterate persons, for whom a companion is permitted to vote on behalf of the elector.[110]

The count   (The actual system of counting votes has already been described in Section 3.)

Save with the permission of the returning officer, the only people who may be present at the count are the returning officer, his clerks and assistants, Gardaí and the agents (the so-called 'tallymen') appointed by the candidates, whose names and addresses have been given to the returning officer two clear days before polling day. No more than five agents may be appointed by the candidate

183

unless the returning officer agrees. The returning officer must provide these agents with the facilities and information to enable them to oversee the proceedings at the count.[111] The returning officer has the power to carry out a re-count if he is not satisfied as to the accuracy of any count. Each candidate has the power to ask for a re-count of the immediately preceding count and, in addition, any candidate can insist once (and once only) on a complete re-examination and re-count of all the ballot papers.[112]

Electoral abuses The Prevention of Electoral Abuses Act, 1923 divided electoral offences, at Dáil or Senate elections, into two classes — *corrupt practices* and *illegal practices*. Corrupt practices, the more serious, include the offence of bribery, personation, threatening, undue influence or knowingly publishing before an election a false statement of the withdrawal of a candidate. Anyone convicted of a corrupt practice, other than personation, is liable to be imprisoned for a maximum period of one year and/or a fine of £1,000.[113] The offence of personation may be committed either by a person applying for a ballot paper in the name of another person or, secondly, by a person who has already obtained a ballot paper applying, in his own name, for *another* ballot paper at the same election.[114] The punishment for a first offence of personation is imprisonment for a maximum of one year and a minimum of two months.[115] However, personation is a very common offence, and district justices frequently use (or abuse) their discretion under the Probation of Offenders Act 1907 to avoid sending the offender to prison.

The other class of electoral offence is an illegal practice, examples of which include the making of a statement likely to mislead voters as to the actual process of voting,[116] or the publication of electioneering posters or placards, without the name and address of the printer and publisher.[117] The punishment is imprisonment for a maximum of six months and/or a fine of up to £500.[118] The Director of Public Prosecutions is under a general duty 'to make such inquiries and institute such prosecutions as the circumstances of the case appear to him to require,'[119] where there is a general complaint of either corrupt or illegal practices. It seems likely, however, that, where a particular accused has been taken and placed in custody at the direction of a presiding officer in a polling place, then a prosecution could be instituted by a presiding officer, returning officer, personation agent or (possibly) a common informer.[120]

11.7 BYE-ELECTIONS

If a vacancy occurs in the membership of the Dáil otherwise than because of a dissolution, then, when the Dáil passes a motion to that effect, the Ceann Comhairle must direct the Clerk of the Dáil to send a writ to the returning officer in the constituency whose TD has ceased to be a member, instructing him to hold an election.[121] Apart from this, the procedure at a bye-election is similar to that at a general election.

The timing of a bye-election is under the control of the Government since it commands a majority in the Dáil. And it is not unknown for Governments to find it in their own interest to allow a considerable delay before the bye-election is called. It is possible that where this delay is unreasonably long (taking into account all the circumstances) it might be held to be unconstitutional. For whilst a voter or constituent has no explicit constitutional right to be represented in the Dáil, it is arguable that such a right is implicit in the right to vote coupled with the requirement that the ratio between the number of deputies and the population, in any constituency, should be the same throughout the country (see Art. 16.1 and 2). For the right to vote would be devalued if the representative in the Dáil for whom one's vote were ultimately cast ceased to be a member in (say) the first few months of the Dáil and there was no opportunity, within a reasonable time, to elect a replacement.

11.8 SENATE ELECTIONS

The Constitution requires a general election to the Senate to take place no later than ninety days after the Dáil has been dissolved,[122] and, in fact, the Senate election usually occurs right at the end of the permitted period. The first meeting of the new Senate takes place on a date fixed by the President on the Taoiseach's advice. The Dáil and the Senate are roughly co-terminous and, as explained in Chapter 6, the Government party always has a majority in the Senate as well as the Dáil. However, it oftens happens that the outoing Senate has to be summoned to pass legislation which has been promoted by the incoming Government and passed by the new Dáil. Even if, during this hiatus, there is a difference of political colour between the Government and the Senate majority, the Senate has almost always resisted the temptation to hold up the legislation.[123]

The subject of the composition of the Senate has been covered in detail elsewhere[124] and so all that is attempted here is to give a sketch of the main constitutional principles which are involved in the nomination and election of senators.

In addition to the qualifications to be explained, in order to be eligible for membership of the Senate, a person must be eligible to become a deputy.[125] Thus the rules already discussed in Section 5 are relevant here too.

The Senate has sixty members, eleven of whom are nominated by the incoming Taoiseach.[126]

University members Six senators are elected to represent the universities, three each for the National University of Ireland and the University of Dublin.[127] In each university constituency, the electorate are Irish citizens, aged eighteen years or over, who have received a degree other than an honorary degree of the university.[128] Oddly enough, there are no rules requiring *candidates* for university seats to have some connection with the university for which they are standing. Candidates must be nominated by two graduates of the appropriate university with the assent of eight others.[129] For each university there is a three-seat constituency and each selector has one, postal, single transferable vote.[130] Should a casual vacancy arise among university senators, the bye-election procedure is similar to that for a general election.[131]

Panel members The remaining senators, forty-three so-called 'panel members,' are chosen according to the vocational principle.[132]

Summary The vocational principle refers to the attempt made to afford the different interests in the State special parliamentary representation. In fact, this vocational principle has not had much effect on the ultimate composition of the Senate,[133] although it has certainly influenced the design of the selection process. The other, contrasting factor which influenced this design was the desire to assign some involvement to the elected representatives of the people, thereby giving considerable influence to the ordinary electors. The integration of these different objectives has resulted in such a complicated system that it may be useful to summarise if before going into more detail. It comprises three elements. First, to be eligible for a panel seat, a candidate must be qualified in one of the five 'interests and services' set out in the Constitution and quoted in the next paragraph. Secondly, a candidate must be nominated either by members of the Oireachtas or by a vocational body concerned with one of the five types of 'interest and service.' Finally, the electorate is composed of the members of the Oireachtas plus all county or county borough councillors.[134]

Qualifications and nominations The Constitution (Art. 18.7.1°) deals with the special qualifications which panel members (as contrasted with other senators) must possess, as follows:

Before each general election of the members of Seanad Éireann to be elected from panels of candidates, five panels of candidates shall be formed in the manner provided by law containing respectively the names of persons having knowledge and practical experience of the following interests and services, namely:

 i. National Language and Culture, Literature, Art, Education and such professional interests as may be defined by law[135] for the purpose of this panel;

 ii. Agriculture and allied interests, and Fisheries;

 iii. Labour, whether organised or unorganised;

 iv. Industry and Commerce, including banking, finance, accountancy, engineering and architecture;

 v. Public Administration and social services, including voluntary social activities.

Nominations to the panels may follow either of two methods. First, any four

186

members of the Houses of the Oireachtas (the in-coming Dáil and the out-going Senate) may make one nomination to any panel, with each Oireachtas member having the right to make only one such nomination.[136] Alternatively, nomination may be by one *Nominating Body* that is, one of the seventy-two (in March 1982) bodies whose names appear on the Register of Nominating Bodies.[137]

The chief criterion to be applied in deciding whether to register a body is (broadly) whether its objects are primarily connected with the interests and services mentioned in Art. 18.7.1° of the Constitution.[138] In addition, a nominating body may not be a branch or affiliate of a body already registered; a profit-making body; or one which is composed of persons employed by the State or by local authorities. There is also a discretion to exclude bodies whose income is below a specified amount or whose system of organisation and administration fails to meet certain, specified conditions.[139]

The person responsible for the Register of Nominating Bodies (which must be revised annually) is the Senate Returning Officer (who is the Clerk of the Senate) and it is he who determines whether a body is qualified to be registered.[140] His decision is final, save for an appeal to an appeal board consisting of a High or Supreme Court judge nominated by the Chief Justice and the Chairman and Deputy-Chairmen of the Dáil and the Senate. This Board may only take into account the information which was available to the returning officer. Appeals to the Board must be delivered or sent to the Clerk of the Dáil.[141]

In order to grasp the system of nominating and voting, it is necessary to appreciate that each panel of candidates is divided into sub-panels, according to whether the candidates are nominated by the nominating bodies or the Oireachtas members. The number of candidates to be elected from each panel — and the *minimum* number to be elected from each sub-panel — are as follows:

Cultural and Education: a total of five, with at least two being elected from each sub-panel

Agricultural: eleven, with at least four from each sub-panel

Labour: eleven, with at least four from each sub-panel

Industrial and Commercial: nine, with at least three from each sub-panel

Administrative: seven, with at least three from each sub-panel.[142]

The maximum number of candidates which each nominating body may nominate is determined as follows. First, the maximum number of senators who may be elected from the particular bodies' sub-panel, is doubled. Secondly, it is divided by the number of nominating bodies registered for that panel. Where the result is a fraction, it is rounded up to the next highest whole number.[143] There are no rules limiting the number of candidates nominated by the Oireachtas sub-panels, apart from the requirement that each candidate be nominated by four members of the Oireachtas.

187

After the closing date for nominations, the returning officer,[144] holds 'the completion of the panels' at which he decides whether the nominations are valid and whether the persons nominated have the qualification set out in the sub-section from the Constitution quoted at the start of this Section. The returning officer may, and must, if he is requested to do so by any person whose name is on a provisional sub-panel, refer any question arising during the completion of the panel to the judicial referee (the President of the High Court or another High Court judge nominated by him), who sits with him at the completion of the panels. The judicial referee's decision is final and is not open to review in any court. The returning officer and the judicial referee each has the power to ask questions, if necessary on oath.[145]

As a result of these proceedings, a certain amount of case law has been built in this field. In addition, there has even been one High Court case.[146] This arose because the returning officer had informally warned a would-be candidate that he was not considered to be qualified for nomination to the Labour Panel. Before a formal ruling could be made at the completion of the panels, the candidate successfully sought a Declaration from the High Court that he was eligible. In this situation the Court held it had jurisdiction, in spite of the rule that the returning officer's decision is said to be final.

Voting The electorate (formerly only Dáil members and seven members from each county or county borough council)[147] is now composed of the members of the Oireachtas (new Dáil and out-going Senate) plus all members of the county or county borough councils.[148] This change had the effect of trebling (approximately) the electorate to about one thousand and consequently terminating the practice of vote-buying.[149]

The election is conducted by registered post and the ballot paper must be filled up in the presence of an 'authorised person,' which category comprises Clerks and Clerks-Assistant or either House of the Oireachtas, county registrars, sheriffs, county and city managers, county secretaries and Garda superintendents.[150] Every elector has one single transferable vote in each of the five panels and the votes for each pane are counted separately.[151] The single transferable vote system is used,[152] and the same quota (which is calculated in the same way as for Dáil elections)[153] applies to candidates in each sub-panel. The result is that candidates are frequently elected for one sub-panel (usually the vocational bodies sub-panel) without reaching the quota and with fewer votes than some of the unsuccessful candidates on the other sub-panel.

Bye-elections In the case of casual vacancy among the vocational senators, if the loss occurred among the members of the Oireachtas sub-panel, a candidate for the bye-election must be supported by nine members of the Oireachtas.[154] Alternatively, if the loss occurred in the other sub-panel, a candidate must be nominated by a nominating body.[155] However, in the case of either sub-panel, the members of the Oireachtas form the entire electorate for the bye-election[156] and in the interests of economy councillors are not involved.

12

The Judicature

12.1 INDEPENDENCE OF THE JUDICIARY

In Chapter 2, we saw that the independence of the judiciary is probably the most significant element of the separation of powers: it is essential to the rule of law that there should be an arm of government, independent of the other organs, which can enforce the law impartially. The easiest way to appreciate the importance of the independence of the judiciary is to consider a period of history when the judiciary was not independent; for this purpose, readers are referred to British seventeenth-century history which includes such significant episodes as the dismissal from the bench of Coke CJ (in 1616) and Pemberton J (in 1680); the later history of the Court of Star Chamber; and Jeffreys' Bloody Assize.[1]

The Constitution declares that: 'All judges shall be independent in the exercise of their judicial functions and subject only to this Constitution and the law.'[2] Judicial independence may be vulnerable at six points, the first of which is appointment. In fact, independence is maintained in spite of, rather than because of, the rules governing appointments. There is no politically-neutral appointment agency, like the Judicial Services Commissions which exist in certain Commonwealth states and which are manned by such figures as the Chief Justice and the Secretary of the Department of Justice.[3] Rather, all judges are appointed by the President, acting on the advice of the Government.[4] Governments have usually appointed supporters of the party in power, but there is no evidence that the appointees have displayed favouritism to the party which appointed them.[5] On his entry into office every judge or district justice must make a declaration by which he promises to execute the duties of his office 'without fear or favour, affection or ill-will towards any man' and to 'uphold the Constitution and the laws' (Art. 34.5).

Secondly, a judge is not eligible to be a member of either House.[6] In the opposite direction, there is a rule of procedure, in each House, that no parliamentary criticism of a judge may be expressed except on a substantive motion,[7] of which there has never been an example in Ireland. Again, no judge is eligible 'to hold any other office or position of emolument,'[8] words which are taken as meaning that a judge may not undertake any other *paid* appointment.[9] Nevertheless the effect and intention of these exclusions is to 'set [judges] apart in many important ways from the life of the community and deny [them] important civil rights in order that they should be independent in the exercise of their functions.'[10]

Thirdly, by Art. 35.5 'The remuneration of a judge shall not be reduced during his continuance in office.' However, the Supreme Court has held, by a three to two majority, that this does not prevent taxes from being levied on a judge's salary in the same way as on the salaries of other members of the community.[11] Judges' salaries may now be increased by Government order.[12] It seems reasonable to suggest that a failure to ensure that judicial salaries keep pace with inflation would amount, in substance, to a reduction in a '. . . judge's [remuneration] . . . during his continuance in office' contrary to Art. 35.5 and that there is thus an obligation to increase judicial salaries in line with inflation. Judicial salaries and pensions are a charge on the Central Fund.[13] Such matters as judicial qualifications, retiring age and pension are dealt with by statute.[14]

The fourth point at which judicial appointment may be vulnerable is removal. The Constitution, in the case of High or Supreme Court judges, and statute law, in the case of Circuit Court judges or district justices, provide that a judge or justice may only be removed from office for 'stated misbehavior or incapacity, and then only upon resolutions passed by Dáil Éireann and by Seanad Éireann calling for his removal.'[15] No removal from judicial office has occurred, though one judge did retire after a motion for his removal for incapacity was put down[16] and on another occasion the threat of a motion for misbehaviour was sufficient.[17] The equivalent British procedure has been used once (to remove an Irish judge, Sir Jonah Barrington, in 1830).

Fifthly, we should advert to contempt of court — the elaborate system of case law which protects judges against any species of disobedient or prejudicial behaviour.[18] One of the purposes of contempt of court is clearly to uphold the independence and authority of the judiciary.

Finally, having created these safeguards to encourage an independent judiciary, the Constitution then goes on, in Art 34.1 (examined in chapter 2.2) to provide that, subject to exceptions, justice may be administered only in the courts manned by these judges. It thereby seeks to guard against any encroachment on judicial independence by indirect means.

12.2 THE COURT SYSTEM[19]

Article 34 of the Constitution deals broadly with the court structure. It envisages a three-tiered edifice. At the top is the 'Court of Final Appeal [which] shall be called the Supreme Court.' Then comes the High Court and, finally, the 'Courts of local and limited jurisdiction' — Circuit and District Courts.[20] As we shall see, the Constitution indicates in very broad terms the jurisdiction of each court and thus creates demarcation lines controlling the type of business which can be assigned to, or withdrawn from, each court. Art. 34 clearly anticipated that new courts of law were to be established under the 1937 Constitution. Until this happened, the existing courts — which had been established by a substantial reforming measure (the Courts of Justice Act,

190

1924) — were continued in being by Art. 58 of the Constitution.[21] Eventually, the courts contemplated by the Constitution were constituted by the Courts (Establishment and Constitution) Act, 1961. Both the jurisdictions of the new courts and their titles[22] are similar to those of their predecessors. Moreover, the judges of the former courts were retained in the new judicial offices, although they had to take fresh oaths of office. However, the establishment of fresh courts has had some consequences: for instance, that the new Supreme Court regarded itself as free to make a change in the precedent doctrine which had been followed in the former Supreme Court.[23]

District Court and Circuit Court   To start at the bottom of the pyramid: the District Court consists of the President and no more than thirty nine justices.[24] Formally, there is only one District Court, as there is only one Circuit Court. However, outside Dublin City, the country has been divided, by an order made by the Minister for Justice, into twenty-three District Court districts and most district justices are assigned, by the Government, to some particular district. Within each district, there is usually a number of District Court areas. The significance of an area (of which there are over two hundred and sixty in the whole country) is that a court must be held in each area.[25]

The Circuit Court consists of the President and no more than twelve ordinary judges.[26] For the purposes of the Circuit Court, the country has been divided, by Government order, into seven circuits.[27]

The District and Circuit Courts are characterised, by the Constitution, as courts of 'local and limited jurisdiction.' They are certainly local for:

While there is one Circuit Court and one District Court for all the country, the jurisdiction of each Circuit Court judge and District Justice sitting in any city, town or village is local in the sense that he has jurisdiction to hear only cases which are brought against defendants living in or which arise out of events happening or property in the county or district for which the Circuit Court or District Justice is sitting.'[28]

But the word 'limited' is ambiguous. Does it mean that the Circuit or District Court's jurisdiction in regard to any particular item of business must be incomplete? This test has the support of one Supreme Court authority.[29] Each court meets this test in most subject areas, in that (as we shall see) it is usually restricted by a financial maximum imposed on the amount of damages which may be claimed. However, in certain areas the jurisdiction is unrestricted. For example, the Courts Act, 1981[30] now grants the Circuit Court unrestricted power under the Illegitimate Children (Affiliation Order) Act, 1930. A second instance which may be mentioned is the Circuit Court's power, with the consent of both parties, to hear subject-matter in excess of the financial limits which would otherwise apply.[31] However, it has been suggested[32] that such jurisdictions as these can be regarded as constitutional if the word 'limited' be given a different meaning. On this view, Art. 34 contemplates two types of courts: the High Court with its unlimited jurisdiction

191

in *all* matters (see below) and, by contrast, the courts of 'local and limited jurisdiction.' On this — it is submitted — realistic analysis, the word 'limited' means only that the Circuit and District Courts may not be erected into a localised replica of the High Court.

High Court   The High Court consists of the President of the High Court and a maximum, at present, of fourteen ordinary judges (or fifteen, if the President or any of the ordinary judges is a member of the Law Reform Commission) together with the Chief Justice and the President of the Circuit Court, as additional judges.[33] Normally, cases (civil or criminal, with or without a jury) are heard by one judge. However, the President of the High Court is empowered, where he considers it necessary, to direct that a case be heard by two or more judges.[34]

As will be seen in Sections 4 and 5, the High Court has always had very wide jurisdiction in civil and, *qua* Central Criminal Court, in criminal cases. It ought to be emphasised, too, in a book on constitutional law that the High Court is the only court of first instance invested with the power either of striking down laws for unconstitutionality or of reviewing the decisions of inferior courts and adminstrative authorities, each of which powers are elaborated elsewhere.[35] The High Court's jurisdiction is underpinned by the Constitution, which in Art. 34.3.1° grants it 'full original jurisdiction and power to determine all matters and questions, whether of law or fact, civil or criminal.' Since the High Court has always had wide jurisdiction, granted to it by statute,[36] it has only been necessary to invoke Art. 34.3.1° in marginal cases. The precise meaning of the provision is the subject of controversy. It is clear, however, on the authority of a majority of four to one, in the Supreme Court case of *R.D. Cox v. Owners of M.V. Fritz Raabe*,[37] that the jurisdiction created by the sub-section encompasses all justiciable controversies, including any new ones created by the Oireachtas. In line with this idea, the Minister for Justice noted during the Dáil debates on the Courts Bill, 1980,[38] which vests various jurisdictions in the lower courts but does not explicitly mention the High Court, that this omission from the Bill could not affect 'the inherent or constitutional jurisdiction of the High Court flowing from Art. 34.3.1°.'[39-40] Moreover, the High Court has jurisdiction over all currently justiciable controversies even though the Court's predecessor would not have had jurisdiction. Thus, in *Cox* itself it was held that the Court had jurisdiction in *in rem* proceedings over ship mortgages which were unregistered. Walsh J classified the difference between *in rem* and *in personam* proceedings as a mere matter of procedure which could not alter the fact that a justiciable procedure was involved and, thus, that the High Court had jurisdiction under Art. 34.3.1°. This result was not affected by the facts that there was no statute which conferred this particular jurisdiction and that the High Court's forerunner — the High Court of Admiralty — would not have had jurisdiction in the circumstances.

The important point which arises next is whether Art. 34.3.1° prevents the

Oireachtas from vesting the decision in regard to certain types of justiciable controversy in some court other than the High Court.

On this important issue, there is a conflict of authority. In *R. v. Att. Gen.*[41] the High Court (Gannon J) read Art. 34.3.1° at its full width and held that no exclusion from the High Court's jurisdiction is permissible. Having reached this interpretation of the Constitution, the learned judge applied the presumption of constitutionality in a rather drastic way to the statutes under examination. Using this technique, he was able to conclude that, although there was no mention of the High Court in the relevant provisions of the Courts Act, 1981 and the Family Law (Protection of Spouses and Children) Act, 1981[42] dealing with *inter alia* barring orders, yet the legislature had not attempted to oust the jurisdiction of the High Court. The result of the law enunciated in *G.* is that the High Court would always have jurisdiction (whether this outcome is achieved by applying the presumption of constitutionality to the legislation, as occurred in *G*, or by striking down the legislation and applying Art. 34.3.1° directly).

The alternative approach was enunciated first in *Ward v. Kenehan.*[43] The defendants relied upon the Courts of Justice Act, 1924, s. 25 (as amended) to argue that, since the damages to which the plaintiff was entitled did not exceed the jurisdiction exercised by the Circuit Court, an order should be made remitting the action to the Circuit Court. The plaintiff naturally sought to reply by an attack on the constitutionality of the provision on which the defendants relied. He failed because McMahon J took into account Art. 36(iii) of the Constitution, which envisages the enactment of laws regulating 'the distribution of jurisdiction and business among the said Courts and judges.' The learned judge regarded Art. 36(iii) as authorising the enactment of exceptions to Art. 34.3.1° and took section 25 to be an example of such an exception. The *Ward* approach was followed in *Tormey v Ireland*[44] in which the High Court (Costello J) held constitutional the statute withdrawing the right, formerly enjoyed by an accused, to have a prosecution which has been initiated in the Circuit Court transferred to the High Court (Central Criminal Court). It is submitted that the *Ward-Tormey* approach is preferable because it affords a sensible way of reconciling Art 34.3.1° and 36 (iii). It must be admitted, however, that this interpretation reduces the effect of Art. 34.3.1° considerably: the only meaning left to the provision would be that, to exclude the High Court from jurisdiction over a justiciable controversy, a statute would have to do so explicitly and unambiguously. This would mean that Art. 34.3.1° would have the same effect in regard to the High Court as does Art. 34.4.3° in the context of the Supreme Court, on which see below.

Even if the more radical view taken of Art. 34.3.1 in *R* is to be preferred, the High Court indicated, in *R*, that it would not necessarily *exercise* its jurisdiction. Where an inferior court and the High Court have concurrent jurisdictions, the High Court would retain a discretion to decline to exercise jurisdiction. This discretion might well come into play to reject the type of fascinating, though not very useful, argument in which a person accused of

193

a summary offence tried to insist on trial before the High Court.[45]

Apart from the demarcation line between the High Court and other courts, the issue also arises of what effect Art. 34.3.1° has on the relationship between the High Court and an administrative authority like a tribunal or a minister. This question is beyond the scope of this work save to say that it seems to have been accepted, on the one hand, that Art. 34.3.1° has not given the High Court *carte blanche* to take over decisions which the legislature has seen fit to vest in a specialised body like a tribunal or minister. On the other hand (as we shall see in Section 5) even at common law, the High Court has always enjoyed the power to review decisions taken by a tribunal or minister if they are taken in breach of the rules of constitutional justice or are otherwise *ultra vires*. The effect of Art. 34.3.1° has been to invalidate statutory exclusion clauses (which are admittedly rather rare) which state that (say) a minister's decision on some factual or legal point relating to jurisdiction is to be 'final' and not reviewable in any court and which thus purport to exclude the High Court's supervisory function completely.[46]

The High Court's supervisory jurisdiction extends not only to administrative authorities but also to 'inferior courts' (Circuit Court, District Court and Special Criminal Court). This means that, apart from the extensive system of appeals on the merits, created by statute and described in Sections 3 and 4 below, the decisions of inferior courts are also subject to review by the High Court if they fall outside the inferior court's jurisdiction or if they are vitiated by some fundamental procedural defect.

A specialised and most important aspect of the High Court's supervisory jurisdiction is its duty in regard to *habeas corpus* orders[47] (as they are known historically, colloquially and in the Rules of the Superior Court, Order 84, though not in the Constitution). *Habeas corpus* is the practical device for implementing the guarantee of personal liberty contained in Art. 40.4.1°. It is an order to the prison governor, police officer or whomsoever is detaining the applicant, instructing him to produce the applicant before the High Court and to certify the grounds of his detention so that the Court can establish whether he is being detained in accordance with law. *Habeas corpus* is not usually sent in the case of persons convicted and sentenced by a criminal court since there are ample appellate procedures in such cases. However, it is an appropriate remedy where it is the place or conditions, rather than the fact, of a prisoner's detention which is in issue.[48] It is also used in extradition, immigration or custody proceedings.

Supreme Court The Supreme Court consists of the Chief Justice, the President of the High Court (who normally, however, sits in the High Court) and four or (if one of them is a member of the Law Reform Commission) five ordinary judges.[49] Where the court is exercising its powers under Art. 12 of the Constitution (removal of the President) or Art. 26 (reference of a bill by the President) the Court must consist of 'not less than five judges.'[50] In other constitutional cases, five judges must sit. In non-constitutional cases,

194

there must be a minimum of three judges and, in fact, the Chief Justice usually does decide on a court of three members.[51]

The Court's most important jurisdiction is not original[52] but appellate: the Constitution provides that no statute may be enacted which excludes the Court's appellate jurisdiction in cases involving a law's constitutionality.[53] In addition, the Court has always had far-reaching statutory jurisdictions in both criminal and civil fields (which are detailed in Sections 3 and 4). Now these jurisdictions have been subsumed in the wider jurisdiction which is created in the following constitutional provision (Art. 34.4.2°)[54]:

The Supreme Court shall with such exceptions and subject to such regulations as may be prescribed by law, have appellate jurisdiction from all decisions of the High Court, and shall also have appellate jurisdiction from such decisions of other courts as may be prescribed by law.

In other words, where High Court decisions are concerned, the Supreme Court has jurisdiction unless this is withdrawn by a clearly-worded statute; with courts other than the High Court, appellate jurisdiction must be conferred by statute.[55] Appeals to the Supreme Court, from the High Court's decision on an appeal from the Circuit Court or (save by leave of the High Court) from the High Court's determination of a case from the District Court are excluded by statute.[56] There has been no comprehensive definition of a 'decision' for the purposes of Art. 34.4.3.° However, drawing on the provision, it has been held that an appeal lies from the High Court against a grant of *habeas corpus*;[57] a discretionary order as to costs in either civil[58] or criminal[59] matters; and committal for civil contempt of court (disobedience to an order restraining defendant from entering certain lands)[60] On the other side of the line, it has recently been decided,[61] by the Supreme Court, that a High Court decision, under Art. 177 of the Rome Treaty, to refer a point of EEC law to the Court of Justice of the EEC does not fall within Art. 34.4.3.° because such a reference has no 'legal effect upon the parties to the litigation,' and is thus not a 'decision of the High Court' for the purpose of Art. 34.4.3°. The other principal reason for the decision, which may be better appreciated after reading the following paragraphs on European Courts, was that Art. 29.4.3 of the Constitution enables EEC law to override Art. 34.4.3°, and the EEC Treaty confers on each national judge an untramelled right of direct access to the EEC Court.

We shall return to Art. 34.4.3° — to consider the provision's operation in the context of criminal appeals — in Section 4.

European Courts[62] EEC law is part of Irish law. This result was brought about by the European Communities Act, 1972 and Art. 29.4.3 which was an amendment added to the Constitution in 1972.[63] Thus, it is true to say of Irish law, as Lord Denning has characteristically said of British law: '. . . when we come to matters with a European element, the treaty is like an incoming tide. It flows into the estuaries and up the rivers. It cannot be held back. [It] is henceforward to be part of our law.'[64]

In most cases, domestic Irish courts have jurisdiction over actions involving EEC law. However, without more, there would be a danger that the domestic court systems of each of the member states would give varying interpretations of EEC law. To meet this difficulty the EEC Treaty (which is part of Irish law, by virtue of the 1972 amendment) includes an article (Art. 177) which provides as follows:

The Court of Justice shall have jurisdiction to give preliminary rulings concerning:

(a) the interpretation of this Treaty;

(b) the validity and interpretation of acts of the institutions of the Community;

(c) the interpretation of the statutes of bodies established by an act of the Council, where those statutes so provide.

Where such a question is raised before any court or tribunal of a member state, that court or tribunal may, if it considers that a decision on the question is necessary to enable it to give judgment, request the Court of Justice to give a ruling thereon. Where any such question is raised in a case pending before a court or tribunal of a member state, against whose decisions there is no judicial remedy under national law, that court or tribunal shall bring the matter before the Court of Justice.

This unique system entails a division of jurisdiction, with the Irish court retaining the power to determine questions of fact and Irish law, whilst EEC law is settled by the court with authority to make an authoritative interpretation. Where this article is invoked, as with a domestic 'case-stated',[65] the *modus operandi* is that the case is suspended at hearing before the Irish court until the EEC court has ruled on the EEC law. Then the Irish court passes judgment by applying the EEC ruling and any other relevant law to the facts.

For the sake of completeness, it should be said that, in contrast with the Treaty of Rome and its offspring, the European Convention of Human Rights is not part of Irish domestic law (although it may be of some persuasive force in interpreting it).[66] This is a consequence of the principle that: 'No international agreement shall be part of the domestic law of the State save as may be determined by the Oireachtas' (Art. 29.6). It means that the Convention is not enforceable through Irish domestic courts but only on the international plane, by way of, first, the European Commission of Human Rights and, in the last resort, the European Court of Human Rights.

12.3 RIGHT TO A JURY TRIAL ON A CRIMINAL CHARGE

In the present context, the law has created two,[67] related distinctions. The first of these, which has been drawn by common law and statute law for centuries,[68] distinguishes between *summary offences*, triable, without a jury,

196

in the District Court and, and on the other hand, *indictable offences*, which are usually tried before a jury in the Circuit Court or Central Criminal Court. Summary offences always carry a relatively light punishment. Usually the statute creating the offence will indicate the category to which it has been assigned, for example:

A person who contavenes subsection (1) of this section shall be guilty of an offence and shall be liable on summary conviction to imprisonment for a term not exceeding six months, or, at the discretion of the court to a fine not exceeding one hundred pounds or to both such prisonment and fine.'[69]

It is not uncommon for an offence to be made triable (at the prosecution's option) either summarily or, with a heavier penalty, on indictment.[70]

Secondly, the idea that a trial for a more serious crime must be heard before a jury is now underpinned by Art. 38.5 of the Constitution which provides that no person shall be tried on any criminal charge without a jury, save that 'minor offences' may be tried by courts of summary jurisdiction (the District Court). (Further exceptions allow for trials in the Special Criminal Court or military tribunals.)[71] The two classifications — summary/indictable and minor/non-minor — are consistent with each other, in most cases. However, as we shall see, it has sometimes been successfully submitted that a summary trial was unconstitutional because the offence charged was not 'minor.' The Constitution offers no definition of a 'minor offence' and the case law is somewhat confused.[72] However, it is clear that the principal criterion is the severity of the punishment for the offence.[73] If the longest sentence for an offence is six months, then it is a minor offence. It may be that the offence would remain minor if the sentence were as long as twelve months.[74] (The question has not been authoritatively decided yet, probably because the maximum penalty for summary offences generally does not exceed six months.)

The recent Supreme Court case of *State (Rollinson) v. District Justice Kelly*[75] may have changed the law on two points which would have the effect of significantly widening the category of minor offence. The first issue is whether the relevant factor to be assessed is the maximum punishment (prison sentence or fine) allowed by statute or whether it is the punishment actually awarded in the particular case before the Court. Pre-Rollinson the former alternative probably held sway.[76] In *Rollinson* only one judge (Hederman J) confirmed the traditional view, whilst three judges (O'Higgins CJ, Henchy and Griffin JJ) preferred to look at the punishment actually awarded. The fifth judge, McCarthy J, found it unnecessary to deal with an issue which arguably was *obiter*. The alternative adopted by the majority provides for greater flexibility in that it enables minor infringements to be heard without the trouble and expense of a jury trial.

The second issue in *Rollinson* arose from the substantial reduction in the real value of money arising from the on-rush of inflation: the question is whether the severity of a fine is to be assessed by reference to the financial standards prevailing at the time when the statute imposing the fine was enacted

197

(or in the case of a pre-1937 statute, at 1937 standards: the difference is not likely to be significant). Alternatively, ought the severity of the fine to be measured by reference to the circumstances prevailing at the time when the fine is imposed? Pre-*Rollinson*, the first alternative held sway[77] and thus, for example, in *Rollinson* in the High Court, Gannon J drew comparisons between the penalty of £500 fixed in 1926, for the offence under examination and a district justice's annual salary, which was £1,000 during the period 1924-47. Not surprisingly, he decided that the offence was not a minor offence. Nevertheless, in the Supreme Court, only O'Higgins CJ applied the traditional rule, whilst the other four judges assessed the severity of the fine against the standards prevailing at the time it was imposed (with Griffin J buttressing his judgment by reference to the Litter Act 1982, s. 15 which imposes a maximum fine of £800 for a summary offence). On a practical level, this seems to be a useful shift in the law. However, it does suffer from a doctrinal difficulty in that it means a provision possibly unconstitutional at the time when it was passed by the legislature would be altered in substance (though not in wording) by the unpredicted fact of inflation and would thus be rendered constitutional, but with a different content from that intended by the legislature. This difficulty looms especially large where a pre-1937 law is involved since, under Art. 50.1, it is deemed to have come over into the post-1937 polity according to whether or not it was consistent with the Constitution *in 1937*.

Unfortunately, the law on the two points under discussion was not definitely settled in *Rollinson*. In addition to the differences mentioned between the judges of the Court, there is, for instance, the fact that Henchy J qualified his statement that the relevant factor is the penalty actually imposed, by the *caveat* 'if I am free to [say] so.' Again, the facts in *Rollinson* were rather unusual and it is arguable that what was said was *obiter*.

A problem arises where among the consequences of the offence is some disadvantage to the offender which is not the central part of the punishment and the severity of which depends peculiarly on the circumstances of the offender. The most obvious example is mandatory disqualification from driving (for twelve months) which the Supreme Court had to consider in *Conroy v. A.G.*[78] The Court held that they would only take into account '[that] which is regarded as punishment in the ordinary sense . . . either the loss of liberty or the intentional penal deprivation of property whether by means of fine or other direct method of deprivation.'[79] Thus, disqualification from driving was too remote to be taken into account (a view which, according to the High Court in the same case, 'would bring the law into ridicule'), as so, too, would be loss of a liquor licence[80] or disqualification from a professional body, even if it followed automatically from the conviction. However, in a subsequent High Court case,[81] the Court felt able to take it into account that the District Court was empowered, in a case of injury to a person resulting from negligent driving, to fine the defendant the probable amount of a civil award of damages and to pay over the amount of the fine to the injured person. Taking this into account, the High Court held that the offence of negligent driving was

198

a non-minor offence. A similar conclusion was reached in a case in which the punishment included the forfeiture of fish and gear worth about £100,000.[82] Whilst the principal criterion is the severity of the punishment, other factors have been taken into account in deciding what is a minor offence. One of these is the degree of immorality (in the contest of 'the ethical or natural law position')[83] entailed in the commission of the offence. And, thus, in *Conroy*, in the High Court, evidence from theologians was taken on the moral quality of the act of drunken driving. In addition, in this area, as elsewhere in interpreting the Constitution, it is usual to consider 'as secondary considerations,'[84] the state of the law and public opinion at the time when the Constitution was enacted. Thus it was regarded as relevant, in support of a six months maximum imprisonment test, that the Irish Free State Constitution created a right to jury save for minor offences and that 'throughout the existence of Saorstát Éireann six months was considered a proper standard not to be exceeded'[85] in the punishment for minor offences.

Nature of a jury   Having said that the accused has a right to a jury trial in serious criminal cases, we ought to examine (briefly) what a jury is. The term is not defined in the Constitution. The leading case on the jury, *de Burca v. A.G.*,[86] held that the selection of jurors on the basis of sex or property qualification is unconstitutional. Speaking *obiter* in *de Burca*, Walsh J gave his opinion as to the essentials of a jury trial in the following passage:

Looking at the essence of trial with a jury, I am of opinion that it does presuppose that the trial should be in the presence, and under the authority of, a presiding judge having power to instruct the jury as to the law and to advise them as to the facts, and that the jury should be free to consider their verdict alone without the intervention or presence of the judge or any other person during their deliberations. I think it also imports an element of secrecy in so far as the members of the jury cannot be compelled to disclose which way they voted if, for example, the verdict is by majority. I do not consider that it is an essential part of trial by jury that the verdict should be simply 'yes' or 'no' (or 'guilty' or 'not guilty'). I think that the jury's verdict may also be taken on the essential components of any question put to them determining liability or guilt.[87]

The learned judge also opined that '[T]he constitutional provision of trial with a jury is not a guarantee that juries must always consist of twelve persons, neither more nor less, or that the verdict must be unanimous.'[87] Accepting this hint, the Criminal Justice Bill, 1983, cl. 25 provides for majority verdicts in criminal trials of 10 to 2 or 11 to 1 or, if it happens that only eleven jurors are present at the end of the trial, 10 to 1.

12.4   CRIMINAL JURISDICTION

District Court   The District Court has several heads of jurisdiction.

1. As already mentioned, many offences are triable summarily in the District Court.[88]

2. There are certain specified indictable offences (for example, larceny of property worth less than £200) which are made triable summarily in the District Court, but subject to two conditions: first, the Court must be 'of opinion that the facts proved or alleged constitute a minor offence fit to be so tried;' secondly, the accused, on being informed of his right to jury trial, does not object to being tried in the District Court. In certain cases, the Director of Public Prosecution's consent is also necessary.[89]

3. In two other instances, the Court has a marginal role in regard to indictable offences. The first of these is the result of the idea, which has been running in the Anglo-Irish system practically since its foundation, that no one should have to undergo trial on a serious criminal charge unless some impartial agency has determined that there is, at least, a case for the accused to answer. This is the basis of the preliminary hearing of the indictable offence which, unless the accused waives it, must be held in the District Court to determine whether there is 'a sufficient case to put the accused on trial for the offence . . .'.[90-91] Another objective of the preliminary hearing is to give the accused advance notice of the prosecution case against him: in practice, this is the more important reason, since the Court seldom does refuse to commit for trial.

4. If the accused wishes to plead guilty to an indictable offence, if the Court is satisfied that he understands the nature of the offence and the facts against him and if the DPP consents, then, subject to certain exceptions, the District Court can sentence him itself. If this course be adopted, the maximum punishment for which the offender is liable is imprisonment for twelve months and/or a fine of £1,000.[92]

5. Where the offence, whether summary or indictable, has been committed by a person under the age of seventeen, then (apart from very grave offences) the Court must sit in a different room or building or at a different time from those at which the ordinary sittings are held. The Court, which is then known as a Juvenile Court, is held *in camera* with a relatively simple procedure.[93]

6. The Court has a plethora of powers in the regulatory field. Typically, a statute will provide that some potentially dangerous or harmful activity constitutes an offence, unless the District Court has decided to grant a licence to allow the applicant to undertake this activity. If this activity is undertaken either without a licence or, where a licence has been granted, in breach of some condition attached to the licence, then an offence is committed. Frequently, jurisdiction to hear the prosecution for the offence will be vested in the District Court. Examples occur under the Auctioneers and House Agents Acts, 1947- ; Intoxicating Liquor Acts, 1924- ; and Pawnbrokers Act, 1964.

Appeals from the District Court   A person convicted in the Court can appeal, against either conviction or sentence, to the local Circuit Court. An appeal against conviction takes the form of a full re-hearing so that, for instance, either party can call fresh evidence.[94] The prosecution cannot appeal: one of several ways in which the criminal justice system is designedly biased in the accused's favour. However, *either* party to District Court proceedings may at any stage of the trial request the justice to refer any legal point to the High Court (sitting as such, not as the Central Criminal Court) by way of *case stated*. The justice may also refer the matter on his own initiative. Having heard the case stated, the High Court may direct the District Court to reverse its decision or to retry the case. An appeal to the Supreme Court lies from the High Court's decision on a case stated.[95]

Circuit Court   The original jurisdiction of this Court which is exercisable in contested cases, before a judge or jury, is confined to indictable offences. It may try any indictable offence, apart from certain specified offences of peculiar gravity, including treason, murder and certain of the offences created by the Offences Against the State Act, 1939.[96]

   This jurisdiction must be exercised by the judge of the circuit either in which the offence occurred or in which the accused was arrested or resides.[97] In a case outside Dublin, on the application of either the accused or the prosecution (which might be made, for example, because it was feared that a local jury might be partisan) the judge must transfer the case to the Dublin Circuit Court.[98] The former right of transfer, to the Central Criminal Court, was terminated because it was being abused by accused persons who wished to take advantage of the long delay before trial in the Central Criminal Court.[99]

High Court (Central Criminal Court)   When exercising its original criminal jurisdiction, the High Court is always known as the Central Criminal Court. The Court consists of a judge or, where the President of the High Court directs that two or more judges sit together, judges nominated by the President of the High Court. The judge (or exceptionally, judges) sits with a jury.[100] As already mentioned, Art. 34.3.1° of the Constitution grants the Court 'full original jurisdiction in and power to determine all . . . criminal [matters],'[101] which is as ample a jurisdiction as well could be. In fact, since only a handful of offences are excluded from the Circuit Court's jurisdiction, relatively few prosecutions are brought in the Central Criminal Court and, in the past (see preceding paragraph) the great majority of these were cases which had been transferred from the Circuit Court to the Central Criminal Court,

Special Criminal Court[102]   Leaving aside courts-martial[103] (which are outside the scope of this work) the remaining court with original criminal jurisdiction is the Special Criminal Court. This Court is exempt from various constitutional rules which apply to the other courts which hear non-minor offences, including the requirement that non-minor offences must be heard by a jury and the rules for the appointment and removal of judges.[104] Art. 38.3.1° of the Constitution defines the scope of this exemption as follows:

Special courts may be established by law for the trial of offences in cases where it may be determined in accordance with such law that the ordinary courts are inadequate to secure the effective administration of justice, and the preservation of public peace and order.

The law establishing the Special Criminal Court is the Offences Against the State Act 1939, Part V (as amended) whose constitutionality has been upheld.[105] Before this code is brought into force, there must be a proclamation, by the Government, along the lines required by the Constitution, 'that the ordinary courts are inadequate to secure the effective administration of justice and the preservation of public peace and order.'[106] The most recent proclamation (which is still in force) was made on 26 May 1972, and four days later the Special Criminal Court was established. Every Court must consist of at least three members who are appointed and removable by the Government.[107] Under the Act, those qualified for membership include: a High Court or District Court judge; a District Court justice; a barrister or solicitor of not less than seven years standing; or an officer of the Defence Forces holding the rank of commandant or above.[108] At present, however, the panel of appointees, from which a Court is drawn as required, includes only judges or justices.

Subject to exceptions,[109] the Court's jurisdiction is confined to 'scheduled offences.' The Government may, by order, declare an offence to be a 'scheduled offence' if it is satisfied that, in relation to that offence, 'the ordinary courts are inadequate to secure the effective administration of justice . . .'. At present such offences include offences against the Malicious Damage Act 1861 or the Explosive substances Act 1883, as well as the 1939 Act itself.[110] In spite of the raison d'être of the Court, not all scheduled offences are politically-motivated and not all politically-motivated offences are scheduled.

Apart from the absence of a jury, broadly speaking the same rules of evidence and procedure apply to the Court as to the Central Criminal Court.[111] However, by the Offences Against the State (Amendment) Act, 1972, a statement by a Garda, not below the rank of Chief Superintendent, that he believes the accused to be a member of an unlawful organisation is to be taken as evidence of that fact.[112]

Court of Criminal Appeal   This Court, like the Supreme Court, has only appellate jurisdiction. The Court of Criminal Appeal is convened once or more each term, according to the amount of business to be done. The Court must consist of at least three judges[113] and usually does consist of three judges. The rules requiring their selection are complicated. They appear to provide that the members are chosen by the Chief Justice and there must be at least one member from the Supreme Court (other than the President of the High Court) and at least two judges from the High Court, of whom one may be the President if he is 'willing to act.'[114]

Appeal lies to the Court of Criminal Appeal against conviction and/or sentence from the Circuit Court, Central Criminal Court or Special Criminal Court.[115] Leave to appeal must be obtained, either from the trial judge (who must decide whether it is 'a fit case for appeal') or (as happens more commonly) from the Court of Criminal Appeal, which must grant leave where a point of law is involved or where the trial was unsatisfactory.[116] The requirement of leave is more a theoretical than a practical hurdle since every application for leave receives a hearing in open court before three judges and the hearing of the application is usually treated as the hearing of the appeal.[117] The case is not fully re-heard in the court. Counsel submit legal arguments or, exceptionally, present fresh evidence. The Court is empowered to affirm the conviction, to reverse it in whole or in part or to reduce or increase sentence.[118]

Although the Court's constitutionality has been upheld,[120] in many ways it is unfortunately designed: it is anomalous that High Court judges should sit on appeal from other High Court judges; an appellant wishing to raise a constitutional point cannot do so in the Court, but only in the Supreme Court; and its changing composition deprives it of continuity. For these and other reasons, the Committee on Court Practice and Procedure has recommended its abolition and the creation of an unqualified right of appeal to the Supreme Court.[121] No action has been taken on these recommendations, although they may be thought to have taken greater cogency from the situation which has now arisen and which will be described at **Supreme Court**, paragraph 5.

Supreme Court Several heads of appellate jurisdiction have been conferred on the Supreme Court.

1. Either side can appeal from the decision, by the High Court, of a case stated from the District Court, provided that they obtain the High Court's leave.[122]

2. A Circuit Court judge may, on the application of either side, in a case pending before him, refer any question of law to the Supreme Court.[123] This power is little used because it necessitates the adjournment of the Circuit Court trial, pending the Supreme Court's decision.

3. Where in any trial on indictment, before the Central Criminal Court or Circuit Court, the judge has directed the jury to bring in a verdict in favour of the accused on a question of law, the DPP (formerly the Attorney General) may refer the point of law to the Supreme Court so as to obtain its decision as a precedent for future cases. But the acquittal of the accused stands, whatever decision the Supreme Court reaches.[124]

4. There may be an appeal from a decision of the Court of Criminal Appeal, if that Court or the DPP or Attorney General certifies that the decision 'involves a point of law of exceptional public importance and that it is desirable in the public interest that an appeal should be taken to the Supreme Court.'[125]

5. The Central Criminal Court is the High Court's *alter ego* and by Art. 34.4.2°, examined above,[126] the Supreme Court enjoys appellate jurisdiction

from all decisions of the High Court apart from any exceptions or restrictions created by statute. This provision has made a considerable impact in the field of criminal procedure. In the first place, it means that a person convicted in the Central Criminal Court has a choice: first, he may appeal to the Court of Criminal Appeal (as already mentioned); if he does this, he may appeal on to the Supreme Court only if he can bring himself with the narrow category ('point of law of exceptional public importance . . .') stated in the previous paragraph.[127] The second alternative was more of a surprise: in *The People (A.G.) v. Conmey*[128] the Supreme Court, by a majority held that if the accused chose not to appeal to the Court of Criminal Appeal then he retained his constitutional right to appeal from the High Court to the Supreme Court. The basis of this view was that a statutory right to appeal from the High Court to the Court of Criminal Appeal amounted to an 'exception' to Art. 34.4.3° only if it were actually exercised. Otherwise, the general principle contained in the constitutional provision, which may only be dislodged by a statute which is clear and unambiguous, holds sway, and an accused convicted in the Central Criminal Court remains free to apppeal to the Supreme Court against conviction or sentence. The anomalies to which this rule leads — a double set of appellate tribunals; possibly more favourable treatment for persons convicted in the Central Criminal Court compared with those convicted in the Circuit Court or the Special Criminal Court — are obvious.

The second consequence of Art. 34.3.1° was even more surprising. Following a period of indecision commencing with an *obiter dictum* in *Conmey*,[129] the Supreme Court has applied the general principle of Art. 34.3.1° at its full, literal width to hold that the prosecutor may appeal to the Supreme Court against an acquittal in the Central Criminal Court. In the hotly-contested case of *The People (DPP) v. O'Shea*,[130] in which this rule was established, the two dissenting judges (Finlay P and Henchy J) relied in vain on the argument that there is, inherently, no appeal from a jury acquittal and on the ancient tradition in the criminal justice system against double jeopardy. Whilst the debate is interesting, the outcome of less importance now that the Minister for Justice has promised[131] to amend the Criminal Justice Bill 1983 to deal comprehensively with all criminal appeals, including the difficulty arising from *O'Shea*. Moreover, one passage in *O'Shea* makes it clear that the Supreme Court has a discretion whether to hear criminal appeals against High Court jury verdicts and that this discretion will only be exercised on certain conditions. This passage is of lasting interest because the discretion applies whether the jury verdict is of conviction or acquittal. Chief Justice O'Higgins said:

A clear practice has developed in relation to appeals brought in respect of civil jury trials. I see no reason why that practice, with appropriate changes. should not apply to appeals resulting from jury trials on criminal charges. Verdicts which are arrived at properly and are supported by evidence, while in theory appealable, would not be disturbed. This Court would be bound by findings of fact at the trial. A conviction would be open to challenge on the sufficiency of the evidence relied on to support it, or on the trial judge's directions or rulings on law. An acquittal duly recorded by a jury on a consideration of the evidence would be immune. Where, however, as in this case, the acquittal resulted from a direction given by the judge, so that the verdict was recorded as a result of the judge's decision and not that of the jury, the Court would consider the appeal in the same manner as a similar appeal in a civil action. If the direction should not have been given, the verdict would be set aside in the same manner as a judgment in favour of a defendant where a case had been wrongly withdrawn from a jury in a civil action. As in civil actions, a new trial would be ordered.[132]

12.5 CIVIL JURISDICTION

District Court Though the District Court is the humblest court in the hierarchy, with a relatively informal procedure, it hears far more cases than all the other courts put together. The various heads of jurisdiction conferred upon the District Court are all subject to the territorial limitations which have already been covered in Section 2 and to financial restrictions. The financial limits, in the area of contract and tort, were increased ten-fold by the Courts Act, 1981 — more than restoring the slippage due to inflation since they were previously fixed in 1971. The Court's jurisdiction includes the following fields: breach of contract or tort (apart from slander, libel, criminal conversations, seduction of title, malicious prosecution or false imprisonment), where the claim does not exceed £2,500;[133] claims arising out of hire purchase agreements where again the maximum claim is £2,500;[134] ejectment for non-payment of rent or overholding, where the annual rent does not exceed £2,500.[135] The District Court also has often-used powers in the field of family law. For instance, it may make a maintenance order against a deserting spouse for the payment of up to £100 per week for the spouse[136] or £30 per week for each illegitimate child.[137] It has extensive powers in the field of guardianship and custody of children.[138] It may also make an order barring a spouse from the family home, if there are reasonable grounds for believing that the safety or welfare of the other spouse or any dependant child requires it. The barring order may be for a maximum period of twelve months, but subject to renewal.[139] (In contrast there is no limit in the case of Circuit Court orders.)

The Courts Act, 1981 made particularly large changes in the family law field and its intended impact may be highlighted by quoting the following passage from the Minister for Justice's speech in the second reading in the Dáil:

. . . in family matters an application to court will often need to cover a number of remedies — a barring order, maintenance and the custody of children being the most common. It is important that a single court should be in a position to grant what one might call the appropriate package on one application. When the Bill becomes law it will be possible for the District Court to deal with all these remedies — excluding only a decree of divorce *a mensa et thoro* — even where the sums sought by way of maintaining are quite substantial. This should cater for the vast majority of cases. The Circuit Court will be enabled to grant the full package without exception or limitation.[140]

In transferring the bulk of family law cases away from the High Court to the two lower courts, the legislature is seeking to provide a cheaper, simple procedure and one which is available closer to the parties' homes.

Circuit Court As just indicated, in the family law area the Circuit judge has unlimited jurisdiction in the areas in which the District Court has a broad, though limited, jurisdiction.[141] In addition, it may grant decrees of divorce *a mensa et thoro* (judicial separation), the effect of which is to suspend the spouses' duty to cohabit and not to free them to remarry.[142] Again, the Circuit Court has jurisdiction under the Family Home Protection Act, 1976 to protect the right of a spouse to reside in the family home. Where the rateable value of the land exceeds £200, then the Court must transfer the proceedings to the High Court, if the defendant so requests.[143]

The Circuit Court has jurisdiction over claims arising from hire purchase agreements, breach of contract cases, and tort actions (apart from criminal conversation), but subject to a maximum of £15,000.[144] It is worth mentioning here that, since 1971, there has been no right to jury trial in civil cases.[145]

Unlike the District Court, the Circuit Court has extensive, though not unlimited, powers in the chancery field. It can, for instance, hear actions concerning the title to land whose rateable value does not exceed £200.[146] A similar limit applies to its jurisdiction over such matters as: the execution of trusts; the dissolution of partnerships; or the grant (or refusal) of probate or letters of administration. But there are no limits to the value of the personalty involved in such cases.[147]

Certain items of business *appear*[148] to have been vested exclusively in the Circuit Court, regardless of the value of the subject-matter involved: for example, granting a new on-licence under the Intoxicating Liquor Code[149] or actions for a new statutory lease under the Landlord and Tenant Acts, 1931.[150]

High Court As mentioned already in Section 2, the Constitution bestows upon the High Court the widest possible jurisdiction and, thus, a description of its jurisdiction consists principally in saying that it bears no equivalent of the limitations as to territory or type of value or subject-matter which affect the lower courts.

It is very significant that, save in 'an action for a liquidated sum, or an action for the enforcement or for damages for the breach, of a contract,' there is an absolute statutory (though not constitutional) right to have a question of fact or damages tried by a jury.[151] This means, for instance, that a negligence case (and about a half of High Court contested cases are negligence cases) can only be heard without a jury where both parties consent and the plaintiff is most unlikely to consent.[152] A majority of nine out of the twelve jurors will suffice to determine the verdict in civil cases.[153]

Appeals to Circuit Court or High Court First, there is an appeal by way of re-hearing, on fact or law, from the District Court to the Circuit Court, whose decision is final.[154] Alternatively, there is the same facility for obtaining an authoritative statement on the law as exists in the criminal justice system, namely the 'case stated' for the High Court, with an appeal lying from the High Court to the Supreme Court.[155]

There is an appeal by way of re-hearing, from the Circuit Court exercising its civil jurisdiction, to the High Court (one judge sitting alone). The High Court on 'circuit' sits in every county and county borough, twice a year. There it hears appeals emanating from the Circuit Courts in the area. However, where no oral evidence has been heard in the case, then the appeal is to the High Court sitting in Dublin.[156]

Supreme Court In any appeal to the High Court from the Circuit Court, the High Court may, on the application of either party, refer any point of law for the determination of the Supreme Court and, if this happens, the High Court action is adjourned pending the Supreme Court's determination.[157] The Circuit Court is also empowerd, on an application by a party, to state a case on a point of law for a decision by the Supreme Court.[158]

The Supreme Court's powers when hearing appeals from the High Court itself vary according to whether the High Court case was heard by a judge sitting with a jury or by judge(s) sitting alone. In the latter case the appellant may ask for the original verdict to be reversed and the Court may make any order which the trial judge could have made. The trial judge may be reversed on a point of law or fact. However, the Court, which has only the short-hand note taken before it, is naturally slow to reverse a finding of fact by a judge who has had the opportunity of listening to the witnesses himself. Where a jury is involved, the appellant can only ask for a re-trial before another jury in the High Court, though the Supreme Court has the power, if it wishes to exercise it, of substituting its own order for the High Court order. The appeal may be based on the submission that the judge misdirected the jury as to law or evidence; that the jury's award of damages was excessive or inadequate; or that the verdict was against the weight of the evidence. However, a successful appeal on a point of fact is even more difficult to sustain in a jury, than in a non-jury, trial.[159]

12.6 JUDICIAL CONTROL OF ADMINISTRATIVE ACTION[160]

Apart from their powers to decide criminal and civil cases, the High Court has also jurisdiction in a variety of other specialised areas. In a work on public law, it seems appropriate to sketch the rules which are applied to control the administrative actions of public authorities, such as ministers or local authorities.

Case study Before going to a more systematic summary, it may be helpful to set the scene by describing a recent British *cause* célèbre in the area, *Bromley v. GLC*,[161] which shows something of the reach of judicial review and the considerable impact which it can make on the decisions of a public authority. The background to *Bromley* was that the newly-elected Labour majority on the Greater London Council had honoured its election promise ('fares fair') to cut London bus and tube train fares by a quarter. The cost of this would have had to be borne by the ratepayers. Accordingly, one of the lower-tier London boroughs (Bromley LBC), which was charged with the duty of levying the rate, sought judicial review of the GLC's action. The actual operation of London's transport services is vested in the London Transport Executive (LTE), whilst the GLC's role is that of policy-maker. By the relevant legislation, the Transport (London) Act 1969, the GLC has power to make grants to the LTE 'for any purpose.' The House of Lords' decision was that this apparently uncontrolled discretion was in fact restricted and the GLC's decision fell outside the restrictions. Summarised very baldly, the House's decision can be put under the following three heads.

(i) By s.7(3) of the Act the LTE is under a duty to avoid a deficit 'as far as practicable.' This provision implies that the GLC is only empowered to make grants to the LTE to make good unavoidable losses and not in order to further a particular social policy (in this case, assisting the travelling public at the expense of the ratepayers). Thus the decision was the result of taking irrelevant considerations into account.

(ii) As a matter of general law (independent of any specific statute) a local authority owes a fidiciary duty to its ratepayers to manage its finances 'responsibly.' Set against this standard, the huge loss which the GLC's policy required, exacerbated by the fact that the GLC's rate support grant had been cut by central government as a punishment for its policy, meant that the decision was regarded by the House as thriftless and, therefore, unreasonable.

(iii) The GLC appeared to regard itself as irrevocably bound by the commitment in the Labour Party's election manifesto to implement the reduction in fares. It had, for instance, gone ahead with its policy in the face of a memorandum from its officials concluding that the transport advantages of the new fares — in terms of increased usage of the transport system — were fairly marginal. This unquestioning loyalty to the doctrine of the electoral mandate meant that there had been, in law, a failure fully and fairly to exercise the GLC's discretion.

The basic idea The law in the area of judicial review of administrative action is untidy and difficult to state in a few simple propositions because it is the product of two conflicting tensions, the balance between which has been set at different points at different periods of judicial thinking. On the one hand, there is the notion that when the legislature allocates a decision in the field of public administration to a specialised public authority, it is reasonable to assume that the legislature does not wish the decision to be taken over by a judge. Judges, after all, are experts in the law and not in public administration; they have not been appointed to strike difficult balances between the claims of different groups in the community; above all, they have not been elected, whereas most, though not all, administrators work under the direction of elected representatives. But on the other hand, the rule of law (on which see Chapter 2.3) requires that an administrative agency should not be left completely free of all legal control and, in particular, that it should not be allowed to wander outside the field staked out for it by the legislature.

Out of the tension between these two policies has emerged a double-barrelled rule which, in its original simple form, may be stated as follows: the High Court will restrain a public authority from acting *ultra vires*, that is, outside the jurisdiction granted to it by the relevant statute, but the Court may not interfere with a public authority's decision simply because it disagrees with the public authority's views of the *merits* of the decision. This doctrine — the *ultra vires* doctrine — has now become more complicated, for two reasons. In the first place, without going into detail, it can be said that there is an inherent difficulty in distinguishing satisfactorily between matters bearing on the merits and those related to *vires* (jurisdiction). This difficulty has been exacerbated by modern developments which have had the effect of shifting the border between merits and *vires* so as to enlarge the scope of judicial review.[162] Secondly, evolving from the simple starting-point which has just been mentioned, the judges have created additional controls over the administrative authorities. However, because the judges were conscious of working in a highly political area, they thought it prudent to proceed stealthily. Thus each of the disparate grounds of judicial review[163] was put under the well-established umbrella of the *ultra vires* principle. These accretions have led to a considerable incoherence in the *ultra vires* doctrine, and it is therefore convenient for the purposes of description to dissect out the six heads of judicial review and to describe them separately.

(i) Correct authority This power may only be exercised by the administrative authority in whom it was vested by the legislature. Thus, for instance, by the *delegatus non protest delegare* rule, the power may only be delegated on to a body other than that in which it is vested by statute, if the legislature has given permission in the statute, explicitly or implicitly, for this delegation to be made. Again, the authority must be properly appointed/elected and, where relevant, properly qualified.[164]

(ii) Pre-conditions The public authority can exercise its powers only over subject-matter which falls within the description, as to facts and circumstances, specified in the statute delineating the authority's field of competence. For example, in one pre-Independence case a local authority was given power to compulsorily acquire land provided that the land was not an orchard. The issue of whether the land which it took was an orchard was reviewed by the High Court.[165] Again, in an English case, a rent tribunal's power to fix a fair rent was confined to cases where a 'contract of tenancy' existed. The question of whether the contract of tenancy had been terminated before the application to the tribunal was made was reviewable by a court; by contrast, the tribunal's decision on the amount of the rent could not be reviewed since that was a question about the merits.[166]

(iii) Within the power   The administrative action must fall within the power conferred by the statute. This is the most straightforward of the heads of review. It means, for instance, that where a tribunal is empowered only to award damages, it cannot make an order for specific performance; again, if a local authority is authorised to make bye-laws dealing with the hours at which vessels may pass a bridge, it is not thereby empowered to levy a charge for the opening of the bridge span.[167]

(iv) Discretionary powers   A statutory discretionary power is frequently drafted so that, read literally, it seems to give the decision-maker *carte blanche*. In fact, even apart from the Constitution, there are limitations upon these discretionary powers: they must be exercised reasonably and *bona fide*; relevant considerations must be taken into account and irrelevant considerations ignored. As has been observed[168] these constraints overlap to a great extent.

The requirement of reasonableness does not, of course, mean that the court would itself have taken the decision in the same sense as the public body in which the legislature vested the decision: as already mentioned, such a rule would clearly subvert the legislature's intention. Instead, the test is the more extreme one, of whether the decision is so clearly wrong that no reasonable body could have reached it. Even with such a test, a decision will sometimes be struck down: see, for example, *Bromley*, above (ground (ii)).

An example of *mala fides* — that is, the knowing abuse of power — occurred in *Listowel v. McDonagh*.[169] A sanitary authority was empowered, by statute: '[to] prohibit the erection . . . of temporary dwellings . . . if they are of opinion that such erection . . . would be prejudicial to public health . . .'. Purporting to act under this power, Listowel UDC made an order banning the construction of temporary dwellings on a number of named streets. The defendant was convicted and fined 10/- for contravening this order. His principal line of defence was to argue that the order had not been made *bona fide* in that the sanitary authority did not genuinely hold the necessary opinion and had made the order simply in order to exclude itinerants. The Supreme Court accepted the legal argument and held that the Circuit Court (to which the case had gone on appeal) was entitled to inquire into the question of what transpired at the Council meeting which considered the passing of the bye-law. In the result, the Circuit Court found that the order had been made *bona fide*.

A case involving an irrelevant consideration is *The State (Cussen) v. Brennan*,[170] which arose out of the selection, by the Local Appointment Commissioners (of whom Mr Brennan was one), of Dr K. in preference to Dr C., as consultant paediatrician and professor of paediatrics at University

210

College Cork (a joint post). It was established that as far as paediatrics was concerned, the LAC had judged Dr C. to be slightly ahead of Dr K., but that Dr K's knowledge of the Irish language had tipped the balance in his favour. According to the relevant statutory provision (Health Act, 1980, s.18), it was for the Minister for Health to lay down the qualifications for the job. The Minister had duly done this and a knowledge of Irish was not among these qualifications. Consequently the LAC's decision had taken into account an irrelevant condition. However, on the facts in this case, the Supreme Court exercised its discretion not to make any order because of what it regarded as Dr C's excessive delay.[171]

However, the 'relevant considerations' are frequently not explicitly stated, as they happened to be, by the Minister, in *The State (Cussen)*. Instead they may have to be deduced by the court from the general tenor of the statute creating the discretionary power. This is a difficult task and the results are sometimes controversial as can be seen from the *Bromley case* (ground (i)). Something of these difficultires also emerges from the Irish *locus classicus, East Donegal v. Att. Gen.*[172] in which the Supreme Court scrutinised the Livestock Marts Act, 1967, which bestowed considerable discretionary power on the Minister for Agriculture to control marts, through the grant (whether absolutely or subject to conditions) or revocation of licences. These powers were couched in such phraseology as '. . the Minster may at his discretion grant or refuse to grant a licence . . .'; or '[t]he Minister may . . . attach to the licence such conditions as he shall think proper . . .' (1967 Act, s. 3). Nevertheless, said Walsh J:

The words of the Act, and in particular the general words, cannot be read in isolation and their content is to be deprived from their context. Therefore, words or phrases which at first sight might appear to be wide and general may be cut down in their construction when examined against the objects of the Act which are to be derived from a study of the Act as a whole including the long title.[173]

Specifically:

The provisions of s. 6 throw considerable light upon the purposes, objects and scope of the Act because they refer specifically to the power of the Minister for Agriculture and Fisheries being directed towards the proper conduct of the places concerned, the proper conduct of the businesses concerned, the standard of hygiene and the veterinary standards in relation to such places and to the provision of adequate and suitable accommodation and facilities for such auctions. Section 6 also provides for the making of regulations dealing with what might be referred to as the mechanics of sale such as book-keeping, accommodation, hygiene, etc. Nowhere in the Act is there anything to indicate that one of the purposes of the Act is to limit or otherwise regulate the number of auction marts as distinct from regulating the way in which business is conducted in auction marts. In the absence of any such indication in the Act, the Minister is not authorised by the Act to limit the number of businesses of the type defined in Section 1.[174]

Not everyone would agree with the last sentence (which is *obiter*): could there not be a connection between the number of marts and their profitability and, on the other hand, considerations which are (as Walsh J indicates) *intra vires*, such as hygiene or accommodation?

(v) Procedural controls, including constitutional justice The requirement that a decision be taken by way of a particular procedure looms especially large in public law. The reason is that public authorities — in contrast with (say) a private individual selling his house — are assumed to be non-partisan bodies taking a decision in the public interest and thus to be open to persuasion by relevant facts or rational argument. If a proper procedure is observed, all the relevant facts and arguments are more likely to emerge and be weighed. There is thus a link between proper procedure and the quality of the decision.

The source of the procedural rule may be the statute creating the decision or some statutory instrument made under the statute. Thus, for instance, as part of the compulsory purchase power, vested in local autorities, an authority is required to serve a notice to treat on the land-owner requiring him 'to state within a specified period (not being less than one month from the date of service of the notice to treat) the nature of the interest in respect of which compensation is claimed and details of the compensation claimed.'[175] In *Healy v. Cork*[176] the period given to the land-owner terminated one month after the date when the notice to treat was *issued*, rather than the date when it was *served*. Applying the presumption that where property rights are concerned, the wording of a statute must be strictly applied against the public authority, the High Court held that the notice to treat was invalid. Hence the local authority would have to initiate the entire process again and, consequently, to pay a much higher sum in compensation.

However, much more important than any particular rules contained in a statute or statutory instrument are the principles which are known as the rules of constitutional justice. First, the decision-maker must not either be biased or appear to be biased, for any reason (for example, financial or political considerations; or the desire to uphold his own previous finding reached at an earlier stage of the decision-making process).[177] Secondly, the 'victim' of an administrative decision should have full knowledge of the case against him and an adequate opportunity of advancing any arguments he may have to rebut it. Thirdly, constitutional justice 'import[s] *more* than the two well-established principles that no man shall judge in his own cause, and *audi alteram partem*.'[178] Thus far, little use has been made of this third rule, which remains an unplumbed reservoir of procedural standards.

In one typical case, involving the second rule of constitutional justice, *Garvey v. Ireland*,[179] the plaintiff's removal as Commissioner of the Garda Síochána was struck down because he had been given no reason for his removal and no opportunity to make representations as to why he should not be removed. A second example of constitutional justice in operation is afforded by the following passage from *East Donegal*, in which Walsh J outlined the manner in which the Minister for Agriculture must exercise his mart-licensing function:

'[The Minister] is required to consider every case upon its own merits, to hear what the applicant . . . has to say, and to give the latter an opportunity to deal with whatever case may be thought to exist against the granting of a licence or for the refusal of a licence or for the attaching of conditions, or for the amendment or revocation of conditions which have already attached as the case may be.[180]

The rules have been applied in a wide range of contexts, in each of which some serious individual interest was at stake. These include: dismissal from public or private employment;[181] other decisions affecting livelihood, such as licence applications or revocations and trade union membership;[182] disciplinary hearings;[183] social welfare grant or pension applications;[184] and planning or compulsory purchase order appeals.[185]

The British equivalent of constitutional justice is known as natural justice. Apart from the additional element contained in constitutional justice (mentioned above), there are two points of contrast between the two concepts: first, it has been stated that constitutional justice is rooted in Art. 40.3.1° of the Constitution[186] and thus it cannot be excluded by statute. Secondly, it has been applied to a greater range of situations than is the case in Britain.[187] To put it briefly, the Irish judges have set the balance between adminstrative efficiency and fair procedure for individuals further in favour of the individual than the British judges.

(vi) Unconstitutionality[188]   It seems likely that Constitutional prohibitions apply in the same way to delegated legislation or other administrative action as they do to Acts of the Oireachtas.[189] A straightforward example of this is the Supreme Court case of *Quinn's Supermarket v. A.G.*[190] which concerned the special exemption on hours of trading granted to proprietors of shops selling Jewish kosher meat, contained in the hours of trading order made under the Shops (Hours of Trading) Act, 1938. The plaintiff (a gentile) was being prosecuted for breach of the order. As a defence he claimed, successfully, that the order was unconstitutional in that it amounted to religious discrimination, contrary to Art. 44.2.3° of the Constitution. The Court held that discrimination is justifiable if it is necessay in the interests of the right to practise religion which is guaranteed by Art.44.2.2 and which the exemption in favour of kosher shops was intended to facilitate. However, in the instant case, the Court struck down the order just because the exceptional hours of opening permitted to the kosher shops went further than was necessary for the practice of the Jewish religion.

General   Finally, it is important to mark two distinctions, the first of which relates to the contexts in which a court may have to review an administrative action. This may occur, first, in the context of specialised proceedings leading

213

to either a state-side order (certiorari, prohibition or mandamus) or an equitable order (declaration or injunction). (An account of the different situations in which the various orders apply would be outside the scope of this work.)[191] In this type of case (for example, *Bromley*; *The State (Cussen)*; *East Donegal* the only questions at issue would be the validity of the administrative action. Alternatively, this question could form only one of the elements for decision during the course of an ordinary criminal or civil case (for example, *Listowel*; *Quinn's Supermarket*). This difference may be illustrated by reference to the situation arising from revocation of a trading licence by an administrative action which did not follow the rules of constitutional justice. In this case, a cautious trader would seek an order of certiorari quashing the revocation. A less cautious trader would continue trading and then, when he was prosecuted, would rely on the invalidity of the revocation as his defence.

It is also significant here to distinguish between a review (which is what we have been speaking about so far in this Section) and an appeal. There are two principal differences. First, an appeal involves a re-taking of the decision, sometimes in its entirety, sometimes partially, as for example, if the appeal is on a point of law only. By contrast, the focus of review is not the merits of the issue but certain characteristics — those which have just been listed — of the original decision, as it was taken by the public authority. Secondly, the High Court always has inherent powers of review over public authorities and, incidentally, over lower courts (District Court, Circuit Court and Special Criminal Court). But an appeal only exists (and then it is not necessarily to a court) if one is created by statute — usually by the statute which creates the power. There is, for instance, in tax matters, an appeal by way of re-hearing from the Revenue Commissioners and thence to the Circuit Court. There is also an appeal by way of case stated — that is, on a point of law only — from the Appeals Commissioners to the High Court and on to the Supreme Court.[192]

Broadly speaking, the legislature is more likely to create an appeal where some important individual interest is directly involved and where there is some code of rules by reference to which the decision must be taken. By contrast, where one is dealing with a policy decision affecting large numbers of people, the only resort from the public authority which took the initial decision will (usually) be to the High Court on review.

214

Notes

NOTES TO CHAPTER 1

1 See Section 5 of this Chapter.
2 See Art. 15.4.
3 Brian Farrell, *The Founding of Dáil Éireann* (Dublin 1971), 83.
4 [1940] IR 146, 179. Cf. too *O'Donovan v A.G.* [1961] IR 114, 136 on which see Chapter 11.2.
5 See Chapter 4.3
6 On which see S.A. de Smith, *Constitutional and Administrative Law* (London 1983), Chapter 2.
7 *Adegbenro v. Akintola* [1963] 3 WLR 63, 70, 73.
8 See further, text above note 27 in Chapter 11.
9 For further detail, see text above note 48 in Chapter 5.
10 See Chapter 5.4.
11 However, see now 'How the Coalition hands out the jobs'), *Irish Times*, 14 February 1984.
12 See J.M. Kelly, *The Irish Constitution* (Dublin 1984), 427-673.
13 Art. 15.4.1°.
14 [1965] IR 294.
15 Kelly, *op. cit.*, 474-75.
16 L.H.Tribe, *American Constitutional Law* (New York 1978), 914-15.
17 [1974] IR 284; see also now Health (Family Planning) Act No. 20 of 1979 and B.M.E. McMahon, *'The Law relating to Contraception in Ireland'* in D.M. Clarke (ed.), *Morality and the Law* (Cork 1982).
18 Heyman and Barzeley, 53 *BUL Rev*, 765, 772-6.
19 Budd (322), Henchy (328); Griffin (333) JJ. Of the other judges, Fitzgerald CJ dissented and Walsh J rested his decision on the more obvious bases of Art. 41 (protection of the family) and Mrs McGee's right to life under Art. 40.3.2°.
20 Unreported judgment on 22 April 1983.
21 *The State (Nicolaou) v. An Bord Uchtála* [1966] IR 567; *In re J.* [1966] IR 295.
22 [1980] IR 32, 55.
23 [1966] IR 345.
24 S. 2(1). See Chapter 4.3.
25 *O'Brien v. Keogh* [1972] IR 144; *O'Brien v. Manufacturing* [1973] IR 334; *Moynihan v. Greensmyth* [1977] IR 55. There is some authority for saying that the right to litigate ought to be located under Art. 40.3.2°.
26 [1972] IR 330.
27 *Murphy v. Stewart* [1973] IR 97, 117.
28 (1973) 109 ILTR 1.
29 [1976] IR 325.
30 [1976] IR 365, 372.
31 [1974] IR 284, 325.
32 [1983] ILRM 156.
33 [1982] IR 241.
34 [1965] IR 294, 312-3.
35 *Buckley (Sinn Féin) v. A.G.* [1950] IR 67, 80.
36 See *Report of the Committee on the Constitution*, 1967 (Pr. 9817). The Committee also submitted

a number of queries (see Annex) on the drafting of the Constitution to the Attorney General. He convened a committee of a dozen or so leading lawyers to examine these queries. The report of this Committee was completed, but never published, except that the Committee's comments on Art. 15.12 (parliamentary privilege) were published as Appendix 1 to the Committee of Public Accounts' Interim Report into the Grant in Aid for Northern Ireland Relief (Prl. 2574).

37 See Arts. 2 and 3; 41.3.3°; and former Art. 44.1., respectively.
38 See F.S.L. Lyons, *Ireland Since the Famine* (London 1973), 381-570; Leo Kohn, *The Constitution of the Irish Free State* (London 1932), Parts I-III; Delaney-Lysaght, *The Administration of Justice in Ireland*, 4th ed. (Dublin 1975), Chap. IV; Brian Farrell, *The Founding of Dáil Éireann* (Dublin 1971) and 4 (1969) *Irish Jurist* 127; John A. Murphy, *Ireland in the Twentieth Century* (Dublin 1975) *passim*; Basil A. Chubb, *The Constitution and Constitutional Change in Ireland* (Dublin 1978), Chapters 1 and 2; A.G. Donaldson, *Some Comparative Aspects of Irish Law* (North Carolina 1957) Chapters 2, 3 and 4; J.F. O'Connor, 'Disturbances in Northern Ireland,' III (1971) *International Relations*, 966.
39 Indemnity Act No. 40 of 1924, s.1; Interpretation Act No. 46 of 1923, s. 2(12); Farrell, 4 (1969) *Irish Jurist* 127.
40 See C. Davitt (1968) *Irish Jurist* 112; and J. Casey, 5 (1970) *Irish Jurist* 321.
41 British Northern Ireland (Temporary Provisions) Act 1972, s. 1(3) and Northern Ireland Constitution Act 1973, s. 31.
42 Irish Free State (Consequential Provisions) Act 1922.
43 For the issue of whether the Treaty was really a treaty or, merely, as the British claimed, 'Articles of Agreement for a Treaty,' see Kohn, *op. cit.*, 56-59. See also O'Connor, *op. cit.*, 971-7.
44 For inter-relationship between the Dáil and the Southern Ireland Parliament, see Lyons, *op. cit.*, 449-50.
45 '. . . one man . . . went to confession and confessed that he had stolen a goat and the penance he got was to read the Dáil speeches on the Treaty debate seven times' (*Dáil Debates*, vol 2, col 2162, 8 March 1923).
46 On which, see Lyons, *op. cit.*, 456-8.
47 See B. Farrell, 5 (1970) *Irish Jurist* 115 and 343; 6 (1971) *Irish Jurist* 111 and 345.
48 See *Select Constitutions of the World* . . . (Stationery Office, Dublin 1922.)
49 Kohn, *op. cit.*, 95-96.
50 On extern ministers, see Chapter 5.2.
51 Act No. 1 of 1922.
52 *The Constitution and Constitutional Change* . . ., *op cit.*, 15. For initiative and referendum, see Chapter 5.2.
53 On which, see text above note 12 in Chapter 6.
54 Constitution (Amendment No. 22) Act No. 45 of 1933. See *Moore v. A.G. for Irish Free State* [1935] AC 484; Kohn, *op. cit.*, Part VII, Chapter IV.
55 Constitution (Amendment No. 21) Act No. 41 of 1933.
56 Constitution (Removal of Oath) Act. No. 6 of 1933.
57 See 1922 Constitution, Arts, 41, 51, 55, 60 and 68. But cf. Kohn, *op. cit.*, 114: 'The monarchical head of the Association into which the Free State had entered had, under the terms of the Treaty, to be introduced into the framework of the Constitution, but it was as a functionary of the Irish people that he appeared therein, almost as the permanent President of an Irish Republic.'
58 Constitution (Amendment No. 27) Act No. 57 of 1936. It was the Executive Powers (Consequential Provisions) Act No. 20 of 1937, which actually abolished the office of Governor-General.
59 1937 Constitution, Art. 29.4.2°. Cf. 1922 Constitution, Art. 51.
60 No. 58 of 1936, s. 3(1).
61 *Dáil Debates*, vol 67, col 60, 11 May 1937.
62 Donaldson, *op. cit.*, 89-93.
63 *Report of the Irish Boundary Commission 1925* (Shannon 1969) with an introduction by G.F. Hand.

64 Treaty (Confirmation of Amending Agreement) Act No. 40 of 1925.
65 Arts. 2 & 3.
66 [1935] AC 472, 481.
67 497.
68 See *B.C.C. v. The King* [1935] AC 500, 520; [1935] IR 487, 497 '. . . the Imperial Parliament could, as a matter of abstract law, repeal or disregard [the statute on which Canada's independence rested]'.
69 [1935] IR 170.
70 On which, see text above note 89 below.
71 See 203, 226 and 239.
72 [1955] IR 176, 216, 17.
73 *Cahill v. A.G.* [1925] IR 70, 76.
74 *Dáil Debates*, vol 67, col 416; Lee 1967 ILTSJ 252
75 For results of the plebiscite, see note 97 below.
76 [1972] IR 242, 216-3, 295-6.
77 263 (Walsh J). See also 295.
78 [1950] IR 142, 152 where the following passage from Sir John Salmond's *Jurisprudence* is quoted with approval: 'Is the commonwealth a body politic and corporate endowed with legal personality, and having as its members all those who owe allegiance to it and are entitled to its protection?' See, too, *Commissioners of Public Works v. Kavanagh* [1962] IR 216, 226.
79 Cf. J.M. Kelly, *The Irish Constitution* (Dublin, 1984) xxix.
80 It seems likely from *Byrne* that the Court would have been prepared to hold, if necessary, that the State was sovereign but at the same time open to being sued in tort: 264.
81 301.
82 Unreported judgment of 8 February 1984.
83 Arts. 16.1.2°; 12.2.2°; 47.3.
84 Unreported judgment, p. 12.
85 See Chapter 5.2.
86 Kohn, *op. cit.*, 112.
87 Cf. the classic formulation of this idea in the U.S. Declaration of Independence, 1776.
88 See, generally, *Report of the Committee on the Constitution*, 1967 (Pr. 9817) paras. 143-48 and Annex 25; Basil Chubb, *The Constitution and Constitutional Change . . .* (Dublin 1978), *op. cit.*; K.C. Wheare, *Modern Constitutions (Oxford 1966), Chapters 5, 6 and 7*.
89 *A.G. v. McBride* [1928] IR 451.
90 Constitution (Amendment No. 10) Act, 1928.
91 [1935] IR 170. Notice that Art. 51 of the 1937 Constitution which provided that the Oireachtas alone could amend the Constitution for the first three years, expressly excluded Art. 46 (the amending article) from its scope.
92 Arts. 46, 47. Notice that it has been decided, in the context of attempts to prevent the Eighth Amendment of the Constitution Bill, 1982 ('the pro-life amendment') from being put to referendum, that the courts have no jurisdiction to scrutinise a bill at this stage: save in the case of Art. 26, a court's jurisdiction is confined to examining the constitutionality of *enacted law*: see *Roche v. Ireland* unreported High Court judgment of 17 June 1983; *Finn v. Minister for the Environment* unreported High Court judgment of 20 July 1983 and Supreme Court judgment of 26 July 1983.
93 Pr. 9817, para. 148. On whether this now appears a correct assumption, see note 97 below.
94 Art. 50.
95 See Chubb, *op. cit.*, 57-60; 14 (1979) *Irish Jurist* 253-4.
96 Art. 34.1. See text above note 15 in Chapter 2.
97 See table on next page.
98 Courts Act No. 11 of 1981, s. 5.

217

RESULTS OF REFERENDA

Note 97

	Total Electorate	Total Poll	Per cent Poll	Votes in Favour	Votes Against
Plebiscite on Draft Constitution	1,775,055	1,346,207	75.8	685,105	526,945
Third Amendment of the Constitution Bill, 1958 [Straight vote, constituency boundary commission]	1,678,540	979,531	58.4	453,322	486,989
Third Amendment of the Constitution Bill, 1968 [Alteration of population per deputy]	1,717,389	1,129,477	65.8	424,185	656,803
Fourth Amendment of the Constitution Bill, 1968 [Straight vote, constituency boundary commission, etc.]	1,717,389	1,129,278	65.8	423,496	657,898
Third Amendment of the Constitution Bill, 1971 [EEC Entry]	1,783,604	1,264,278	70.9	1,041,890	211,891
Fourth Amendment of the Constitution Bill, 1972 [Votes at 18]	1,783,604	903,439	50.7	724,835	131,514
Fifth Amendment of the Constitution Bill, 1972 [Termination of special position of Catholic Church]	1,783,604	903,669	50.7	721,003	133,430
Sixth Amendment of the Constitution (Adoption) Bill, 1978	2,179,466	623,476	28.61	601,694	6,265
Seventh Amendment of the Constitution, 1979 [Election of Members of Seanad Éireann by Institutions of Higher Education) Bill	2,179,466	622,646	28.57	552,600	45,484
Eighth Amendment of the Constitution Bill, 1983 [Pro-life Amendment]	2,385,651	1,266,000	50.3	841,233	416,136
Ninth Amendment of the Constitution Bill, 1984 [Extension of the Dáil Franchise]	2,051,165	895,022	43.7	726,310	168,712

NOTES TO CHAPTER 2

1 See M.C.J. Vile, *Constitutionalism and the Separation of Powers* (Oxford 1967); Geoffrey Marshall, *Constitutional Theory* (Oxford 1971), Chapter V.

2 Letter in *Life of Mandell Creighton* (London 1904) 372.

3 *Constitutional and Administrative Law, op. cit.*, 36.

4 O. Hood Philips, *Constitutional and Administrative Law* (London 1979) 13.

5 See Kelly, *op. cit.*, 210-249; Casey, 24 (1975) *ICLQ* 305. In Australia, where the constitutional structure is similar, it has also been held that this principle means, *inter alia*, that powers alien to the judicial cannot be vested in courts: *A.G. for Australia v. R. and the Boilermakers Society* [1957] AC 288. There has been no occasion for this question to arise in Ireland.

6 Or anyone else: for contempt of court, see Kelly, *op. cit.*, 249-255.

7 *Buckley v. A.G.* [1950] IR. 67.

8 [1973] IR 140. For a similar situation to *Maher*, with a similar outcome, see *McEldowney v. A.G.* unreported Supreme Court judgment of 26 July 1983.

9 Id., 146.

10 [1963] IR 170, 183. *Cf. State (O'Rourke) v. Kelly* unreported Supreme Court judgment of 28 July 1980.

11 *The State (Sheerin) v. Kennedy* [1966] IR 379; see, too, *The State (O) v. O'Brien* [1973] IR 50; *The State (C) v. Min. for Justice* [1967] IR 106.

12 *Murphy v. Dublin No. 1* [1972] IR 215, 233; see, also, *The People (A.G.) v. Simpson* [1959] IR 105; *Geraghty v. Minister for Local Government* [1975] IR 300; *Folens v. Minister for Education* [1981] ILRM 21, *State (Crawford) v. Governor of Mountjoy Prison* [1981] ILRM 86; *Hunt v. Roscommon* unreported High Court judgment of 1 May 1981; *State (Hanley) v. Holly* unreported High Court judgement 24 June 1983.

13 [1961] IR 411.

14 [1971] IR 217. On the particular facts of the case, the Court was able to apply the presumption of constitutionality on this point.

15 But *cf. G. v. An Bord Uchtála* [1980] IR 32, 70, 72; *Cowan v. A.G.* [1961] IR 411, 419-21.

16 Art. 37.2 inserted by the Sixth Amendment of the Constitution (Adoption) Act 1979.

17 [1933] IR 74

18 For example, *Foley v. I.L.C.* [1952] IR 118, 156; *Madden v. Ireland* unreported High Court judgment of 22 May 1980.

19 [1960] IR 239. See also Solicitors (Amendment) Act No. 37 of 1960, ss. 56-58; Medical Practitioners Act No. 4 of 1978, s. 46.

20 275. For High Court, see 251.

21 *Lynham (No. 2)* at p. 113; *In re Solicitors Act, 1954 and D, a Solicitor* 95 ILTR 60; *Central Dublin v. A.G.* 109 ILTR 69.

22 289-69.

23 109 ILTR 69.

24 *'Constitutional Theory'*, op. cit, 119.

25 *In re Solicitors Act*, 1954 [1960] IR 239, 271.

26 [1964] IR 239, 247-48. The actual decision in *State (Shanahan)* involved the Attorney General's (now the Director of Public Prosecution's) power to order the trial, on indictment, of an accused although the District Court had held that there was no case to answer. Davitt P held that this constituted an interference with the administration of justice. His decision was reversed in the Supreme Court. However, it was the High Court's view which prevailed in the recent Supreme Court case of *Costello v. Director of Public Prosecutions* [1984] ILRM 413.

27 [1965] IR 217, 230-1.

28 *Cf. Prentis v. Atlantic Coast* 29 Sup. Ct. Reports 67, 69.

29 109 ILTR 69.

30 Prl. 3632, paras. 94-101.

31 For Australian authority on this, see *Shell Co. of Australia v. Federal Commission of Taxation* (1930) 44 CLR 530; *Rola Co. v. The Commonwealth* (1944) 69 CLR 185; *R. v. Macfarlane* (1923) 32 CLR 518.

32 *In re Solicitors Act 1954* at 273.
33 *McDonald* at 231.
34 232.
35 241-2.
36 [1980] IR 381, 398-9.
37 [1983[ILRM 429; [1984] ILRM 208.
38 For *ultra vires*, see Chapter 12.5.
39 [1967] IR 106, 118.
40 [1972] IR 215, 237-39.
41 See Art. 28.4.2°; Ministers and Secretaries Act, 1924, s. 5; see also Chapter 4.3.
42 For short accessible accounts, see R.F.V. Heuston, *Essays in Constitutional Law* (London 1964), Chapter 2; Hood Philips, *Constitutional and Adminsitrative Law, op. cit.*, 35-40; H.W.R. Wade, *Administrative Law* (London 1982), 23-28; Sir Ivor Jennings, *The Law and the Constitution* (London 1959) Chapter II, Section 1 and appendix II.
43 See e.g. Philip Kurland, *Watergate and the Constitution* Chicago 1978), Chapter 6. There were three articles of impeachment: obstructing justice by attempting to cover up the Watergate break-in; repeated violation of the constitutional rights of citizens, for example, by harassing political opponents by causing discriminatory tax investigations into their affairs; failing to produce the papers sub-poena'd by the Judiciary Committee of the House of Representatives.
44 [1966] IR 345.
45 P.P. O'Donoghue, *The Citizen versus the State* in F.C. King (ed.), *Public Administration*, Vol. III (Dublin 1954).
46 For the rule of law in the context of a British Government's attempt to enforce a non-statutory pay policy through its control over contracts and subsidies, see [1978] *Public Law* 333. See, too 'Dukes [Min. for Finance] denies any outside pressure to block pay deal,' *Irish Times*, 11 May 1983.
47 Wade, *op. cit.*, 23.
48 Art. 15.5. which does not, however, ban retrospective increases in punishment.
49 For comment on retrospective taxation legislation, see *Irish Law Times*, August 1983, 63.
50 Art. 34.1.
51 *State (Buchan)v. Coyne* (1936) 70 ILTR 185; *McDonald v. Bord na gCon* [1965] IR 217, 242; *In re Haughey*, [1971] IR 217, 263-64.
52 Art. 38.5; see Chapter 12.3.
53 *The State (Healy) v. Donoghue* [1976] IR 325, 350-2, 62

NOTES TO CHAPTER 3

1 See Michael McDunphy, *The President of Ireland* (Dublin 1945). Mr McDunphy was Secretary to the President when he wrote. See also *Magill*, June 1983. These two works constitute extreme opposites so far as reticence-revelation is concerned.
2 Art. 12.1.
3 Quoted in Dunphy, *op. cit.*, 4. The original statement in Irish is less grandiloquent.
4 Kohn, *op. cit.*, 264. By Ombudsman Act No. 26 of 1980, s. 2 the President also now appoints the Ombudsman.
5 Art 13.4, 5 and 10.
6 Act No. 18 of 1954, s. 17(1).
7 Art. 13.5.2°; Defence Act, 1954, Part IV, Chapter 1.
8 Art. 13.6. The section also provides that, save in capital cases, the powers of commutation or remission may be conferred on other authorities, on which, see Criminal Justice Act, 1951, s. 23; Road Traffic Act, 1961, s. 124.
9 Red Cross Act No. 20 of 1944 s. 1.
10 The Republic of Ireland Act No. 22 of 1948, s. 3.
11 Art. 13.9 and 11.
12 Art. 14.

13 Chubb, *The Constitution* . . ., *op. cit.*, 28-29.

14 *Dáil Debates.* vol 67, col 51.

15 Not included are the President's powers in regard to the appointment or removal of members of the Council of State: Art. 31.

16 Art. 22.2. See text above note 53 in Chapter 8.

17 Art. 24. See text above note 9 in Chapter 7.

18 Art. 27.4. See text above note 14 in Chapter 7.

19 Art. 26.2.1°. See text above note 88 in Chapter 7.

20 Art. 13.2.2°. See text between notes 31 and 32 in Chapter 5.

21 Art. 13.2.3°. See note 22 and text above it.

22 The Council of State met to advise on the exercise of this function on 20 December 1968.

23 However, see Art. 14.4.

24 Arts. 31, 32.

25 Presidential Establishment Act No. 24 of 1938, ss. 6, 7; Dunphy, *op. cit.*, 91.

26 Consider, for example, the dismissal of the Australian Prime Minister by the Governor-General in 1975 (see [1976] Public Law 217); the Governor General's dissolution of the constituent assembly in Pakistan in 1955: see B.O. Nwabueze, *Constitutionalism in the Emergent States* (London 1973), 185-88.

27 Notice that in 1945, President Hyde was subjected to some criticism by the Government during the election campaign for his successor because he had used his Art. 26 power to refer the School Attendance Bill, 1942 to the Supreme Court (*Round Table* vol. 35 (1945), 307, 312-13).

28 See *In re Emergency Bill, 1976* [1977] IR 159; for more elaborate description and comment, see M. Gallagher, *Parliamentary Affairs*, vol. XXX, 373-84; Gwynn Morgan, 13 (1978) *Irish Jurist* 67.

29 Art. 13.7. For the other view on this point, see Kelly, *op. cit.*, 65-66. The President is also debarred from leaving the State except with the Government's consent: Art. 12.9. For the difficulties presently arising, in Italy, from the outspokeness of the ceremonial President (Pertini), see, for example, *Irish Times*, 12 January 1984.

30 Art. 13.8.1°.

31 Unreported. See *Irish Times*, 14 May 1981.

32 [1982] ILRM 501.

33 Art. 13.8.1°.

34 *Dáil Debates*, vol 93, col 2469, 2483; vol 107, cols 133, 141; vol 96, col 2325.

35 Art. 12.11. Presidential Establishment Act No.24 of 1938, s. 1(2). Under the Presidential Establishment (Amendment) Act No. 18 of 1973, s. 2 the President's personal remuneration is equal to that of the Chief Justice plus 10%.

36 Art. 12.6.3°.

37 Art. 12.10. 13.8.2°.

38 Art. 12.3.1°.

39 Art. 12.2.2°. Electoral Act, 1963, s. 5.

40 Art. 12.1-8.

41 No. 32 of 1937.

42 Act No. 19 of 1963, Part IV.

43 Art. 12.4.1°, 6.2°, 3.2°.

44 Art. 12.4.2°. In 1959, Eoin O'Mahony secured nominations from three councils but failed to find the fourth nomination.

45 Art. 12.4.4°.

46 Art. 12.2.3°.

47 See, for example, *Report on the Constitution*, 1967, paras. 21-27 and annexes 1 and 2.

NOTES TO CHAPTER 4

1 Arts. 13.1.1°; 28.1; 28.5.1°.
2 *Government and Politics* (Dublin 1970), 166.
3 For the distinction, see Section 3 below.
4 Formerly, he had a second principal function, that of responsibility for all prosecutions on indictment. He lost most of this function on the creation of the office of Director of Public Prosecutions: Prosecution of Offenders Act, 1974; see J.P. Casey, *The Office of the Attorney General in Ireland* (Dublin 1980), Chapter 7.
5 Art. 30.
6 See M. Ó Muimhneacháin, *The Functions of the Department of the Taoiseach* (Dublin 1969).
7 Ministers and Secretaries Act No. 16 of 1924, s. 1(i).
8 For the first statutory reference to Government committees, see Ombudsman Act, 1980, s. 7 (1) (b). The existence of Government committees is usually secret. One example of a long-established committee is the Cabinet Security Committee whose membership usually includes: Taoiseach; Tanaiste; Minister for Foreign Affairs; Minister for Justice; Minister for Defence; and Attorney General.
9 During the 1948-51 Coalition Government, the Chief Whip took the minutes because of Mr Sean MacBride's conviction that, after eleven years' continuous service under Mr de Valera, the Secretary to the Government ought not to be privy to the Government's discussion: B. Farrell, *Chairman or Chief?* (Dublin 1971), 46.
10 Statistics Acts 1926 No. 12 of 1926 and No. 34 of 1946; S.I. No. 142 of 1949.
11 National Board for Science and Technology Act No. 25 of 1977; S.I. Nos. 1 and 37 of 1980.
12 Arts Act No. 9 of 1951.
13 *McLoughlin v. Minister for Social Welfare* [1958] IR 1, 20.
14 *Report of the Public Services Organisation Review Group*, Prl. 792, para. 12.7.5.
15 See generally Farrell, *Chairman or Chief?*, *op. cit.*, and Basil Chubb, *Government and Politics*, 2nd ed. 201-05.
16 Arts. 13.1.1°; 28.5.1°.
17 See Section 3.
18 Art. 13.2.1° *Cf.* Art. 28.2 and 29.4.1°.
19 *Irish Press*, 3 February 1969, quoted in Chubb, *op. cit.*, 203.
20 See text above note 50 in Chapter 5.
21 For circumstances of Dr Browne's dismissal of 1951, see Farrell, *op. cit.*, 50-52.
22 Brian Farrell, 'Coalitions and Political Institutions: The Irish Experience' in Bodlanor (ed.) *Coalition Government in Western Europe* (London, forthcoming), 7.
23 Art. 13.1.2°. On the interaction between the executive and the Dáil, see Chapter 5.
24 Art. 28.7.
25 Senator Connolly (1932-37); Senator Moylan (March-November, 1957). The most recent Senator Minister, James Dooge, was Minister for Foreign Affairs during a period (1981-2) when his Government could not afford the absence of a single supporter from the Dáil.
26 Art. 28.8.
27 Ministers and Secretaries (Amendment) Act No. 36 of 1939, s. 7. See also Art. 28.12.
28 Art. 28.9; 13.1.3°; 13.9.
29 Art. 28.10 and 11.1°.
30 Art. 28.11.1°.
31 Art. 28.11.2°.
32 It is arguable on a strict reading of Art. 28.11 that where the existing Taoiseach is returned to office, there is no need for a formal nomination and appointment by the President but nevertheless this is what happened in, for example, 1969 (*Dáil Debates*, vol 241, col 22) and 1965 (vol 215, col 19).
33 *Report of the Committee on the Constitution*, Pr. 9817, para. 32.
34 Art. 28.6. It was stated in the Report on the Constitution that this does not exhaust all the grounds on which a Taoiseach may be unavoidably absent. But see Act. No. 36 of 1939, s. 7.
35 Farrell, *op. cit.*, 11.

36 M. and S. Act, 1924, s. 7.
37 M. and S. (A) (No. 2) Act No. 28 of 1977, s. 1; M. and S. Act No. 2 of 1980, s. 2.
38 For example, Public Service (Delegation of Ministerial Functions) Order, S.I. No. 117 of 1978.
39 1977 Act, s. 2. In *Geraghty v. Min. for Local Government* [1976] IR 153, 154, 160 the power
    was exercised by the parliamentary secretary but the Minister was the defendant. See also
    M. and S. (A) Act, 1980, s. 6.
40 DSO 88(3) 56, 14, 54, 70, 112(3), 118, 119 and SSO 9, 50 and 83. Compare *Dáil Debates*,
    vol 301, col 726ff and DSO 54.
41 For example, Interpretation Act No. 38 of 1937, Sched., item 18; Civil Service Regulation
    Act No. 46 of 1956, s. 2(1) (d).
42 M. and S. (A) No. 2) Act, 1977, s. 4; *Dáil Debates*, vol 301, col 62-63.
43 *Dáil Debates*, vol 301, col 59-62, 2 November 1977 (Mr Colley).
44 M. and S. (A) (No. 2) Act, 1977, s. 1(1).
45 Compare M. and S. Act, 1924 s. 7(1), on which see Farrell, *op. cit.*, 14-15.
46 M. and S. Act, 1924, s. 7(2).
47 M. and S. Act, 1977, s. 1.
48 For the supercession of the title 'Ministry' by 'Department' in 1924, see Fanning, *The Irish
    Department of Finance, 1922-5* (Dublin 1978) 39.
49 S. 2(1).
50 M. and S. (A) Act No. 36 of 1939, s. 6(3).
51 *Murphy v. Dublin No. 1* [1972] IR 215, 238 and *Geraghty v. Min. for Local Government* [1976]
    IR 153, 179. But contrast the English case of *Bushell v. Secretary of State for Environment*
    [1980] 2 AER 608, 613 which, it is submitted, is in closer contact with reality.
52 M. and S. (A) Act, 1939, s. 6(2). Rules of this type are always vulnerable for breach of Art.
    34.3.1°. See *Murren v. Brennan* [1942] IR 466.
53 M. and S. Act No. 16 of 1924, s. 1(ii).
54 M. and S. (A) Act No. 36 of 1939, s. 2.
55 M. and S. (A) Act No. 38 of 1946.
56 Id.
57 M. and S. (A) Act No. 21 of 1956.
58 M. and S. (A) Act No. 17 of 1959.
59 M. and S. (A) Act No. 18 of 1966.
60 M. and S. (A) Act No. 14 of 1973.
61 M. and S. (A) Act No. 27 of 1977.
62 M. and S. (A) Act No. 40 of 1983.
63 Minister for Supplies (Transfer of Functions) Act No. 21 of 1945, s. 3.
64 Act No. 36 of 1939, s. 6(1). The words quoted in the text constitute a rare example of a 'Henry
    VIII clause,' on which see text above note 100 in Chapter 7.
65 Economic Planning and Development (Transfer of Departmental Administration and Ministerial
    Functions) Order, S.I. No. 1 of 1980.
66 Economic Planning and Development (Alteration of Name of Department and Title of Minister)
    Order, S.I. No. 112 of 1980.
67 Energy (Transfer of Departmental, Administration and Ministerial Functions) Order, S.I. No.
    9 of 1980. To complete the story of the departmental re-arrangement which occurred when
    Mr Haughey became Taoiseach, those interested should also see: Tourism (Transfer of
    Departmental Administration and Ministerial Functions) Order, S.I. No. 8 of 1980; Industry,
    Commerce and Energy (Alteration of Name of Department and Title of Minister) Order, S.I.
    No. 10 of 1980; Tourism and Transport (Alteration of Name of Department and Title of
    Minister) Order, S.I. No. 11 of 1980.
68 Art. 55.
69 As of February 1984, the full list of departments of State is as follows: Taoiseach; Environment;
    Foreign Affairs; Energy; Defence; Public Service; Fisheries and Forestry; the Gaeltacht;
    Communications; Finance; Industry, Trade, Commerce and Tourism; Health; Social Welfare;
    Agriculture; Justice; and Education.
70 M. and S. (A) Act, 1946, s. 4. replacing M. and S. Act 1924, s. 3. which had significantly
    limited wording.

71 M. and S. (A) Act, 1939, s. 4. The device of a minister without portfolio has only been availed of twice: once during 1939-45 when a Minister for the Coordination of Defensive Measures was appointed; and, secondly, for a few months in 1977, during a period when a Minister for Economic Planning and Development was appointed before the office had been constituted by the M. and S. Act, 1977.

72 For collective and individual responsibility to the Dáil, see Chapter 5.

73 Art. 28.4.2.; M. and S. Act, 1924, s. 5.

NOTES TO CHAPTER 5

1 See Sections 3, 4 and 5 below.

2 See, generally Sir D.L. Keir *The Constitutional History of Modern Britain since 1485* (Oxford 1968), 273-74, 400-18, 462-72; C.R. Lovell, *English Constitutional and Legal History* (New York 1962) 469-99.

3 For example, 'The electorate returns Deputies to the House. The Deputies in turn elect the Taoiseach . . .' (J. Lynch in *Dáil Debates*, vol 249, col 179, 29 October 1970: motion of confidence in the Taoiseach and other members of the Government arising out of the Arms Trial).

4 See F.S.L. Lyons, *Ireland Since the Famine*, op. cit., Part II, Chapters 1 and 3.

5 Kevin Boland, a Fianna Fáil TD, resigned from the Fianna Fáil Government over the Arms Crisis yet voted confidence in the Government because he had signed the party pledge: *Dáil Debates*, vol 249, col 454, 29 October 1970.

6 Cf. Lord Melbourne's famous remark: 'Now is it to lower the price of corn or isn't it? It does not much matter which we say, but mind, we must all say the same.'

7 For this reason, the distinction which Mr Colley, when Tánaiste, sought to draw in December 1979, between loyalty to Mr Haughey *qua* Taoiseach and absence of loyalty to Mr Haughey *qua* party leader seems to be impracticable.

8 For interaction of individual and collective responsibility, see Section 4 of this Chapter.

9 See, generally, L. Kohn, *The Constitution of the Irish Free State*, op. cit., Part VI, Chap. II; Nicholas Mansergh, *The Irish Free State, Its Government and Politics* (1934), 156-71; J.L. McCracken, *Representative Government in Ireland* (Oxford 1958) 161-69; Basil Chubb, *Cabinet Government in Ireland* (Dublin 1974).

10 See *Dáil Debates*, vol 1, col 1556-60, 12 October 1922 (K. O'Higgins), quoted in Chubb, op. cit., 23.

11 Irish Free State Constitution, Art. 54.

12 Ibid., Arts.51, 55.

13 Ibid., Art. 55.

14 Ibid.,Art. 56.

15 'Mr J.J. Walsh .. . freely availed himself of his . . . right to criticize the Executive Council . . . and this did not make for cohesion': Donal O'Sullivan, *The Irish Free State and its Senate* (London 1940) 89.

16 Constitutional (Amendment No. 5) Act No. 13 of 1927.

17 Irish Free State Constitution, Art. 53. Notice, too, that in contrast with British practice and with the 1937 Constitution (Art. 13.2.1°) it was the Dáil itself which fixed the date of conclusion of the annual session and of the re-assembly: Arts. 24 and 28 and Kohn, op. cit., 233-35.

18 1937 Constitution, Arts. 13.2.2°. See text between notes 31 and 32 of this Chapter.

19 1922 Constitution, Arts. 47 and 48.See, generally, Kohn, op. cit., Part III, Chap.VIII; F.S.L. Lyons, *Ireland since the Famine*, op. cit., 476-78, 498-99.

20 Constitution (Amendment No. 10) Act No. 8 of 1928.

21 Basil Chubb, *Government and Politics* (Dublin 1982), 183-84.

22 The Labour Party's decision to form the 1981-82 Coalition Government was taken at a special delegate party meeting (at the Gaeity Theatre, Dublin) which agreed that the Labour Party should enter the Government. Fine Gael's consent to the terms of the Coalition was signified

by way of a meeting of the parliamentary party: *Irish Times*, 29 June 1981. For the celebrated 'Gregory deal', see *Irish Times*, 8-13 March 1982.

23 Thus, for instance, in November 1982, the Workers' Party voted against the Fianna Fáil Government and brought it down at least partly because an upheaval in the Labour Party, its rival on the Left, made this seem an auspicious time for the Workers' Party to fight an election.

24 *Dáil Debates*, vol 24, cols 239-42, 27 March 1930 and cols 276-468, 3 April 1930.

25 In 1938, a private members' motion to establish compulsory arbitration in civil service pay disputes was carried against the Government's wishes (*Dáil Debates*, vol 71, cols 1866-67, 25 May 1938). In 1944, the Government was defeated on the second stage of a Transport Bill (*Dáil Debates*, vol 93, col 2469-2504, 10 May 1944).

26 See, generally Basil Chubb, *Government and Politics*, op. cit., 183-84 and *Cabinet Government in Ireland*, op. cit., 54-56; J.L. McCracken, op. cit., 168.

27 [1963] 3 WLR 63.See S.A. de Smith, *The New Commonwealth and its Constitutions* (London 1964), 88-90; Macintosh, (1963) 11 *Political Studies* 126, 137-55.

28 Annex 27, p. 153. The same suggestion was made in respect of Art. 13.2.2° where the same phrase is used.

29 [1978] *Public Law* 360 (Philip Morgan).

30 *Irish Times*, 8 July 1981.

31 *Dáil Debates*, vol 337, col 521.

32 S.P.O.G. 1/3 quoted in R. Fanning, *The Irish Department of Finance 1922-58* (Dublin 1978), 641-42, note 36.

33 Arts. 28.11.1°; 30.5.4; Ministers and Secretaries (Amendment) (No. 2) Act No. 28 of 1977, s. 1(3).

34 The wording of Art. 54 of the 1922 Constitution is similar.

35 See text above note 50 in this Chapter.

36 An episode involving the scope of the subject matter within the rule arose in 1982 when two ministers resigned rather than vote for the then Taoiseach (Mr Haughey) to continue as party leader and (consequently) Taoiseach. The ministers asserted that this was not a matter regarding the business of government but was a logically earlier and distinct question and thus not a matter of collective responsibility, which members of the Government could be required to agree upon: see *Irish Times*, 6 October 1982.

37 Circular dated 10 September 1928 (F 200/9/28) quoted in Fanning, op. cit., 573.

38 For example, resignation of Frank Cluskey: see *Irish Times*, 9 December 1983.

39 See text above note 6 in Chapter 1.

40 One Coalition minister, Patrick McGilligan, SC (Professor of Constitutional Law at University College, Dublin 1934-59) asked rhetorically: 'Have we got to the stage when men, because they join the Government circle must all, as one deputy said, when they go out of the Council chamber, speak the same language?' (*Dáil Debates*, vol 119, col 2521, 23 March 1950). But a member of a later Coalition, Garret Fitzgerald, said more moderately: 'When I became a Minister I did not feel I had given up my right to express personal opinions in areas outside the framework of Government decisions and Government policy' (*Dáil Debates*, vol 275, col 181, 24 October 1974.

41 Commenting on the breaches of collective responsibility arising from the dissensions within Fianna Fáil in 1969-70, Professor Chubb oberves: 'In eventually taking decisive and successful action, however, Jack Lynch made it clear that the principle was still regarded as at least the norm' (*Cabinet Government in Ireland*, op. cit., 38-39).

42 J. McGrath and R. Mulcahy (1924, The army mutiny); E. MacNeill (1925, The Boundary Commission); N. Brown (1951, The 'Mother and Child' scheme); P. Smith (1964, Increased power of trades unions); C. Haughey, N. Blaney, (1970, Dismissed as a result of the Arms Crisis); K. Boland (1970, Resigned in sympathy with Messrs. Haughey and Blaney); M. Ó Moráin (1970, Resigned, officially for health reasons): see note 50 below; D. O'Malley and M. O'Donogue (1982, Mr Haughey's leadership); F. Cluskey (1983, Ownership of Dublin Gas Co.). A Parliamentary Secretary (Paudge Brennnan) also resigned in sympathy with Messrs. Haughey and Blaney.

43 '. . . In a country with parliamentary democracy, which is not a presidential system, it is vital

that the Government act collectively and together, vital that the Government should take clear-cut decisions clearly written down and communicated and abided by and inspected to make sure they are abided by. Otherwise there is chaos . . .': Garret Fitzgerald, *Dáil Debates*, vol 249, col 433, 3 November 1970 (debate on Arms Crisis).

44 'Collective responsibility is often elevated by writers to the level of a "doctrine" but is in truth little more than a political practice which is commonplace and inevitable . . . In a political world, where the Opposition are anxious to reveal disagreements or disputes within ministerial ranks, no other principle of political action is workable': T.C. Hartley and J.A.G. Griffith, *Government and Law* (London 1975) 60-61.

45 For the British practice, see S.E. Finer, 'The individual responsibility of Ministers,' (1956) 34 *Public Administration* 394.

46 For case study, see text above note 55 in this Chapter.

47 de Smith, op. cit., 174.

48 See Gwynn Morgan, 'The Emergency Powers Bill — I', 13 (1978) *Irish Jurist* 67, 68-70.

49 *Dáil Debates*, vol 256, col 1473-1501, 9 November 1971; col 1732-66, 10 November 1971 (motion of no confidence in Mr J. Gibbons).

50 *Dáil Debates*, vol 246, col 641ff, 6 May 1970. For the resignation (in sympathy with the two dismissed ministers) of the Minister for Social Welfare and Local Government and the Parliamentary Secretary to the Minister for Local Government, see id. cols 743ff and 932ff. The Minister for Justice was said to have resigned on health grounds (id., col 641) though this was doubted by the Opposition. (The debate, formally on the appointment of successors to these Ministers, lasted thirty five hours.) See, too, vol 246, cols 1394-1586, 13-14 May, 1970 (motion of confidence in Government); and vol 249, cols 176-257; 400-544; 603-728, 29 October-4 November 1970 (motion of confidence in Taoiseach following on conclusion of Arms Trial).

51 *Dáil Debates*, vol 249, col 202, 29 October 1970.

52 *Dáil Debates*, vol 246, col 1174, 9 May 190.

53 *Dáil Debates*, vol 249, col 807, 8 May 1970 (Deputy Thornley).

54 Including the votes of the two dismissed ministers. Mr Boland, however, abstained in the November 1970 confidence motion.

55 *Dáil Debates*, vol 187, col 19-59, 32 (Mr Sweetman), 7 March 1961. (The discussion of ministerial responsibility occurred in a debate on the passing of an indemnity bill, the Mental Treatment (Detention in Approved Institutions) Bill, 1961)

56 Id., col 57 (Mr MacEntee).

57 20 July 1954, *H.C. Deb.*, vol 530, col 159.

58 See K.C. Wheare, *Maladministration and its Remedies*, (London 1973), Chapter 3.

59 Id., 53

60 (Devlin) Report of the Public Services Organisation Review Group (1966-69), para. 7.1.2.

61 Cf. (British) Parliamentary Commissioner Act 1967, s. 6(3).

62 Fifty-fifth Report of the Committee (Prl 6169), 15. See, also, *Senate Debates*, vol 83, col 1450, 31 March 1976 (Senator Robinson). In the context of civil service anonymity, it is worth drawing attention to the celebrated Report on Economic Development (1958) prepared by T.K. Whitaker when he was Secretary to the Department of Finance. The Taoiseach agreed that, in this case, the rule could be waived and the Report published in Dr Whitaker's name. See Earl of Longford and T.P. O'Neill, *Eamon de Valera* (London 1970), 445.

63 For New Zealand's movement in a Devlin-direction, see *Parliamentary Affairs* 36 (1983) 334, 343.

64 Id., para. 13.1.3.

65 Id., appendix 1 (Note on Administrative Law and Procedure, prepared by a committee chaired by Ó Dálaigh CJ).

66 T.K. Whitaker, 'The Civil Service and Development; *Administration* 9 (1961), No. 2.

67 See Mary Robinson, *Administration* 22 (1974), No. 1.

68 All the writers who have examined the question have bemoaned the feebleness of the House of the Oireachtas.See *Cabinet Government in Ireland* (Dublin 1974) Chaps. 6 and 7; M. Robinson, 'The Role of the Irish Parliament,' *Administration*, 22 (1974) No. 1, 21 ('. . . still basically a nineteenth century debating forum which has failed to adapt to the greatly expanded role

of the government . . .'); Ward, 'Parliamentary Procedures and the Machinery of Government in Ireland,' *Irish University Review* (1974) 225, 241 ('[The legislature lacks] any but the most nominal role in the formulation of public policy and the management of the State.' 'Modern Ireland was born in an age of party Government and its parliamentary institution have never acquired the dignity and respect of older bodies which knew real power in the nineteenth century'); B. Desmond, 'The Houses of the Oireachtas — A Plea for Reform, *Administration,*' 23 (1975) 425 ('. . . the part-time legislative inspector of a continuous Government activity'); J. Stapleton, 'Parliamentary Reform: The Irish Situation,' *Adminstration,* 24 (1976) 212, 219 ('There are influences at work which indicate that the Irish parliament may be moving towards a more central and assertive role in the political System.'); *Reform of the Dáil*: Fine Gael Policy on reform of the Dáil (Dublin 1980) 1 ('. . . during the past twenty years power has moved away from the Oireachtas to various sectoral interests representing some but by no means all, of many sections of the community'); Basil Chubb, *Government and Politics*, op. cit., 228 ('The Irish parliamentary representative, we have argued, is more a factor in administration and a "consumer representative" than a legislator . . . this kind of activity by public persons and this kind of relationship between them and their clients are deeply rooted in Irish experience'). Recently, there have been several newspaper articles on the same theme; for example, *Irish Independent*, 26 August 1982 (Maurice Manning); *Irish Times*, 28 September 1982 (Michael Keating); *Cork Examiner*, 6 November 1982: Jim Corr, 'Why I quit (the Dáil)': 'The contribution which a back-bencher can make towards framing policy is quite insignificant.
69 *Government and Politics*, 182.
70 See text above note 22 in this Chapter.
71 Art. 28.3.1°.
72 Art. 15.6.1°.
73 See generally (1979) *Irish Jurist*, 252-64.
74 Art. 29.5.2°.
75 See text above note 112 in Chapter 7.
76 Thus, when Mr Haughey the responsible minister, styled the compromise contained in the bill 'an Irish solution to an Irish problem' Dick Walsh of the *Irish Times* labelled it 'a Fianna Fáil solution to a Fianna Fáil problem.' For Mr Jim Gibbons' abstention on this bill, see text above note 92 in this Chapter.
77 For both the examples, see Chapter 9.2.
78 See Chapter 9.4.
79 Art. 13.2.1° cf. Arts. 13.2.3°; 15.7 For Senate, see Art. 18.8; Senate S.O. 21(3).
80 Oireachtas (Allowances to Members) and Ministerial and Parliamentary Offices (Amendment) Act No. 22 of 1973, s. 14.
81 See generally Bernard Crick, *The Reform of Parliament* (London 1964).
82 However, see Ministerial and Parliamentary Offices Act 1938-73, Part III as amended.
83 For a convenient collection of these constitutions, see Basil Chubb, *A Source Book of Irish Government* (Dublin 1983), Chapter 8.
84 Lyons, *Ireland since the Famine*, op. cit., 494-495.
85 There is no such thing in the Irish parties as a three-, two- or one-line whip.
86 Labour Constitution, Section 3, *Coru agus Rialachta*, rule 7; Fine Gael Constitution and rules, rule 45.
87 For examples, see Labour Annual Report 1978, 11 (Senator Noel Browne not ratified as Dáil candidate because he had been a member of Labour Party without taking Labour whip).
88 For the debate over withdrawal of whip from Mr O'Malley, see newspapers for 19 and 20 May, 1984.
89 *Dáil Debates*, vol 249, col 724, 4 November1970.
90 For example, George Colley (December 1979; Loyalty to the leader); Charles McCreevy (April, 1980; the Economy); Bill Loughnane (May 1981; H-Blocks).
91 Cf. *Dáil Debates*, vol 126, col 2028 and vol 123, col 589 (Mr de Valera); Farrell, *Chairman or Chief?* 34
92 *Irish Times*, 5 May 1979. For the Taoiseach's statemet, hinting at a more liberal regime for the future, which seems not to have come about, see*Irish Times*, 5 May 1979 quoted in Chubb,

A Source Book . . ., op. cit., 63.
93 See Mary Robinson, *Irish Times*, 24 July 1974, quoted in Chubb., op. cit., 63. See, generally, *Irish Times* for early July 1974. A further example occurred in November 1981: the Coalition Government did not introduce a bill to abolish capital punishment because a few members of their own precarious majority were reluctant to support the measure and because the Opposition (led by Mr C.J. Haughey, a committed opponent of capital punishment) was expected to vote against the proposed bill and to allow no conscience examptions.
94 Yet in January 1944, General Richard Mulcahy was made president of Fine Gael, although he had lost his Dáil seat in 1943 and was not to regain it until May 1944.
95 *Irish Times*, 4 February 1983.
96 See *Irish Times*, 26 February 1982, 7 October 1982 and 1-8 February 1983.

NOTES TO CHAPTER 6

1 See Chapter 11.8 below;*Report of the Committee on the Constitution* (1967 Pr. 9817), 26-33 and Annexes 18-23; Garvin, *The Irish Senate* (Dublin 1969); McGowan Smyth, *The Theory and Practice of the Irish Senate* (Dublin 1972).
2 Art. 35.4.
3 See text above note 112 of Chapter 7.
4 Art. 21.2.
5 Art. 23.1.2°
6 Art. 27. See Chapter 7.2.
7 Notice the constitutional crisis which ensued in 1975, when the Australian Senate flexed its muscles: see e.g. 1976 *Public Law* 217.
8 Joint Committee on the Constitution of Seanad Éireann, 16 May 1928; Commission on Second House of Oireachtas, 1 October 1936; Commission on Vocational Organisation 1943; Joint Committee on Seanad Panel Elections, 13 May 1947; Second Electoral Law Commission, 28 March 1959; Report of the Committee on the Constitution 1967, paras. 64-86 and annexes 18-23.
9 See Art. 18.4 and 7.
10 For discussion on this, see Garvin, op. cit., 89.
11 Parts of this passage may be unclear unless the reader has read Chapter 11.8, on Senate elections.
12 See, generally, D. O'Sullivan, *The Irish Free State and its Senate* (London 1940).
13 Art. 31 of the 1922 Constitution.
14 Constitution (Amendment No. 7) Act No. 27 of 1928.
15 O'Sullivan, op. cit., Appdx. F.
16 Constitution (Amendment No. 13) Act No. 14 of 1928.
17 O'Sullivan, op. cit., 304-15, 324-25.
18 *Dáil Debates*, vol 64, col 1608 (Mr de Valera in the Constituent Assembly).
19 Various explanations have been suggested to account of the interesting political phenomenon, for example: loyalty on the part of the nominated Independents to the Taoiseach; poor whipping in the Fine Gael and Labour Parties; variety of views among Independents; presumption against voting against the popularly-elected chamber; memories of what happened in the Irish Free State Senate. There are fewer divisions in the Senate than in the Dáil.
20 The bill was rejected by 486,989 to 453,322 (approx. 50% to 46%); whilst, on the same day, Mr de Valera was elected as President by approximately 538,003 to 417,536 (approx. 55% to 43%).
21 E. Marnane, '*A constitution for Ireland*' (M.Comm thesis in UCC Library 1976), 82.
22 Pr. 9817, para 67.
23 All figures from: Pr. 9817, annex 22; E. Marnane, op. cit., 53-54; and author's own research. Total number of bills for 1938-66 and 1967-80 were 714 and 399, respectively, of which 159 and 48, respectively, were amended. For comparison, during 1922-36, 489 Dáil bills were received from the Senate and a total of 1,831 amendments were made to 182 of these bills (O'Sullivan, op. cit., Appdx. B).
24 During 1967-77 a total of twenty-three Government bills were launched in the Senate.

25 Greece has approx. one deputy to 25,000 inhabitants.
26 Op. cit., 94.
27 G.A. Wood in *Parliamentary Affairs*, Summer 1983, 334.
28 *Senate Debates*, vol 70, col 965, 7 July 1971 (Criminal Law Amendment Bill, 1971 rejected at first reading). Cf. also *Senate Debates*, vol 77, col 205, 20 February 1974. The Senate was also the only House to debate (but defeat, by thirty four to two) a motion of censure on the Censorship Board for censoring *The Taylor and Ansty*: *Senate Debates*, vol 27, cols 121, 300 (9 December 1942).
29 *Senate Debates*, vol 90, col 683, 5 December 1978.
30 *Senate Debates*, vol 99, col 1, 30 September 1982.

NOTES TO CHAPTER 7

1 Art. 15.4.
2 Art. 15.2.1°.
3 On which, see Section 5 below.
4 Private members are responsible for drafting their own bills with some limited assistance from the staff of the Oireachtas Bills Office.
5 *Dáil Debates*, vol 339, col 688-70, 2 February 1983 (J. Kelly).
6 Art. 20.1,2
7 Arts. 21, 22
8 On which, see Chapter 8.4.
9 To be distinguished from an emergency under Art. 28.3.3° of the Constitution on which, see Gwynn Morgan, 14 (1979) *Irish Jurist* 252. A meeting of the Senate must be convened within eight days to consider Art. 24 bills: SSO 81(2).
10 See SSO 98; McGowan Smyth, op. cit., 66-67.
11 Art. 20.2.2°. This subsection was invoked in the passing of, for example, Protection of Animals (Amendment) Bill, 1965.
12 Game Preservation Bill, 1929 (T.65); Intoxicating Liquor Bill, 1942 (T.108).
13 The two were: Third Amendment of the Constitution Bill, 1958 and Pawnbrokers Bill, 1964 (For Dáil resolutions that bill deemed to have been passed by both Houses, see *Dáil Debates*, vol 174, col 1314; and vol 212, vol 271 respectively) the Irish Free State Senate was more independent and its differences with Fianna Fáil Governments considerable. Consequently, the Dáil had to pass resolutions under Art. 38 of the Constitution relatively frequently. For example, Constitution (Removal of Oaths) Bill, *Dáil Debates*, vol 47, col 421. See also Report of the Committee on the Constitution (Pr. 9817), paras. 91-94.
14 For detailed rules regarding this petition, see Constitution (Verification of Petition) Act No. 8 of 1944, ss. 1-3.
15 Constitution (Amendment No. 10) Act No. 8 of 1928. See also text above note 20 in Chapter 5.
16 DSO 130-32; SSO 116-17, 81(1).
17 Note that this part of the Committee's functions was first suggested in *Reform of the Dáil: Fine Gael Policy* (Dublin 1980) drafted by John Bruton, TD. Cf. Crick, *The Reform of Parliament* (London 1964), 77; Note that the recommendations of the Joint Commitee on Electoral Law (T. 184 (Pr. 6363)) led to the Electoral Act, 1963.
18 For Order of Reference in full, see *Dáil Debates*, vol 344, col 1716. See, also, *Senate Debates*, vol 101, col 281 (Professor Dooge).
19 See DSO 88, SSO 79, 80.
20 See *Informal Committee Report of Dáil Procedure* (Prl. 2904), paras. 23-24.
21 DSO 88(3), 85, SSO 80.
22 DSO 89, SSO 83. See *Informal Committee Report*, para 26.
23 In the Dáil (DSO 89(1)9i)) though not the Senate, there is also a third way of opposing a bill at a second stage, namely to amend the motion by replacing the word 'now' by 'this day six months.' This device is never used. It had some meaning in the British context (where

it originated) if the House's session was to finish before the period of postponement, because of the rule 'that a bill which does not pass all its stages in a session is lost.' But this rule does not exist in Ireland: see text above note 51 in this Chapter.

24 DSO 90-96; SSO 84-89.
25 *Dáil Debates*, vol 24, cols 1108-16, 21 June 1928.
26 DSO 91, 28; SSO 85, 25.
27 DSO 92-96; SSO 86-89.
28 *Dáil Debates*, vol 23, cols 2349, 2357.
29 DSO 93(2). The wording is slightly different in the Senate: SSO 87(2).
30 DSO 95(3); SSO 88.
31 The Informal Committee Report (Prl. 2904), para. 31 rejected such a system because of the Dáil's small size. Cf. Appdx. 4 (p. 54) to the Report.
32 DSO 90(1); SSO 84(1).
33 DSO 90(1), 83, 94 and 99; SSO 84(1), and 92. For Joint Committee on Legislation see *Dáil Debates*, vol 344, col 1419, 6 July 1983. In the case of a select committee, a joint committee — i.e. with members from both Dáil and Senate — may be set up; furthermore, DSO 90(2) and SSO 84(2) provide for the commital of some sections of a bill to a Committee of the whole House whilst the remainder are allocated to a special committee. See also McGowan Smyth, op. cit., 83.
34 On which, see *Dáil Debates*, vol 19, col 794-803, 12 December 1934.
35 DSO 97; SSO 92.
36 The two bills are: Meath Hospital Bill 1950 (*Dáil Debates*, vol 123, col 1883); Seanad Electoral (Panel Members) Bill 1952 (*Senate Debates*, vol 41, col 381). During 1922-33, fifteen bills were committed to select committees in the Senate. In some cases — for example, Private Witnesses Oaths Bills, 1924 and Oireachtas Witnesses Oaths Bill, 1924 (which were considered together) — witnesses gave evidence before the committee.
37 The only such bills since 1964 are: Value Added Tax Bill, 1971 (Committee appointed 7 June 1972); Law Reform Commission Bill, 1975 (4 February 1975), Family Law (Maintenance of Spouses and Children) Bill, 1975 (30 July 1975-T244); Misuse of Drugs Bill, 1973, (30 July 1975-T247); Corporation Tax Bill, 1975 (5 February 1976-T246); Wildlife Bill, 1976 (7 April 1975-T250); National Board for Science and Technology Bill, 1976 (7 December 1976-T251); Value Added Tax (Amendment) Bill, 1977 (28 June 1978).
38 McGowan Smyth, op. cit., 82.
39 For order of reference, see *Dáil Debates*, vol 344, col 1716,
40 See text above note 95 in Chapter 9.
41 See note 39.
42 DSO 97-102; SSO 90-96. See Dáil, *Informal Report* . . . para. 35.
43 *Dáil Debates*, vol 56, col 1400-91.
44 *Dáil Debates*, vol 30, col 163; vol 56, col 1490; vol 191, col 97. SSO 93;
45 DSO 100.; SSO 93; *Dáil Debates*, vol 28 col 1833-34; vol 73, col 1370; vol 191, col 97.
46 DSO 98, 101; SSO 90, 91, 94.
47 *Dáil Debates*, vol 178, col 259, 19 November 1959.
48 DSO 103; SSO 97(1).
49 *Dáil Debates*, vol 79, col 1710; vol 44, col 2057; vol 229, col 791-95.
50 DSO 103; SSO 97(2). See also DSO 104; SSO 100,
51 DSO 105; SSO 101. See, for example, *Dáil Debates*, vol 339, col 417 and 680, 26 January, 2 February 1983.
52 T.115 (Dáil Report); R.61 (Senate Report) 11. The two reports are, in substance, identical.
53 DSO 107-117; SSO 103-113.
54 See, for example, *Dáil Debates*, vol 323, col 120, 160.
55 DSO 107(1)-(3); SSO 103(1)-(3).
56 Fisheries (Consolidation) Act 1959; Income Tax Act 1967; and Social Welfare (Consolidation) Bill 1980.
57 DSO 107(4); SSO 103(4). These were waived, by agreement, for the Social Welfare (Consolidation) Bill.

58 DSO 108(1); SSO 104(1).
59 *Dáil Debates*, vol 344, col 1716; DSO 109-113; SSO 105-109.
60 DSO 114, 116; SSO 110, 112.
61 DSO 117; SSO 113.
62 DSO 85(2).
63 DSO 86(2).
64 DSO 83.
65 McCracken *Representative Government*, op. cit., 167.
66 The six are: Meath Hospital Bill, 1951; Agricultural Workers (Weekly Half Holidays) Bill, 1951; Local Government (Sanitary Services) (Joint Burial Board) Bill, 1952; Friendly Societies (Amendment) Bill, 1953; Local Government Bill, 1953; Law Reform (Personal Injuries) Bill, 1958.
67 *Irish Times*, 26 April 1978 (Senator Robinson).
68 For further detail, see McGowan Smyth, op. cit., Chapter 14. See also (British) Parliamentary Costs Act 1865 as adapted by the Private Bill Costs Act, No. 52 of 1924.
69 *Parliamentary Practice* (London 1971), 817. On the question of whether a particular bill is a private bill, see *Dáil Debates*, vol 19, col 477; vol 46, col 575-78.
70 It is submitted, though, that the enactment of a private act does not amount to an 'administration of justice' — because private acts are not the result of the application of pre-existing principles. Consequently Art. 34.1 of the Constitution — which provides that justice may only be administered in a court (see Chapter 2.2) — is not engaged.
71 State Harbours Bill, 1924; Auctioneers, Valuers, House and Estate Agents' Bill, 1931; Architects (Registration) Bill, 1941. Only the first measure was enacted. See *Senate Debates*, vol 26, col 9-10, col 163-215; *Dáil Debates*, vol 19, col 477; vol. 46, col 576-78.
72 DSO 106; SSO 102.
73 E.g. Cork City Management (Amendment) Act No. 5 of 1941, s. 25. For the provisional order confirmaton act fixing the border between Cork County and Cork Corporation, which generated some controversy, see Act No. 2 (Private) of 1965; *Dáil Debates*, vol 215, col 775, 2088-2132; vol 216, col 200-205.
74 For examples, see reference in previous note.
75 See generally McDunphy, *The President of Ireland*, op. cit., Chapter XIV.
76 Cf. 1922 Constitution Art. 12. The reference to the King was removed by the Constitution (Amendment No. 27) Act, 1936.
77 Kohn, op. cit., 264.
78 Art. 25.1.2
79 Art. 25.4.1°
80 For Rule of Law, see Chapter 2.3.
81 Arts. 13.3.2°; 25.4.2°.
82 Art. 25.4.3° provides for the possibility that a bill may be passed in both or either of the two official languages.In fact, almost all bills are passed in English only.
83 Art. 25.4.5°.
84 Art. 25.2.1°. Surprisingly, a case (*In re McGrath and Harte* [1941] IR 68) has arisen on this point. Notice that only two amending acts were passed under the Art. 51 dispensation.
85 Art. 25.2.2°. The formula commonly employed in such a motion is: 'That pursuant to Art. 25.2.2° of the Constitution, the Senate concurs with the Government in a request to the President to sign the [e.g., Finance Bill, 1979] on a date which is earlier than the fifth day after the date on which the Bill shall have been presented to him': see e.g. *Dáil Debates*, vol 92, col 296, 31 May 1979.
86 Art. 25.3.
87 Art. 34.3.2°
88 Art. 26.2.2° See, also, Art. 34.4.5°.
89 Art. 26.1.2°, 2.1°
90 Art. 26.3.1.° Art. 26.3.2° envisages an unlikely possibility involving Art. 27.
91 [1940] IR 470; [1961] IR 169; [1977] IR 129; [1977] IR 159; [1943] IR 334; [1983] ILRM 246; *Irish Times*, 9 February 1984.

92 On three occasions — the Health Bill, 1947; Income Tax (Consolidation) Bill, 1966; Criminal Justice Bill, 1984 — the Council of State was convened to decide whether a bill should be referred but the bill was not referred. In the case of the 1966 Bill the reason was that a promise was given by the Government that the provision would be repealed by a later statute. *Dáil Debates*, vol 227, col 113..

93 Art. 34.3.3.°

94 247-48 (italics in origin). In addition, President Hillery took the opportunity of his inauguration in December 1983 to complain of the way in which Governments have legislation, which may be unconstitutional, passed by the Oireachtas and then depend on the Art. 26 system to ascertain whether it is constitutional before it comes into effect.

95 248.

96 S.I. No. 65 of 1977.

97 See preamble to S.I. No. 72 of 1962.

98 Municipal Corporation (Ireland) Act 1840 s. 125, Local Government (Ireland) Act 1898.

99 See text above 36 in Chapter 2.

100 *Cityview v. An Chomhairle Oiliúna* [1980] IR 384, 399.

101 On these powers, see text above note 64 in Chapter 4.

102 On which, see Jackson, 1962 *Public Law* 432-3; Kelly, *Fundamental Rights in the Irish Law and Constitution* (Dublin 1967) 321-2.

103 Act No. 44 of 1947.

104 Cf. Civil Service Commissioners Act No. 45 of 1956, s. 32.

105 On the practical difficulty of this distinction, see H.W.R. Wade, *Administrative Law* (Oxford 1982), 733-34.

106 See Report of Senate Select Committee on Statutory Instruments, T.162-Pr. 4685, 15.

107 1947 Act, s. 2(1).

108 1947 Act, s. 2(4)(3)(5). See also *The State (Gleeson) v. Min. for Defence* [1976] IR 280, 82, 87.

109 1947 Act, s. 3(1), as amended by Statutory Instruments (Amendment) Act No. 26 of 1955, s. 1. The imposition of the burden of proof of notice on the prosecution was the result of a Senate amendment to the 1947 Bill. See Jackson, op. cit., 422.

110 For further discussion of position in Britain, see Wade, op. cit., Chapter 22; Foulkes, *Administrative Law* (London 1982), Chapter 3.

111 O'Sullivan, *The Irish Free State and its Senate* (London 1940), 526.

112 Local Government (Planning and Development) Act, 1963, s. 10(2). For the position regarding statutory instruments which may be annulled by either House within a period which is not expressed in *sitting* days, see Houses of the Oireachtas (Laying of Documents) Act No. 10 of 1966, s. 3(1)(c).

113 See text above note 25 in Chapter 8.

114 Smyth, *The Theory and Practice of the Irish Senate*, op. cit., 90. See e.g. *Senate Debates*, vol 48, col 471; vol 68, col 226.

115 Jackson, op. cit., 426; T152, Appendix IV(6).

116 See McGowan Smyth, op. cit., 85-90; Jackson, op. cit., 422-28; McCracken, op. cit., 180-82; *Senate Debates*, vol 13, col 56, 141-70; vol 34, col 1345, 1525; vol 35, col 590; vol. 67, col 477-50; *Dáil Debates*, vol 94, col 1651. For select committees generally, see Chapter 9.4.

117 On which, see text above note 82 in Chapter 9.

118 See Chapter 12.6.

119 [1978] IR 297.

120 Municipal Corporations (Ireland) Act 1840, s. 125; Local Government (Ireland) Act 1898, s. 125. For another example of procedural *ultra vires*, see *The State (Devine) v. Larkin* [1977] IR 24.

NOTES TO CHAPTER 8

1 Courts (Supplemental Provisions) Act No. 39 of 1961, s. 46(4).

2 Comptroller and Auditor General Act No. 1 of 1923 s. 2.

3 S.I. No. 329 of 1972.

4 For example, Irish Shipping Limited Act No. 37 of 1947, ss. 2, 3; Gas Act No 30 of 1976, s. 22.

5 Local Loan Funds Act No.16 of 1935, s. 4 as amended most recently by the Local Loan Funds (Amendment) Act No. 16 of 1983. The Fund is a channel for the provision of capital for local authorities. The resources for the fund come from the Exchequer by way of repayable advances. They are used for the construction of housing, sanitary services etc. In 1983, such spending was £375 million. i.e. 20% of the Public Capital Programme. The statutory ceiling on issues from the Fund was increased to an aggregate figure of £3,500 in 1983: *Dáil Debates*, vol 343, col 260.

6 Finance Act 1970 s. 54(1), (2) as amended by Finance Act, 1978, s. 49 and Finance (No. 2) Act 1981, s. 18. See, generally, Appropriation Act 1965, s. 4. and Income Tax Act 1967, s. 464.

7 DSO 118 and sessional order printed at *Dáil Debates*, vol 338, col 68-69, 15 December 1982. Cf. *Dáil Debates*, vol 198, col 1015-16.

8 DSO 120. It is no longer the case, as it was before 1974, that the expenditure of non-voted money requires a Money Resolution: see DSO 119(2) (1963 edition of standing orders) and Informal Committee on Reform of Dáil Procedure (Prl. 2904), 11-12.

9 DSO 119(1) (1963) and *Informal Committee . . .*, 11, 12.

10 DSO 118, 119(1), 120, 121. An amendment to a bill which would have the effect either of imposing or increasing a charge either on the people or on the revenue must be moved by a member of the Government or a minister of state: DSO 118(3); 119(3).

11 DSO 121.

12 Art. 17.2; DSO 119(2). A specimen message reads as follows:

'Local Loan Fund (Amendment) Bill, 1980: For the purpose of Article 17.2 of the Constitution the Government commend that it is expedient to authorise such charges on and payments out of the Central Fund or the growing produce thereof and such payments out of moneys provided by the Oireachtas as are necessary to give effect to any Act of the present session to amend the Local Loans Act, 1935 to 1978.

Given on this 9th day of December, 1980
(Signed Charles J. Haughey Taoiseach

13 See *A Better Way to Plan the Nation's Finances* (Pl. 299, 1981), Chapter 1.

14 This timetable differs from that which was followed before 1 January 1975 when the financial year was 1 April — 31 March. The Exchequer and Financial Years Act No. 3 of 1974, s. 2 made the financial year co-extensive with the calendar year.

15 Art. 28.4.3°

16 DSO 122.

17 Art 17.1.1° requires the Estimates to be considered 'as soon as possible' after their presentation to the Dáil.

18 Pl. 299 (1981), Chapter 1.0-1.7.

19 The word 'budget' derives from the French, *bougette* or bag, a reference to the brief-case in which the Minister for Finance carries his secrets.

20-21 E.g. that 'it is expedient to amend the law relating to customs and inland revenue (including excise) and to make further provision in connection with finance.' Arguably, there is a constitutional requirement (under Arts. 28.4.3° and 17.1.1°) for a debate on state receipts and expenditure, which may be fulfilled by this debate.

22 Provisional Collection of Taxes Act, 1927, s. 2.

23 Finance Act No. 27 of 1974, s. 85; Finance Act No. 6 of 1975, s. 55.

24 On which, see text above note 36 in Chapter 2.

25 Imposition of Duties Act No. 7 of 1957, ss. 1, 2, as amended by the Finance Act No. 15 of 1962, s. 22.

26 1957 Act, s. 2(1). N.B. also the unusual s. 2(3).

27 *City View v. An Chomhairle Oiliúna* [1980] IR 384, 399. See further, text above note 36 in Chapter 2.

28 E.g. Arts. 17,2; 22.

233

29 See *Dáil Debates*, vol 339, col 640-2, 650-1 in which the existence of this power to impose tax by order was recently criticised by two former ministers, Messrs. O'Malley and Kelly.
30 Act No. 26 of 1965, s. 2. The question arises whether the 1965 Act removes the need for the Appropriation Act. However, in fact the Appropriation Act in one year is necessary to operate with the 1965 Act in the *subsequent* year (see 1965 Act, s. 3). It is also helpful to have a single schedule listing all estimates and supplementary estimates together. Finally, the Appropriation Act is important in meeting the requirement, in Art. 11 of the Constitution, that appropriation be made 'by law.'
31 1965 Act, s. 4.
32 1965 Act as amended by S.I.No.293 of 1974, Second Schedule.
33 On which see Section 7 of this Chapter.
34 Pl. 299, 12.
35 The Grant-in-Aid for Northern Ireland Relief was not subject to audit by the CAG and this episode led to a strengthening of the régime for contolling grants in aid. See, in particular, confidential Department of Finance Circular 2/72 published as Appdx. 9 to *CAP (Final Report) into the Grant in aid for N.I.Relief* (Pr. 2574). See also paras. 59-61 and 81 of this report; *PAC (Final Report) for 1970-71* (Prl. 4077) para. 7 and appdx. 2a; *PAC (Final Report) for 1971-72* (Prl.4357) para. 6.
36 Public Accounts and Charges Act 1891, s. 2(2).
37 See, generally, *A Better Way to Plan the Nation's Finances* (Pl. 299); *Dáil Debates*, vol 339, col 730-33, 908-13 (Mr Alan Dukes).
38 Pl. 1637, 1983.
39 DSO 41.
40 DSO 41, 125.
41 For debate on the publication, to certain deputies, of copies of the budget statement, a few hours before the Minister for Finance reads it to the House, see *Dáil Debates*, vol 333, col 481-89.
42 For its order of reference, see *Dáil Debates*, vol 343, col 2444-45. Note that it must refrain from publishing confidential information if so requested; and that any member of the Government or minister of state has a right to attend and to speak, but not to vote, at its meetings.
43 Art. 26. See Chapter 7.7.
44 Art. 27, 23.1. See Chapter 7.2.
45 See *Report of the Committee on the Constitution, 1967* (Pr. 9817) 33 and Annex 24.
46 Art. 21. A meeting of the Senate must be convened within eight days to consider money bills: SSO 81.
47 *Report . . .*, Annex 23 and research by the writer.
48 Clause 4 of Finance Bill, 1976. See *Dáil Debates*, vol 290, col 1742. See also Finance Bill, 1971, cl. 27; *Dáil Debates*, vol 255, col 1168, Cf. too Finance Bill 1978, s. 47(1).
49 See Report of the Committee of Privileges, dated December 1935.
50 The case of *Kildare Co. v. The King* [1909] 2 IR 100, 104, 105 was relied upon as an authority.
51 Para. 34.
52 Art. 22.2. See also DSO 127.
53 See British Parliament Act 1911, s. 3; Erskine May, *Parliamentary Practice* (London 1971), 788-89.
54 Fanning, *The Irish Department of Finance 1922-58*, (Dublin 1978) esp. Chap. 12 and Epilogue; Devlin Report, Chapters 8.2, 12, 20, 34, 36, 37.
55 See text above note 53 in Chapter 4.
56 Central Bank Act No. 22 of 1942, ss. 3, 6(2), 7.
57 In its comments on the draft of the 1937 Constitution, the Department submitted, unsuccessfully that the Minister for Finance should be, *ex officio*, Tanaiste.
58 T.K. Whitaker, 'The Finance Attitude' *Administration* 2 (1954) 61.
59 Art. 17.2., DSO 119(2).
60 See text above note 33 of this Chapter.
61 S. 2(4). For similar provisions in regard to other areas of expenditure, see e.g. Employment Equality Act No. 16 of 1977, s. 54; Social Welfare (Consolidation) Act No. 1 of 1981, s. 4.
62 Cf. the very similar Art. 61 of the 1922 Constitution.

63 Constitution (Consequential Provisions) Act 1937, s. 6(1).
64 *Comyn v. A.G.* [1950] IR 142, 159.
65 Central Bank Act 1971 s.49.
66 Art. 33.1 See also Comptroller and Auditor General Act 1923, s.7. For Art. 33.1. in the context of Irish Government funds, kept abroad, see: *PAC Report for 1969-70* (Prl. 3609) para. 14 and appdx. 48 and *PAC (Final Report) for 1970-71* (Prl. 4077), p. 159.
67 For further detail, see *An Outline of Irish Financial Procedures* (Stationery Office, Dublin undated) 19-20 and appdx. 1; J.B. O'Connell, *Financial Administration of Ireland* (Dublin 1961), Chapter VIII.
68 Art. 33.2 and 4. See Comptroller and Auditor General Act No. 1 of 1923 and *Dáil Debates*, vol 32, col 1040, 7 November 1929.
69 Art. 33.3 and 5.
70 (British) Exchequer and Audit Department Act 1921, s. 1. Elements of the (British) Exchequer and Audit Department Acts 1866 and 1921 are incorporated by reference, in the Comptroller and Auditor General Act 1923, s. 7(3). See also Adoption of Enactments Act No. 2 of 1922, s.2. See, too, circular sent by Minister for Finance to accounting officers, published as appdx. to Minute of Minister for Finance of 29 January 1969: see *PAC Report for 1967-68* (Pr. 766), Appendix 2. For the suggestion that the CAG cannot investigate waste, etc. because this function is not mentioned in any statute. See *Dáil Debates*, vol 237, col 800-810, 20 November 1968. The argument found little favour with other deputies.
71 *PAC (Final Report) for 1977* (Prl. 8562) para. 44.; *Report of CAG for 1982* (reported in *Irish Times*, 3 November 1983).
72 *PAC (Final Report) for 1977*, para. 48
73 See *Irish Times*, 27 April 1983.
74 1866 Act, s. 28.
75 Appdx. to Minute of Minister for Finance, 29 January 1969 in Pr. 766. See also *PAC (Interim Report) for 1966-67* (Pr. 274). See also *Dáil Debates* vol 237, col 783-84, 20 November 1968. The only other occasion on which the CAG was denied access to documents occurred when the Board of Assessors refused to divulge information regarding its award of pensions under the Military Service Pensions Act 1924. See *Dáil Debates*, vol 32, col 1011ff., 7 November 1929; *PAC (Final Report) for 1924-25*, para. 18; *PAC (Final Report) for 1925-26*, para. 42.
76 1921 Act s. 22.
77 Id., s. 23.
78 Id., s. 22.
79 Id., s. 22.
80 1866 Act, s. 21.
81 1921 Act, s. 2.
82 1921 Act, s. 2.
83 1921 Act, s. 4.
84 *PAC (Final Report) for 1969-70*, para. 5, 15 ques. 34-47 and appdx. 5; *PAC (Final Report) for 1970-71*, para. 10 and p. 159.
85 For example, the holding by the Civil Service Commissioners of competitions for posts when it already had waiting panels of several thousand qualified applicants: *Irish Times*, 7 April 1984.
86 Cf. *Dáil Debates*, vol 237, col 801, 20 November 1968.
87 *PAC (Final Report) for 1927-28*, para. 1(vi) and for 1928-29 para. 2(c) and Minutes of Minister for Finance of 26 June 1930 and 16 July 1931 which are appended to the PAC reports mentioned.
88 The Appropriation Accounts and CAG's Report for 1982 were published on 2 November 1983. See newspapers for following day.
89 The triple elections in 1981-82 meant that it was only in June 1983 that a PAC was constituted to examine the appropriation accounts for the years ending 31 December 1980 and 1981 and to complete the examination for 1979. See *Dáil Debates*, vol 343, col 522, 2 June 1983.

NOTES TO CHAPTER 9

1   Dáil Debates, vol 1, col 59, 11 September 1922. The Third Dáil adopted, for the interim period, the standing orders of the First and Second Dáil.
2   Dáil Debates, vol 1, col 716ff.
3   Dáil Debates, vol 16, col 2361.
4   Dáil Debates, vol 69, col 2939-40.
5   In re Haughey [1971] IR 217, 23, 58.
6   Art 15.10 For adoption of Senate SO, see Senate Debates, vol 21, col 13, 27 April 1938.
7   DSO 87(2); SSO 78(2).
8   DSO 73; SSO 69.
9   Report of Informal Committee on Reform of Dáil Procedure, 1972, Prl. 2094 (hereafter Informal Committee Report). See Dáil Debates, vol 250, col 1176.
10 Dáil Debates, vol 274, cols 1869-1900, 2324-53.
11 The current edition of the SSO was published in 1979. See Senate Debates, vol 92, cols 855-56, 10 July 1979.
12 DSO 140; SSO 124.
13 DSO 50; SSO 45. See Dáil Debates, vol 24, cols 561-70.
14 Report of Committee on Procedure and Privileges on the ruling of the Cathaoirleach with regard to the Local Government (Guarantee Fund) Bill, 1935. R59/1935.
15 Dáil Debates, vol 192, col 1232; vol 194, col 731; vol 228, col 305.
16 See text above notes 30 and 41 in this Chapter.
17 Dáil Debates, vol 301, col 72.
18 O'Sullivan, The Irish Free State and its Senate, Chapter X.
19 Whilst the Constitution (Art. 15.7) uses the term 'session', in the British sense, as the period of months during which the chamber sits each year, in practice, in Leinster House (and in this work) 'session' is used to refer to the period of the entire life of the Dáil or Senate, as, for example, sessional order or sessional committee.
20 Tues., 2.30-9.00 p.m.; Wed. 10.30 a.m.-9.00 p.m. with a break from 1.30-2.30 p.m.; Thurs. 10.30 a.m.-5.30 p.m.: DSO 20(1), (2), 21 and sessional order at Dáil Debates, vol 338, col 68, 15 December 1982, originally made in 1976. The press of business is such that the maximum period is always used. The times may be varied by resolution. For the Senate, see SSO 21.
21 Chubb, The Government and Politics of Ireland (2nd ed.), 213.
22 See McGowan Smyth, op. cit., 91; Garvin, op. cit., 52-54.
23 DSO 25.
24 DSO 29.
25 For notice of motion and order of the day, see text above note 45 in this Chapter.
26 DSO 25. For an example of a failure to reach agreement (arising over the Local Government (Planning and Development) Bill 1983, see Dáil Debates, vol 344, col 536-50.
28 For obstruction and the consequent closure of debate, see text above note 58 in this Chapter.
29 See DSO 38.
30 Dáil Debates, vol 339, col 409, 26 January 1983.
31 Id., col 407. See also Dáil Debates, vol 326, col 541-43.
32 SSO 22.27.
33 However, DSO 26 lays down an order of priority for private members' business, in case there is no agreement.
34 DSO 85. See SSO 80.
35 See Informal Committee Report, paras. 45-46, Appdx. 8.
36 DSO 82.
37 SO 86. Cf. Informal Committee Report, paras. 50-52.
38 DSO 20, and sessional order at Dáil Debates, vol 338, col 68; SSO 28(2)-(5).
39 See text above note 125 in this Chapter.
40 DSO 30; SSO 29.
41 Informal Committee Report, paras. 19-22.

42 May, op. cit., 358-59.
43 DSO 89(1); cf. DSO 87(1); SSO 78(1).
44 For Journal, see text above note 167 in this Chapter.
45 DSO 28, 29; SSO 23, 25.
46 DSO 45, SSO 38.
47 If the amendment be to delete words (with or without any substitution) the question is: 'That the words proposed to be deleted stand part of the original motion.' If the amendment be to add words then the question is: 'That the words be there added.'
48 SSO 25, 33.
49 DSO 41, SSO 35.
50 DSO 39, SSO 31.
51 See e.g. *Dáil Debates*, vol 197, col 1407. But the Ceann Comhairle has also ruled that 'Independent deputies will get their turn in relation to their numbers as against Parties in this House,' brushing aside claims that 'so far as the House is concerned there are no parties': *Dáil Debates*, vol 129, col 699-700. Probably, however, an Independent or a member of a small party has a better chance of being called than a member of a large party.
52 On which, see text above note 33 in this Chapter.
53 DSO 49; SSO 44.
54 *Dáil Debates*, vol 148, col 249; vol 33, col 1399, 1402.
55 *Dáil Debates*, vol 340, cols 2430-64. See also *Dáil Debates*, vol 339, cols 689-94.
56 DSO 57-60; SSO 51-54.
57 DSO 135; SSO 24.
58 For a recent example of a guillotine, see *Dáil Debates*, vol 344, col 976-1035 and 1089-111, 30 June 1983 — on the Local Government (Planning and Development) Bill, 1983.
59 Jennings, *Parliament* (London 1957), 125-26.
60 DSO 55; SSO 49.
61 On which, see *Reform of the Dáil: Fine Gael Policy* (1980).
62 *Dáil Debates*, vol 339, cols 418-71 (26 January 1983); cols 510-80 and 632-64 (27 January); cols 685-732 and 907-70 (2 February); cols 1011-74 and 1129-52 (3 February); 1257-77 (8 February). For earlier discussion of parliamentary reform, see Informal Committee on Reform of Dáil Procedure (Prl. 2904) debated at *Dáil Debates*, vol 250, col 1176; vol 274, cols 1869-20, 2324-5.
63 See Chapter 8.3.
64 *Dáil Debates*, vol 343, col 2380 (21 June 1983) Mr Haughey was speaking on the motion to constitute some of the new committees. See also *Dáil Debates*, vol 330, cols 913-15, 2 February 1983 (Mr Lenihan).
65 *Dáil Debates*, vol 339, col 1258.
66 See text above note 39 in Chapter 7.
67 *Report of the (Senate) Committee on Procedure and Privilege on Select and Special Committees* T. 257 (Prl. 7640), para. 6.
68 DSO 67; SSO 61.
69 [1971] IR 217. See also *Dáil Debates*, vol 250, cols 49-53. On *In re Haughey*, see text above note 7 in Chapter 10.
70 But see now text above note 12 in Chapter 10.
70a For constitutional justice, see text above note 177 in Chapter 12.
70b Prl. 2574, para. 17.
71 At 263. For clarification, it should be emphasised that the conduct of Mr Haughey referred to, in the quotation in the text, is entirely distinct from the supposed offence arising from his refusal to answer the Committee's questions.
72 DSO 72; SSO 68.
73 DSO 73; SSO 69. See e.g. T.257 (Prl. 7640), para. 1. For procedure in breach of privileges cases, see Chapter 10.4.
74 See, for example, *Report on the Office of the Leas-Cheann Comhairle* (1928); Report T. 116 and 117 (1946).
75 *Standing Orders of Dáil and Seanad relative to Private Business* (1939), no. 56(a). On private

bills, see Chapter 7.6.
76   *Dáil Debates*, vol 343, col 2439; *Senate Debates*, vol 101, col 261.
77   *Dáil Debates*, vol 270, col 1153; *Senate Debates*, vol 77, col 124-5.
78   *Dáil Debates*, vol 339, col 1267.
79   *Dáil Debates*, vol 344, col 1716.
80   See text above note 18 in Chapter 7.
81   See text above note 59 in Chapter 7.
82   See text above note 117 in Chapter 7.
83   *Dáil Debates*, vol 343, col 2444.
84   DSO 126.
85-86 See text above notes 42 and 85, respectively, in Chapter 8.
87   Journal of the Dáil for 8 March 1960; Journal of the Senate for 29 March 1960. For report, see Pr. 6363, T. 184.
88   E.g. *Dáil Debates*, vol 192, col 1419, 7 December 1961.
89   *Dáil Debates*, vol 339, col 681.
90   *Dáil Debates*, vol 344, col 1722.
91   *Dáil Debates*, vol 344, col 1727.
92   *Dáil Debates*, vol 344, col 1728.
93   Vol 344, col 1726.
94   *Dáil Debates*, The Order of Reference for each of these three committees will be found at *Dáil Debates*, vol 343, cols 2360, 2435 and 2442 and *Senate Debates*, vol 101, cols 224, 247 and 265 respectively. The Commercial State-sponsored Bodies Committee was first established by the Dáil on November 1976 (see *Dáil Debates*, vol 293, col 1403. See also *Dáil Debates*, vol 319, cols 169-202). And see Robinson, *Irish Parliamentary Scrutiny*, 16 *C.M.L.R.* (1979) 9.
95   DSO 65; SSO 58. In committees, members may speak more than once on the same question. There is no need for a seconder in a Senate committee although one is needed in the House itself.
96   *Senate Debates*, vol 83, col 1458 (Senator Alexis Fitzgerald referring to special committee on Companies Bill, 1962).
97   DSO 83.
98   See *Dáil Debates*, vol 339, col 565 (in West Germany, '. . . the committee system results in something like 85 per cent consensus on most legislation . . .') 573, 77, 917, 925, 1266.
99   *Dáil Debates*, vol 339, cols 681-84.
101 *Dáil Debates*, vol 344, col 1731. Cf. also, Robinson, op. cit., 20.
102 *Dáil Debates*, vol 339, col 1259.
103 In 1973, the first Joint Committee on European Secondary Legislation sought fourteen, and was granted four, officials: Robinson, op. cit., 17-18.
104 Final Report of the Committee of Public Accounts, T. 230 (Prl. 2574), 67.
105 *Sunday Tribune*, 27 November 1983.
106 Cf. *Dáil Debates*, vol 339, col 657-61 (Mr John Kelly): '[A deputy] would get to his feet at 8.45 knowing that he would get low media coverage . . . . [He would] womble through until 10.30 [this was before 1975] because he knew that if he did that . . . he would be first in at 10.30 in the morning when, of course, the press would in that gallery, bright-eyed and bushy tailed . . .'.
107 For the order of business, see text above note 30 in this Chapter. Visitors, including media reporters, may be present unless the committee decides otherwise: DSO 74; SSO 76. Before 1983, committees have usually interviewed witnesses in public but deliberated in private. After 1983 committees have been encouraged, by the Leader of the House, to do as much business as possible in public. See discussion of privacy versus publicity in T.257 (Prl.7640), para. 7 and (Final) Report of the Committee of Public Accounts T.230 (Prl. 2574), paras. 4, 13, 83.
108 D. 21, No. 4, Col. 68 (24 February 1976) (Mr D. O'Malley). The rest of this exchange (cols. 55-69) contains an unusually explicit statement of factors militating against increased use of committees. Note also that each of the Government members of the special committee

on the National Board of Technology Bill, 1976, whose work was much praised, lost their seat at the following general election in 1977. It was suggested, in the Reform of the Dáil debate, that a meeting with the Press Gallery (apparently the first such meeting) ought to be held to discuss the problem and also that it should be a condition of any agreement to broadcast proceedings that adequate attention should be paid to committees. See *Dáil Debates*, vol 339, cols 649, 657-60, 700, 1265.

109 But the matter is mentioned in DSO 72, in the case of the Dáil Committee of Selection.
110 See e.g. *Senate Debates*, vol 101, cols. 241-45.
111 DSO 70(1); SSO 64; *Dáil Debates*, vol 344, col 1719.
112 DSO 71; SSO 67.
113 *Senate Debates*, vol 95, col 1711, 22 October 1981.
114 Certain of the Committee's functions are created by the European Communities (Amendment) Act No. 20 of 1973, s. 1.
115 *Senate Debates*, vol 89, col 64, 10 May 1978.
116 *Senate Debates*, vol 88, col 1001, 3 May 1978. See 55th Report of the First Joint Committee (Prl. 6169), 11-12.
117 *Dáil Debates*, vol 343, col 2446.
118 *55th Report of the First Joint Committee* (Prl. 6169), 9.
119 *Dáil Debates*, vol 339, col 1057.
120 *Dáil Debates*, vol 293, col 1411. The type of conflict of principle canvassed in the paragraph in the text appears to have arisen in connection with Garda Commissioner Wren's partial refusal to give evidence before the Dáil Committee on crime, lawlessness and vandalism: *Irish Times* 25 July 1984.
121 Prl. 8063 (25 May 1978), para. 14.
122 Prl. 8808 (12 March 1980), para. 55.
123 5th report of Joint Committee (10 October 1979), para. 29.
124 The three examples given in this paragraph are taken from the order paper for 18 February 1981.
125 1924 Act, s. 1(i); J.P. Casey, *The Office of the Attorney General in Ireland* (Dublin 1980), 68-70.
126 DSO 33.
127 Vol 275, col 47.
128 DSO 31.
129 Id.
130 DSO 34 as amended by sessional order: see *Dáil Debates*, vol 338, col 68-69, 15 December 1982.
131 DSO 36.
132 DSO 35. Subject to sessional order identified in note 130.
133 Sessional order identified in note 130 referring to Informal Report (Prl. 2904), para. 14. The seniority list is determined by the order in which ministers join the Government, save that the Taoiseach is always first and the Tánaiste is always second. Where, as at the start of a new Dáil, a number of ministers are appointed at the same time, then their names will be announced (and seniority determined) according to their respective lengths of service in the Dáil.
134 *Dáil Debates*, vol 339, col 661.
135 *Informal Committee Report*, Appendices 3 (Mr J.C.B. Deane) and 4 (Senator Neville Keery).
136 See, in spite of its age, T. Troy, 'Some Aspects of Questions', 7 (1959) *Administration* 251, 57.
137 According to a recent survey by *Relate*, the National Social Services' Board's bulletin (summarised in *Irish Times*, 20 January 1984) out of 357 questions answered by the Minister for Social Welfare 333 concerned individual problems. Only ten questions covered matters of general policy. *Relate* accused deputies, in certain areas, of deliberately encouraging the belief that they could pressurise departments to circumvent the rules. Again, many of the questions could have been answered by looking at the *Summary of Social Insurance and Social Assistance Services* issued by the Department. It must also be said that many

questions do have the effect of cutting short a lot of departmental delay. It remains to be seen to what extent the Ombudsman will take over this function from deputies and, in addition, will create better and quicker communication between the Department of Social Welfare and its 'clients,' without the need for intervention by third parties.

138 See *Dáil Debates*, vol 339, cols 662-3, 1269.

139 Standing orders deal comprehensively with: e.g. the election of the Chairman at the commencement of a new sssion (DSO 6, 7; SSO 4, 5); a vacancy in the office occurring during the course of the session (DSO 9; SSO 10).

140 DSO 5, 14, SSO 4(1), 9.

141 Under DSO 13 and SSO 7, the term of office of the Chairman is the term of the House. But 'for the purpose of these Standing Orders'(e.g. supervising the preparation of Official Reports) (DSO 81, SSO 75), he continues in office until this successor has been appointed. For certain other purposes, too, the Chairman is regarded as a continuing office, e.g. payment of his salary (Ministerial and Parliamentary Offices Act No. 38 of 1938, ss. 5, 6); membership of Commission which operates (under Art. 14) in the absence or incapacity of the President; membership of appeal board which polices the Registry of Political Parties (Electoral Act,1963, s. 13): see *Loftus v. Att. Gen.* [1979] IR 221, 243.

142 DSO 13; SSO 8.

143 Art 16.6; Electoral Act No. 19 of 1963, s. 14(1); see e.g. Electoral (Amendment) Act, 1980, s. 5.

144 Constitution (Amendment No. 2) Act No. 5 of 1927; *Dáil Debates*, vol 18, col 167.

145 The four are: Michael Hayes (Cumann na nGaedhael, 1922-32); Frank Fahy (Fianna Fáil, 1932-51); Paddy Hogan (Labour, 1951-67); Cormac Breslin (Fianna Fáil, 1967-73).

146 Art. 15.11 (admittedly the drafting of this sub-section is not very clear).

147 *Dáil Debates*, vol 52, col 278.

148 *Dáil Debates*, vol 20, col 1749.

149 *Dáil Debates*, vol 3, col 1331.

150 *Dáil Debates*, vol 329 col 121 (7 July 1981) and vol 33, cols 163-66 (23 March 1982).

151 DSO 51(1); SO 46(1). For an example, see vol 250, cols. 498-518.

152 DSO 52, SSO 47.

153 For constitutional justice, see text above 177 in Chapter 12.

154 DSO 51(1); SSO 46(1).

155 DSO 52; SSO 47.

156 DSO 51(2); SSO 46(2). Similarly, censure must be carried out in the House itself, if the disorder occurred in a committee of any type: DSO 50, 52; SSO 45, 47(1).

157 DSO 53; SSO 48.

158 *McLoughlin v. Min. for Social Welfare* [1958] IR 1, 17, 25.

159 DSO 78; SSO 72.

160 R. 57/1934 — (Senate) *Report of the Committee on Procedure and Privileges on the Exclusion of Certain Duly Authorised Visitors*; O'Sullivan, *The Irish Free State and its Senate*, 355ff.

161 See e.g. Act No. 38 of 1959, ss. 8(1) 11, 21, 23(2)(c).

162 DSO 79; SSO 73.

163 DSO 1, 137 and see text above notes 70, 121, 140 and 144 in Chapter 11.

164 Oireachtas (Allowances to Members) Act, 1938, s. 5.

165 DSO 3, 6; SSO 2, 4.

166 See e.g. DSO 28, 31, 33, 138, 128, 129; SSO 25, 79, 122, 114, 115.

167 DSO 76; SSO 70.

168 DSO 52; SSO 47.

169 Documentary Evidence Act, 1925, s. 2.

170 *Wavin Pipes v. Hepworth*High Court, 8 May 1981; reported in [1982] 8 Fleet Reports 32. For comment, see (1981) DULJ 110. See also *Rowe v. Law* [1978] IR 55 (O'Higgins CJ) and comment at 1984 *Senate Law Review* (forthcoming).

NOTES TO CHAPTER 10

1 The term *'parliamentary privilege'* is sometimes used, in the singular, when it connotes the idea of an entity. Alternatively and more usually, in Ireland, *'parliamentary privileges'* is used and implies the existence of several, separate privileges.

2 Erskine May, *Parliamentary Practice* (19th ed., London 1976), 67.

3 See de Smith, *Constitutional and Adminstrative Law* (1983), Chapter 14. Westminister's right to regulate its own composition has been heavily qualified by statute.

4 1922 Con., Art. 73; 1937 Con., Art. 50.

5 Cf. style of reasoning in *In re Electoral (Amendment) Bill.*, unreported judgment of 8 February 1984. See text above note 41 in Chapter 10. Contrary to the argument in the text (that pre-Independence common law privileges did not continue into independent Ireland), it was stated by S.F. Egan SC (as he then was), in an opinion for the Public Accounts Committee investigation into the Grant-in-Aid for Northern Ireland Relief that although Art. 15.12 and 13 do not apply to proceedings in a committee of the Oireachtas these proceedings would still be absolutely privileged *by virtue of ordinary substantive law* and the English authority of *Griffin v. Donnelly* (1881) 6 QBD 307 was cited. (This opinion is reproduced at Prl. 2574 T.230, 11.) It will be clear from the text that I disagree with this part of Mr Egan's opinion.

6 The following authorities are relevant: (i) *The People (A.G.) v. O'Callaghan* [1966] IR 501, 518 (Walsh J); (ii) Irish Statutes, 4 Wm and Mary Chap 1 (1692), An Act of Recognition of their Majesties undoubted Right to the Crown of Ireland; (iii) In *In re Haughey* [1971] IR 217, 257, 260, the Supreme Court assumed that it had jurisdiction to pass judgment on whether the Dáil had obeyed its own standing orders, even though the Bill of Rights provides that '. . . proceedings in Parliament ought not to be impeached . . . in any court . . .'. The entire question of the immunity of parliamentary proceeding from review was not mentioned in the Supreme Court. (Nor was there any discussion in *Haughey* of 'the great respect which one organ of State owes another' (*Buckley v. A.G.* [1950] IR 67, 80) which might be thought to be relevant). (iv) The question of whether the Bill of Rights is in force in Ireland was canvassed before, but explicitly not decided by, the Tribunal appointed by the Taoiseach in July 1975 (Prl. 4745).

7 [1971] IR 217.

8 See *Interim and Final Reports of Committee of Public Accounts 1970*, T.230 (Prl. 2574).

9 Act No. 22 of 1970.

10 Ss. 2, 3(2) of the 1970 Act were similar to the Committees of the Houses of Oireachtas (Privilege and Procedure) Act No. 10 of 1976, s. 2 with the important difference that the 1970 Act extended to witnesses.

11 At pp. 248-52.

12 It is worth noting, too, that s. 3(4) of the Committees of the Oireachtas (Privilege and Procedure) Bill No. 7 of 1976 made it a summary offence — triable and punishable by the High Court — for a witness to refuse to appear before any committee. This provision thereby probably avoided the constitutional defects of s. 3(4) of the 1970 Act (cf. *In re Haughey*, 248-51). However, this part of the bill never became law. Secondly, Garret Fitzgerald, TD suggested that similar powers should be given to the Committee on Procedure and Privileges to equip it for its inquiry into telephone bugging in Leinster House (*Irish Times*, 24 June 1982).

13 Contrast the position in the USA where, although there is no express power to sub-poena witnesses in the Constitution, this power exists as an implied concomitant of the power to legislate and oversee the executive, notwithstanding the existence of an equivalent of Art. 34.1 of the Irish Constitution in Art. III. 1 of the U.S. Constitution: see Novak, Rotunda, Young, *Constitutional Law*, 221ff.

14 The difference between Arts. 15.10, 12 and 13 of the 1937 Constitution and their equivalents in the 1922 Constitution (Arts 20, 19 and 18 respectively) are insignificant.

15 In England the Bill of Rights, 1688, art. 9 has been used to prevent a plaintiff from relying upon statements in Parliament as evidence of malice in respect of statements made outside

Parliament: *Church of Scientology v. Johnson Smith* [1972] IQB 522. Since the wording of Art 15.13 is similar, on this point, to that of the Bill of Rights, the same result would probably obtain in Ireland.

16   Report of the Tribunal appointed by the Taiseach on 4 July 1975: Prl. 4745, paras. 26-28 (the Tribunal consisted of Henchy, Parke and Conroy JJ). See also Report of the Tribunal appointed by the Taoiseach on 7 November 1947, para. 6.

17   But quaere (i) Is the word 'amenable' (from the French *amener* = to lead) apt to cover a situation in which the only power the Tribunal exercised was the power to make a factual recommendation rather than a mandatory order? (ii) By comparing the wording of Art 15.13 with Art 15.10 it seems as if Art 15.13 applies only to members individually and not to the House as a collective entity. Thus, it would not cover an intrusion into the affairs of Parliament. Would Art. 15.10 which protects the House against interference, not have been more relevant?

18   Prl. 4745, para. 28.

19   See now, Committees of the Houses of the Oireachtas (Privilege and Procedure) Act No. 10 of 1976, s. 2(2)(b).

20   In the English language, an utterance may be either oral or written. However, the Irish equivalent of utterance in Art. 15.12, *caint*, means 'talk.' Where there is a conflict between the English and Irish versions, the Irish version prevails.

21   See *Senate Debates*, vol 69, col. 240-48, 17 December 1970; Report of Attorney General's Committee on legal points referred to the AG by the Committee on the Constitution (published in the 1970 Report of the Committee on Public Accounts (Prl. 1574, T.230, 10); L. Kohn, *The Constitution of the Irish Free State* op. cit., 229-30. By Defamation Act, 1961, s. 24 and second Sched., a fair and accurate report of any proceedings in public of the legislature of any foreign state is given *qualified* privilege; it would be strange if there were no similar protection in respect of reporting of the Oireachtas.

22   Compare e.g. Defamation Act No. 40 of 1961, s. 24.

23   This possibility was suggested by Pádraig Haughey: see *In re Haughey*, esp. 255-56.

24   S. 3 of the Bill which would have extended the privilege to witnesses and also have made it an offence for a witness not to attend the first being regarded as a *quid pro quo* for the second. Both were deleted as a result of Opposition pressure: see *Dáil Debates*, vol 291, cols. 310-25, 25 May 1976.

25   See Report of Attorney General's Committee . . ., *Senate Debates*, vol 69, cols 240-48, 17 December 1970.

26   The reason why legislation was considered to be necessary was the fear that the fact that committees usually sit in public might mean that there was no qualified privilege at common law.

27   See e.g. 21 *MLR* 465.

28   *R v. Rule* [1937] 2 KB 375.

29   *McCarthy v. Morrissey* 1939 Ir. Jur. Rep. 82; *Lindsay v. Maher, Irish Times*, 18 February 1984. Mr Morrissey was a deputy and a local councillor whilst Mr Maher was a MEP.

30   See Chapter 10.1(iv).

31   Para. 36.

32   Id., paras. 35-42; Annex 3 with appendix. See also note 12 in this Chapter.

33   However, Irish statute law already provides certain protections for the Oireachtas: Offences Against the State Act No. 13 of 1939, ss. 6, 7, 28.

34   T.143 (Pr. 1973) (July 1953).

35   The phrase '*attempt* to corrupt' (my italics) was probably used to avoid the suggestion that any member of the Oireachtas could possibly be corrupted. Yet the phrase would probably cover even a successful attempt: for a successful act is an attempt, at some point in its career.

36   *Report of the Committee on Procedure and Privileges re fracas between two Members of the Dáil on 24th April, 1947*, T.119 ('contempt of an aggravated nature'); *Report of the Committee on Procedure and Privileges on the Assault Committed by a Member on another Member in the Oireachtas Restaurant on 31st January, 1952*, T.133 ('contempt'). It was regarded as

an aggravating factor, in regard to the first case, that the violence took place almost within view of the House while in session and that a challenge was issued and accepted across the floor of the House and, in regard to both cases, that the violence was in retaliation for words spoken in the House.

37 Report of the Committee on Procedure and Privileges on Statements relating to a Member made by Minister in Dáil Éireann on 14th December, 1948, T.120, T.133, para. (vi) (Dáil Debates, vol 129, col 273).Report of the Committee on Procedure and Privileges arising from Allegations made by two Members against the Minister for Local Government in the Dáil, T.242; Report of the Committee on Procedure and Privileges on a statement made by Deputy Crowley in the Dáil on 3rd March, 1976, in relation to the Minister for Posts and Telegraphs, T.248 (Prl. 5482).

38 Report of the Committee on Procedure and Privileges on a Newspaper Article in Sporting Press, T.155 (Pr 3589) ('The Committee finds that the article — in so far as its meaning can be followed — is scurrilously abusive of members in the performance of their Parliamentary duties. It considers, however, that the article is not a responsible one or one calling for attention, and accordingly recommends that it be ignored'). Report of the Committee on Procedure and Privileges on a statement reported in the Press to have been made by a Member, T.200 (Pr. 7720). (It was alleged that a TD had stated that many TD's make claims for travel expenses when they travel in other deputies' cars. The TD denied that he made this statement and his denial was accepted.

39 Dáil Debates, vol 50, col 1674 (Mr Noonan); Irish Times, 23 April 1983.

40 However, in a straightforward case, the Ceann Comhairle may refer the matter to the Committee on his own motion (as happened in Report . . ., T.242 (Prl. 4705).

41 The wording of SO 73 ('. . . as and when requested to do so . .') which gives the Committee jurisdiction over privileges cases assumes that the cases have to be referred to it, rather than being considered of the Committee's own motion.

42 McMahon and Binchy, Irish Law of Torts (Oxford 1981), 358-60.

NOTES TO CHAPTER 11

1 See generally, Casey, 'The Development Electoral Law in the Republic of Ireland,' 28 NILQ (1977) 357; Lawless, 'The Dáil Electoral System, 5 (1957) Administration 57; Coakley, 'Constituency Boundary Revision . . .,' ;28 (1980) Administration 291.

2 No. 19.

3 T.184, Pr. 6363.

4 The British legislation is the Parliamentary Elections Act 1868 which was retained in force by way of the statutes listed in the only post-Independence petition, Dillon-Leetch v. Calleary, unreported judgment of the Supreme Court (Henchy J) on 25 July 1973. See also substantive judgments delivered on 31 July 1973. There has only been one electoral petition in the history of the State.

5 S.I. No. 246 of 1963 as amended by S.I. No. 115 of 1972.

6 S.I. No. 169 of 1963 as amended by S.I. No. 381 of 1977.

7 S.I. No. 78 of 1964 as amended by S.I. No. 115 of 1972.

8 S.I. No. 195 of 1961.

9 For 'Southern Ireland', see text above note 41 in Chapter 1.3.

10 The Report of the Committee on the Constitution, 1967, Pr. 9817, 17-19, made a unanimous recommendation to reduce these limits to 17,500 and 22,500, respectively.

11 In re Art 26 and the Electoral (Amendment) Bill, 1961, [1961] IR 169, 180-81.

12 [1961] IR 114.

13 Act. No. 30 of 1959.

14 [1983] 1 AER 1099.

15 [1961] IR 114, 136.

16 Casey, op. cit., 365.

17 Art. 16.2.4°. The previous, valid revision was in 1947.

18   *In re Art. 26 and the Electoral (Amendment) Bill, 1961* [1961] IR 169.
19   P. 132 quoted with approval, at 182-83 in *In re Art. 26* . . . The plaintiff relied on alleged differences between the English and Irish texts in urging this point.
20   Pp. 122, 146-8. See also *Report of the Dáil Éireann Constituency Commission* (April 1980), Chapter 3.
21   P. 146.
22   Coakley, op. cit., 307.
23   Commission Report, Summary and Chapters 1 and 3. See *In re Art. 26* . . ., 183.
24   P. 201. Paradoxically, the effect of the High Court decision was that the Electoral (Amendment) Act, 1961 had to be enacted and this Act broke the first obligation contained in Art. 16.2.4° in that it was passed thirteen years after the last, valid act. The Supreme Court, in *In re Art. 26* . . ., 179-80, excused the infringement because the act had been carried out as soon as possible and because there was a satisfactory explanation.
25   Any revision must be based on the results of the last *completed* census: *In re Art, 26* . . ., 180-81.
26   See Coakley, op. cit., 315-19 and footnote 67 for the variants on the word 'gerrymander': Kellymander (1934), Bolander (1968) and Tullymander (1973), which were coined to celebrate t draftmanship of various Ministers for Local Government. The sponsor of the 1959 and 1961 Electoral (Amendment) Bills, Neil Blaney, had a bi-syllabic surname, yet his name was not thus immortalised. History does not relate the reason for this injustice. Fortunately, gerrymandering is not a precise science and the Government has probably only gained a significant advantage from it on two occasions: 1935 and 1969.
27   There was in fact a good deal of history leading up to this achievement, including the provisions constituting an electoral commission which were contained in two (defeated) constitutional amendments (the Third Amendment of the Constitution Bill, 1958 and the Fourth Amendment of the Constitution Bill, 1968). See *Report of the Committee on the Constitution*, 1967, 19-21; Coakley, op. cit., 210-11; Casey, op. cit., 366-67.
28   Oireachtas debates on boundary revision bills lasted for nine hours in 1946-47; fifteen in 1959; 24 in 1961; 53 in 1968-69; 82 in 1973-74; but only five in 1980: Coakely, op. cit., 315.
29   See text above note 8 in Chapter 1.
30   See, generally, Lawless, op. cit., 64-67. For the history and merits of proportional representation in Ireland, see Report of the Committee on the Constitution, 21-26 and annexes 9-17.
31   Art. 16.2.5°.
32   In the list system, the voter chooses not between individual candidates but between lists of candidates sponsored by parties and the seats are distributed in proportion to the number of votes cast for each party. Generally, each party's seats are filled by members according to the order in which the party had arranged their names on its list.
33   Art. 16.2.6°.
34   Third Amendment of the Constitution Bill, 1959; Fourth Amendment of the Constitution Bill, 1968. An amendment to the 1968 Bill — the so-called 'Norton Amendment' — which would have substituted a single transferable vote in *single-member* constituencies in place of the straight vote system was narrowly rejected. It was said that this compromise would have offered the best of both the straight vote system and proportional representation. The idea of the single transferable vote system in single member constituencies was revived at the 1984 Fianna Fáil Ard Fheis: *Irish Times*, 2 April 1984.
35   Act No. 12 (s. 17).
36   1923 Act, Third Sched., rules 3, 4. To illustrate this formula in operation, consider the example of a three-seater constituency where the vote totalled 15,000. The quota would be 3,751 so that three successful candidates would take up a total of 11,253 leaving at most 3,747 votes for any other candidate which figure does not reach the quota. So the formula suffices in that it produces the smallest number of votes which will return the requisite number of members while being just big enough to prevent any more being elected. The quota is known as the 'Droop quota' after H.R. Droop who invented it in 1872.

37   Id., rules 5, 6. A point to notice here is that some or all of these may have to be re-distributed again in accordance with the third preference of the voters. Although the system seems complicated, wasted votes run at only about 1%.

38   Id., rule 7. Where the total of the two or more lowest candidates' votes is less than the number of votes credited to the next highest candidate, the returning officer may, at the same count, exclude the two or more lowest candidates and transfer their votes.

39   Id., rule 9.

40   Art. 16.1.2° (as amended by the Third Amendment of the Constitution Act, 1972 which reduced the voting age from twenty one to eighteen years). See also Art. 16.1.3°. On reduction of voting age, see *Report of the Committee on the Constitution*, 1967, Pr. 9817, 16-17. See, also Art. 16.1.3° which bans discrimination on the ground of sex in regard to the right to vote or stand for election.

41   See *In re Art. 26 and the Electoral (Amendment) Bill 1983*, unreported judgment, 8 February 1984.

42   Electoral Act, No. 19 of 1963, s. 26(1), (4)(a).

43   Id., ss. 5(1) 6(1) and Registration of Electors . . . Regs. (S.I. No. 169 of 1963). These Regulations are the source for all dates given in this and the succeeding paragraphs in the text.

44   See *Connacht Tribune*, 9 April 1981.

45   *Fox v. Strik* [1970] 3 WLR 147.

46   67 *LQR* 32; 11 (1962) ICLQ 1153.

47   1963 Acts, ss. 6(1), 7(1).

48   Id. s. 7(2)(c).

49   Id. s. 8.

50   See *Irish Times*, 14 and 15 February 1973.

51   Unreported judgment of 10 February 1984.

52   The meagreness of postal voting facilities is criticised by Casey, op. cit., 361-62.

53   See note 118 below.

54   Art. 16.1.1°.

55   The Joint Oireachtas Committee on Electoral Law would have swept away all disqualifications (save that persons convicted of treason or of an offence under the Official Secrets Act would be disqualified from membership, if a member; but not from standing at subsequent elections). 'The Committee feels that electors must be regarded as mature enough to elect representatives of the type they want and to take the consequences of their choice should the persons elected become incapable of acting during their period of office by reason of imprisonment, mental instability or bankruptcy. It is noteworthy that this principle actually applies to the office of President, for which there are no statutory disqualifications': *Report*, T.184, para. 100.

56   Electoral Act, 1923, s. 51(2), (4). Note the proviso to s. 51(2).

57   Electoral Act, 1963, s. 3 and First Sched. excising the Prevention of Electoral Abuses Act, 1923, s. 6(3).

58   Art. 12.6.

59   Art. 33.3

60   Art. 35.1 and 3. Report T.184, 175.

61   Electoral Act, 1923 s. 51(3), (4); Defence Act No. 18 of 1954, ss 48-74.

62   See Central Bank Act No. 22 of 1942, ss. 19(4)(a), 23(6).

63   E.g. Gas Act No. 30 of 1976, First Sched., arts. 3, 9(1).

64   T.184, para. 161.

65   E.g. Gas Act 1976, s. 16.

66   T.184, paras. 105-7.

67   See 'Lost job candidate in appeal to Eurocourt,' *Irish Independent*, 1 November 1979. Note that there is also a deal of arcane law lurking in the coverts of nineteenth century British legislation regulating the candidacy of, for instance, clergyman and British peers: see Casey, op. cit., 368-69.

68   Department of Finance Circulars Nos. 23/1925; 21/1932; 20/1934; Department of the Public Service Circular No. 22 of 1974. See statment made by the Minister for the Public Service

on 6 March 1974, reproduced as Appdx. 8 of Dooney, *The Iirsh Civil Service* (Dublin 1976).
69   S. 10. See also Art. 16.5
70   Art. 13.2.
71   Electoral Act, 1963, s. 11.
72   1963 Act, s. 12 and Second Sched. Part 1. See also DSO 1-4.
73   Art. 16.3.2°, 4.2°. There is thus a potential gap of up to two months when no Dáil is in being, a gap which was closed by the General Elections (Emergency Provisions) Act, 1943, passed under Art. 28.3.3, which was, however, repealed by the Electoral (Amendment) Act, 1946.
74   Electoral Act, 1963, ss. 18, 24.
75   Id., s. 9(2) referring to Electoral Act No. 12 of 1923, s. 60.
76   1963 Act, s. 21, rule 3.
77   Id., s. 20.
78   Id., s. 18 and s. 21, rules 1(1), 6.
79   Id., s. 21, rule 9(2), (4), (6).
80   Id., s. 21, rule 9(3).
81   Id., s. 13(1), (2), (5). See, too, European Assembly Elections Act No. 30 of 1977, s. 8.
82   Id., s. 13(8).
83   [1979] IR 221. Mr Loftus changed his name to include 'Christian Democrat' for the 1973 General Election and later also added 'Dublin Bay' to his name, since the protection of the Bay's environment was one of his campaign planks.
84   At p. 242.
85   Electoral Act 1963, s. 13(4).
86   At p. 242.
87   Cf. Electoral Act, 1963, s. 13(7).
88   Another argument raised in *Loftus* was that the advantage enjoyed by parties represented in the Dáil in 1963 amounted to 'political discrimination' against Art. 40.6.2°, but the Court confined this expression to discrimination motivated by political belief rather than by status.
89   [1979] IR 245-48. All the quotations in the text are from this reference.
90   S. 3 and Third Sched.
91   T.184 (Pr 6363) *Second Interim Report*, paras. 34-42.
92   Casey, op. cit., 372-74.
93   Prevention of Electoral Abuses Act No. 38 of 1923, s. 50. See, too, Dáil Elections Free Postage Regulations, 1961 (S.I. No. 195 of 1961).
94   Unreported Judgment delivered on 3 June 1981.
95   Henchy J at p. 10. See too Kenny J at p. 4.
96   Broadcasting Authority Act No. 10 of 1960, s. 20(4).
97   Id., s. 18(2).
98   Id., s. 18.
99   [1982] IR 337. For statutory provisions, see Act No. 10 of 1960, s. 31 as amended by Act. No. 37 of 1976, s. 16.
100   Electoral Act, 1963, s. 22.
101   Id., s. 23.
102   Id., s. 25 substituting a new s. 35(1)-(3) in the Electoral Act 1923.
103   Electoral Act, 1923, s. 31.
104   Electoral Act, 1963, s. 30.
105   Id., s. 25. Prevention of Electoral Abuses Act, 1923, s. 22.
106   Electoral Act, 1963, s. 26.
107   1963 Act, s. 24(1)(b). But see id., s. 34 ('Advance polling on islands').
108   *McMahon v. Attorney General* [1972] IR 69, 111; 7 (1972) Irish Jurist 349.
109   Electoral Amendment Act No.4 of 1972, s. 1.
110   1963 Act, s. 27.
111   Electoral Act, 1963, s. 41.
112   1923 Act, Third Sched., rule 10, as amended by Electoral Act, 1963, s. 39.

113   Prevention of Electoral Abuses Act No. 38 of 1923, s. 6(1) as amended by Electoral Act, 1963, s. 90(2).
114   Prevention of Electoral Abuses Act No. 5 of 1982, s. 1. Those interested in the salacious details of the acquittal of Mr C.J. Haughey's agent, Mr O'Connor, on a charge of personation are referred to Peter Murtagh and Joe Joyce, *The Boss* (Dublin 1983), Chapter Six.
115   Prevention of Electoral Abuses Act, 1923 s. 6(1), (2), as amended by Electoral Act, 1963, s. 90(1)-(3). For those convicted of a second offence of personating the penalties are even stiffer.
116   Id., s. 13A as inserted by Electoral Act, 1963, s. 90(4).
117   Id., s. 13.
118   Id., s. 15 as amended by the Electoral Act, 1963, s. 90(5). The provisions (1923 Act, ss. 6(3)(4), 7, 15 and 16) imposing disqualification from holding office or voting, on those guilty of a corrupt or illegal practice and, in the case of corrupt practice, rendering an election void if the candidate was involved, were excised by the Electoral Act, 1963, s. 3 and First Sched.
119   1923 Act, s. 44 and Prosecution of Offences Act, No. 22 of 1974, s. 3.
120   *State (Duff) v. Judge Davitt* [1934] IR 282, 289-89; *State (Ennis) v. District Justice Farrell* [1966] IR 107; Casey, *The Office of the Attorney General in Ireland*, op. cit., 90-94.
121   Electoral Act 1963, s. 12(2); DSO 137.
122   Art. 18.8
123   See e.g. *Senate Debates*, vol 98, col 18, 13 May 1982 (Senate motion not to insist on amendment which it had originally made to Housing (Private Rented Dwellings) Bill, 1982).
124   John McGowan Smyth, *The Theory and Practice of the Irish Senate*, op cit., Chapters 2-6; Thomas Garvin, *The Irish Senate* (Dublin 1969), Chapters I-III.
125   Art. 18.2. Seanad Electoral (University Members) Act No. 20 of 1937, s. 16(2).
126   Art. 18.1 and 3. Art. 18.3 was amended by the Second Amendment of the Constitution Act, 1941 so as to make it clear that it was the *incoming* Taoiseach. See also Art. 18.10.2°.
127   Art. 18.4.1°. See, now, Art. 18.4.2° and 3°, added by the Seventh Amendment of the Constitution Act, 1979 against the possibility that in the future the NUI would be dissolved and its constituent colleges reconstituted as independent universities.
128   Seanad Electoral (University Members) Act No. 30 of 1937, s. 7, as amended by the Electoral (Amendment) Act No. 3 of 1973, s. 3. In the University of Dublin, the holders of certain scholarships are included, as well as graduates.
129   1937 Act, s. 16(1).
130   Id., s. 6; Art. 18.5.
131   1937 Act, ss. 13, 3.
132   For the vocational principle, see text above note 9 in Chapter 6.
133   Basil Chubb, 'Vocational Representation in the Irish Senate,' *Political Studies*, II (1954) 97.
134   Art. 19 does authorise a simpler system in that it provides for the passage of a law allowing 'the direct election' of senators by an vocational group. However, no such law has been passed and the universities remain the only group to enjoy the privilege of nominating their own candidates without outside assistance and then of electing their representatives themselves.
135   These professional interests have been defined as law and medicine: Seanad Electoral (Panel Members) Act No. 42 of 1947, s. 3(2).
136   Id., s. 25.
137   See 1947 Act, Part II (ss. 8-20) as amended by the Seanad Electoral (Panel Members) Act No. 1 of 1954, ss. 3-6.
138   1947 Act, s. 8(2)(b).
139   1947 Act, s. 8(2),(3),(4). The summary in the text is too terse to do justice to the complexity of this section.
140   1947 Act, ss. 9-11.
141   1947 Act, ss. 12-20.
142   1947 Act, s. 53. See also Art 18.7.2°.
143   Id., ss. 26 (as substituted by the 1954 Act, s. 7) and 34(2). Cf. 1947 Act, s. 52.

144   1947 Act, s. 4(1). The returning officers for the university constituencies' seats are the Vice-Chancellors of the NUI and the Provost of Trinity: Seanad Electoral (University Members) Act, 1937, s. 14.

145   1947 Act, ss. 36-43 as amended by the 1954 Act, s. 10.

146   *Ormonde and Dolan v. MacGabhann and the Attorney General*, High Court, unreported judgment of 9 July 1969 quoted in Smyth, op. cit., 31-34.

147   Act No. 43 of 1937, ss. 36, 37. The 1937 Act was entirely repealed by the 1947 Act, s. 7.

148   1947 Act, s. 44. Persons with plural qualifications receive only one set of votes.

149   Garvin, op. cit., 24-27. Figures of £20-£60 were mentioned as the price of a Senate vote in a court case in 1944.

150   1947 Act, s. 51; First Sched., rule 8. See generally, Part IV, Chap. III of the Act.

151   Id., s. 53; Second Sched.

152   Art. 18.5.

153   See Part III of the 1947 Act.

154   1947 Act, s. 67(1)(c).

155   Seanad Electoral (Panel Members) Act No. 1 of 1954, s. 11 creating a new s. 58A(1) in 1947 Act.1

156   1947 Act s. 69(2) and 1954 Act s. 11 creating a new s.58A(8) in 1947 Act.

NOTES TO CHAPTER 12

1   See, for example, F.W. Maitland, *The Constitutional History of England* (Cambridge 1908) 261-75; 311-20; C.W. Lovell, *English Constitutional and Legal History* (New York 1962) 324-35.

2   Art. 35.2; see *Clune v. D.P.P.* [1981] ILRM 17, 20-21.

3   S.A. de Smith, *The new Commonwealth and its Constitutions* (London 1964) 136-43.

4   Arts. 35.1; 13.9.

5   Paul C. Bartholomew, *The Irish Judiciary* (Dublin 1971) Chapter 2.

6   Art. 35.3.

7   *Dáil Debates*, vol 340, cols 2430-64, esp. 2438.

8   Art. 35.3.

9   See *In re the Solicitors Act and Sir James O'Connor* [1930] IR 623.

10   *O'Byrne v. Min. for Finance* [1959] IR 1,40 (Lavery J, dissenting).

11   *O'Byrne v. Min. for Finance.*

12   Courts (Supplemental Provisions) (Amendment) (No. 2) Act No. 21 of 1968, s. 1(b)

13   Courts (Supplemental Provisions) Act No. 39 of 1961, s. 46(1). For Central Fund; see

14   Chapter 8.1.

      In many cases, by Act No. 39 of 1961. See, too, Art. 36 and *State (Walsh) v. Murphy*]1981] IR 275.

15   Art. 35.4; Courts of Justice Act, 1924, s. 39; Courts of Justice (District Court) Act, 1946, s. 20.

16   Bartholomew, *The Irish Judiciary*, op. cit., 6.

17   When Mr Gerry Boland was Minister for Justice, he encountered the Circuit Court judge for the Western Circuit, in St Stephen's Green, at a time when the judge should have been presiding in Galway. Mr Boland threatened the judge with a motion for his removal unless he went to his court straightaway, which he duly did.

18   For a description of the case law, see Kelly, op. cit., 249-60.

19   See, generally, Delaney-Lysaght, *The Administration of Justice in Ireland* (Dublin 1975).

20   See *Clune v. D.P.P.* [1981] ILRM 17, 19-20; J.P. Casey, 14 (1979) *Irish Jurist* 14.

21   *Sullivan v. Robertson* [1954] IR 161; *The State (Killian) v. Min. for Jus*, [1954] IR 207. Articles 51-63 of the Constitution (the transitory provisions) are no longer printed in post-1938 texts of the Constitution.

22   The suffix 'of Justice' was dropped from the formal titles of the former 'Supreme Court of Justice', 'High Court of Justice' etc.

23   *State (Quinn) v. Ryan* [1965] IR 70, 125; *A.G. v. Ryan's Car Hire* [1965] IR 642, 653.

24 Courts (Establishment and Constitution) Act No. 38 of 1961, s. 5; Court Acts No. 11 of 1977, s. 1(3).
25 Courts (Supplemental Provisions) Act No. 39 of 1961. s. 32; Courts of Justice Act No. 32 of 1953 ss. 21, 22 and Sixth Schedule.
26 Act No. 38 of 1961, s. 4; Courts Act No. 11 of 1981 s. 30(a).
27 Act No. 39 of 1961,. s. 20(2); Courts of Justice Act No. 32 of 1953, s. 16.
28 *Fifth Interim Report of Court Practice and Procedure* (Pr. 8936) 31 (Kenny J).
29 *Grimes v. Owners of S.S. Bangor Bay* [1948] IR 350, 358.
30 Act No. 11 of 1981, s. 14.
31 Pr. 8936 17-19, 31. The Committee on CPP recommended expanding the consent procedure and also extending it to the District Court.
32 Casey, op. cit., 15.
33 Act No. 38 of 1961, s. 2; Courts (No. 2) Act No 31 of 1981, ss. 1, 2. See also Local Government (Planning and Development) Act No. 20 of 1976, s. 4(5). *In extremis* the Chief Justice, at the request of the President of the High Court, may request an ordinary judge of the Supreme Court to sit on the High Court.
34 Rules of the Superior Courts, 0.49 r.1.
35 See Chapter 1.2 and Chapter 12.6 of this book, respectively.
36 See Act No. 39 of 1961 s. 8(2).
37 Unreported judgment of 1 August 1974.
38 See text above note 140 in this Chapter.
39-40 *Dáil Debates*, vol 324, col 86. But cf. vol 328, col 2388.(Minister of State at Department of Justice seemingly suggesting that Circuit Court takes *exclusive* jurisdiction under Family Law (Protection of Spouses and Children) Act, 1981).
41 Unreported judgment of 16 February, 1984 criticised at (1984) 6 *DULJ* (forthcoming) (G.W. Hogan).
42 See note 39-40 above.
43 Unreported judgment of 21 December 1979. Cf. also *Macaulay v. Min. for Posts* [1966] IR 345, 58; *Ronayne v. Ronayne* [1970] IR 15, 23.
44 Unreported Judgement of 10 May 1984. It is expected that this case will be appealed to the Supreme Court.
45 See also *In re Haughey* [1971] IR 217, 53-4; J.P. Casey, 14 (1979) *Irish Jurist* 14, 28.
46 *Murren v. Brennan* [1942] IR 466.
47 On habeas corpus see Art. 40.4; Ryan and McGee *The Irish Criminal Process (Dublin 1983)* 450-63.
48 *For example, State (McDonagh) v. Frawley* [1978] IR 131 in which the applicant applied for habeas corpus (unsuccessfully) on the ground that he was not receiving proper medical treatment and, thus, that his right to bodily integrity (under Art. 40.3.1°: see text above note 30 in Chapter 1) was being violated.
49 Act No. 38 of 1961, s. 1(2); Act No. 39 of 1961, s. 4(1) Law Reform Commission Act No. 3 of 1975 s. 14(1)(a). Mr Justice Walsh has been a member of the LRC since 1975. The Chief Justice is also empowered (by s. 1(4) of Act No. 38 of 1961) to summon High Court judges to sit on a particular case. Thus, for example, Pringle J sat on the Court in *Boland v. An Taoiseach* [1974] IR 338 because Walsh and Henchy JJ had been members of the Anglo-Irish Law Enforcement Commission. See Casey, op. cit., 33.
50 Art. 12.3.1°; 26.2.1°.
51 Act No. 39 of 1961, s. 7(3), (4).
52 It has been said that there is nothing in the Constitution to render additional original jurisdiction created by statute unconstitutional: *The People (Attorney General) v. McGlynn* [1967] IR 232.
53 Art. 34.4.4°. See also Art. 40.4.3°.
54 See, also Act No.39 of 1961, s. 7(2). For a survey of the case law on Art. 34.4.3°, see Kelly, op. cit., 332-41.
55 *The People (Att. Gen.) v. Conmey* [1975] IR 341, 360; *State (Browne) v. Feran* [1967] IR 147, 156.

56   Act No. 39 of 1961, ss. 48, 52; Courts of Justice Act No. 48 of 1936, s. 39; *Andrews v. Gaiety* [1973] IR 295; *B. v. B.* [1975] IR 54, 63.
57   *State (Browne) v. Feran* [1967] IR 147.
58   *Vella v. Morelli* [1968] IR 11.
59   *People (Attorney General) v. Bell* [1969] IR 24.
60   *State (H) v. Daly* [1977] IR 90. But the point was decided *sub silentio.*
61   *Campus Oil v. Minister for Industry* No. 2, unreported Supreme Court judgment of 17 June 1983. For strong criticism, see D. O'Keeffe (1984) *ELRev* 87; F. Murphy [1985] *ECR,* forthcoming.
62   See Hartley, *The Foundation of European Community Law* (London 1981) Chapter 9; (1977) *Journal of Irish Society for European Law,* 36.
63   Third Amendment of the Constitution Act, 1972.
64   *Bulmer v. Bollinger* [1974] 2 AER 1226, 1231.
65   See text notes 94 and 95 in this Chapter.
66   *In re Ó Láighléis* [1960] IR 93; *Application of Woods* [1970] IR 154; *Norris v. A.G.,* unreported judgment of 22 April 1983, O'Higgins CJ, 44; Henchy J, 5, 31 (1982) *ICLQ* 856, note 22.
67   A third distinction, that between a felony and misdeanour is not relevant to the court structure. So far as it retains any significance, it is in regard to power of arrest and certain consequences of conviction: see Ryan and McGee, op. cit., 2.
68   Cf. the Great Charter of Ireland granted in 1216 which is quoted in *Conroy v. A.G.* [1965] IR 411, 415: 'No freeman shall be taken or imprisoned or disseised or outlawed or exiled or in any otherwise destroyed: nor will we pass upon him nor send him but by the lawful judgment of his peers or by the law of the land.'
69   Road Traffic Act No. 24 of 1961, s. 49(2).
70   For example, Official Secrets Act No. 1 of 1963, s. 13.
71   Art. 38. For the right to jury trial in the context of criminal contempt, see *State (D.P.P.) v. Walsh* [1981] IR 112.
72   For an up-to-date list of authorities see *Charlton v. Irelnd* [1984] ILRM 39. For the generally accepted principles, see *Melling v. O'Mathhgamhna* [1962] IR 1, 13-15; *Conroy v. A.G.* [1965] IR 411, 435-8.
73   For example, *State (Sheerin) v. Kennedy* [1966] IR 379, 393; *In re Haughey* [1971] IR 217, 247.
74   *R (Eustace) v. D.J. of Co. Tipperary* [1924] II IR 69, 75, 84 as explained in *Melling* 17; *Conroy v. A.G.* [1965] IR 411, 418, 436-8; *State (Sheerin)* 393; *Melling* 16-17; *State (Rollinson) v. Kelly,* unreported Supreme Court judgment of 31 January 1984 (Hederman J) reversing *State (Rollinson) v. Kelly* [1982] ILRM 249 (HC). *State (Rollinson)* also confirmed the obvious principle that where several offences are being tried together, they are examined separately to see whether any of them is a non-minor offence; one does not aggregate the punishments for all the offences.
75   See note 74 above.
76   *In re Haughey* [1971] IR 217, 247-48, though see *O'Sullivan v. Hartnett* [1983] ILRM 79, 80; *Melling* 17.18.
77   See, for example, *Melling* 35; *Charlton* 43.
78   [1965] IR 411, 441.
79   At 418-9.
80   *State (Pheasantry) v. D.J. Donnelly* 1982 ILRM 512, 14, see, too *Charlton* 413.
81   *Cullen v. A.G.* [1979] IR 394.
82   *Kostan v. Ireland,* unreported High Court judgment of 10 February 1978.
83   *Conroy v. A.G.* [1965] IR 411, 435.
84   *Conroy* 443.
85   *Melling* 47 (O'Dalaigh J as he was then).
86   [1976] IR 38;
87   P. 67.
88   The Courts of Justice Act No. 10 of 1924, s. 77. For history, see *The State (McEvitt)*

v. *Delap* [1981] IR 125, 129.
89   Criminal Justice Act No. 2 of 1951, s. 2; Criminal Procedure Act No. 12 of 1967, s. 19.
     See *The State (Hastings) v. Reddin* [1953] IR 134; *The State (Vozza) v. O Floinn* [1957]
     IR 227; *The State (Nevin) v. Tormey* [1976] IR 1; *Clune v. D.P.P.* [1981] ILRM 17.
90-91 For preliminary hearing, see Criminal Procedure Act No. 12 of 1967, Part II. See also
     Court of Justice Act No 48 of 1936, s. 62 by which, in exceptional circumstances, the
     Director of Public Prosecutions may commit the accused for trial even if the preliminary
     hearing decides that there is no case to answer: *State (Shanahan) v. Att. Gen.* [1964] IR
     239). See, generally, *First Interim Report of the Committee on Court Practice and Procedure*
     (Pr. 7164).
92   Criminal Procedure Act 1967, s. 13 as amended by Criminal Procedure (Amendment)
     Act No. 16 of 1973 s. 1; Genocide Act No. 28 of 1973 s. 6; see also *The State (Hunt)
     v. O'Donovan* [1975] IR 39. Criminal Justice Bill 1983, cl. 17 (assuming that this Bill
     becomes law).
93   Children Act, 1908, s. 111 as amended by the Children Act 1941, s. 26. See also The
     Courts of Justice Act 1924, s. 80 as amended by Courts of Justice (District Court) Act,
     1946, s. 4.
94   Courts of Justice Act No. 15 of 1928, s. 18 carries over the British statutes which, in most
     types of case, are the authority for the appeal. For appeal against sentence, see Act No.
     39 of 1961, s. 50.
95   Act No. 39 of 1961, s. 52(1).
96   Id., s. 25(1)(2).
97   Id., s. 25(3).
98   Courts Act, 1981, s. 31 and Schedule repealing Courts Act, 1964, s. 6.
99   *Dáil Debates*, vol 328, col 131.
100 Act No. 39 of 1961, s. 11. Historically the Central Criminal Court was a development
     of the old Dublin Commission where all serious crime was tried: see Delaney-Lysaght,
     The Administration of Justice in Ireland (Dublin, 1975), op. cit., 40.
101 See also Act No. 39 of 1961, s. 11(4).
102 See M. Robinson, *The Special Criminal Court* (Dublin 1974); Ryan and McGee, *The Irish
     Criminal Process* (Dublin 1983), Chapter 14.
103 On which see Defence Act No. 18 of 1954.
104 Art. 38.3, 5 and 6.
105 *The People v. Doyle* 77 ILTR 108; *Re MacCurtain* [1941] IR 83.
106 Act No. 13 of 1939, s. 35(2).
107 Id., s. 39(1).
108 Id., s. 39(3).
109 For the exceptions, see id., ss. 46, 47(2), 48.
110 Id., s. 36; S.I. No. 142 of 1972.
111 1939 Act, s. 41(4). For Special Criminal Court Rules, see S.I. No. 147 of 1972.
112 Act No. 26 of 1972, s. 3(2).
113 See Courts (Establishment and Constitution) Act No. 38 of 1961, s. 3.
114 Id.
115 The Courts of Justice Act No. 10 of 1924 s. 28; Act No. 39 of 1961, ss. 48(2); Offences
     against the State Act No. 13 of 1939, s. 44.
116 Act No. 10 of 1924, ss. 31, 23, 63; Act No. 39 of 1961 ss. 12, 48; Act No. 13 of 1939,
     s. 44; *The People (A.G.) v. Giles* [1974] IR 422, 430.
117 *Seventh Interim Report of the Committee on Court Practice and Procedure* (1966) (Pr. 9168)
     para. 13.
118 Act No. 10 of 1924, s. 34.
119 Courts of Justice Act No. 15 of 1928, s. 5.
120 *The People (A.G.) v. Conmey* [1975] IR 341, 349.
121 *Seventh Interim Report*, para. 24.
122 Act No. 39 of 1961, s. 52(2).
123 Courts of Justice Act No. 20 of 1947, s. 16.

124   Criminal Procedure Act No. 12 of 1967, s. 34.
125   Courts of Justice Act, 1924, s. 29; Act No. 39 of 1961, s. 48(3). According to *The People v. Giles* [1974] IR 422, 431, during 1924-74, only twenty-two certificates were awarded, fifteen of them by the Court of Criminal Appeal.
126   See text above note 54 in this Chapter.
127   *The People (A.G.) v. Conmey* [1975] IR 341.
128   At 354, 360. See also *State (D.P.P.) v. Lynch* [1982] IR 64.
129   See *Conmey* at 353, 59-60, 65-66; *State (D.P.P. v. Walsh* [1982] IR 1, 42, 47, 62; *State (D.P.P.) v. Lynch* [1982] IR 64, 68, 87. For comment, see Casey, 16 (1981) *Irish Jurist* 271; Kelly, op. cit., 334-39.
130   [1982] IR 384.
131   *Dáil Debates*, vol 352, col 223-25 (21 June 1984).
132   At 404-5.
133   Courts Act No. 11 1981, ss. 6, 10.
134   Id., s. 18.
135   Id., s. 6.
136   Id., s. 12.
137   Id., s. 14.
138   Id., s. 15.
139   Family Law Protection of Spouses and Children Act No. 21 of 1981, s. 2.
140   *Dáil Debates*, vol 324, col 83 (Mr G. Collins).
141   Courts Act, 1981, ss. 12, 14 and 5.
142   Id., s. 5.
143   Id., s. 13.
144   Id., s. 2.
145   Courts Act No. 36 of 1971, s. 6.
146   Courts Act, 1981, s. 2(1)(d).
147   Id., s. 2(1)(a), (d).
148   See text above note 41 in this Chapter.
149   Act No. 39 of 1961, s. 24.
150   Landlord and Tenant Act No. 55 of 1971, s. 5.
151   Act No. 10 of 1924, s. 94; Act No. 39 of 1961, s. 48.
152   For a discussion of the pros and cons of the jury in civil actions, see *Irish Times*, 18 and 19 May 1982.
153   Act No. 10 of 1924, s. 95.
154   Act No. 10 of 1924, s. 84; Act No. 39 of 1961, s. 48.
155   Act No. 39 of 1961, s. 52.
156   Courts of Justice Act No. 48 of 1936, Part IV.
157   Id.
158   Courts of Justice Act No. 20 of 1947, s. 16.
159   Act No. 39 of 1961, s. 7(2); Delaney-Lysaght, op. cit., 64.
160   See, generally, S.A. de Smith *Judicial Review of Administrative Action* (London 1980); D. Foulkes, *Administrative Law* (London 1982) Chapter 6-9. Foulkes is a particularly clear introductory work.
161   [1981] 1 AER 129; 1982 *Public Law* 171.
162   See de Smith, op cit., Chapter 3, *Anisminic v. F.C.C.* 1969 2 A.C. 147; *State (Abenglen) v. Dublin* [1982] ILRM 590 (S.Ct.); *State (Cork) v. Fawsitt*, unreported High Court judgment of 13 March 1981; *I.P.B.S. v. Registrar of Building Societies* [1981] ILRM 242.
163   The sole exception to this is error of law on the face of the record (on which see de Smith, op. cit., 400-08), which will not be considered here.
164   *State (Walshe) v. Murphy* [1981] IR 275.
165   *R. v. Queen's County Justices* [1908] 2 IR 285.
166   *R. v. City of London Rent Tribunal ex p. Honig* [1951] 1 KB 641.
167   *Waterford v. Murphy* [1920] 2 IR 365.
168   See *Associated Picturehouses v. Wednesbury* [1948] 1 KB 223, 229 generally on this area.

169   [1968] IR 312.
170   [1981] IR 181.
171   The legislature has now, in the Local Authorities (Officers and Employees) Act No. 1 of 1983, s.2, effectively reversed the legal rule established in *The State (Cussen)* by providing that the LAC may take into account a knowledge of the Irish language.
172   [1970] IR 317.
173   P. 341.
174   Pp. 342-43.
175   Housing Act No. 21 of 1966, s. 79(1).
176   Unreported High Court judgment of 2 February 1981.
177   For example, *R (Donoghue) v. Cork County Justices* [1910] 2 IR 271; *The King (De Vesci) v. Justices of Queen's Co.* [1908] 2 IR 285; *O'Donoghue v. Vet Council* [1975] IR 398 *Corrigan v. I.L.C.* [1977] IR 317; *State (Curran) v. I.L.C.*, unreported High Court judgment of 12 June 1978.
178   *McDonald v. Bord na gCon* [1965] IR 217, 242.
179   [1981] IR 70.
180   [1970] IR 17, 344.
181   *Garvey; State (Gleeson) v. Min for Defence* [1976] IR 280; *State (Duffy) v. Min. for Defence*, unreported Supreme Court judgment of 9 May 1979. *Glover v. B.L.N.* [1973] IR 388.
182   *Moran v. A.G.* [1976] IR 400; *Kilkenny v. Irish Engineering* [1939] *Irish Jurist* 52.
183   *State (Gallagher) v. Governor of Portlaoise Prison*, unreported High Court judgment of 6 March 1978; *State (Boyle) v. G.M.S. (Payment) Board* [1981] ILRM 14.
184   *Kiely v. Min. for Social Welfare Nos. 1 and 2* [1971] IR 21; [1977] IR 267; *State (Williams) v. Army Pensions Board* [1983] ILRM 332.
185   *Murphy v. Min. for Local Government* [1972] IR 215; *Geraghty v. Minister for Local Government* [1975] IR 301; *Clarke v. I.L.C.* [1976] IR 375.
186   *In re Haughey* [1971] IR 217, 263-65; *State (Furey) v. Min. for Defence*, unreported Supreme Court judgment of 2 March 1984.
187   Contrast, for example, *Bushell v. Secretary of State for Environment* 1980 3 WLR 22 with *O'Brien v. Bord na Móna (the High Court judgement) unreported judgment of 18 March 1981*, and *McInnes v. Onslow* 1978 3 AER 11 with *E. Donegal* at p. 347 (application for licence not attended by natural justice in England).
188   See also Chapter 1.2.
189   See *The State (Quinn) v. Ryan* [1965] IR 70, 130.
190   [1972] IR 1.
191   See Law Reform Commission Working Paper No. 8 of 1979.
192   Income Tax Act No. 65 of 1967, Part XXVI.

Supplement

SUPPLEMENT TO CHAPTER 1

1.2 FUNDAMENTAL RIGHTS: ART. 40.3.1

There has been the usual torrent of litigation involving this ubiquitous sub-section, either as a foundation or a make-weight. Here we have only space for the following highlights.

Right to Privacy For a period of several months during 1982, the telephones of three journalists were tapped on the (purported) authorisation of the Minister for Justice. This activity led eventually to *Kennedy v. Ireland* [1988] ILRM 472[1] a major case on the right to privacy. Here the High Court confirmed what was clear from *Norris v. Attorney General* namely, that the personal rights bestowed by Article 40.3 include a right to privacy. In regard to the content of this right, Hamilton P adopted the description of a U.S. judge that it was 'the right to be left alone'. As Hamilton P stated this leaves open the question of the extent of the right. However, in the present case, he was able to rest his decision on the basis that: 'The dignity and freedom of an individual in a democratic society cannot be ensured if his communications of a private nature, be they written or telephonic, are deliberately, consciously and unjustifiably intruded upon and interfered with' (at 477). Damages — £20,000 each in the case of the two principal plaintiffs — were awarded for this breach of constitutional right. In assessing these damages, two features are of general interest. First, the amount was increased by the fact that 'the infringement was carried out deliberately ... consciously and without justification by the executive organ of the State, which is under a constitutional obligation to respect, vindicate and defend that right' (at 478). Secondly, there was a mitigating factor, especially in regard to any claim the plaintiffs might otherwise have had under the head of 'good name'. This factor arose from the fact that, in early 1983, the incoming successor Minister for Justice had openly acknowledged (at 478):

that both the telephones referred to in this case were in fact 'tapped', that the system of safeguards which successive Ministers for Justice have publicly declared in Dáil Éireann to be an integral part of the system was either disregarded or, what amounted to the same thing, was operated in such a way as to be rendered meaningless and that the facts showed that there was not justification for the tapping of either of the two telephones and what occurred went beyond what could be explained as just an error of judgment.

Right to a livelihood　As might be expected at a time of economic stress, the right to earn a living has been invoked on a number of occasions. *Cafolla v. Attorney General* [1985] IR486[2] is an instructive case in this context because it concerns an example of a rather significant category, namely economic regulation of trading in the public interest. The Gaming and Lotteries Act, 1956 regulates the operation of gaming facilities in amusement halls: it fixes maximum amounts for the stakes to be wagered (2p) and the prizes offered (50p) which have never been raised, although between 1956 and the date of the proceedings the cost of living had risen nearly tenfold and excise duty had been imposed on the machines. The plaintiff submitted, unsuccessfully, that these factors constituted an unjustifiable interference with his right to earn a livelihood. Costello J, with whose judgment the Supreme Court (briefly) agreed, noted, first, that there was recent authority *(P.M.P.S. v. Attorney General* [1983] IR 339) that laws could be enacted which even prohibit an existing activity altogether. He also held that it was not necessarily the case that, because limits operated more restrictively on the plaintiff's business at the time of the case than when they were originally imposed, they were not required by the exigencies of the common good. He said in the central passage of his judgment (at 495):

This court has neither the ability not the jurisdiction to decide what level of restrictions are reasonably necessary to curb gaming in licensed amusement halls; these are matters peculiarly within the jurisdiction and competence of the Oireachtas. It can, however, consider whether they are capable of being so justified. Let me ... consider a hypothetical re-enactment now by the Oireachtas of the 1956 Act in its present form (suitably adjusted to conform with the provisions of the Decimal Currency Act). The plaintiff has not, in my opinion, shown that it would be unreasonable for the Oireachtas to conclude that present day social conditions required the maintenance of the limits set in 1956 even though the value of money has greatly declined since that time. And he has not shown that there would be any disproportion between the aims of the 1956 Act and the imposition of controls operating more restrictively than they did in 1963.

On the basis of the result and reasoning, in both this case and in *Attorney General v. Paperlink* [1984] ILRM 373, it seems that any plaintiff who wishes to assail a legislative restriction upon trade on the basis of the right to livelihood has an uphill battle.

Right to beget children　At least two new unspecified rights have recently been divined. The first of these is a spouse's right to beget children. This right, it was said in *Murray v. Ireland* [1985] IR532, is a basic human right which a person enjoys by virtue of membership of a family, as opposed to the rights of the family under Art.41 which are defined as relating to the constitution and authority of the family as an institution. However, Costello J held that nothing turned on this distinction because — and this is a most significant general point — irrespective of the language of Art.41 ('antecedent and superior to all positive law') there is no hierarchy of constitutionally protected rights. In consequence, it could not be said that a right enshrined in its own special article, such as the rights of the Family in Art. 41, necessarily ranks higher than one of the unspecified rights with which Art. 40.3.1 is pregnant.

The facts in *Murray* involved a married couple each of whom had been convicted of murdering a Garda and imprisoned for life. When the age which the wife would have reached by the time her sentence expired was taken into account, this would have meant that the couple would be unable to beget children. Accordingly, they claimed bail, or appropriate facilities within prison, to enable them to exercise this right. This argument was rejected by the High Court on the straightforward grounds, first, that bail is clearly incompatible with the restriction on their liberty which is constitutionally permitted by their imprisonment, and, second, that the provision of such facilities within prison for all the prisoners, who would be entitled to them, would impose unreasonable demands on the prison service.

Right to communicate   The other new right is the right to the basic human faculty of communication[3] which was invoked in *Kearney v. Ireland* [1986] IR 116 which arose out of the Rules for the Government of Prisons, 1947. These Rules provide for the compulsory inspection and, if the contents are 'objectionable', the censorship, of prisoners' letters. The High Court held that this infringement of the right to communicate was justifiable because of the public interest in security, provided that the only types of letters regarded as 'objectionable' were those which might violate security. This was in fact the practice normally followed. However, since in this case, there had been a failure to deliver innocuous letters by virtue of the unauthorised actions of prison officers, damages (which, in the circumstances of the case, were only nominal) were awarded.

The right to communicate was also invoked in *Attorney General for England and Wales v. Brandon Books* [1987] ILRM 135. This case concerned an application by the British Government for an interlocutory injunction to restrain the publication of *One Girl's War*, the memoirs of a member of what is laughingly called the British Secret Service. The general significance of the case is slightly undermined by the fact that Carroll J held that there was no question of any (Irish) public interest being affected by publication. There was, thus, no countervailing value to balance against that of the right to communicate. Nevertheless, from the tone of the judgment, there is no doubting the importance which the learned judge set on the right to communicate. Holding that the plaintiff had failed to make out his case, Carroll J said (at 138):

The exercise of a constitutional right cannot be measured in terms of money: what is at stake is the very important constitutional right to communicate now and not in a year or more when the case has worked through the courts.

The right to communicate was unsuccessfully invoked in *Attorney General (ex. rel. SPUC) v. Open Door* [1987] ILRM 477 (High Court); [1988] 2 CMLR 433 (Supreme Court)[4]. It was held that the right to disseminate information (which in this case included counselling about abortions in Britain) had to give way before Art. 40.3.3., which protects the right to life of the unborn.

1.5 AMENDMENT

Details of the two most recent referenda on proposals to amend the Constitution are given in the footnotes.[5]

Of the two major cases, stated in the Text (at 32) to be pending before the European Commission of Human Rights, both have by now been decided by the European Court: one against, and the other in favour of, Ireland. In *Norris v. Ireland* (1988) 10 EHRR 300,[6] the European Court followed its decision in the Northern Irish case of *Dudgeon v. U.K.* (1982) 4 EHRR 149 and held that the law making a criminal offence out of homosexual acts between males, even adult Consenting males, was contrary to the European Convention of Human Rights. Mr Norris thereby brought about effectively the change which he had failed to achieve by invoking the Irish Constitution, in the High and Supreme Courts: see Text at 16.

Manifestly the legislation under attack violated Art. 8.1 of the Convention ('Everyone has the right to respect for his privacy and family life . . ') in that it interfered with homosexual acts, even if committed in private. The kernel of the Court's decision lay in the issue of whether this prohibition could be brought within the exception authorised by Art. 8.2. For this, a law must both have an aim which is legitimate under the Paragraph and be 'necessary in a democratic society'. The law succeeded at the first hurdle in that it was aimed at the protection of morals, but failed at the second stage. The Court said (at para. 46) in a passage which includes a quotation from its judgment in *Dudgeon:*

As in the Dudgeon case, . . . not only the nature of the aim of the restriction but also the nature of the activities involved will affect the scope of the margin of appreciation. The present case concerns a most intimate aspect of private life. Accordingly, there must exist particularly serious reasons before interferences on the part of public authorities can be legitimate for the purposes of paragraph 2 of Article 8.

Yet the Government have adduced no evidence which would point to the existence of factors justifying the retention of the impugned laws which are additional to or are of greater weight than those present in the aforementioned Dudgeon case.

The Irish Government's reaction to this defeat was to indicate that the law would be changed in the case of adults whilst some protection is retained for vulnerable groups, like juveniles: plainly, this will involve a difficult question of degree for the Oireachtas. The Government would not commit itself to a timetable and although the Court's decision was handed down on 26 October 1988, no bill has yet been published.

In *Johnston v. Ireland* (1986) 8 EHRR 200, the first two applicants, an unmarried couple who had been living together, in a stable relationship for more than ten years, failed in their claim that a right to divorce is implied

258

by Art. 12 of the Convention: 'Man and woman of marriageable age have the right to marry . . .'. However, their daughter, who was the third applicant was successful in her contention, namely that Art. 8 (right to respect for family life) was violated by the absence of an appropriate legal regime to reflect her natural family ties. To substantiate this claim, the third applicant was able to point to such matters as: her status of illegitimacy, the impossibility of her being adopted by her parents, and her lack of succession rights vis a vis her parents. Subsequently, the legal position of illegitimate children, including those in the third applicant's position, was improved by the Status of Children Act, 1986, the bill for which had, however, been published some months before the decision in *Johnston*.

SUPPLEMENT TO CHAPTER 2

2.2 SEPARATION OF POWERS IN THE IRISH CONSTITUTION

The Court's rigorous enforcement of Article 34.1 has attracted a substantial jurisprudence. In regard to the first limb of the Article — the notion that there must be no interference with the judicial process — it was established in *Pine Valley v. Minister for Environment* [1987] IR 23, that the parliamentary draftsman had drawn the correct lesson from the classic teaching of *Buckley v. Attorney General* [1950] IR 67. Two cases are relevant, each undertaken by the same benefactor of Irish Public Law. In the earlier case, *State (Pine Valley) v. Dublin Co. Co.* [1987] IR 407 the Supreme Court had held that the Minister for the Environment (the appellate authority, in pre-Bord Pleanála days) had no power to grant planning permission, if it contravened the development plan. This decision came as a surprise to the legal profession which has always assumed that the opposite was the case. Accordingly the Local Government (Planning and Development) Act, 1982, s.6(1) was passed to restore the law to the position which it has been thought (erroneously) to occupy until the first *Pine* case and to do so, moreover, with retrospective effect. However, s.6(2) of the 1982 Act, in slightly circuitous language, excluded Pine Valley itself from this bounty. Thus, in the second *Pine* case, the applicant developers, who had been disadvantaged by the results of the first case, claimed that this sub-section was unfairly discriminatory. Rejecting this argument, the Court held that the discrimination could be justified because it was necessary in order to prevent the invasion of the judicial domain through an attempt to bestow validity on a planning permission which had been declared invalid by the courts.

Another form of interference with the judicial process involved the Director of Public Prosecutor's (formerly the Attorney General's) power to order a return for trial on indictment, even though a District Court had ruled that there is no prima facie case against the accused. Correcting a surprising wobble in *State (Shanahan) v. Attorney General* [1964] IR 239, the Supreme Court held in *Costello v. Director of Public Prosecution* [1984] IR 436[6a] that this power violates Article 34.1 by enroaching on the District Court's exercise of its judicial power.

On the opposite side of the same line was *State (Divito) v. Arklow UDC* [1986] ILRM 123. The background to the case was that the Gaming and Lotteries Act, 1956 makes the use of gaming slot-machines an offence unless the relevant local authority area is covered by a resolution of the local authority adopting Part III of the 1956 Act. In this case, the sequence of events was this: first, as required, the applicant had published in the newspapers a statutory notice of his intention to apply for a certificate from the District Court which was necessary to allow him lawfully to run the machines; next, the local authority rescinded the existing resolution under the 1956 Act.

Before the Supreme Court, the applicant argued, *inter alia*, that the withdrawal of the resolution amounted to an unconstitutional invasion of the judicial domain. Henchy J rejected this argument on the stringent ground that (at 126):

> there was no list before the District Court when the council intervened. There was no pending proceedings of which the District Court was seised. All that happened was that the applicant had served and published a statutory notice of intervention to make an application for a certificate in the District Court on a specified date.

No point was taken that in deciding whether to grant a gaming certificate, the Court was not administering justice. It may be, in view of cases like *State (McEldowney) v. Kelleher* [1983] IR289, that it is too late in the day for this point to be taken.

Pre-trial cases Two Supreme Court cases have raised queries about the conformity of aspects of the pre-trial criminal procedure with Article 34.1. In the first of these cases, *State (Lynch) v. Ballagh* [1986] IR 203, the issue before the Court was whether the power of the Gardai to grant bail was *ultra vires* the District Court Rules. Against this background Walsh J (alone of the five judges, who all gave judgments) dealt with a peace commissioner's power to grant bail. He remarked (at 212):

> It appears to me that those particular functions which the various statutes have purported to assign to a peace commissioner are really judicial functions because they purport to have given power to hear evidence and having heard the evidence, to exercise a discretion as to whether prisoners shall be remanded in custody or on bail. These are functions which when carried out by the District Court are clearly judicial functions. As peace commissioners in the exercise of these functions are not within the provisions of either Article 34 or 37 of the Constitution, their position appears to be somewhat constitutionally dubious.

This hint was acted on in *State (O'Mahony) v. Melia* High Court, 6 July 1989; *Irish Times* Law Report, 6 November 1989. Here Keane J. granted a Declaration that the legislation empowering a peace commissioner to remand an accused in custody was unconstitutional.

The second of the two Supreme Court cases, *State (Clarke) v. Roche* [1986] IR 619[6b], centred on the procedure for the issuing of a District Court summons. Under the relevant legislation (Petty Sessions (Ireland) Act, 1851, ss. 10, 11) complaint could be made to *inter alia* a District Court clerk. The point which was taken by counsel for the prosecutor was that there was no proof that the issue of a summons against the prosecutors had been made by the District Court clerk, as opposed to some person under his general supervision. It thus became relevant to ascertain whether 'the activity of a District Court in deciding to issue a summons is not the carrying out of a judicial act but is rather the carrying out of an administrative or ministerial acts' (at 640). The reason for this categorisation was that in the case of a judicial, in contrast to an administrative or ministerial act, no delegation would be possible . Having concluded that the act was judicial for the purpose of non-delegation, Finlay CJ went on to make a separate point which, however, relied upon the same terminology (at 64):

No argument in this case was submitted to the Court with regard to the consequences from the point of view of constitutional validity of a conclusion that the powers given to the Peace Commissioner and District Court clerk to receive a complaint and issue a summons constituted the carrying out of a judicial act in a criminal matter. I, therefore, express no view upon it, but would refer to the query raised by Walsh J. In his judgment in *The State (Lynch) v. Ballagh* [1986] IR 203 as to the constitutional validity of giving to a Peace Commissioner powers to grant bail.

As a comment, it is submitted that the category of a 'judicial act' for the purpose of the non-delegation doctrine, including as it does, for example, a quasi-judicial decision is different from and wider than an administration of justice for the purpose of Article 34.1 which was the subject of Walsh J's query in *Clark*. More important, as regards both *Lynch* and *Roche*, it can be said that the functions involved (although they were incidental to the judicial function) were discretionary and also lacked the element of finality and conclusiveness. This feature, which was not considered in the judgments, militates against there being an administration of justice: see Text at 39-40. It is submitted that the wiser teaching is to be found in the classic case of *Macauley v. Minister for Posts and Telegraphs* [1966] IR 345 which involved the Attorney General's former power, under the Ministers and Secretaries Act, 1924, s. 2, to grant or withhold his fiat in an action brought against a Minister. Rejecting the suggestion that the Attorney General's fiat violates Art. 34.1, Kenny J said (at 355):

The nature and features of the fiat are, I think, an answer to this. The Attorney General may exercise the power to grant or withhold the fiat in any way he thinks fit: he is not bound to hear the parties — and he has not to give any reasons for his decision. If he refuses to grant it, he may subsequently change his mind and give it. His decision to refuse it decides nothing. The function of the Attorney General in granting or withholding the fiat is not an administration of justice in any sense.

However, this criticism notwithstanding, the suggestion which was made by Finlay CJ in *State (Clarke) v Roche* has been accepted by the High Court?

In regard to the particular point at issue in *Clarke* the law has been amended to meet the difficulty by the Courts (No. 3) Act, 1986 which provides that proceedings in the District Court in respect of an offence may be commenced, by the issuing, as a matter of administrative procedure, of a '[summons] by the appropriate officer of the District Court'. And in regard to the issue of summonses issued at a date *before* the decision in *Clarke*, it has been held, by the High Court, that the decision should not be regarded as operating retrospectively in the absence of an express declaration to that effect by the Supreme Court: *White v. Hussey* [1989] ILRM 109.

Nevertheless, there remain myriad pre-trial decisions taken by non-judges, for example, the rule that an extradition warrant may not be brought before an Irish court unless the Attorney General is satisfied that there is sufficient evidence (Extradition (Amendment) Act, 1987, s.2); or the Master's extensive interlocutory jurisdiction in the High Court, in regard to which the *Lynch-Clarke* line of development may, if it is followed, have considerable effect.

Tax cases   *Deighan v. Hearne* [1986] IR 603 involved an Inspector of Taxes' power to raise an estimated assessment of income tax in respect of a person who has failed to make a return of income when required to do so. Such an assessment must be notified to the taxpayer and then, in default of a notice of appeal (as a result of the Income Tax Act, 1967), the assessment becomes 'final and conclusive'. Is such an assessment an 'administration of justice'? No, according to Murphy J in the High Court. Because the taxpayer was deemed, by the legislation, to have acquiesced in the Inspector's assessment, it follows that: 'The assessment does not pre-suppose any dispute or controversy between the taxpayer on the one hand and the Inspector on the other' [at 613].

A second point in this case concerned the right given by the legislation, to the sheriff to execute the Inspector's assessment, without the intervention of a Court Order. The taxpayer contended that the execution was an integral part of the administration of justice. This argument was rejected on alternate grounds: first, if a landlord can distrain for rent arrears, without recourse to a court, there is no reason why the Public Exchequer should have a lesser right. In any case, it was held that the power of executing even the judgment of a court has always been an executive rather than a judicial function.

In *State (Calcul) v. Appeal Commissioners* High Court, 18 December 1986, in contrast to *Deighan*, there was a dispute between the Revenue Commissioners and the taxpayer, which had gone, on appeal, to the Appeal Commissioners. The High Court (Barron J) held that the Appeal Commissioners were not administering justice, principally because they lack the power to enforce their decision or to impose liabilities (see Text at 40). According to Barron J (at 18-19 of the judgment):

Essentially their decisions are enforced by the institution of legal proceedings to recover the amount of tax determined by them as being payable. Equally in those cases where penalties may become payable proceedings must be instituted before they can be recovered.

... undoubtedly, questions of fact and law require to be decided to determine taxable income. I am sure that a spectator at a hearing before the Appeal Commissioners will see no material difference between the conduct of the hearing and the conduct of many hearings in the Courts. In each case, there will be an adversarial procedure with each side seeking to establish the law and the facts to suit its own case.

This, however, is not the test. This lies in the orders which the Appeal Commissioners are empowered to make. Such orders obviously impose liabilities upon the taxpayer concerned, but they do not deprive him of anything nor impose penalties nor limit his freedom of action. They declare his liability for tax upon the basis of the facts as found by them. Having declared this liability, they have not power to enforce their decision.

In *Cacul*, the High Court offered an alternative ground for its decision — namely, that the Appeal Commissioners, even if it were judicial, was 'limited' and, thus, fell within the protection of Art. 37.1. The somewhat surprising reason offered for this (at 21) was that '[tax] payments cannot have far-reaching effects on the fortune of the taxpayer ... since in each case the liability is relative, being proportionate either to his income or his turnover'.

In *Kennedy v. Hearne* [1988] ILRM 52, the third case in which a taxpayer failed to establish that the Revenue Commissioners were administering justice, Murphy J held that their action lacked that quality of conclusiveness which is of the essence of a court order. He said (at 61-2):

... even if the Commissioners' order had been implemented fully and the property of the plaintiff seized and disposed of [the legislation] still provides that the amount to be paid by the employer is to be that in respect of which he assesses himself and that any excess over that amount however collected by the revenue authorities is to be repaid. The purpose of s.7 is to procure the prompt payment of an amount which an employer is estimated to be holding as a result of deductions of tax which he has or should have made and which have not been accounted for or paid over to the appropriate authorities. The section is then clear in its provisions that when the sum for which the employer is admittedly liable is remitted this emergency action by the revenue authorities is not merely discharged but the status quo restored ...

Courts in other jurisdiction, faced with essentially the same phenomenon — tax collection administered, for good reasons, by bodies to other than courts — have reached the same conclusion as the Irish Courts[8]. The US Courts[9] have, indeed, gone so far as even to exclude public regulatory power generally from the sweep of their equivalent of Art. 34.1. There is some support for this approach in the dictum of Johnson J in *Lynham v Butler No. 2* [1933] IR 74, 115 but this has not taken root in traditional Irish jurisprudence. The tax administration cases just described may, however, provide some support for a restriction on the scope of Art. 34.1, even where public regulatory functions other than taxation are involved.

Arts. 28.2 and 29.4.1° The analogous provision to Art. 28.2 in the field of foreign affairs is Art. 29.4.1°, which proclaims that: 'The executive power

263

of the State in or in connection with its external relations shall ... be exercised by or on the authority of the Government.' Like its counterpart, this is of course an aspect of the Separation of Powers. In this context it is relevant to note a major conceptual point: there is a tension and sometimes conflict between the Separation of Powers and the notion that, as Justice Walsh stated in *Crotty v An Taoiseach* [1987] ILRM 400, 454: 'to the judicial organ of government alone is given the power to decide if there has been a breach of constitutional restraints.' This quotation contains a fundamental rule of government, the Supremacy of the Constitution as interpreted and enforced by the Courts. This is really a re-statement of the first and most important facet of the Rule of Law (Text at 42-3). It was illustrated recently in *Crotty*. In *Crotty*, the plaintiff sought a declaration and injunction restraining the Government from ratifying the Single European Act, the critical parts of which provided for improved cooperation in the sphere of foreign policy. The plaintiff's successful argument was that since Art. 29.4 vests the Government with the power to conduct foreign affairs, it is not open to the State to fetter the Government's authority by a treaty which would oblige it to make foreign policy with a greater measure of cooperation with other nations of the EEC. The plaintiff's argument succeeded by a majority of three to two.

The first ground of difference between the minority and majority judges in *Crotty* was that the minority held that the terms of the SEA were so loose that it involved no significant changes, especially bearing in mind the Separation of Powers, which meant that the court could intervene only in the case of a clear breach of the Government's constitutional duties. This argument was grounded on the fact that the treaty in question was couched in very loose language, for instance: 'endeavour to avoid' and 'as far as possible'. The majority was unimpressed by such nuances. It held that an obligation is an obligation, however qualified. It also decided that the SEA went beyond any evolution of the EC which might have been contemplated at the time of the original constitutional amendment which inserted Art. 29.4.3° and authorised the State to join the EC *as it was in 1973*.

The minority's alternative ground may be classified as a standing-cum-ripeness argument: even if their reading of the SEA was incorrect, they averred that the court has jurisdiction to intervene only where there is an actual or threatened breach of constitutional rights and, necessarily, this had not materialised at the time of the case. The majority swept aside such caution with Justice Henchy remarking (at 464): 'if Ireland were to ratify the Treaty it would be bound in international law to engage actively in a programme which would trench progressively on Ireland's independence and sovereignty in the conduct of foreign relations.'

To an American observer, the really striking thing about *Crotty* would be that neither the majority nor the minority judgment examined what is known in the United States as 'the political question' doctrine. By this is meant that there are certain constitutional questions which are inherently non-justificable.

One might have thought that such an argument would have been apt: not only were foreign affairs involved, but the basis of *Crotty* was the hobgoblin of sovereignty and its alleged erosion. In a world of highly qualified sovereigns, this is an issue par excellence of political judgment. Furthermore, the flip-side of the issue was relations with that unique and evolving complex, the EC. Thus it might at least have been argued that the chief issue in *Crotty* involved a political question. In fact, no one mentioned the political question doctrine in *Crotty*. Moreover, it appears likely, in view of the present judicial temper, that the suggestion of a judicial no-go area, a *fortiori* one which is not explicitly mentioned in the Constitution, would have been viewed with disfavour by the judges.

The sequel to *Crotty* was the Tenth Amendment of the Constitution Act 1988 which made the necessary amendment to enable Ireland to ratify the SEA. Out of twelve member states of the EC, in only two, Ireland and Denmark, were referenda necessary before the SEA was ratified.

The case of *McGimpsey v. Ireland* [1989] ILRM 209 is also relevant in this context. In *McGimpsey*, the plaintiffs unsuccessfully sought a declaration that what is popularly known as the Anglo-Irish Agreement, signed at Hillsborough in 1985, was unconstitutional. One of their major arguments[10] arose from the fact that the Agreement establishes an Intergovernmental Conference and Secretariat and commits each state to 'make determined efforts . . . through the Conference . . . to resolve any differences, on matters relating to Northern Ireland.' Founding on *Crotty*, it was said that this obligations fetters the power of the Irish Government to regulate its own external/foreign affairs and so contravenes Art. 29.4.1°. However, Barrington J distinguished *Crotty* and found against the plaintiff. The kernel of his judgment is as follows (at 227):

We are not dealing in [*McGimpsey*] with a multilateral treaty conferring powers on supranational authorities. We are dealing with a bilateral treaty between two sovereign Governments. The clear implication of Article 29, Section 5 is that the State is entitled to enter into international agreements. This means that the State may commit itself to deal with some aspect of foreign policy in such a way rather than in another. But this is something quite different from purporting to transfer the conduct of the foreign policy of the State to some supranational authority or even to some other State . . .

It is clear that the Conference, though served by its own Secretariat, is merely a forum in which the representatives of the two Governments find it convenient to meet on a regular basis to discuss matters of common interest relating to Northern Ireland. Article 2 provides that 'in the interest of promoting peace and stability, determined efforts shall be made through the conference to resolve any differences'.
But the Article also provides that:

There is no derogation from the sovereignty of either the Irish Government or the United Kingdom Government, and each retains responsibility for the decisions and administration of government within its own jurisdiction.

Under these circumstances it appears to me that the present case is totally different from the Crotty case and that it does not involve any unconstitutional fettering of the executive powers of government. The High Court decision was confirmed by the Supreme Court, on substantially the same grounds, on 1 March 1990.

SUPPLEMENT TO CHAPTER 3

3.4 THE PRESIDENT'S INDEPENDENCE

Draper v Ireland (Text at 50) was, in substance, followed in the case of *O'Malley v An Taoiseach*, High Court, 23 May 1989. Just before the dissolution of the Dáil, in May 1989, Chris O'Malley sought an interim injunction in the High Court instructing the Taoiseach not to advise the President to dissolve the Dáil. Hamilton J accepted the substantive point in the case, namely that there had been a breach of the constitutional obligation to revise constituency boundaries (see *infra*, chapter on *Elections*). However, applying Art. 13.8, he refused the injunction sought, on jurisdictional grounds:

> The constitutional duty of dissolving the Dáil is vested in the President and he is not answerable to any Court for the exercise and performance of this duty. The constitutional duty of advising the President in relation to this question is vested in the Taoiseach and in my opinion the Courts have no jurisdiction to place any impediment between the President and his constitutional advisor in this important matter, which is solely the prerogative of the President.

In short, where the front door was barred, it would be wrong to permit an attack by the back door.

SUPPLEMENT TO CHAPTER 4

4.3 THE LEGAL FRAMEWORK OF THE MINISTERS AND DEPARTMENTS

On the reorganisation of the Coalition Government in February 1986[11] the tourism functions of the Minister for Industry, Trade, Commerce and Tourism were transferred to the Minister for Fisheries and Forestry, leaving the original Minister re-titled simply the Minister for Industry and Commerce. When the Fianna Fáil Government was formed in 1987, further, extensive changes to the structure of government were made in order to reinforce the portfolios with the greatest potential for wealth and employment creation.[12] The most important change was that two new Ministers and Departments were created. The Minister for Tourism, Fisheries and Forestry was re-christened the Minister for the Marine,[13] retaining the marine functions of the original Minister and also receiving a transfer of transport functions from the Minister for Communications.[14] The second new Minister, the Minister for Tourism and Transport, received transfers of the remaining transport functions from the Minister for Communications;[15] and of tourism functions from the Minister for Marine. This combination was based on the idea that the transport system should be regarded as an aspect of tourism policy. To complete this change, forestry was transferred to the Minister for Energy.[16]

The Minister for Communications (with a rump of functions, following the loss of transport, consisting mainly of radio and t.v.) remained in being as a separate corporation sole, but one which was held in tandem with another portfolio.

The second change was that all the functions of the Minister for the Public Service were transferred to the Minister for Finance,[17] who thenceforth became known as the Minister for Finance and the Public Service. The reason given for this was 'the interests of better co-ordination of pay and staffing matters with budgetary requirements and of better utilisation of highly-qualified staffing resources.' This was the justification for vesting the personnel function in the Minister of Finance which was always given before the establishment of the Minister for the Public Service. The statutory shell — the corporation sole — thus vacated by the Minister for the Public Service was used to constitute the Minister for Tourism and Transport[18] so that there was no need for a Ministers and Secretaries (Amendment) Act to create a new corporation sole. (see text at 61-63, on constituting the Minister for Energy).

Thirdly the Minister for Agriculture was re-named the Minister for Agriculture and Food[19].

Finally, according to the Taoiseach (Mr Haughey)[20]:

In order to give greater thrust to certain development areas, I intend to create Offices attached to a number of Departments. Each of these Offices will be under the direct control of a minister of State. A headline for this kind of Office already exists, in the Office of Public Works and the Office of the Revenue Commissioners, which are attached to the Department of Finance, but which exercise separately their own distinct functions and responsibilities.

However, the only legislation found necessary to implement this change was the delegation, under the Ministers and Secretaries Code (see Text at 60), of, for example, certain functions of the Minister for Agriculture and Food to each of the Ministers of State in that Department.[21]

The changes made in 1987 were substantially retained following the 1989 election.

SUPPLEMENT TO CHAPTER 5

5.3 COLLECTIVE RESPONSIBILITY TO THE DÁIL

Nomination of a Taoiseach: an inter-regnum[22]   In July 1989 it appeared possible that the Dáil elected in 1987 would be unable to produce a majority to nominate any candidate as Taoiseach.[23] This possibility actually materialised for a period in the case of the Dáil elected in 1989. In these circumstances, it seems appropriate to examine the events of 1989 in order to see what lessons they teach for the future.

After the election of a Ceann Comhairle, in both 1987 and 1989, the outgoing

Taoiseach was re-nominated. (It was suggested that in recent years, a practice had developed by which the nomination of any outgoing Taoiseach should be taken first before other candidates[24].) In each case, this motion was defeated. In 1987 Mr Haughey was then nominated, with the vote on this motion being 82:82. The Ceann Comhairle then gave his vote in favour of the motion. In view of the importance of this vote, it was perhaps unfortunate that he did not give a explanation (to be recorded, as normal, in the Journal on the House and the Dáil Debates) to show why he exercised his vote in this way: as regards the two accepted guiding principles for the casting vote[25] one of them — preservation of the status quo — was really not relevant as Dr Fitzgerald had just been defeated; the other general principle — to exercise the Chair's vote so as to provide, if possible, that the House would have an opportunity to review the decision reached — would militate in favour of casting the vote against Mr Haughey. But such a vote might appear rather precious in regard to a matter of such great moment, when, moreover there was no real alternative candidate likely to become available.

In 1989, when the 26th Dáil reconvened after the general election, no candidate could secure a majority for nomination as Taoiseach.[26] The first constitutional provision to be relevant here is Art. 28.10:

The Taoiseach shall resign from the office upon his ceasing to retain the support of a majority in Dáil Éireann unless on his advice the President dissolves Dáil Éireann and on the reassembly of Dáil Éireann after the dissolution the Taoiseach secures the support of a majority in Dáil Éireann.

It seems to have been assumed that Mr Haughey had 'ceased to retain the support of a majority' before the 1989 election, an assumption to which we return. However, accepting its correctness for the sake of argument it follows that having failed to secure the support of a majority in the Dáil which reassembled after the dissolution, Mr Haughey was then under an obligation to resign. Mr Haughey accepted this but said that his Attorney General had advised that he could remain in office for a few days so as to have consultations with other party leaders. Following opposition protests, however, he resigned within hours of the defeat on the motion to renominate him. Dr Fitzgerald said that his Attorney General's advice, in 1987, was that had Mr Haughey not been nominated in 1987, Dr Fitzgerald would still have been under an obligation to resign forthwith as substantive Taoiseach. This view appears to be correct: the injunction to resign is not qualified by any such formula as 'within a reasonable period'. Nor is it necessary to read in any such restriction in order to make sense of the provision in view of the fact that a Taoiseach is allowed about two weeks before the Dáil meets, in order to negotiate, if necessary, with other parties.

The other relevant provision is Art. 28.11.1° by which:

If the Taoiseach at any time resigns from office the other members of the Government shall be deemed also to have resigned from office, but the Taoiseach and the other members of the Government shall continue to carry on their duties until their successors shall have been appointed.

The eminently sane policy of the second part of this provision ('but the Taoiseach...') is to ensure that the State is not without a Government. It achieves this by providing what came to be called an 'acting Government' headed by an 'acting Taoiseach'. In 1989, this Administration held office for about three weeks until it was replaced by a Taoiseach nominated by the combined votes of Fianna Fáil and Progressive Democrats deputies.

The interesting question is about the status and powers of any acting Taoiseach and acting Ministers. In what way are these restricted in comparison with their substantive equivalents?[27] An argument could be drawn, from the fact that such a Taoiseach does not enjoy Dáil support coupled with the rather spare language of the provision — 'carry on their duties' — that an acting Government has the minimum of powers necessary to keep the country ticking over. It would follow, for instance, that such a Government would not have authority to take any decision which could reasonably be left to its substantive successor. However, when one comes to apply to this extremely vague yardstick to concrete situations — for example, the appointment of judges, the extradition of offenders, the making of delegated legislation — one sees how very inadequate it is. A Court would probably be very reluctant to decide where to draw the line and, so, might refuse to strike down any of these decisions.

One question of peculiar importance here is whether an acting Taoiseach would have authority to advise a dissolution. The argument against is squarely based on Art. 28.10: this appears to allow a Taoiseach defeated in the Dáil one opportunity, at one point only, to precipitate another election. To allow a caretaker Taoiseach to do so would seem to fly in the face of this. The contrary argument appeals to common sense on the ground that such a liberal interpretation would mean the polity would be trapped in a revolving-door, in that there could be no dissolution (since the President cannot dissolve without the advice of a Taoiseach). However, this logic is not impeccable since it would be open to the Dáil to nominate some person as Taoiseach simply on the basis that he would go to the President to advise a dissolution. The significant point, however, about this is that it would mean that there could be no dissolution unless a majority of the Dáil wished it. By contrast, the normal situation is that it is the Government which has the prerogative of dissolving the Dáil. It is part of the Government's authority which, it is assumed, will be exercised responsibly.

How long could an acting Taoiseach continue, on the assumption that estimates, finance resolutions etc. either had been passed or a majority could be found to do so? Certainly there is nothing explicit in Art. 28.11 to restrict the period with which an acting Government could order the affairs of the State. On the other hand, the assumption appeared to be made by some politicians in July 1989, that it would be improper for this constitutional irregularity to continue for longer than was required for the prosecution of meaningful negotiations to put together majority support for some candidate as Taoiseach. However, to suggest any limit, however vague, immediately raises the question of what should happen after termination of the acting Government. Since the absence of any Government whatsoever is the ultimate evil in the eyes of a constitution, this line of thought presumably leads to the idea that the acting Taoiseach becomes, at some point, under an obligation to advise a dissolution. There are several difficulties with this, one of which is noted in the previous paragraph.

The question has sometimes been raised as to whether in the circumstances of constitutional upheaval presently being discussed the President would have a role going beyond that expressly marked out for him in Art. 13.2, namely automatically granting a dissolution to a Taoiseach who retains the support of the Dáil or exercising a discretion as to whether to grant a dissolution to a Taoiseach who does not. Certainly the Constitution does not say that, in the conditions of a hung Dáil, the President has any role in (say) encouraging the formation of a Coalition Government, but then it is not necessary that it should and the important point is that it does not expressly forbid him to undertake any such task (as, for instance, in Art. 13.7, it forbids him to issue a message to the Nation, without Government approval). However, his only concrete bargaining counter, the authority to grant or not grant a dissolution to a Taoiseach who has ceased to retain a Dáil majority, would only be helpful in (say) encouraging politicians to form a coalition of alien spirits, only in certain circumstances. He could, for instance, offer to consent to a dissolution on the advice of a Taoiseach, provided that the Taoiseach tried and failed to run the Government without a secure majority. Apart from this bargaining counter, the President has only the advantage that as the *paterfamilias* of the State and usually a former Minister, a President should be in at least as good a position as (say) an archbishop or (as occurred briefly in 1989) the Leader of the Labour Party to act as an honest broker. But the fact remains that, with the exception of Erskine Childers (Text at 47) all the Presidents have taken a minimalist view of their powers and duties and that this has almost come to be accepted as the norm. And in 1987 and 1989, whilst events never quite raised the issue of the President's refusing a dissolution, there was no indication of a departure from this norm. In short, whilst the hour may produce the man, the President is not a recourse on which to rely in this type of situation.

Finally, we ought to return to examine briefly a lacuna which was assumed, without discussion, at the start of this section. This is a restriction which appears to apply to Art.28.10, namely that it seems to be drafted to cover the classic nineteenth-century case in which a Taoiseach calls an election after he has lost a vote of confidence in the Dáil. The more usual twentieth-century pattern has been that a Taoiseach has called an election towards the end of the five-year period of the Dáil, without losing any vote. This occurred, for example, in 1973, 1977 and 1981. In these circumstances, Art. 28.10 would apply rather awkwardly in that it would seem to mean that a Taoiseach would begin to fall within the section only after the Dáil had reassembled after the election and there had been a failure to renominate him. If this occurred, would such a Taoiseach have the right, under Art. 28.10, to advise an immediate dissolution, even though a majority could be found for another candidate as Taoiseach? If he does have such a right, as appears to be the case, one would expect that, at least in a clear cut case, the President would exercise his discretion against accepting the advice to dissolve in these circumstances. In relation to this query, there was one conclusion which emerged tolerably clearly from the recent episodes. It was that although neither Dr. Fitzgerald in 1987 nor Mr Haughey in 1989 actually lost a Dáil vote of confidence before the respective elections, they were probably not entitled to advise a further dissolution under Art. 28.10. Dr Fitzgerald actually stated that his Attorney General's advice had been to this effect.

Government-Dáil relations   As mentioned, the 1987-89 Fianna Fáil Government was in a minority in the Dáil and so it was not unnatural that it should be defeated — in fact six times[28] — in the Dáil. The Government did not always adjust its policy to take account of these defeats: for example, it did not heed the motion, passed in private members' time, 'directing' the Minister for Health to rescind his proposal to close a Limerick hospital. There is nothing surprising in this. As a British author remarks: '[apart from votes of confidence] any other adverse vote ... will have whatever effect is prescribed by the terms of the vote, but no other.'[29] The more interesting point is in regard to the question of what constitutes a matter of confidence, defeat on which requires the resignation of the Government and (almost inevitably) a general election (see Text at 71). For the Government did not resign or even call for an early vote of confidence following any of these defeats; nor was it credibly suggested that it should have taken either of these courses. Too much should not be made of this as showing a definitive change of rule as to what constitutes a matter of confidence (not least because there can be no definite rules in this area). After all, the Government has explained its refusal to adopt either of the two courses classically required on the basis that all but one of the defeats were in private members' time, whilst the exception (the vote to hold a debate on the motion regarding Deputy Lawlor's replacement on the Joint Oireachtas Committee on State Sponsored Bodies) was merely procedural. Nonetheless, it is noteworthy that earlier, on two occasions, Government defeats (in 1938 and 1940) on relatively minor issues were seized on as at least passable excuses for a rush to the hustings which resulted in the return of a Government with a more secure majority; whilst, in 1930, a Government resigned but was re-elected without an election, following defeat on a minor issue (see Text at 70).

At this point, it may be objected that the reason why the Government's reaction to the defeats in 1987-89 was different to those in earlier cases was not from any excess of political virtue, but stemmed simply from the fact that the political circumstances were different. Specifically, throughout the present period, it has been the conventional wisdom that the electorate, or a sufficient number of them, would vote against any party which was perceived as causing an 'unnecessary election'. However, this begs the question of what constitutes an 'unnecessary election'. The simple point being advanced here is that during most of the two-year period over which these defeats were sustained, the Government party was riding high in the opinion polls, yet it chose not to cause an election and some part of the reason for this was that a resignation on foot of these minor issues would have been widely regarded as leading to an 'unnecessary election'. In other words, the Government's failure to call an election suggests a perception that the category of issues requiring resignation has narrowed. We are safe in assuming that this perception is not the Government's only reason for refraining from resigning, so far. The Government will also be influenced by the possible danger of losing an election. Nevertheless, if one considers the future significance of its actions, one can say that the existence of these six defeats, followed by no election, makes it that much more difficult for a future Government to claim that it was obliged to resign on foot of some trivial defeat in the Dáil. Eventually, it is true, in May 1989, the Taoiseach dissolved the Dáil, giving as his reason the need for a Government majority so that it could be confident of securing the passage of its business in the Dáil (notwithstanding that it had suffered no defeat on a major item of business). The Opposition replied that this was an unnecessary dissolution, and the election resulted in the loss of four seats by the Government. This proves little since the election was largely fought on other issues. However, it does mean that a future Government will be somewhat less anxious to seize on any trivial Dáil defeat as an excuse for a dissolution.

This perception of narrowing in the class of issues which might be regarded as matters of confidence is reflected in both media comment and British practice. If it is maintained, its effect will be to uncouple the fate of the Government from the question of who wins a Dáil vote on a minor matter. This will slightly reduce the ascendancy of the Government over the Dáil and may, over the years, lead to an increase in free votes in areas which are not central to the Government's programme — for example, family law reform. It may be a sign of things to come that the 25th Dáil saw the passage into law of the first private member's bill since the 1950s, the Judicial Separation and Family Law Reform Act, 1989.

SUPPLEMENT TO CHAPTER 6

6.6 THE PLACE OF THE SENATE

Writing in 1986, Senator Professor James Dooge remarked on:[30]

the tendency for criticism of the Seanad to vary in intensity with some degree of regularity. Indeed attempts to deal with this criticism seem to recur at quite regular intervals of about ten years.

The major criticism of the second Seanad during the first 10 years of its existence related to the dangers of corruption due to the small electorate concerned . . . At the end of the first ten years, legislation had been introduced providing for 5 separate panel elections and the extension of the electorate to include all members of City Councils and County Councils.

The next major Oireachtas debate on the Seanad arose in November, 1957 when Dr Noel Browne moved that Seanad Eireann as at present constituted should be abolished. An Inter-Party Government amendment suggesting reform rather than abolition was supported by Fianna Fail. In the following year a commission of Seanad Electoral Law was established which reported in February, 1959 (Pr. 4985). This Commission recommended in a majority report that vocationally nominated Seanad candidates should be directly elected by a vocationally established electorate representative of the Nominating Bodies . . .

No action was taken on the 1959 Commission Report and there was no serious discussion for another ten years when the position of the Seanad was considered by the Report of the Committee on the Constitution published in 1967 (Pr. 9817).

About ten years later the Seanad Committee on Procedure and Privileges made two attempts to consider a major overhaul of the methods of working of the Seanad but in each case the only outcome was some desirable but relatively minor changes in the Standing Orders. Since a further ten years have now elapsed one can expect the present time to be once again a high season for criticism of the Seanad.

Sure enough, in June 1987, with the dictates of cyclical rhythm probably strengthened by the Progressive Democrats' proposal for the abolition of the Senate, the Senate debated and passed a motion 'that Seanad Eireann calls on the Government to carry out an urgent review of the powers and functions of the Seanad and the methods of election of its members.'[31] The upshot of this motion, which was carried without a division, was that a sub-committee of the Committee of Procedure and Privileges was directed to propose reforms of the Senate procedure, as a preliminary, so it was said, to the Senate and the Government grasping the nettle of electoral reform. In any event, thus far the main reform made concerns 'Dissenting procedure' (covered in the Supplement in the chapter on Procedure in the Houses of the Oireachtas).

Another feature of the Senate's deliberations is that during the 1983-87 Senate, it made a point of debating the reports of the Joint Oireachtas Committees, devoting a half day (or, if there was no pressure of legislation, a whole day) on Thursdays, to the debate. Thus, in 1985, ten of these reports were debated in the Senate; compared with only one in the Dáil. An even more significant change is the increase in legislation which was initiated in the Senate. The figures are as follows:

	Total No. of Bills Introduced in Both Houses	SENATE BILLS	
		Government	Private Members
1984	27	4	3
1985	24	6	1
1986	39	12	1
1987	34	14	3
1988	35	3	2
1989 (1 Jan-1 May)	12	3	1
compared to e.g.			
1979	41	3	0

Note: None of the Private Members Bills became law.

SUPPLEMENT TO CHAPTER 8

8.2 FINANCIAL PROCEDURE IN THE DÁIL

The suggestion made in the Text at 116-7 — that the delegation of legislative power given to the Government by the imposition of Duties Act, 1957 was unconstitutional — was accepted in *McDaid v. His Honour Judge David Sheehy* High Court, 18 January 1989.[32] The case arose on an application to quash a conviction for keeping, in the fuel tank of a motor vehicle, hydrocarbon oil, on which a rebate of duty had been allowed under the Imposition of Duties (No. 221) (Excise Duties) Order. The decision that the Government's authority was unconstitutional was based on the fact that the Government was left totally free in the exercise of the power: it was not a case of the Government only filling in the details, within a principle fixed by the Oireachtas. In spite of this holding, the applicant's action failed on the ground that the 1975 Order had been 'confirmed' by the Finance Act, 1976. It was said that this had embossed the Order with the status of a permanent statutory provision.

8.3 REFORMS IN THE DÁIL

Addressing the question of progress in regard to various reforms listed in the Text at 121-3, it can be said, first, that the Comprehensive Public Expenditure Programmes have become a permanent feature of the landscape. Secondly, in the autumns of 1987 and 1988, the Government was able to publish an abridged version of the Estimates for the Public Services, for the following years.[33] Thirdly, the Estimates were immediately debated on a general 'take note' motion with each separate Estimate then being debated in the year in which the money was spent (during the period between the enactment of the Finance Bill and the summer recess). The procedural modifications mentioned in the Text — multiple, brief interventions etc. — remain under discussion by the Dáil CPP. Next, a summary of the Public Capital Programme was debated as part of the 'take note' Estimates debates of 1987 and 1988, already mentioned. Finally, however, no Public Expenditure Committee was reconstituted in the 1987-88 or 1989- Dála. In part, no doubt, this was because there had been some feeling in the previous Dáil that there was an overlap between the work of the Committee and that of the Public Accounts Committee. Indeed, even the Coalition Government, which had set up the PEC, had suggested (though without taking any action) the amalgamation of the two Committees to form a Committee of Public Management whose brief would be:[34]

. . . to examine and report on the adequacy of the systems used to ensure the efficient management of departments including the extent to which aims and objectives are clearly defined, staff and other resources cost-effectively deployed, and the outcomes monitored. The Comptroller and Auditor-General would be give additional staff and the necessary skills to enable him to assist the new Committee.

However, there was another and probably stronger reason for the non-revival of the PEC. Take the following passages as examples of that Committee's work:

The Committee discussed aspects of the Public Capital Programme with the Minister and he agreed generally with the Committee's findings on lack of control in some areas of capital expenditure.[35]

I agree with the Committee that the state of affairs existing before the implementation of Circular 1/83 [appraisal of capital projects] was in many regards most unsatisfactory.[36]

Many of the report's findings mirror the Minister's thinking and, indeed, that of the Government. Others represent the view from a slightly different angle and provide an additional insight into the problems of the public service today. . .[37]

In contrast, with the rather bold approach of the Committee disclosed by these extracts, Mr Haughey, who became Taoiseach in 1987, had taken the view even as Leader of the Opposition that '... the running of the country, particularly the running of the economy, is a matter for clear, hard decision by the Government.'[38] This statement is of course antithetical to the type of work which the PEC had been doing and it is easy to infer from it that the Fianna Fáil Government would consider the Committee too intrusive and not reconstitute it.

SUPPLEMENT TO CHAPTER 9

9.1 SOURCES OF PROCEDURE

Notwithstanding the apparent supremacy of standing orders, there are some cases in which practice has been accepted as superseding standing orders. One example concerns standing orders themselves. These contemplate either (in DSO 144) their own explicit amendment or, alternatively (in DSO 143(1)) their suspension only 'for the day's sitting, and for a particular purpose'. Notwithstanding this, there is a long-standing practice by which standing orders have been suspended, either indefinitely or for the session (as with sessional orders), or for a specified period (for example, 'until the Adjournment for the Christmas Recess'). In each case, this has been done merely by an ordinary motion. A recent example is the Order introducing the new Questions system (explained *infra*), initially as an experiment for one year.[39]

9.2 ARRANGEMENT OF BUSINESS

A more controversial case of practice superseding standing orders concerns the Taoiseach's prerogative under DSO 25 to fix the order in which the Government business on the Order Paper is to be taken (Text at 136). Theoretically his power is confined to fixing the sequence of business. Thus if the Taoiseach wishes to make any proposals to curtail debate or the scope of the Dáil's decision — as by taking an item without debate or within a set time or to exclude amendments other than those put down by the Government — then such proposals are motions of substance in their own right. This would mean that they must be attended by the full procedure specified in DSO 28 (see Text at 140) so that, theoretically, due notice must be given and the text of the motions be on the Order Paper or, in a case of permitted shorter notice, on a supplementary Order Paper.

In fact, what customarily happens is that, for example, out of the first 41 sittings of the 1987-89 Dáil, there was a proposal, made by the Taoiseach, to curtail debate in some form on 27 sittings. It is true that on at least one occasion[40] this was disputed and there was a vote in favour of the guillotine, but there was no advance notice of it or any mention on the Order Paper.

How has this practice come about? In recent Dála, minor curtailments of debate as to, for instance, time limit on speeches, were occasionally allowed to be moved on the Order or Business. However, these were proposed with the agreement of all parties concerned. Proposals regarding restriction of debate, slipped in as part of the Taoiseach's announcement on the Order of Business, gathered momentum in the 1982-87 Dáil. They followed from daily agreement between the whips of the Coalition Government and the then main opposition party (Fianna Fáil). This type of arrangement continued into 1987-89 Dáil in which it was Fianna Fáil which was the Government party and Fine Gael the main opposition party. However, the significant difference was that, leaving aside independents and members of smaller parties, there were two other parties which were sufficiently large to be recognised as 'groups' (see Text at 138) and which had not been consulted. Eventually, from the autumn, 1987 session, for the rest of the 1987-89 Dáil consultation regarding the curtailment of debate, without the necessary notice, was extended to include all three of the Opposition 'Groups'. And, subject to agreement among the four whips, this widening of the Taoiseach's prerogative appears to have been accepted, even though it is not in accord with standing orders; the agreement is reached outside the House; and it does not extend to the independent deputies or smaller parties.

9.3 FORM OF DEBATE: SUB IUDICE

Increasingly, matters of political controversy are cast, at some point, in the form of legal proceedings. There has, thus, been an increase in the situations in which the stringent Oireachtas *sub iudice* rule bars discussion in the Oireachtas of some matter which otherwise it would be the function and duty of the Oireachtas to debate. The purpose of this rule is to prevent either discussion which might prejudice a fair trial or the criticism of a judge, which might be thought to interfere with judicial independence. In 1986, a minister of State was dismissed. He issued a libel writ in respect of some of the media coverage of his dismissal and, as a result, the Taoiseach was prevented from giving the Dáil an explanation for the dismissal. The Ceann Comhairle took the unusual step of explaining his ruling on this point, as follows:[41]

> The purpose of the sub judice rule, which has operated in the House for over 60 years, is to protect litigants, plaintiffs and defendants, and ensure that actions coming before the courts are not prejudiced by being discussed in this House which enjoys absolute privilege. If the rule were to be ignored, the House used as a sort of a pre-trial forum or as an alternative for other court procedures — I have in mind interrogatories and discovery — in my opinion it would undermine our system of justice, bring about unfair judgments, and influence unfairly tribunals, judges and juries.

In 1987, on the next occasion, when the matter came up, the Dáil unusually exercised its undoubted freedom to pass a motion setting aside (for one debate) its normal practice 'in relation to references in debate to matters which are awaiting or under adjudication in the courts'.[42]

The matter arose again the following year, when the Ceann Comhairle refused to allow discussion of the rod licence dispute, a matter of grave public concern, because a plenary summons had been issued, in relation to some episode in the dispute. As a result, the *sub judice* rule was referred to the Committee of Procedure and Privileges to consider what reform might be appropriate.[43]

Plainly, there is a deal of scope for reform since the basic rule was fixed in the Westminister Parliament, some centuries ago, at a time when the courts themselves operated a very strong version of their own *sub iudice* rule for the distinct purpose of determining whether someone was guilty of contempt of court. By contrast, contemporary Irish courts set a much greater value on free speech than did these by-gone English courts. It is true that although (because of Art. 15.13) there is no possibility of a deputy or senator being disciplined by a court, nevertheless the Oireachtas still wishes not to interfere in the fair administration of justice. However, there is no reason for the Oireachtas to conform to an absolute standard — of no discussion whatsoever of court proceedings — which the courts themselves no longer consider necessary.

Various significant details will have to be considered by the CPP including whether any general rule should be open to modification by such factors as that: a jury trial is involved; an appellate court is hearing the case; the proceedings are civil rather than criminal; or the case is being heard in a foreign court.

Finally, it is worth mentioning an unusual and indirect enforcement of the *sub iudice* rule, involving a foreign parliament.[44] This occurred, in 1988, at a time when Father Patrick Ryan's extradition from Ireland was sought by the British authorities. Certain remarks were made about Father Ryan in the British House of Commons which might have prejudiced a fair trial in a British court. In view of this, the Irish Attorney General refused to recommend his extradition from Ireland to Britain.

Dissenting in the Senate   The Senate has modified its voting procedure to meet the defect that in recent times the only way in which a Senator could

277

be formally recorded as dissenting was by an adverse vote, upon which his name would be shown in the Journal of Proceedings as voting against. By contrast the Dáil still continues on an earlier assumption which does not raise this problem. This is that if a member rises to claim a vote, and fewer than the specified number of members (seven in the Dáil; five the Senate) support the claim so that no vote is taken, those who did claim the vote will be taken as having dissented. In the Senate, however, the point had been made that claiming a vote does not necessarily mean that a deputy is opposed to a motion: for the motivation may, instead, be (say) to force another deputy to come down on one side or the other. Furthermore, the effect of the restoration of the traditional rule must have been to increase the overall number of divisions. For example, in the 1987-88 session, in the Senate in a quarter or so of the divisions the oppositions mustered a vote in single figures. To meet both of these difficulties, a new procedure has been produced which, while not affecting the right to claim a vote, provides for an alternative procedure by which a Senator may have his dissent recorded in the Journal without the need for a division. To take advantage of this procedure, a member must either raise his hand when called upon to do so by the Cathaoirleach or sign, prior to the putting of the questions, but on the same day, a register maintained by the Cathaoirleach.[45]

9.4 OIREACHTAS REFORMS

Committees   Before listing the surviving committees in the 1987-89 Oireachtas, we ought to note the judgements reached on the innovative committees of the previous Oireachtas, by the two scholars who have written obituaries of them. According to Professor Zimmerman:[46]

The new committee system is forcing senior executive officials to justify their positions with facts and explain alternative courses of action, thereby improving executive accountability. Committee probing, while increasing work for senior executive officials, can sharpen and increase administrative efficiency. In spite of the negative experience of a few senior executives in their early appearances before committees, the committees serve as contact points for members to gain a better understanding and appreciation of the role played by the officials and the problems they encounter in carrying out their duties. Michael O'Kennedy, Vice Chairman of the Committee on Public Expenditure, stated in 1985:

It is not just a question of our having the opportunity of criticising the public services. Equally, what we must encourage . . . . is that public servants would, in a very healthy and outspoken way, also tell us where we . . . . create conditions that they find incur extra public expenditure.

Dr Atkins writes: [47]

Where policy has derived in some way from select committee recommendations, the relevant government spokesmen have not hesitated to make a formal acknowledgement.

The Department of Labour policy document on the amalgamation of the unemployment and training agencies cordially acknowledged the similar proposals contained in the PEC reports. Announcing the decision to give officials of Customs and Excise powers of arrest in matters relating to drug smuggling, the Department of Justice paid tribute to the recommendations outlined in the CLVC report.

. . . Each committee made some impact in the area of its investigations, if not directly then at least indirectly by highlighting important issues. While it is the case that at least five reports were ignored for every one which received direct government acknowledgement or general media coverage, it is also the case that committees may have had some impact merely by deciding to investigate a subject. Quite possibly, for example, it was the sheer existence of an SSBC enquiry which prompted government action in relation to Ostlanna Iompair Eireann, Irish Shipping, and Udaras na Gaeltachta. Certainly the situation in each of these companies altered radically within weeks of committee hearings. In each case government action eclipsed SSBC reports and recommendations, nevertheless each enquiry served to reveal vital information which might otherwise have remained undisclosed.

One should not over-emphasise the impact which these committees made. It was only the Public Expenditure Committee which was guaranteed debating time for its reports in the Dáil and, in fact, few committee reports were debated in the Dáil, though most were debated in the Senate. Nor was there any obligation, as in certain other parliaments, for the executive to respond formally to report recommendations. Whilst membership of a committee certainly helped to inform its members, its impact on the course of government was fitful and marginal. However it must be said that more could not have been expected in the experimental stages.

Of the ad hoc select committees, only three were re-constituted in the 1987-89 Oireachtas,[48] namely Joint Committees on Women's Rights, the Irish Language, and Commercial State Sponsored Bodies. The Joint Committee on Legislation was not revived. Its non-revival meant *inter alia* that there was no parliamentary body to examine domestic (as opposed to EC) delegated legislation. If this were to persist in future parliaments, the Senate would doubtless consider the re-establishment of the Senate Committee on Statutory Instruments (Text at 98 and 110). The fate of the Public Expenditure Committee is dealt with *supra* under the heading of Finance.

Other reforms Even apart from the committee system, the path of Oireachtas reform has not run smoothly. There have been some changes in regard to Questions *(infra)*; and the earlier publication and debate of Estimates (see under head of Finance). A new edition of the Dáil Standing Orders was issued in 1986 (the current edition of the Senate Standing Orders is still the 1979 edition) which consolidated a number of changes which had depended upon sessional orders, among them the hours of sitting (see Text at 236). However, the main thrust of reform waits on a report from a CPP sub-committee. For: in May, 1988, in Private Members' time, the Dail passed the following resolution unanimously:[49]

279

That Dáil Éireann requests the Committee of Procedure and Privileges to report to it within [twelve] months with
(a) proposals, with necessary safeguards, for the televising of Dáil proceedings, and
(b) proposals for a more general programme of reforms to Dail procedure, covering limitations on the length of speeches, procedures for dealing with urgent matters and the relevancy and admissibility of Parliamentary Questions.

One of the strongest points to emerge from the debate was the intimate connection between the televising of the Dáil and the matters mentioned in (b); 'If we were to televise the proceedings without a reform of Standing Orders bewilderment would grow among the public rather than be reduced.'[50] Later additions to the brief for investigation were: making sound broadcasting permanent (which has been introduced experimentally since November 1986); the *sub iudice* rule *(supra)*; the question of privilege from defamation, including how it should be applied to Committee proceedings and the related issue of whether committees whould be given, by legislation, power to sub-poena witnesses. (This means that the legislation mentioned in the Text at 164 is still under consideration.) The CPP established a working group composed of the whips of the four larger parties, to examine all these matters. Following its recommendation, the Dáil has now approved the televising of its proceedings (to begin from the 1991 Budget). The Committee's proposals on reform are to be submitted to the Dáil by late 1990.

9.5 QUESTIONS

Certain changes designed to improve Questions were introduced on an experimental basis in June 1985 and confirmed as a permanent feature in what are now DSO 31-40 (of the 1986 edition) of Standing Orders. [51] There are two aspects to these changes: first, improvements in the existing system; and, secondly the introduction of a new type of Question, the Priority Question.

As regards the first set of changes, the most significant improvement was designed to promote greater topicality, its absence being a particular sin in politics, which is so dependent on the fickle attention of the news media and public. Under the former system, a minister continued to answer Questions for however many sessions were necessary to exhaust all the Questions down for oral answer by him. Under the new scheme, one minister answers Questions for at most one session, with the minister next in line on the rota taking the following session and any unanswered Questions to the original minister being either answered in writing or, if the Questioner so requests, put to the minister on the next occasion when he is answering Questions. This change has been weeks — before the rota of ministers can go full cycle. However, as the then Chief Whip said in 1986: [52]

In a comparison made between two nine month periods, one in 1984-85 under the old system, the following emerged: in the period under the old scheme, Questions relating to four Government Departments were taken on three occasions; Questions relating to four other Departments twice only; Questions relating to a further three Departments once only; while, in the case of five Government Departments, Questions relating to their activities were not reached at all during the period. The Departments not reached at all were Social Welfare, Agriculture, Justice, Education and Labour. By contrast in a similar period in 1985-86, under the new procedures, Questions relating to all Departments were reached on at least four occasions, and in the case of six of those Departments, on five occasions.

A second change is that, under the original system, a deputy could put down as many Questions as he wished, so that the early bird could enjoy a monopoly. Under the new system, a deputy is confined to two Questions per minister and the sequence in which Questions are put is determined by a lottery, at which deputies may attend. Finally, the rule that a Question is not acceptable if it goes over ground already covered in the recent past has been slightly relaxed by reducing the time limit from six months to four months.

The other major development is the establishment of Priority Questions, the object of which is again to enable a topic to be agitated whilst it is still topical. There is no restriction on the subject matter which may be covered in these Questions (as there is, for instance, with a Private Notice Question, on which see Text at 154). But the Questions must be in the name of a deputy nominated by a 'group' and the groups always nominate their front-bench spokesman on the relevant subject-area. In addition, it is only the deputy who put the substantive Question who may put supplementary questions. The fact that Priority Questions are confined to groups (on which, see Text at 138) means that independent deputies and members of smaller parties are excluded unless they number, in all, at least seven and have organised themselves to claim this privilege.

SUPPLEMENT TO CHAPTER 10

10.1 GENERAL

Two episodes in early 1990 illustrated the reach of Irish parliamentary privilege, although it seems likely that neither will yield an authoritative court ruling.

The first of these episodes involved Art 15.13 of the Constitution:

The members of each House of the Oireachtas shall except in case of treason as defined in this Constitution, felony or breach of the peace, be privileged from arrest in going to and returning from and while within the precincts of, either House.

According to reports[53], the incident involved a Senator who had allegedly refused a blood or urine sample to gardai after he had been arrested on suspicion of driving with more than the permitted blood-alcohol level. The reports stated that the Senator had indicated that he intended to invoke the immunity just quoted and that the D.P.P. had withdrawn charges. It was also said that this was the third occasion in the preceding decade that a member of the Oireachtas had relied upon this privilege.

Against this background, it may be worth attempting to dissect this constitutional privilege. In fact, it probably does not grant such a wide immunity as might have been supposed. The first limitation stems from the fact that it is confined to misdemeanours (other than breach of the peace) and arrest for a misdemeanour is usually unnecessary anyway. Secondly, the immunity only restrains arrest and not prosecution. This point of distinction of course is relevant in regard to the case mentioned in the previous paragraph, on which the facts unfortunately are unclear. It is uncertain whether the arrest occurred before the refusal to give the sample so that the refusal occurred while the Senator was unconstitutionally detained. On that assumption, the prosecution for the refusal would probably have been tainted with the unconstitutionality of the detention and the Senator would have had to be aquitted (if he chose to plead the privilege). On the alternative assumption, the refusal and, hence, the crime of refusing came *before* the arrest and, on that assumption, it seems less likely that the privilege would apply.

The third restriction on this privilege is that it is confined to: '[an] arrest in going to and returning from, and while within the precincts, of either House'. The point of difficulty, here, is how close, in distance and time, the member must be to the House in order to fall within the words 'going to and returning from ... the precincts...' One of the surprising features of the present case is that the episode was said to have occurred several hours after the Senator's attendance at the Senate.

The second episode concerned the issue of a House's right to control its own proceedings. It is well-known that the Westminster Parliament counts it as one of its leading privileges that it may regulate its own proceedings, free of outside control by a court or anyone else. The closest parallel to this privilege, which the Irish Constitution offers, is contained in Art 15.10 by which: 'Each House shall make its own rules and standing orders, with power to attach penalties for their infringement...'

The situation (which was also widely reported)[54] in which this provision became relevant arose out of an attempt to discipline a Senator, by suspending him from the Senate for one week, on the recommendation of the Committee on Procedure and Privileges. This was normal procedure, as was the fact that the Committee was chaired by the Cathaoirleach who was also in the Chair when the Senate adopted the Committee's recommendation. What was unusual in this case was that the breach of procedure of which the Senator had been found guilty and for which he was being punished was that of making a grave accusation against the Cathaoirleach. On that basis, the Senate's procedure almost certainly violated constitutional justice[55] (even if the Senate had been required to follow that procedure by Senate Standing Order (2) which states that: 'A Senator may be named only when the Cathaoirleach is in the Chair') The first rule of constitutional justice — *Nemo iudex in sua causa* — was breached because it might seem that the Cathaoirleach was partisan. The second rule — *Audi alteram partem* — was breached in that the Senator was not allowed certain rights (for example, the right of appearing to put his case to the Committee) to which it seems, from *In re Haughey* (see Text at 145) that the Senator was entitled.

The major issue, however, in this episode, concerned not constitutional justice, but rather the question of whether the High Court had jurisdiction to supervise the Senate's internal, disciplinary proceedings. The Court did grant the Senator leave to apply for a judicial review of his disciplining but this is not significant since only the most hopeless cases fall at this preliminary stage. At the time of writing, it appears either that there will be no substantive hearing of the Senator's claim for review or if there is, that the central issue will not be fully considered because the fact that the Senator's punishment was withdrawn and he received an apology will mean that the High Court may well rule that the issue is moot.

If this matter were to be fully investigated by a court, the starting point would be the provision mentioned earlier. This states that the House has authority to 'make its own rules and standing orders...' The first difficulty with this formulation is that, read literally, it only refers to *making* rules with penalties and *not* to their *enforcement*.

It is true that there is a long standing practice in most parliaments (and the Dáil and Senate are no exception) of exercising jurisdiction to apply their rules in respect of such matters as the organisation of debates, disorder and discipline, and taking votes. It is appropriate and convenient that they should do so. But to ground the Senate's action in the field on discipline on this basis might mean that it was put on a non-constitutional footing. And this would weaken the argument for saying that the Senate had exclusive authority. In any case, even if the Senate's action could be grounded upon Art 15.10, this does not (explicitly or even probably implicitly) give the Senate exclusive authority. And, given the activist temper of the contemporary Irish judiciary[56], by Art 34.3.1 [Text at 192-94] it seems that a court would be unlikely to find that it did not have jurisdiction.

Moreover, there is a fairly close precedent. For the Separation of Powers is not relevant here since the case has nothing to do with legislation (see Text at 40-42) but concerns the disciplining of an individual. In the line of cases[57] involving attempts to stop the progress of the pro-life constitutional amendment before the referendum, the plaintiffs failed just because the cases were held to be attempts to get the court to interfere with the legislative process. The more relevant precedent here is *Re Haughey* in which the Supreme Court was prepared to exercise jurisdiction over the Dáil (in fact, the Dáil Public Accounts

Committee) and its procedure. It is true that the person involved in that case was not a member of the Oireachtas. However, even if this be a relevant point of distinction, there are in the *Haughey* case more exact precedents, namely that the Court was prepared to check that the Dáil Standing Orders had been properly made and, secondly, to determine whether the Committee had wandered outside its terms of reference.

In short, it seems likely that if the Senator's penalty had not been withdrawn, that the High Court would have exercised jurisdiction to quash the penalty.

SUPPLEMENT TO CHAPTER 11

11.2 'ONE MAN: ONE VALUE'

O'Donovan v. Attorney General (Text at 171-73) was, in substance, followed in the high-profile case of *O'Malley v. An Taoiseach*, High Court, 23 May, 1989. Just before the dissolution of the Dáil in May, 1989, Chris O'Malley MEP sought an interim injunction in the High Court, founded on the fact that there had been changes in the distribution of the population since the Electoral (Amendment) Act, 1983, with no corresponding amending of electoral boundaries. (The recommendations of the 1988 Dáil Constituency Commission Report, chaired, as it happens, by Mr Justice Hamilton had been made the basis of a bill, the Electoral (Amendment) Bill, 1988, but this was not proceeded with by the Government because it seemed, from Opposition protests at its terms of reference, that it did not enjoy the support of a Dáil majority.) Mr O'Malley complained that out of the forty one constituencies, the deputy/population constituency varied by at least 7% from the national average in seventeen constituencies and 10% in the case of eight of these. Secondly, under Art. 16.2.3⁰ and 4⁰, the constituencies must be revised with due regard to changes in population and if a census return discloses major changes — as the 1986 census had done — there is an obligation on the Oireachtas to pass legislation revising the constituencies. Hamilton P, accordingly opined, in a considered *obiter dictum*, that the Oireachtas was in breach of its constitutional obligation to revise the constituencies. (Though for the outcome of the case, see Chapter on the President *supra*.)

11.4 FRANCHISE AND REGISTRATION

Following *In re Art. 26 and the Electoral (Amendment) Bill, 1983* (1984) IR 268 (Text at 28-29), Art 16.1.2⁰ of the Constitution was amended (Text at 175-176) to empower the Oireachtas to widen the Dáil franchise (but not the franchise in referenda or Presidential elections) to include non-citizens. This invitation was accepted by the Electoral (Amendment) Act, 1985. This extends the franchise to (as of April 1989) about 11,000 British citizens (as so defined 'under the Act of the British Parliament entitled the British Nationality Act 1981': 1985 Act, s.2). In addition, the franchise may be further extended by order of the Minister for the Environment, which is subject to the unusual requirement of positive resolution of each House. Such an order may only be made in respect of the citizens of a member state of the EC, provided also that the Minister is of opinion that the electoral law of that state permits Irish citizens resident in the state to vote for members of its National Parliament on an equal footing with its own citizens. However, apart from Britain (which has always allowed Irish citizens not only to vote but even to be members of Parliament) no state yet fulfils this requirement.

Two relevant recent cases involved broadly similar facts — namely, certain undoubted imperfections in the Dáil electoral system. The law laid down and, particularly, the judicial attitude adopted were also broadly similarly. The future is likely to bring to light several other imperfections in a rather tense area and it may be helpful if these two cases are described together in order to bring the essential similarity in the judges' approach into sharper focus. The grievance in *Draper v. The Attorney General* (1984) IR 285 (mentioned briefly in the Text at 177) was that there was, at that time, no postal vote facility for those, like the plaintiff, who were physically incapable of going to a polling booth to cast their vote. Evidence from the Irish Wheelchair Association was given to show that some five hundred of its members were unable to leave their homes without assistance and more than two hundred could not do so, even with assistance. In the other case, *O'Reilly v. Minister for the Environment* (1986) IR 143, which, unlike *Draper*, was not appealed to the Supreme Court, the plaintiff's complaint was that the listing of candidates on the ballot paper in alphabetical order resulted in a bias in favour of those surnames beginning with letters at the start of the alphabet. Evidence from politicians and political scientists, much of it of great intrinsic interest — was led, which 'prove(d) conclusively' (according to Murphy J) that in Dáil elections over a forty year period, there had been a significant over-representation of candidates whose surnames began with letters at the start of the alphabet. Moreover, a system in use in Calfornia State elections was described which would have obviated this defect. Put simply, this system consisted of having a number of different types of ballot paper, in each system, so that each candidate would have the chance of appearing at the top in the case of some of the ballot papers.

The relevant provision is Article 16.1.2° by which: 'Every citizen. . . . who is not disqualified by law and complies with the provisions of the law relating to the elections of members. . . shall have the right to vote.' Read very literally the references to 'disqualifi[cation] by law' and 'the provisions of the law relating to the election of members . . .' might just be taken to mean that the Oireachtas could totally subvert the right to vote which appears to be conferred by the Article. In fact, in these two cases, a balanced and less literal interpretation was adopted. In a central passage, in the Supreme Court's judgement, in *Draper*, O'Higgins CJ said at 290:

Elections to Dáil Eireann and the constitutional right of citizens, not disqualified, to vote in such elections must be regulated by law.... The State has an obligation to make such a law operative and effective by providing throughout the country for appropriate facilities for the conduct of the poll, by the employment of sufficient officers to supervise it, and by providing protection for voters and their ballot until the result is decided. In making this regulating law and in taking the other necessary steps the State must act reasonably and, having regard to the requirements of secrecy in the ballot and the dangers of intimidation and other electoral abuses, must strike a balance which will serve the common good.

Postal voting may, without extraordinary and complex safeguards, be open to abuse. . .

In the opinion of the Court, the present law, contained in the Electoral Act, provides a reasonable regulation of elections to Dáil Eireann, having regard to the obligation of secrecy, the need to prevent abuses and other requirements of the common good. The fact that some voters are unable to comply with its provisions does not of itself oblige the State to tailor that law to suit their special needs. The State may well regard the cost and risk involved in providing special facilities for particular groups as not justified, having regard to the numbers involved, their wide dispersal throughout the country and the risks of electoral abuses.

This passage was quoted with approval by Murphy J in *O'Reilly* (at 150-51).[58] Murphy J applied the principle contained in it, in the following comment on the Californian State election code (explained *supra*) which the plaintiff had offered as a practicable alternative to the alphabetical arrangement of candidates's names (at 152):

But even accepting that the system advocated is an improvement in those respects on the existing system it does not necessarily follow that the existing system is unreasonable or unconstitutional.

In each of the cases, because of the wide exception, already mentioned, to the right to vote in Article 16.1.2°, the plaintiffs had recourse to what they hoped might have been greener pastures. The first of these was Art. 40.1 — the equality provision — on which, in *Draper*, the plaintiff built the argument that it was unconstitutionally discriminatory for members of the Defence Forces or the Garda Siochana to be allowed a postal vote, when handicapped people were not given this privilege. The Court, however, decided that there was a justification for this difference of treatment in that soldiers or gardaí were people, in respect of whom the possibility of abuse was low.

In *O'Reilly*, a similarly-based argument was made that the undeserved bonus to candidates with surnames beginning with letters placed early in the alphabet was discriminatory. There is a rather literal line of cases which hold that since Article 40.1 speaks of 'All citizens . . . as human beings (being) held equal before the law' consequently the equality provision should be restricted, in its scope, to the essential attributes of human beings. Surprisingly, although this line of authority had not been invoked in *Draper*, it was adopted in *O'Reilly* (where *Draper* was not mentioned in this context). Accordingly the merits of the plaintiff's argument on this point were not canvassed.

The other submission which each plaintiff made was founded on the idea that the right to vote is one of the unenumerated personal rights protected by Article 40.3.1°. This point was explicitly left open in the Supreme Court in *Draper*. By contrast in *O'Reilly* Murphy J gave it as his view that 'wherever the right to vote was grounded, the extent of the obligations on the Oireachtas would be the same. . . . Nevertheless it may be appropriate to indicate that in my view the obligation placed on the legislation in this regard derives from Article 16 and not Article 40' (at 150). It is submitted, with respect, that this view is correct. There seems indeed little point in having a relatively detailed provision like Article 16, if it has to give way before a sub-section of the generality of Art. 40.31°.

In conclusion, it may be said that each of these decisions displays a robust common-sensical attitude. Whilst a different section of Article 16 was involved in *McMahon v. Attorney General* [1972] IR 69 (Text at 183) it is worth querying whether with the attitude displayed in *Draper* and *O'Reilly*, the majority in *McMahon* would have swung the other way.

Notwithstanding the plaintiff's failure in *Draper*, the legislature has now amended the law to allow handicapped persons a postal vote. By the Electoral (Amendment) (No. 2) Act, 1986, each registration authority — the county council or county borough council for the area — must draw up a list of 'special voters'. To come within this category, a person must be: 'unable to go in person to vote at the polling place for his polling district by reason of physical illness or physical disability suffered by him.' This must be a continuing condition. In addition, a special voter must also be of sound mind. All these matters must be confirmed by a medical certificate. It is necessary for a voting paper to be personally delivered to the special voter by the 'special presiding officer' (who is appointed by the returning officer) and a Garda, both of whom must wait in the special voter's presence, as he votes. Apart from this, the elector votes, as the Act says, in 'secret' unless assistance is necessary. Registration as a special voter is on an annual basis and whilst a substantial advertising campaign attracted the registration of about 6,000 such voters on 1 April 1987, by 1989 this figure was only about 3,000.

SUPPLEMENT TO CHAPTER 12

12.1 INDEPENDENCE OF THE JUDICIARY

A radical piece of interpretation occurred in the case of *Eccles v. Ireland* ([1985] IR 545; [1986] ILRM 343). The plaintiff, who had been convicted before the Special Criminal Court, of capital murder, argued that there was a potential danger to the Court's independence. This arose, he claimed, from the fact that (under the Offences Against the State Act 1939): each of its members is removable at the will of the Government; and secondly, the members' remuneration is fixed — and theoretically may be reduced — by the Minister for Finance. At first sight, it would seem that such an argument would fall on barren ground in that the Independence of the Judiciary is established by

Art. 35 whilst Art. 38.6 provides explicitly that the Special Criminal Court is to be excluded from the scope of Arts. 34 and 35. Consequently the plaintiff's argument had to be founded upon the ubiquitous Article 38.1 which provides that: 'No person shall be tried on any criminal charge save in due course of law.' In the High Court, Barrington J rejected this argument: 'It appears to me that it would not be a valid interpretation of Art. 38 to hold that what was specifically excluded by Art. 38.6 was included by implication , in s.1' ([1986] ILRM at 348). However, in a two-page judgment, basing itself on a purposive rather than a literal interpretation, the Supreme Court reached a different view. It held that although the Special Criminal Court did not attract the Article 35 guarantee of judicial independence yet 'it does have, derived from the Constitution (sc. Article 38.1), a guarantee of independence in the carrying out of its functions.' ([1985] IR at 351).

Notwithstanding this, the Supreme Court invoked the general presumption that the constitutional interpretation is the one intended by the Oireachtas and, thus, read the 1939 Act as requiring the Court to carry out its functions independently. Consequently, since no one had suggested that the judges of the Court had ever been less than independent, the Court upheld the plaintiff's conviction.

One long-established emblem and guarantee of an independent and honest court system is that justice should be administered in public. In articulating the significance of this principle, Walsh J stated, *In re R* [1989] ILRM 757, 763-64:

[This is] a fundamental principle of the administration of justice in a democratic state ... The actual presence of the public is never necessary but the administration of justice in public does require that the doors of the court must be open so that members of the general public may come and see for themselves that justice is done. It is in no way necessary that the members of the public to whom the courts are open should themselves have any particular interest in the cases or they should have had any business in the courts. Justice is administered in public on behalf of all the inhabitants of the State.

This desideratum is established by Article 34.1 which provides that: 'save in such special and limited cases as may be prescribed by law, [justice] shall be administered in public'.

In re R is the leading contemporary case[59] in this field. This case was brought by a petitioner who had been the chief executive of the respondent company and a substantial shareholder in it. He alleged that the company was being run by its directors in a way which was likely to damage its interest. Now the Companies Act 1963 gives a court discretion to order an *in camera* hearing where a public hearing 'would involve the disclosure of information the publication of which would be seriously prejudicial to the legitimate interest of the company'. The High Court, with whom a minority of the Supreme Court agreed, had made an order that the proceedings be held *in camera*. However, speaking for the Supreme Court majority and founding himself upon *'the overriding consideration of doing justice'* (at 766), Walsh J reversed the High Court. The relevant statutory provision required the party seeking protection to satisfy the court that disclosure would prejudice its legitimate interests. In addition, Walsh J inferred from the constitutional provision, quoted earlier, that there is a second pre-condition, namely, that 'a public hearing of ... the proceedings which it is sought to have heard other than in a public court would fall short of the doing of justice' (at 766).

One obvious argument which arises from this interpretation is that since it was common ground between the parties that a public hearing would entail a serious prejudice to the company's legitimate interest did it not follow that an open hearing would involve an injustice to the company? Consider, for instance, the fact that, according to one of the dissenting judges, correspondence entered into on behalf of the petitioner prior to instituting the petition was open to the construction of constituting a clear threat of publication of the petition, unless his claim was satisfactorily settled. Walsh J repulsed this line this line of argument (at 766-67) on the basis that:

... it is the affairs of a juristic person created by the Companies Acts which are under review. That puts the case in a quite different category from the private affairs of a human person. It is difficult to see why the disclosure of evidence of this type must necessarily be deemed to be a failure to do justice in the case of a juristic person where it would not be such in the case of a human person or of any unincorporated body of persons. The defendants as well as the petitioner are entitled to a fair and public hearing by the courts set up under the Constitution. Is ... the statutory condition precedent namely a serious prejudice to the legitimate interest of the company to be regarded as necessarily ... equivalent to those exceptional circumstances where public knowledge of the proceedings is likely to lead to an injustice or to defeat the object of the courts in doing justice? I do not think so even though it might be thought that this appeal proceeded on the basis that it does. While in one sense the quarrels between a shareholder or shareholders in a limited company and the company itself might be regarded in the nature of a family squabble it is in no way comparable to family disputes in the true sense. A limited company is the creature of the law and by its very nature and by the provisions of the law under which it is created it is open to public scrutiny.

I do not say that there can never be circumstances where the public hearing of cases such as this would prevent justice being done. However I am of opinion that in the present case no circumstances, so far at least, have been shown which would justify the court at arriving at such a conclusion.

The message which emerges from this gloss on Article 34.1 is that, whatever the relevant legislation says, it is only in fairly extreme circumstances that *in camera* proceedings will be permitted.

12.2 THE COURT SYSTEM

In *State (Boyle) v. Neylon* [1986] ILRM 337 (High Court); [1986] IR 551 (Supreme Court) the prosecutor had been charged with several offences allegedly committed in County Wicklow and returned for trial to Wicklow Circuit Court.

Then, however, the DPP had exercised his power under the Courts Act, 1981, s.31 (1)(a) to have the prosecutor's trial transferred to the Dublin Circuit Court. The prosecutor argued that this provision was unconstitutional in that the Circuit Court was a court of local and limited jurisdiction (in the language of Article 34.3.4°) and accordingly Dublin Circuit Court could not be granted jurisdiction to try matters with no connection with Dublin Circuit.

The first point contained in the Supreme Court judgment, given by Walsh J, was that the wording of Article 34.3.4° does not confine courts of first instance to either the High Court or courts of local and limited jurisdiction and, consequently, the Oireachtas is free to set up courts which fall outside either of these categories. However, counsel for the Attorney General had not put his case on the basis that the Circuit Court was (so to speak) a court of the third kind. Consequently Walsh J went on to decide the case on another ground. Nevertheless, this significant point remains open to be taken by the Attorney General — with a fair wind from Walsh J's *obiter dictum* — in a future case. Moreover, if this point were successful, it does not appear that there would be any corresponding disadvantage to the State in being thus freed from the straitjacket of the 'local and limited jurisdiction' formula.

In fact, Walsh J met the prosecutor's argument by adopting a purposive interpretation of the Constitution. According to the learned judge (at 556-57):

The purpose [of courts of first instance of local and limited jurisdiction] is . . . [to] provide local and cheaper venues for litigants than would be the case if they had to go to the High Court. They would also in most cases be more convenient. It was left to the statute to decide how this would be achieved. . . . It is quite clear that the whole structure of the courts is based upon the exercise of its jurisdiction locally. . . . It does not, however, follow that for a legitimate reason the Oireachtas may not provide that in certain cases another locality would be properly available for the trial of a case whether civil or criminal, as may be provided for by an Act of the Oireachtas. Experience has shown that justice itself would require a provision of this kind to avoid the risk of an injustice to one party or another by reason of local circumstances or conditions. The ability to transfer the trial of a case from one locality to another does not alter the essential local exercise of a jurisdiction of the Circuit Court.

It seems probable that the fact that the statutory provision under examination at least required an accused to be formally transferred by a court with which the offence did have a local connection — in this case Wicklow Circuit Court — is not a major part of this reasoning. Rather Walsh J was emphasising that all that the Constitution requires is that the Circuit Court's jurisdiction be *essentially* local. The tolerance thus allowed would presumably extend to the requirement that the Circuit (or District) Court's jurisdiction be 'limited'. If this assumption be correct, it affords some support for the view hazarded in the Text (at 192) that this requirement does not mean that the Circuit (and District) Court's jurisdiction for every particular item of its jurisdiction must be incomplete. This would of course mean giving the word 'limited' a different interpretation from the same word in Article 37 (see *Re Solicitors Act*: Text at 38). But the contexts are totally different.

Supreme Court The fact that the Supreme Court's appellate jurisdiction from High Court decision, absent express provision to the contrary, extends even to discretionary, procedural points was confirmed in *S.E.E. v. Public Lighting Services* [1987] ILRM 255, 258 and *Jack O'Toole v. MacEoin Kelly* [1987] ILRM 269, 271, 275. In each of these cases, the precise point involved a trial court's discretion (under the Companies Act, 1963, s. 390), in an action in which the plaintiff is a limited company, to require the plaintiff to give security for the defendant's costs. Whilst it was held that this discretion could be reversed by the Supreme Court, it was also said that the Supreme Court should give due weight to the views of the trial judge.

In regard to the Supreme Court's appellate jurisdiction in civil matters arising from Article 34.4.3°, there have been some recent developments which make a brief survey of this area of the Court's jurisdiction worthwhile, not least in order to chart some open points. Broadly speaking it remains the case, notwithstanding Art. 34.4.3°, that the Supreme Court has appellate jurisdiction from High Court decisions at first instance, on points of law, but not (subject to the qualifications noted *infra*) points of fact. The reason for this restriction, as regards points of fact, remains the traditional one. As it was put by Henchy J, in *Northern Bank Finance v. Charlton* [1979] IR 149 at 189:

. . . . comprehensive as it is, [a verbatim transcript] is necessarily an imperfect record of the oral hearing because what was adduced viva voce in the sight and hearing of the trial judge has had to be converted into a written transcript. It cannot recapture the mood of the trial, the demeanour of witnesses, the essential nuances of particular responses, and many other features of the trial which, although they may have been crucially determinative in the judicial ascertainment of the facts, may have become blurred or lost when the oral evidence was reduced to writing. Herein lies the source of this Court's restricted jurisdiction in regard to matters of fact. It cannot put itself in the position of the trial judge. He has had opportunities of judicial assessment that are denied to this Court.

This explanation would of course apply as much to the decision of a judge as to that of a jury. However, it has sometimes been said that: 'a judge's finding of fact was not necessarily sacrosanct in the way a jury's finding might be regarded' *(Northern Bank Finance* at 179: O'Higgins CJ). On the other hand, in *Holohan v. Donoghue* [1986] ILRM 250 at 255, Finlay CJ remarked: '. . . . this Court may not substitute for findings of fact made by a court of trial *(whether consisting of a judge sitting without a jury or with a jury)* which are supported by evidence, its own findings of fact' (my italics). Up until the virtual abolition of civil jury actions in the High Court, by the Juries Act, 1988 this difference was not of much practical significance. However, now it awaits definitive resolution as an issue of practical importance. It will presumably be a matter for the Court's discretion. The significance of the Supreme Court's discretion can be seen in the fact that it has already been given as the basis of the Supreme Court's refusal to hear a High Court appeal on a point of fact. This restriction is nowhere stated in Art. 34.4.3°. As has been said in *The People v O'Shea* [1982] IR 384 at 404: '[Article 34.4.3] means no more than that the Court is given a competence to entertain such appeals. How, and to what extent, that competence will be exercised is a matter for decision by the Court' (O'Higgins CJ).

The statement that there is no appeal to the Supreme Court from a High Court decision on a point of fact calls for some qualifications. In the first place, the Court may intervene not where it disagrees with the finding of fact, but rather on a more stringent test where it considers that there is no evidence to support the finding of fact which has been reached. Secondly, it may intervene where what is at issue is not a factual resolution of conflicting evidence but rather in the nature of a characterisation (as in negligence) or, alternatively, a deduction from some fact which has already been found or admitted. Here it is long established that the Supreme Court may set aside such findings. The question in doubt is whether, if it does so, it must order a re-trial or whether it may substitute its own decision. The precise point has not arisen, at any rate in the context of Article 34.4.3°. However, a related point arose in *Holohan v. Donoghue* [1986] ILRM 250, in which the defendant had appealed successfully against the assessment of general damages in a personal injuries action. By a majority of four to one, the Supreme Court went on to hold that in an appropriate case, it could substitute its own assessment of damages for that of the trial court. Seemingly, the principal factor to be taken into account, in determining what is an appropriate case, will be whether disputed facts are involved in the assessment. According to Finaly CJ (at 256; see also Henchy J at 261):

In this case, although the plaintiff has, through her counsel, expressed a strong desire to have her damages, if they are found to be excessive, assessed in a new trial by a jury, no reason has been advanced as to why it is not possible for this Court, on the evidence adduced, and contained in the transcript, to make an assessment of the damages. This is a case in which there was no conflict of evidence from medical witnesses. It is a case in which no query was placed by the medical evidence as to the probable future consequence of these injuries. It is not a case in which the veracity or bona fides of the plaintiff has been challenged by any evidence with regard to her injuries.

In my view, therefore, this Court can fairly and properly access the damages to which the plaintiff is entitled on the information which is before it.

It must be said that, so far as the content of its decision is concerned, *Holohan* merely confirmed the earlier case of *Gahan v. Engineering Products* [1971] IR 30 which had also held that the Court had jurisdiction to reassess damages. *Gahan*, however, rested on the assumption that the Supreme Court's jurisdiction derived from the Courts of Justice Act, 1924, s.96 (as expressly re-enacted by the Courts (Supplemental Provisions Act, 1961), itself a capacious provision, rather than the Constitution. The significance of *Holohan* is that it shows that 'the court's jurisdiction to make such an order has a constitutional and not a statutory basis' (Henchy J at 260) and that the Court's inherent jurisdiction under the Constitution extends to 'making such order in an appeal before it as the justice of the case require[s]' (Henchy J at 261). The full extent of this jurisdiction remains to be seen. Does it mean — to return to the question posed in the previous paragraph — that if the Supreme Court decides that there is no evidence to sustain a High Court finding of fact, it may substitute its own view on this, without the need for a re-trial?

12.3 RIGHT TO A JURY ON A CRIMINAL CHARGE

Minor offences   A doubt was introduced by *State (Rollinson)* (Text at 197-8) as to whether when a range of penalties is provided for an offence, the relevant issue, in determining whether the offence is minor, is the maximum punishment prescribed by the state or the penalty actually imposed by the court. The latter view — what may be called the revisionist line — was adopted by the High Court in *Cartmill v. Ireland* [1988] ILRM 430, 433-4 and 436, though not without a bow in the other direction.

Another principle followed in *Rollinson* [1984] IR 248, 267 — explicitly by Hederman J and implicitly by the other judges — was adopted by the High Court in *State (Wilson) v. Neilan* [1985] IR 89, 98, when Carroll J stated:

I am of the opinon that, in determining whether an offence is or is not a minor offence, each one must be looked at separately. It seems to me that an offence which is a minor offence cannot change into a non-minor offence merely because an accused is charged with a number of similar minor offences.

What Murphy J in *Cartmill* called the 'troublesome area' of the distinction between primary and secondary punishments — the latter not being counted in assessing the severity of sentence when classifying an offence as minor — was the other point which came up in *Cartmill*. Here the offence with which the plaintiff was about to be prosecuted in the District Court was providing facilities for gaming by means of a slot-machine. Among the consequences of conviction would have been the possible exercise of the District Justice's power to order the forfeiture of the machines, worth in the instant case about £120,000. Founding himself on the *Conroy-Pheasantry Ltd.* line of authority Murphy J refused to take the value of the machines into account. He also gave the following statement of the policy underlying this area of the law (at 434-5):

It was clearly recognised in the Conroy case that there may be good executive and administrative reasons for depriving a citizen of the right to use equipment or exercise functions which are themselves valid and proper because the citizen has displayed an incapacity or unwillingness to use the equipment or discharge the functions in a proper manner. How much more should there be an administrative or executive power to deprive a citizen of equipment, in the present case gaming instruments, which are inherently designed for the commission of a criminal offence?

The idea seems to be that the forfeiture of the gaming machines would be regulatory (an exercise of the administrative or executive power) as opposed to punitive and, consequently, not relevant in assessing the severity of the crime.[60]

All relevant factual issues for the jury   In connection with Art. 34.1, we have encountered attempts by the Oireachtas to withdraw some element of a decision from a court of law and vest it elsewhere (Text at 36). An analagous problem in the context of Art. 38.5, arises where some factual point is withheld from the jury, as occurred in *Curtis v. Attorney General* [1986] ILRM 428. The offence involved here was the evasion of customs duties. The relevant legislation provided that the offence could be tried summarily or on indictment, depending on the value of the goods involved. It was thus convenient for the District Justice to be vested with the decision as to the value of the goods. In addition — and this is the point of contention — the Justice's determination was made 'final and not appealable'. In the first place, this violated the principle that in a criminal case, on indictment, all relevant issues should be left to the jury. For the amount of the goods smuggled might be relevant in regard to the accused's guilt because they might be relevant to *mens rea*. In addition, the learned judge held that as regards punishment, 'if the value put on the goods by the prosecution is challenged by an accused, there would have to be a question put to the jury to decide the value in order that the relevant fine would be imposed. . . . ' (p. 432). Finally, it was held (presumably as a result of Art. 38.1) that there could be no fragmentation of issues in a criminal trial, between two courts, even if both had jurisdiction.

In *The People (DPP) v. Conroy* Supreme Court 31 July 1986, it was held (by a majority and contrary to the views of two Supreme Court justices in *The People (DPP) v. Lynch* [1982] IR 64) that there was a well established exception to the principle that all relevant issues should be left to the jury: this exception existed in the case of an issue of fact relevant to the admissibility of evidence. This exception was justified on the ground that a jury informed of the content of a rejected statement would no longer be impartial.

Criminal charge   The catchment area of Art. 38.2 and 5 depends not only on what is a minor offence but also on the category of 'criminal charge', an expression which is also used in Art. 38.1 (requiring trial or a criminal charge to be 'in due course of law') and in a slightly different version in Art. 37.1. The meaning of 'criminal charge' came up for examination (probably in the context of Art. 38.1, though this is not significant) in *McLoughlin v. Tuite*[1986] ILRM 304. The Income Tax Act, 1967 imposes penalties for failure to make tax returns and provides that if the taxpayer fails to pay these penalties, he can be sued in civil proceedings in the High Court. The plaintiff had been the victim of such proceedings which he argued were unconstitutional in that they had been enforced without allowing the protections required by a trial on a criminal charge. Although the High Court accepted that the proceedings were essentially punitive, it found that, in every other feature, the indicia of a criminal offence were missing. Thus, for example, non-payment of the penalty does not lead automatically to imprisonment; the prosecution did not have to establish mens rea; no ethical stigma attached to failure to fill up a form.

12.4 CRIMINAL JURISDICTION

The Supreme Court case of *The People v O'Shea* [1982] IR 384 [Text at 204] which held that an appeal does lie to the Supreme Court from an acquittal in the Central Criminal Court (the High Court under a different name) has now led to another Supreme Court decision, *The People (DPP) v Quilligan No. 2* [1989] ILRM 245. In *Quilligan* the main question was whether the Court's jurisdiction to hear an appeal against acquittal carried with it a concomitant jurisdiction to order a re-trial. According to Walsh J, who was on this occasion one of two dissenting judges (at 247): 'The jurisdiction to set aside erroneous decisions in law must necessarily carry with it the necessary competence to ensure that the interrupted proceedings are brought to a conclusion in accordance with the law'. The majority rejected this reasoning on the basis that in the case of statutory jurisdictions, authority to order a re-trial is always specifically conferred. But this perhaps overlooks the fact that here it was the Constitution and not a statute which was being interpreted.

In fact, to appreciate why the result in *Quilligan* was different from that which might seem to have been required by *O'Shea,* it is best to see the case as a continuation of the judicial differences in *O'Shea*. Many of the arguments rehearsed in the *Quilligan* judgements, on each side, were the same as those in *O'Shea*. More significant was the judicial line-up in the two cases. Henchy J, who dissented in *O'Shea* with Finlay P, was joined in *Quilligan* by Griffin J (in place of Finlay P). On the other side, Walsh J who concurred in *O'Shea*, with O'Higgins CJ, was joined, in *Quilligan,* by McCarthy J. The reason for the contrasting results in such similar cases was that Hederman J acted, as it were, as 'the swing vote', holding in *O'Shea* that the Court had jurisdiction to hear an appeal against acquittal and in *Quilligan* (in a half-page judgment) holding that, nevertheless, the Court could not order a retrial.

One of the general lessons which emerges from this saga is the Court's lack of respect for its own recent precedents. The other is the legislature's lack of interest in the area. Contrary to the prediction made in the Text at 204, no bill has been brought forward to resolve the doubts in this area and none seems likely for the forseeable future.

295

Notes

1. See, further, G.W. Hogan [1987] PL 509. One of the sequels to the episodes which gave rise to the *Kennedy* case was the publication by the Government of the Interception of Postal Packets and Telecommunications Messages (Regulation) Bill, 1985 which provided that phone-tapping or the interception of letters would only be lawful on warrant of the Minister for Justice which could only be issued for purposes of state security or a criminal investigation. This Bill never became law but the question of new legislation was said to be still under consideration at *Dáil Debates*, vol. 373, col. 1767, 13 May 1987.
2. The right to a livelihood was also invoked unsuccessfully in the more unusual circumstances of the monopoly to convey letters (which was then vested in the Minister for Posts and Telegraphs): *Attorney-General and Minister for Posts and Telegraphs v Paperlink* [1984] ILRM 373.
3. According to Costello J in *Paperlink* at 381, where this right includes the right to communicate information, it derives from Art. 40.3.1° and it is to be differentiated from the narrower right under Art. 40.6.1° (i) to express freely convictions and opinions. This is an extremely fine distinction. It was not followed in *Brandon Books, infra*.
4. For comment, see J. Friedman, (1988) 10 *DULJ* 71. See also *SPUC Ireland v Coogan* [1990] ILRM 70.
5.

	Total electorate	Total poll	Per cent poll	Votes in favour	Votes against
Tenth Amendment of the Constitution Bill, 1986 [Removal of Divorce Ban]	2,360,000	1,480,000	62.7	538,279	935,844
Tenth Amendment of the Constitution Bill, 1987 [Ratification of SEA]	2,461,790	1,080,400	43.9	755,425	324,977

   On each referendum, see 3 (1988) *Irish Political Studies* at 43 (O'Leary and Hesketh) and 77 (Gallagher), respectively.
6. For comment, see T. O'Malley, (1988) 6 *Irish Law Times* 279.
6a. Followed in different circumstances in *Irish Commercial v Plunkett* [1986] IR 258,267 and *Director of Public Prosecutions v Olympic* [1987] ILRM 320.
6b. In *Rederij Kennemerland v Attorney General* [1989] ILRM 821, 839-41, 842-3, it was held that a claim founded upon *Lynch* and *Clarke* was distinguishable. Since, in authorising the applicant's continued detention, a peace commissioner did not hear evidence and merely signed a form he knew to have been prepared in advance, the peace commissioner had not exercised any judicial function. However, the applicant succeeded on the ground, *int. al.*, that the peace commissioner had not lawfully exercised his statutory power.
7. See *Joyce v Esmonde* [1987] ILRM 316; *Rainey*; and *White* (though in each of these cases, the plaintiff failed, for other reasons).
8. B.O. Nwabueze, *Judicialism in Commonwealth Africa* (London 1975), Chap.1.
9. See L. Tribe, *Constitutional Choices* (London 1985), Chap. 7.
10. The other major argument, which was grounded on a point outside the scope of this book, was that the Agreement violated Art. 2 of the Constitution, which states that: 'The national territory consists of the whole island of Ireland . . .'. The plaintiff submitted that this Article amounted to a recognition of the present constitutional arrangements in Northern Ireland and thus to a violation of Art. 2 of the Constitution. Barrington J rejected this. On his characterisation 'the two Governments merely recognise the situation on the ground in Northern Ireland'. From a general perspective it is more significant that (on a point which had not been argued before him) the learned judge gave it as his opinion that the claim to national unity in Art. 2 exists in the political, rather than the legal, realm. However, the Supreme Court took the reverse view: See *Irish Times*, 14 March 1990.

11. *Dáil Debates*, vol. 363, col. 2774.
12. *Dáil Debates*, vol. 371, col. 52-59.
13. Tourism, Fisheries and Forestry (Alteration of Name of Department and Title of Minister) Order S.I. No. 82 of 1987.
14. Communications (Transfer of Departmental Administration and Ministerial Functions) Order, S.I. No. 91 of 1987.
15. Communications (Transfer of Departmental Administration and Ministerial Functions) (No. 2) Order, S.I. No. 92 of 1987.
16. Forestry and Wildlife (Transfer of Departmental Administration and Ministerial Functions) Order, S.I No. 96 of 1987.
17. Public Service (Transfer of Departmental Administration and Ministerial Functions) Order S.I. No. 81 of 1987
18. Public Service (Alteration of Name of Department and Title of Minister) Order S.I. No. 83 of 1987.
19. Agriculture (Alteration of Name of Department and Title of Minister) Order No. 97 of 1987.
20. *Dáil Debates* vol. 371, cols. 56-57. The Offices are: the Office of Science and Technology and the Office of Trade and Marketing (each attached to the Department of Industry and Commerce); the Office of Food Industry and the Office of Horticulture (each attached to the Department of Agriculture); the Office of Forestry (attached to the Department of Energy).
21. Agriculture and Food (Delegation of Ministerial Functions) Orders S.I. Nos. 163 and 164 of 1987.
22. See generally, Gallagher, 'The President, the People and the Constitution' in Farrell (ed.), *De Valera's Constitution and Ours* 85-88; *Report of the Committee on the Constitution* (Pr. 9817), 11-13.
23. *Dáil Debates*, vol. 371, cols. 20-51.
24. *Irish Times*, 2 March 1987.
25. See e.g. *Dail Debates* vol. 3, col. 1331; vol. 52, col. 227.
26. See newspapers for the period 17 June - 13 July 1989, especially *Irish Times* for 30 June, July, 1, 4, 7 and 13.
27. For specific example, see Art. 19 (Nomination of Senators).
28. The six Dáil defeats were as follows: *Dail Debates,* vol. 375, col. 1645, 24 November 1987 (Government amendment to Fine Gael motion on pupil-teacher ration circular defeated; but motion also defeated); vol. 376, col. 602, 2 December 1987 (motion 'instructing' Government to rescind its decision to abolish National Social Services Board passed); vol. 378, col. 259, 17 February 1988 (motion 'directing' Minister for Health to rescind his proposal to close Barrington's Hospital in Limerick passed); vol. 384, col. 2247, 29 November 1988 (Report stage motion to re-commit Judicial Separation and Family Law Reform Bill, 1988 passed); vol. 387, col. 922, 21 February 1989 (Government motion that Committee of Selection report recommending appointment of new member of Joint Committee on State Sponsored Bodies be adopted without debate defeated); 26 April 1989, *D.D.* reference not yet available (motion to set up haemophiliacs trust fund passed).
29. R. Brazier, *Constitutional Practice* (London 1986) 176.
30. 'The Role of the Senate' in Lynch and Meenan, (eds.) *Essays in memory of Alexis Fitzgerald* (Dublin 1987), p.146. See also *Irish Times,* 13 April, 1989 (article on Senate by F. O'Toole).
31. *Senate Debates* vol. 116, col. 625.
32. See further Hogan and Morgan, *Administrative Law* (1986), 15-16; G.W. Hogan, 'Note on the Imposition of Duties Act 1957' (1985) 7 *DULJ* (n.s.) 180.
33. See e.g. *Dáil Debates*, vol. 374, col. 684.
34. *Serving the Country Better: A White Paper on the Public Service* (1985 pl. 3262), p.26.
35. Report of the Committee on Public Expenditure 1984-85 (1986), p. 12.
36. *Dail Debates*, vol. 362, col. 532 (Minister for Finance).
37. *Dail Debates* vol. 360, col. 732. (Minister for Labour speaking on behalf of the absent Minister for the Public Service).

39.   *Dail Debates*, vol. 358, col. 2200.
40.   *Ibid.*, vol. 373, col. 1994-2012.
41.   *Ibid.*, vol. 369, col. 11-18, 265.
42.   *Ibid.*, vol. 373, col. 1155-65. The motion was passed over the strenuous protests of Deputy Tom Fitzpatrick, who has been Ceann Comhairle on the previous occasion referred to in the Text (see cols. 1156 and also 1206).
43.   *Dáil Debates*, vol. 379, col. 213-15.
44.   See *Irish Times*, 14 December 1988.
45.   See *Senate Debates*, vol. 121, cols. 1460 ff.
46.   J.F. Zimmerman 'An Oireachtas Innovation: Backbench Committees', 36 (1989) *Administration* 265. Professor Zimmerman usefully reproduces an extract from the Department of Public Service's circular, 'Guidelines for civil servants appearing before or providing information to Oireachtas committees'.
47.   A. Atkins, 'The committees of the 24th Oireachtas', 3 (1988) *Irish Political Studies* 91.
48.   See *Dáil Debates*, vol. 373, col. 2016-2028.
49.   *Ibid.*, vol. 380, col. 1612ff. and 1876ff., 17 and 18 May, 1988. The motion originally said six months. Then, by a motion of 3 November 1988, moved by the Government Chief Whip, twelve months was substituted in place of six months *(Dáil Debates*, vol. 383 col. 1678ff., 3 November 1988).
50.   *Dáil Debates*, vol. 383, col. 1688.
51.   See *Dáil Debates*, vol. 358 cols. 2100-2300; vol. 369, cols. 2271-2308.
52.   *Dáil Debates* vol. 369, col. 2277.
53.   See *e.g. Irish Independent*, 7 March, 1990; *Irish Times*, 30 March and 14 April, 1990. The matter was discussed in the Senate on 3 April, 1990.
54.   See *e.g.* Senate proceedings for 15 and 26 March and 4 April, 1990.
55.   On which see, Hogan and Morgan, *Administrative Law*. Chap. 9.
56.   *Id.* Chap. 10.4.
57.   See J. M. Kelly, *The Irish Constitution* (1984), 686-87.
58.   Murphy J also offered what may be regarded as an alternative ratio. He said (at pp. 152-53), 'The established propensity of the electorate in favour of candidates whose names appear towards the top of the ballot paper is not, as I see it, so much a defect in the present electoral system but rather it is a measure of some degree of indifference by the electorate or some part of it as to how their voices - and in particular their second and subsequent preference votes - are cast. . . . It would seem therefore, that what is described as a bias in favour of the candidates whose names appear at the top of the ballot is not so much a defect in the system itself as a defect or a want of care or a want of interest by the electorate.'

       But surely the law must judge any system according to how it is operated by the generality of people, including in this case, a number of voters who show a want of interest. It is not relevant that any system would work well, if the people operating it were better than they are. This reflection leads on to the query of what would happen if Irish people became so apathetic that (say) a majority did not vote (something which shows no sign of happening). Would the Constitution require voting to be made compulsory, as in Australia?
59.   Though see also: *In re Redbreast*, 91 ILTR 12; *In re Singer*, 97 ILTR 130, and *Beamish v Crowley* [1969] IR 42.
60.   However, it does not seem possible to use this ground to distinguish *Cartmill* from *Kostan v. Ireland*, High Court, 10 February 1978. It is certainly true that there is a distinction (drawn in the passage quoted) between equipment which could be used for a lawful purpose but, in the instant case, had been abused and, on the other hand, equipment which is 'inherently designed for the commission of a criminal offence'. And this distinction can be applied to distinguish *Kostan* from *Cartmill* since the equipment in *Kostan* — the fishing boat and equipment — was certainly capable of being used lawfully. However, so far as this distinction is relevant, it would seem to mean that it was the *Cartmill* equipment which should have been taken into account and *Kostan* equipment which should not. The reason is that since the *Kostan* equipment could have been used for a lawful purpose, even after a crime had been established, there would have been a regulatory discretion for the District Justice to exercise in *Kostan* rather than in the case of *Cartmill* where the machines could only be used for crime.

Table of Constitutional Articles

Table of Statutes

(Br) indicates that the statute was enacted by the Westminster Parliament.

Table of Irish and Foreign Cases

Index

finance, cont.
procedure in the Dáil 115-121;
peculiarity of financial procedure in
the Dáil 112-115; the senate's
inferior status re 123-125
Finance Bill, 1976 124
Finance, Department of 61, 95: three
divisions of 125; and collective
responsibility of Government 72f
Finance, Minister for 58, 62, 114f, 148:
control by 125-127; and the Public
Service 267; *see also* finance;
Finance, Department of
Fitzgerald, Garret 55, 58
Foreign Affairs, Department of 56, 263f
franchise and registration of voters
175-177
freedom of speech: of members of
Parliament 162-165; *see also*
privilege, parliamentary

Gardaí 11; and Offences Against the
State Act 202
Garvin, T. 92
Gibbons, Jim 85
Government, the 54-63: appointment of
68f; its control over the Dáil 64,
79ff; responsible to the Dáil 64,
267-272; its control of departmental
admninistration 76-79; and
appointments of judges 189; legal
framework of ministers and
departments 61-63; resignation of
ministers of 73; meetings of 55;
members of 58f, 68f; motion of no
confidence in 156, 271; and parties
64ff; its party majority in the Senate
185; has sole executive power 42;
removal of 69-71; replacement of
71f; collective responsibility of 65f,
68-73; and separation of powers 33ff
Government Chief Whip 55
Government Information Service
(formerly G.I. Bureau) 55, 56f
Government Procedural Instructions 95
Government Secretariate 54-63, 95
'Grand Inquest of the Nation' 82, 91
Griffith, Arthur 170
grants, bulk 120
grants-in-aid 120
habeas corpus orders 194, 195
Haughey, Charles 55, 57f, 75, 86, 87,
144, 194, 195

Health (Family Planning) Bill, 1978 80,
85
Health, Minister for 62
'Henry VIII clause' 108
Hewart, Lord 110
High Court 192ff, 206, 207, 209, 214,
290; appeals to 201; rules of 108;
see also Central Criminal Court
Hillery, Patrick 52
homosexual acts 258
Housing (Private Rented Dwellings) Bill
106, 107
Hyde, Douglas 52, 53

International Monetary Fund 115
Incorporated Law Society 37: limitation
on members entering 17
Industry, Commerce and Energy,
Minister for 62, 63, 266
Initiative, the (in 1922 Constitution) 29,
67, 68
'intention of the legislature' 159
instruments, statutory 107-111: Senate
Committee on 110, 146, 148, 149
Iris Oifigiúil 105, 109
Irish Free State: *see under* Constitution
of IFS
Irish Party at Westminster 65, 143

James I 43
Jennings, Ivor 143
Journals of the Proceedings of the
Houses of the Oireachtas 105, 158
judges: appointment of 189;
independence of 189; removal of
189f; salaries of 190
judicature 189-214: the court system
190-196; civil jurisdiction 205-207;
criminal jurisdiction 199-205; and
separation of powers 33ff; judicial
control of administrative action
110f, 207-214; independence of
judiciary 189-190, 287ff; right to
jury trial on criminal charges
196-199; publics reaction to
appointments to bench 14
jurisdiction, civil 205-207
jurisdiction, criminal 199-205, 295
jury, right to trial by on criminal charges
196-199, 293
justice, administration of 38ff; by a
body not a court of law 161

316

317

Oireachtas, cont.
  Houses of 157; has unique power to
  make laws 40ff; *see also*
  Cathaoirleach; Ceann-Comhairle;
  committee(s) of the Oireachtas;
  legislation; privilege, parliamentary
O'Kelly, Sean T. 52
O'Malley, Chris 266
O'Malley, Desmond 72(n36), 84
Ombudsman 14, 44, 78, 79, 81
Ombudsman Bill, 1979 103
One Girl's War 257
order papers and sequence of business in
  Dáil 136f, 275f; in Senate 137
O'Sullivan, Donal 110

Parliament: *see* Oireachtas
Parliamentary secretary: *see* Minister of
  State
parties, parliamentary/political 64ff,
  82-87: and election to Dáil 179ff;
  breach of discipline in 84;
  conscience exemption 85; free vote
  85; pledge 83; meetings 85; election
  or review of leader 86f; whip 83f;
  Register of 180
Pawnbrokers Bill, 1964 90
Paymaster General 126, 127, 130
people, sovereignty of 27ff
phone-tapping 167
Plato 33
poll, in election to the Dáil 182
power, public authorities' statutory
  discretionary 210
President 46-53: and Art. 24 bills 96;
  and Art. 27 of the Constitution 97:
  reference to bills to Supreme Court
  under Art. 26 106f; appoints
  Comptroller and Auditor General
  128; his discretion to grant
  dissolution of the Dáil 67, 71f, 269f;
  appoints all judges 189; and
  legislation 105-107; removal of
  194; and separation of powers 33ff;
  restricted power of 270; election of
  51; independence of 50f, 266;
  Guardian of the Constitution' 47f; as
  head of state 46f; and 'hung' Dáil
  270f
privacy, right to 255; of a juristic person
  289
private bills 103f
private members' bills 102f

private members' business 138
private notice questions 154
privilege, parliamentary 160-169: Art.
  15.10 165-168; procedure in the Dáil
  168; freedom of speech 162-165; in
  general 160-162, 281ff; freedom
  from arrest 281ff
Privy Council 13, 25f, 70
Procedure in Government 55
procedure in Houses of Oireachtas
  133-159: arrangement of business
  135-139; chairmen and
  administration 155-159; forms of
  debate 140-143; Informal
  Committee on 133, 139; questions
  152-155; reforms of 144-151;
  sources of 133-135, 275
provisional order confirmation bills 104
Provisional Sinn Féin 182
public authorities' statutory discretionary
  power 210
Public Accounts, Audit of 128-132
Public Accounts (Select) Committee of
  the Dáil 122f, 131f, 145, 146, 148,
  283f
Public Expenditure Committee 122,
  146, 149, 274f, 278
Public Capital Programme 114, 115,
  122, 125, 274f
Public Sector Borrowing Requirement
  114
Public Service, Minister for and
  Department of 62, 79, 94, 131, 135,
  148, 150, 168, 267

questions in the Dáil 152-155, 275, 279,
  280ff: Devlinisation of 155; subject
  matter (three kinds) 152f; procedure
  154; rules about 153; supplementary
  154; value of 154f; priority 281

Radcliffe, Lord 13
Referendum: in 1922 Constitution 29,
  67, 68; in 1937 Constitution 30ff
Register of Nominating Bodies 187
Register of Political Parties 180
registration of voters 175-177
Reports of parliamentary debates,
  Official 154, 158
representation, proportional 173ff
Revenue Commissioners 126, 130, 214,
  262f

rights of the individual 11f, 15ff, 255ff;
the Constitution a reservoir of
unspecified 15-20
Rome, Treaty of 195f
rule of law 42-45, 264
Rules of the Superior Courts 108
rulings from the Chair 134

Sale of Goods and Services Bill, 1978 71
secrecy at election 183
Senate: Clerk and his staff 157-158;
Clerk and elections to 187; in
disagreement with the Dáil 96ff;
members can be in Cabinet 58;
rulings by Chairman of 134;
elections to 185-188; in Free State
constitution 89f; Government is not
responsible to 68; and delegated
legislation 107ff; legislation powers
of 95f, 272f; Minutes and Journal of
158f; and money bills 123-125; the
place of 88-93; standing orders of
92, 103, 133(n6), 134, 279; a
'revising' chamber 90; vocational
character of 88f; desenting in 277f;
disciplining of members 282ff; see
also procedure
Senate Commitee on Procedure and
Privileges 134
Senate Committee on Statutory
Instruments 110, 146, 148, 149
Senate Debates 135, 158
separation of powers 33-36, 259ff
sessional orders 133
single transferable vote 81
Sinn Féin (1920s) 21, 170
Social Welfare, Minister and Department
of 62, 155
Special Criminal Court 194, 197, 201f,
214, 287f
speeches in Oireachtas 141
standing orders 133
State, principal organs of the 11
State-sponsored bodies 11, 56, 113, 114,
120, 122, 130, 163, 178, 272;
appointment to 14; and questions in
the Dáil 153
State Paper Office 56
statutory instruments 107-111
Succession Bill, 1965 91
Sunday Express 167

Supplementary Estimates 120
Supplies, Minister for 62
'Supply Services' 112
Supreme Court 194f, 291ff: appeals to
201, 203ff, 207, 214; its appellate
jurisdiction 195, 291f; reference of
bills by President to 106f; rules of
108

Tanaiste 58, 59
Taoiseach: appointed by President 68;
and his Department 54-58; and
dissolution of Dáil 81, 179: and
summoning of Dáil 181; nominated
by Dáil 68f, 267ff; his power 56-58,
275f; removal of 68ff; his residual
responsibility for public business
153; 'acting Taoiseach; 269f
taxes *see* Revenue Commissioners;
Appeal Commissioners
Third Amendment of the Constitution
Bill, 1958 31(n97), 90
Tourism and Transport, Minister for 266
Transport and Power, Minister for 62
Treaty, the Anglo-Irish, 1921 22

Udarás na Gaeltachta 162, 164
ultra vires 209
University of Dublin 185
university members in Senate 185f

vires 209
Vote, excess 121
Vote, a passed Estimate becomes a 117
vote, postal 177, 285f
vote, right of British citizens to in Irish
elections 28, 31, 51
vote, single transferable 173-175
vote system, straight 174
voters, registration of 175-177
voting, system of in elections to
Oireachtas 173-187, *passim*
voting in the Oireachtas 142

Walsh, Brian 172, 173
White Paper on Receipts and
Expenditure 115
'white print' 95
whip, chief 83f, 95, 149
Wild Life Bill, 1975 91
Women's Affairs, minister of state for
55